Politics in
FRANCE

The Little, Brown Series
in Comparative Politics

Under the Editorship of
GABRIEL A. ALMOND
JAMES S. COLEMAN
LUCIAN W. PYE

LIBRARY OF CONGRESS CATALOG CARD NO. 75-152815

THIRD PRINTING

Published simultaneously in Canada
by Little, Brown & Company (Canada) Limited

PRINTED IN THE UNITED STATES OF AMERICA
66618

A COUNTRY STUDY

Politics in

FRANCE

Second Edition

Henry W. Ehrmann
McGill University

Boston
LITTLE, BROWN AND COMPANY

TO

A.G.   B.G.   F.G.

S.H.   G.L.   M.M.

R.R.   J.T.   *all of Paris*

AND TO

G.Z.   *of Berlin*

Foreword

The publication of the second edition of Henry Ehrmann's *Politics in France* opens a new phase in the Little, Brown Series in Comparative Politics. The conceptual innovations initiated by the Series have now been widely accepted in the literature of Comparative Politics. Revisions of the various volumes in the series and new contributions both to the *Country Studies* and to the *Analytic Series* will now reflect the pedagogic experience we have had and the significant conceptual innovations that have occurred in the years since the Series began. There will be greater stress on policy-making processes, on developmental patterns and prospects, and on the performance of political systems.

The Fifth Republic has now existed for two years without the dominating leadership and personality of de Gaulle. The two institutions that emerged under his leadership and seemed to contribute most to its viability — a powerful, popularly elected presidency and a political party broadly representing all strata and elements of French society with a safe majority of seats in the National Assembly — have survived his resignation and death. In his second edition, Henry Ehrmann pursues as a central theme the persistence of these and other significant changes in French politics and society. Uniquely qualified by a lifetime of research and writing on France, he weighs the most recent evidence on the economy of France, its social structure, its political processes, its political and governmental institutions, the ends and effectiveness of its public policies. He points to the possibility of a significant shift in the French polity toward stability and more effective and responsive performance, but underlines the tentativeness of these developments, the shallow quality of the system's legitimacy, and the many problems still besetting its institutions and processes.

Gabriel A. Almond
James S. Coleman
Lucian W. Pye

Preface
to the Second Edition

One reason for revising and updating a book published less than three years ago is its gratifying success. Fairly widespread classroom adoption of the first edition has proved to publisher and author that American undergraduates are quite receptive to a study which shuns oversimplification in explaining a complicated political culture and which introduces general concepts to enhance comparability.

Another reason for the revision is of course the changes in the political scenery of France. The first edition was rescued from immediate obsolescence by a hastily written Postscript reporting, without the benefit of any historical distance whatsoever, on the upheaval of May–June, 1968. Although this Postscript has elicited, and for good reasons, interest from student readers in particular, the temptation to treat these events in a special chapter of the second edition had to be resisted in a book not given to chronological treatment. What by now has become in French political parlance *les événements* (and rendered by me as "the Events" with a capital E) are here discussed in different chapters dealing with problems for which the Events had paramount significance (e.g., Chaps. VII and III). The reader who wishes to obtain a more coherent picture may consult the Index where he will find numerous entries listing all passages referring to the Events, their etiology and their aftermath.

The passing of General de Gaulle from the political stage made
: necessary to survey the immediate consequences of this change

in politics and to evaluate the general conditions under which the
Fifth Republic will have to operate in its post–de Gaulle phase.
But when examining the first edition, I realized that many features
of the political landscape of previous years appear changed now
that the providential leader has stepped down, and under somewhat surprising circumstances. Finally, the abundance of serious
monographic studies on French politics that has appeared in both
French and English during the last few years invited further
revisions.

There was danger that adding new information and thoughts
would increase unduly the size of the book. I therefore have
found it necessary to shorten, wherever possible, earlier discussion
and to eliminate entirely certain materials dealing with the first
years of the Fifth Republic. Needless to say, like any author, I
regretted doing this. The unusually curious reader must be
referred to the first edition.

Friends and colleagues in both France and the United States
have been generous and helpful with suggestions for improvement.
Serge Hurtig, Mark Kesselman, Alain Lancelot, Georges Lavau,
Val Lorwin, William Safran, Stanley Rothman, Sidney Tarrow,
and Gordon Wright have earned the gratitude of the author and
of the readers, some by careful page-by-page criticism, others by
spirited comment on details. The staff of Little, Brown and Company was as attentive, fast, and obliging in helping along the
second edition as it was for the first.

This is written at a time when one of the foremost French
political commentators has characterized the year just passed as
"a halt in the history of an unstable people." Friends of France
everywhere (and the authors of textbooks on French politics in
particular) can only wish that the next forward surge of a
dynamic country will enhance and not destroy that stability without which even Frenchmen cannot do.

                                                                    H.W.E.

January, 1971

Preface
to the First Edition

The Frenchman Montesquieu once remarked that those nations are happy whose annals of history are boring to read. To the extent that this is true, France is of course an "unhappy" country — for her history has been fascinating and turbulent, not boring. No wonder that the political systems under which she has lived have invited unending and frequently passionate comments by Frenchmen and foreign observers alike.

Such an abiding interest is caused in part by high expectations — expectations which the present leader of the French Republic is not the first to have voiced. Because the country has been the beacon of Western enlightenment, the performance of its political system is measured by exacting standards. There are puzzling inconsistencies in the political and social life of every nation. Those of France have frequently aroused irritation; explanations that have been offered are stubbornly contradictory because they fasten on different aspects of the country's internal contradictions. Does the turbulence of political life hide a pattern of basically undisturbed fundamental values? Or is, in a rapidly changing environment, an all too persistent adherence to basic values responsible for political explosions?

When discussing "Some Characteristics of Historians in Democratic Times," [1] Alexis de Tocqueville suggests that the lot of

[1] Alexis de Tocqueville, *Democracy in America* (New York: Vintage oks, 1954), Vol. II, pp. 90–93.

historians writing in an aristocratic age was an easy one. They were content simply to detach from the mass of general events "the particular influence of one man or of a few men." Anyone trying to explain the present French regime cannot quite fail to comment upon the "influence of one man." Yet present-day political science fits well, as it must, the characteristics which Tocqueville attributes to the historians of democratic times. We seek, as he puts it, to "assign general causes" to a mass of incidents and are "given to connect incidents together so as to deduce a system from them." Instead of attempting to discern the influence of individuals we prefer "talking about the characteristics of race, the physical conformation of the country, or the genius of civilization" — now conveniently summarized under the heading of "political culture."

Just because France shares with other democracies many political institutions which have worked adequately elsewhere but have failed her, a discussion of the country's political culture as a major variable determining political behavior has always appeared to be particularly relevant. It also provides the main theme of this book. To avoid the stereotypes which a discussion of this kind easily invites, the functional approach suggested in the writings of Gabriel Almond and common to this series in comparative politics has proved particularly, and to this author almost surprisingly, helpful. The categories here employed seem to clarify where choice and where circumstances have shaped the structures of the French political system and how they have determined the functioning of these structures. By sorting out what is unique and what is common to societies of similar development, our classifications should serve the purposes of comparison.

All comparative studies suffer from the limitations imposed by the paucity of strictly comparable data. I do not share the optimism of those who believe that the growing number of comparative statistical studies of national politics are sufficient to test general propositions. Where I have used such data I have regarded them as suggestive illustrations, not as evidence. Until quite recently most French statistics were notoriously unreliable and were, for that reason alone, unlikely to mirror reality better than subjective judgments. I have regarded polling and surve͏ data, also, as suggestive illustrations. French techniques in th͏ field have been refined greatly and their results, too, provide interesting comments. But they "prove" little and, as some French political scientists have shown, to me convincingly, even less than in some other countries.[2]

This study is one of an old country undergoing rapid development. My footnotes should show how much I have profited from the literature on political development — some of which appears in this series. Circumstances have not permitted me to investigate in necessary detail the impact which the international environment has had on French domestic politics. It is obvious that the political development of a country such as France has been drastically affected by her frequent exposure to large-scale wars and more recently to the tensions caused by the cold war.

Yet however heavy the heritage of past events, whether generated within the national borders or outside, present-day France is not just a prisoner of its past. The "silent revolution" described on many pages of this book as taking place in many fields, would not be possible, if a nation's values were foreordained and unalterable. The limits and constraints conditioning the ongoing development must be clearly understood if France is to hold, as she has so often in the past, pertinent lessons for general and democratic political theory. But again Tocqueville reminds his disciples not to get embroiled too far in "doctrines of necessity" and, instead, to "acknowledge the strength and independence of men united in society." For, as he concludes, "the great object in our time is to raise the faculties of men, not to complete their prostration."

The research for and the writing of this book were substantially aided by Dartmouth College. Its generous leave policy, grants awarded by its Committee on Research, and altogether an atmosphere in which research and teaching are equally recognized made this study possible. But the book also owes much to my earlier musings and wanderings supported by the Social Science Research Council, the Rockefeller Foundation, and the Ford Foundation.

My colleagues and friends to whom this book is dedicated have

[2] See Association Française de Science Politique, *Les Sondages et la Science Politique* (Paris: Mimeographed, 1966).

contributed more than they might wish to acknowledge when they see the results of their counsel. Whether they have read, with great attention to ideas and details, parts of the manuscript, whether they have answered precisely my manifold inquiries or engaged with me, over many years, in lengthy discussions of French politics, their knowledge and understanding were indispensable. In the United States, Gabriel Almond, Lewis Edinger, and Richard Rose have commented helpfully and with acumen on parts of the manuscript. My colleague and friend at Dartmouth, Professor Howard Bliss has gone with great care over the entire manuscript. His thoughtful suggestions have resulted in many improvements of content and style. To be edited by as competent a staff as that of Little, Brown and Company is an intellectual joy. The efficiency of the staff of Baker Library at Dartmouth and especially of its Order Department should prove attractive to any scholar.

One of my students, Mr. Roger Witten of the Dartmouth Class of 1968 proved his mettle as an untiring research assistant. Mrs. Louise Spiess can only be described as a paragon among secretaries. The reader is bound to profit from Mrs. Joan Erdman's skill as a judicious indexer.

My wife Claire made no suggestions whatsoever, nor did she proofread. She did not even read. Ever since we met more than thirty years ago in Paris — to be sure in the midst of acute political crisis — we have talked, lived, and breathed French politics, with a frown or a smile, in France and from afar. This book will teach her nothing. But all through the writing process she fulfilled her usual and indispensable function. She never ceased insisting that there are broader horizons and more urgent problems in the world at large than a work-centered author will admit. For this my undivided thanks go to her.

H.W.E.

March, 1968

Table of Contents

Illustrations and Tables

Politics in
FRANCE

CHAPTER I

Origins and History of the System

A NATION OF PATRIOTS — DIVIDED

As one of the oldest nation-states of Europe, France has been free of many of the tensions characteristic of countries which have found their national unity and identity only in more recent times. Many of her borders are not determined by natural barriers as are those of the British Isles. Yet, except for some relatively minor though hotly contested frontier areas, France's territorial limits were determined far earlier than those of other continental countries. Brought together over centuries by accidents of history rather than by facts of geography or of ethnical origin, Frenchmen have developed a strong sense of national identification. Theirs is an adult "civilization," a term which to them is more meaningful than "culture" or *"Kultur."* It not only denotes a long-term achievement but also encourages missionary zeal to spread its values.

Geographically the country is at once Atlantic, Continental, and Mediterranean, and hence occupies a unique place in Europe. Ethnically, no such thing as a French race exists. "We are a race of half-breeds," a French historian has written; but he added wistfully: "Mongrels are often more intelligent than purebred dogs." [1] Which of their gifts and deficiencies French-

---

[1] Charles Seignobos, as quoted in André Siegfried, "Approaches to an Understanding of Modern France" in Edward M. Earle (ed.), *Modern*

men owe to the Latins, the Celts, or the Germanic tribes is far less significant than the fact that in a nation fashioned by common historical experience, neither regional nor linguistic, nor even differences between Catholics and Protestants, are divisive factors as they have been for all of France's neighbors. Moreover, the existing diversities have been encompassed by a strong national unity.

The French monarchy played an outstanding role in national integration. It also gave to French national feeling some of its distinguishing characteristics. Unlike other European monarchs, the French kings claimed and received, for close to a thousand years, sacerdotal and religious dignity. Such status has marked not only French Catholicism but all concepts of authority.[2] A French monk described the first crusade as *Gesta Dei per Francos:* the Franks were presented as the chosen instruments of God. There are other nations that from time to time have claimed to be pacesetters for the rest of the world. But among Frenchmen a belief in the universal value of their own civilization has remained strong whatever the setbacks of their national destiny. Only recently André Malraux, one-time left wing intellectual and during the years of General de Gaulle's rule the Fifth Republic's Minister of Cultural Affairs, voiced the conviction that "with the exception of the Revolution [!] the universal calling of France has never been as striking as at present."

Claims that attribute general significance to a national civilization have been common to the political Right and Left. The very term "nationalism" in its pejorative sense was coined to reproach the Jacobins for their all too burning desire to export ideals at the point of French bayonets. In 1793, at the height of the Terror, "patriotism" described the resolve not only to defend the soil of *la patrie,* but also to cultivate civic and republican virtues and to share with other nations the blessings of the Revolution. The Paris Commune of 1871, hailed by Karl Marx as the harbinger of a worldwide class struggle,

---

France. Problems of the Third and Fourth Republics (Princeton: Princeton University Press, 1951), p. 4. In some respects Siegfried's article contains still valid generalizations about the political culture of the country.

[2] Ernst Robert Curtius, *The Civilization of France* (New York: Vintage Books, 1962), pp. 72 ff.

was in fact an act of defiance addressed to the "Prussian" Bismarck as well as to the bourgeois government at Versailles. The language and thought of communist and socialist resistance movements during the Second World War showed the same amalgam of patriotism and democratic values.

Even an insistence on the nation's greatness, its *grandeur,* is not the monopoly of any particular political orientation, for it is raised in the name of a civilization rather than in defense of martial ventures. Jules Michelet, influential historian of the Revolution, wrote sweepingly that the concept of French national *grandeur* belonged to a tradition which was common to the National Convention of 1792 and to St. Louis, the first Bourbon king. More recently, the opening sentences of General de Gaulle's memoirs have given to such a mythology of the nation an expression that already has become classical.

> All my life I have thought of France in a certain way. This is inspired by sentiment as much as by reason. The emotional side of me tends to imagine France like the princess in the fairy stories or the Madonna in the frescoes, as dedicated to an exalted and exceptional destiny. . . . In short, to my mind, France cannot be France without *grandeur*.[3]

However deep the roots of a common national mythology, Frenchmen are divided by conflicting views as to which political system is most appropriate to attain the goal of greatness. If every Frenchman loves France, this does not preclude his poorly concealed contempt for the Frenchmen outside of his own immediate or political family. When the momentary destiny of the country appears mediocre, he is inclined to impute this to the faults of his fellow citizen, while the genius of the land remains unimpaired in his eyes.

In all nations, historical events that have created deep divisions have produced a political culture in which the citizens are full of mutual mistrust and low in agreement on fundamentals.[4] It was natural enough that the Revolution of the eighteenth century opened long drawn-out controversies be-

[3] Charles de Gaulle, *War Memoirs, I: The Call to Honour* (New York: The Viking Press, 1955), p. 3.
[4] See the observations by Sidney Verba in Lucian W. Pye and Sidney Verba (eds.), *Political Culture and Political Development* (Princeton: Princeton University Press, 1965), p. 556.

tween monarchists and republicans. But it also shook and split, on the most sensitive level, the conscience of elites and common people. The Revolution amounted not merely to a collective apostasy from the Catholic Church, but to such a violent break with Christianity as, prior to the bolshevik seizure of power, no other European nation had experienced. From then on France became the champion of emancipated reason and yet remained a refuge for Catholic faith.[5] The sharp political discontinuities, the revolutions and counter-revolutions of the nineteenth and twentieth centuries, were in part a consequence of the rift between believers and nonbelievers, although they also added new sources of conflict.

The more vividly the conflicts of the past are remembered, the more heavily they weigh on the behavior of political actors and onlookers. Edmund Burke spoke of society as "a partnership . . . between those who are living, those who are dead and those who are to be born." French society frequently appears overcommitted to the experiences of past generations. A habit of historical thinking can prove a bond, but also — as the American Civil War shows — a hindrance to consensus. Frenchmen are so fascinated by their own, admittedly exciting, history that the feuds of the past are constantly superimposed on the conflicts of the present. The passionate use of historical memories, resulting in seemingly inflexible commands and warnings, narrows the scope of authoritative and private decision-making. The old country that is France is, again in de Gaulle's words, "weighed down by history." [6]

The very nature of political conflicts is in part determined by the style which defines them. "Politics are ideas," a modern French writer has claimed.[7] Hence at least at a certain level, the style of politics will remain as ideological as it became in the age of the enlightenment when the Old Regime, in order to compensate for the servile condition to which it had confined the educated classes, left them free to voice their views on many topics. Philosophy, religion, ethics, and even politics could be discussed provided the discussion remained on a general

[5] Curtius, *op. cit.*, p. 123.

[6] Charles de Gaulle, *op. cit., III: The Salvation* (New York: Simon and Schuster, 1960), p. 330.

[7] Albert Thibaudet, *Les Idées Politiques en France* (Paris: Stock, 1932).

and abstract plane. At about the same time, the bourgeoisie was compelled to abandon those local administrative functions which it had exercised previously. Hence its political initiation, sophisticated though it was, was derived entirely from men of letters and philosophers. "Thus alongside the traditional and confused, not to say chaotic, social system of the day there was gradually built up in [these Frenchmen's] mind[s] an imaginary ideal society in which all was simple, uniform, coherent, equitable, and rational in the full sense of the term." [8]

Since then the urge to discuss a wide range of problems, even the most trivial ones, in broad philosophical terms has not diminished; nor has the endless search to find a solution to the problems of the day in a system, a doctrine, or a faith. In all countries conservatives seek the Platonic idea to which they want to make society conform. But in France the enemies of the republican regime have gone to the extreme of defining their image of France as the *"pays réel,"* the real country, compared to which the existing institutions deserve the contemptuous label of the *"pays légal,"* the merely legal institutions. Yet their opponents can be just as bigoted and doctrinaire when they reject a compromise between conflicting ideologies as an offense to the method prescribed by Descartes.

Symbols and rituals perpetuate the political style. A pretender to the throne, the Comte de Chambord, might have been able to restore the monarchy in 1873 had he been less unyielding on the issue of a flag for the nation. Today, two rural communities which fought on opposite sides in the French Revolution, pay homage to different heroes nearly two centuries later. In the eyes of an American observer who knows them both, they have no real quarrel with each other. Yet inherited symbols have kept them apart so that their political and religious habits have remained disparate.[9] Formal symbols to which all Frenchmen respond are not entirely lacking but rare. After

[8] Alexis de Tocqueville, *The Old Régime and the French Revolution* (New York: Doubleday Anchor Books, 1955), pp. 64, 146. For a succinct analysis of the political and social situation during the decades preceding the Revolution, see also Gabriel Almond and G. Bingham Powell, Jr., *Comparative Politics: A Developmental Approach* (Boston: Little, Brown and Company, 1966), pp. 320 f.

[9] Laurence Wylie, "Social Change at the Grass Roots," in Stanley Hoffman et al., *In Search of France* (Cambridge: Harvard University Press, 1963), p. 230.

1940 the Vichy regime found it necessary to replace on every public building the time-honored "Liberty-Fraternity-Equality" with another triad. In every town and city a considerable number of streets change names with every change in political fortunes. Whether a Paris street should bear the name of Maximilien Robespierre became quite recently the subject of a passionate debate in the Municipal Council.

Abiding faiths create deep hatreds. Ever since the Jacobins denounced their opponents as "enemies of the people," such accusations have belonged to the arsenal of French political polemics (long before they entered the terminology of modern totalitarianism). In every democratic country, a scandalous mistrial such as that of Captain Dreyfus with its backdrop of intrigue, motivated by anti-Semitism and caste spirit, would have provoked indignation and possibly prolonged unrest. What was characteristically French was the fact that at the turn of the century *L'Affaire* became a violent conflict over values among the country's elites. Both sides went to fanatical extremes; guilt or innocence of Dreyfus was not a question of evidence but of unshakable dogma. The legacy bequeathed by the upheaval and its aftermath was the confinement of the officer corps and a majority of the practicing Catholics for many decades to a political ghetto, in which they lived apart from the mainstream of national life.

For all its drama, the Dreyfus affair was only one, if characteristic episode in the political history of a nation united by almost universal admiration for a common historical experience yet divided by conflicting interpretations of its meaning.

TENSIONS BETWEEN REPRESENTATIVE
AND PLEBISCITARIAN TRADITIONS

Although the controversies between monarchists and republicans have continued well into our century, their effect on the various political systems that have emerged in rapid succession since the Revolution has been less significant than the opposition between the temptations of two other patterns of government. One is identifiable with a representative tradition of democracy, the other with a plebiscitarian.

In the early days of the Revolution, mere lip service was

paid to Rousseau's concept postulating the direct participation of the citizenry in the political process. The system then established was based on a belief, shared by most of the middle-class deputies to the National Assembly, that the intentions of the sovereign people could be expressed validly only through its elected representatives; that legislative as well as constituent power should be exclusively in their hands. But a few years later, the constitution of 1793 rejected such views, and denouncing "representative despotism," it tried to organize the general will by annual elections and referendums. But before this Constitution could come into existence it was superseded by revolutionary rule which climaxed in Napoleon's rise to power.[10] His rule set the pattern for a system which was as hostile to the representative ideas of Abbé Siéyès, of the American Constitution, and of the parliamentary monarchies of Europe, as it was to the absolute monarchy of the Old Regime. It was more than a device of political cleverness that for several years French coins bore the double inscription: "French Republic — Napoleon Emperor." Bonaparte claimed to continue the Revolution rather than to abrogate it.

Hence France, just freed from its old shackles, experienced within the short span of a decade two novel and different forms of authority. They were to form the opposite poles between which French political life has moved ever since, even if some of the sixteen constitutions under which Frenchmen have lived since the Revolution have aimed at combining elements of both traditions. Almost invariably, political life under a given regime has been determined by one or the other of the major trends. With each change of regime the tradition which was temporarily eclipsed lived on as a strong undercurrent creating perpetual internal tensions.

Since Napoleon Bonaparte was the first to develop the pattern of a political system which claimed that its rule was sanctioned by the voice of the sovereign people, practices of direct democracy in France are easily identified with bona-

---

[10] The historical background of the two traditions is traced in greater detail by Henry W. Ehrmann, "Direct Democracy in France," *American Political Science Review,* LVII:4 (1963), pp. 883 ff. Cf. also Stanley Hoffmann, "Paradoxes of the French Political Community," in *In Search of France,* p. 14.

partism. Shorn of all accidentals, the theory and practices of the two Napoleons scorned intermediaries in state and society which might stand between the unorganized masses and the popularly acclaimed head of the executive. There was in their system room neither for a totalitarian party nor for voluntary associations. Accordingly, the role of the legislative branch was reduced; the political life of the nation was carefully circumscribed and potentially extinguished. Any infringement of constitutional and other laws by the ruler could be given legitimacy by popular approval. The Napoleonic plebiscites combined the threat of social chaos which would follow the demise of the providential leader with the flattery of the people by giving them the opportunity of choosing their master directly — or of perpetuating his rule. The temper of the regime was anti-individualist: Napoleonic codes and legislation strengthened the authority of the head of the family, of the employer, of the administrative official.[11]

What distinguishes French bonapartism from other forms of caesarism is the allegiance it paid to certain Jacobin traditions of the Revolution. At all times, Napoleon's appeals to the masses over the heads of the traditional notables had egalitarian undertones. During the Hundred Days, the returning emperor discovered the possibilities of a "people's bonapartism." From then on the Napoleonic legend, on which Napoleon's nephew Louis Bonaparte would draw in his campaign for a popularly elected republican presidency, was distinctly tinged with egalitarian socialism — or at least with its terminology. The constitution of the Second Empire (as would that of the Fifth Republic) explicitly referred to the "principles of 1789" and boasted of having given the constituent power back to the people.

With the demise of Napoleon III, the opposite, representative tradition established itself firmly and exercised its sway with only short interruptions until turmoil in Algeria returned General de Gaulle to power. But during every crisis of

[11] For the plebiscitarian ideology of bonapartism cf. Robert Michels, *Political Parties* (New York: Collier Books, 1962), pp. 212–219 and the excellent recent treatment by René Rémond, *La Vie Politique en France, Tome I* (Paris: Armand Colin, 1965), pp. 221–247 and *Tome II* (id., 1969), pp. 131–169.

the Third and Fourth Republics, the critics of the existing system liked to argue in terms established by bonapartism. All political parties were condemned as hampering the expression of
a general will — assumed to be unequivocal on all major political decisions. Parliament was likened to a broken mirror mis-
representing the true interests of the electorate. Popular sovereignty should be reestablished by giving the voters the
amending power and the right to vote in referendums. The
executive should be enabled to rule efficiently above and despite political and social divisions. Such detailed and fundamental criticism of the parliamentary regime, to be sure, came
either from a vocal minority of intellectuals and publicists or
from men that put themselves forward as an alternative to the
existing regime. But antiparliamentary feelings, both vague
and vehement, were at times quite widespread and frequently
associated with longings for a strong-arm rule. The tenacity
of this mood even during the height of the representative
regime tended to put the latter's protagonists on the defensive
and drove them to exaggerations.

To the authentic spokesmen of the representative tradition,
the essence of democratic government consisted in the close
control of an ever-suspected executive and in the defense of
constituency interests, however fragmented they might be. For
such tasks the deputy, "entrenched, fortified and undefeatable
in his constituency like the feudal lord of old in his castle," [12]
was superbly qualified. He could be counted upon to decide
for himself, without directives from an extraparliamentary body
— even a political party — how best to resist authority. Any
direct appeal to the people was viewed as a manifestation of
"supreme decadence." In fact, historical experiences had instilled
in deputies and senators such fear of executive leadership
and of the popular acclaim it might seek, that they frowned

[12] Alain, *Éléments de la doctrine radicale* (Paris: Gallimard, 1925), p.
42. The (unfortunately untranslated) writings of the curious philosopher-
journalist Alain are indispensable for an understanding of the French
version of the representative system and of the period during which it
flowered, i.e., the first thirty years of the present century. For a recent
evaluation of Alain's significance, see Roy Pierce, *Contemporary French
Political Thought* (London and New York: Oxford University Press,
1966), pp. 4–10.

upon any address by a political leader which was not made either from the tribune of parliament or within the narrow confines of his small constituency. Paul Reynaud, perennial deputy throughout three republican regimes, gave perfect expression to this tradition during the debate on President de Gaulle's proposal for a constitutional referendum. He condemned the very idea of consulting the French electorate on a question of constitutional revision. "For us republicans," he scorned, "France exists only here [in parliament] and nowhere else."

It will be explained below (Chaps. VI and VIII) why republican France has never developed a modern party system of the kind which, in other democracies, has accomplished the necessary transformation of parliament "from the representative corporation which it was into a plebiscitary expedient." [13] In the absence of such a system, the tensions created by the oligarchic deformations of the representative traditions and the caesaristic temptations of plebiscitarian regimes have never been resolved.

TENSIONS BETWEEN BUREAUCRATIC
TRADITIONS AND INDIVIDUALISM

To both distrust government and expect much from it is a widespread ambivalence of modern times, which might well betray some unresolved inner conflict about the interaction of government and society.[14] In most countries this ambivalence is a consequence of the rise of the modern service-state which is unavoidably burdened with ever new tasks. But in France such feelings can again be traced to centuries-old traditions. The Old Regime, and especially the long reign of Louis XIV, gave the country a rigidly centralized administration, recruited and operated according to functional criteria. Its activities reached deep into many phases of economic and social life. It proved so all pervasive that it "deprived Frenchmen of the possibility and even the desire to come to each other's aid. When the Revolution started it would have been impossible to

[13] Gerhard Leibholz, "The Nature and Various Forms of Democracy," *Social Research,* VII (1938), p. 99.

[14] Cf. Felix Frankfurter, *The Public and Its Government* (New Haven: Yale University Press, 1930), pp. 3–4.

ind . . . even ten men used to acting in concert and defending their interests without appealing to the central power for aid." [15] What sheltered the individual from constant interference by governmental authorities was, in an age of underdeveloped communications, the relative remoteness of the central government which had not abolished the existing patchwork of local privileges and traditions of lax enforcement.

The Jacobins and Napoleon took over the techniques and, frequently, the men that the monarchy had bequeathed to them and used them for their political ends. The egalitarian temper of sans-culottism, bent as it was on uprooting privileges wherever they had survived, soon became hostile to hopes for a federal structure of government alive during the early days of the Revolution. The demand for equality was to be satisfied by the greatest possible uniformity of rules, over which an ever stronger, better qualified, and more centralized administration was to watch. The more significant the central power became, the more tenacious grew the fight for its control. Because the stakes were high, political forces not only denied the wisdom of their opponents, which is normal, but contested the very legitimacy of their power or of their claim to power.

The French citizen's fear and distrust of authority and his simultaneous need for strong authority feed on both his individualism and his passion for equality. In France social mobility has remained steady if limited; a preindustrial mentality shared by the peasantry and the bourgeoisie has persisted (for details see Chaps. II and III). Such a country produces a self-reliant individual who is convinced that he owes to himself (and perhaps to his immediate family) what he is and what he may become. In his eyes the obstacles in his way are created by the outside world, the "they" that operate beyond the circle of the family, the family firm, the village. Most of the time, however, "they" are identified with the government.

> The government is made up of incompetents, swindlers or fools, who are usurping the function of the state. The government is that which prefers someone else. The government is

[15] Tocqueville, *op. cit.*, p. 206.

that which threatens the family property through taxes. The
government is that which threatens the established order through
partisan legislation. The government is that authority which must
be checkmated or exploited through seduction, silence and systematic obstruction.[16]

A stock of memories reaching possibly all the way from the
eighteenth century through the most recent wars is used to
justify a state of mind which is one of latent, even if seldom
actual, insubordination. If the government is nefarious, it must
be controlled and is not looked upon as a possible source of
reform. The authentic republican tradition is again exemplified
by Alain's "radical doctrine": the government deserves distrust
without revolt, and obedience without commitment. A strong
government is considered *ipso facto* reactionary, even if it pre-
tends to follow a politically progressive course of action. Such
deeply ingrained beliefs explain why, over the span of history,
authoritarian regimes have originated more fundamental transformations of society and state than representative regimes.

Since the citizen feels that no one but himself can be entrusted with the defense of his interests, he is inclined to shun
constructive cooperation. He fears that the discipline involved
in any cooperation might put social constraints on him. Where
he participates in public life, he hopes to weaken authority
rather than to encourage change, even when change is overdue.

At times this commitment to individualism is tainted with
outright anarchistic tendencies. Yet, inasmuch as it is wedded
to a sharp sense of equality, it is quite able to accommodate
itself to bureaucratic rule. Especially on the lower level of
administration, the government may act through incompetent
civil servants whom the citizens are wont to criticize as unjust
masters. Another French philosopher, Charles Péguy, has spoken
sarcastically of that one true division between Frenchmen, more
marked than all class division — the one between those who wait
in front of an official's window and those who sit behind it.

But however despised the government and its officials, the
abstract entity that is the state is indispensable since it safe-

---

[16] Jesse R. Pitts, "Continuity and Change in Bourgeois France," in *In
Search of France,* p. 260. For some recent observations modifying such
extreme statements, see below Chapter III.

guards the uniform rulings which guarantee equality of treatment. The farther removed that entity is, the more acceptable are the solutions which it imposes from above. They permit the citizen to escape responsibility for resolving conflicts and to avoid face-to-face relationships with either his peers or his superiors.[17] This in turn gives to the administration enough leeway to stand firm amidst the vagaries of the political system. Its rulings may meet with the derision and bitterness of the citizenry; they will still be condoned as guaranteeing egalitarian standards. This explains the often noted paradox that traditionally France, the country of weak governments, appears as a strong state until an acute crisis reveals the feebleness of state *and* government. For this, the dramatic Events of May, 1968, offered the most recent evidence.

Individualism and administrative centralization, both fostered by the same Jacobin temperament, are complementary and able to mitigate their mutual effects. The pattern of authority created thereby is neither liberal nor totalitarian, but has been characterized as the coexistence of *limited* authoritarianism and *potential* insurrection against authority.[18]

The attitudes of the deliberately distrustful French are quite different from those of the British who in their political attitudes reflect the basic trust characteristic of their social relationships. In neither (and no) society is equality fully achieved. But in England it is often not valued as a goal,[19] while in France the concern for equality far outranks the value placed on liberty.

CONSEQUENCES FOR THE POLITICAL SYSTEM

There have been long-standing discussions among Frenchmen and among foreign observers of the French political scene as to the moment when the political system became unable to deal successfully with the tasks incumbent upon it.

---

[17] All the writings of Michel Crozier have emphasized the basic avoidance of face-to-face relationships in French society. They are summarized and expanded in his study, *The Bureaucratic Phenomenon* (Chicago: The University of Chicago Press, 1964), esp. pp. 220 ff. For more detailed treatment see below, esp. Chaps. III and VI.

[18] Hoffmann, *op. cit.*, p. 8.

[19] Richard Rose, *Politics in England* (Boston: Little, Brown and Company, 1964), pp. 39, 43.

The apparent contradictions in the behavior of individuals
and of groups are, in fact, the result of tensions, themselves
the consequence of historical experiences reaching back to the
period of the absolute monarchy.

Even though in fact the Revolution of 1789 did not effect as
complete a break with the past as is commonly believed, it has
conditioned the general outlook on crisis and compromise, on
continuity and change. Sudden rather than gradual mutation,
dramatic conflicts couched in the language of opposing and
mutually exclusive, radical ideologies — these are the experiences that excite Frenchmen at historical moments when their
minds are particularly malleable. Even at the end of the nineteenth century, history itself appeared to an illustrious French
historian, Ernest Renan, as a "kind of civil war." In fact, what
appears to the outsider as permanent instability is a fairly
regular alternation between violent crises and more or less
prolonged periods of routine.

It is perhaps noteworthy that in France there is an abundance of political biographies of the figures of exalted times,
but hardly any of the great parliamentary leaders, to say nothing of administrators or judges. To contend that Frenchmen,
whether illustrious or humble, "love" crisis may be invidious.
But they have become accustomed to think that no thoroughgoing change can ever be brought about except through a
major upheaval. Since the great Revolution, every adult Frenchman has experienced — usually more than once in his lifetime —
occasions of political excitement followed by disappointment.
This leads periodically to moral exhaustion and almost permanent and widespread scepticism regarding any possibility of
change. The aphorism that "The more things change, the more
they stay the same," may be quite worn, but it still expresses
general feelings.

In addition to the factors discussed so far, wars and other
pressures from the international environment have constantly
sharpened crises. Before the Revolution the very development
of the French nation and state was closely related to many of
the dynastic conflicts of Europe. Since then many of the political upheavals and constitutional breaks were caused by,
or at least connected with, wars in which the country became

embroiled. Whether they originated within the country or were brought about by international conflicts, each of the frequent national emergencies has resulted in a constitutional crisis. Each time, the social and political forces emerging temporarily triumphant codified their norms and philosophy, usually in a comprehensive document. Hence, to give only a few examples, the constitutions of 1791, 1830, 1875, and 1946 enshrined the representative principle and Montesquieu's precepts; those of 1793 and of 1848 belong partly, those of 1852 and of 1958 (especially as amended in 1962) more frankly to the plebiscitarian tradition. Because of such practices, constitutions have never played the role of fundamental charters, nor have they laid down generally accepted rules for the political game. Their conflicting norms are satisfactory only to one segment of public opinion and are hotly contested by the others. This in turn invites a lack of respect for fundamental norms which are viewed as being forever in flux.

The highly ideological and historically oriented language of politics has deepened the chasm between actual and declared policies. To wrap the political discontent of the day in metaphysics, to give to the tritest discussion the dignity of philosophy, has not furthered the French contribution to political theory, in spite of some brilliant thinkers.

The prevailing style of debate has encouraged a proclivity for "false conflicts." To the degree that behavior of the political actors and of the electorate corresponds to past alignments, it is unsuited to the solution of actual conflicts. On the other hand, when finding solutions and accommodating conflicting interests by compromise finally becomes unavoidable, such agreements are reached without any reference to fundamentals. This increases the contempt not only for politicians but for the political way of life itself as seemingly betraying the principles by which men ought to live. Middle-of-the-road politics are considered an eternal "swamp" which muddies every forthright action. As far as possible, the political system is put outside the rational and emotional loyalty of the citizens, which strengthens their nonparticipatory disposition. "Turbulence on the one side," a French sociologist has concluded, "and a nearly unbelievable tolerance of the provisionary and the confused on the other, are evidence that the French do not take social situations seriously." [20]

The high sensitivity of the public at moments of crises and its withdrawal into apathy during periods of unexciting routine are again only different aspects of the same phenomenon. Although the pulling back of the public from the political game and its exclusive devotion to private life is observed not only in France, the absence of a modern party system mediating between the public and its government, the insensitivity of parliament and of the administration to currents of public opinion has at different periods rendered the alienation of the French citizen more acute than in other modern democracies, even though electoral participation remains generally high. An approaching major crisis is usually foreshadowed rather precisely by a lack of support for the regime, a lack that sometimes is expressed in the flash successes of extremist parties,[21] in tax evasion or outright resistance to tax collection, and in fiery debates on the next, and better, constitution.

That Frenchmen are people difficult to govern is a commonplace voiced in over-quoted statements by Caesar, Tocqueville, and, most recently, by one of the country's present preceptors, the first Prime Minister of the Fifth Republic, Michel Debré. Historical events have brought this about. The subsequent chapters will show in greater detail the mutual influence of values and beliefs, of political institutions, and of the economic and social setting.

[20] François Bourricaud, "France" in Arnold M. Rose (ed.), *The Institutions of Advanced Societies* (Minneapolis: University of Minnesota Press, 1958), p. 520; cf. also Otto Kirchheimer, "France from the Fourth to the Fifth Republic," *Social Research,* XXV:4 (1958), pp. 382–83.

[21] In all elections held between 1947 and 1956, extremist parties, opposed to the very foundations of the existing order, obtained about 40 per cent of the votes.

CHAPTER II

The Economic and Social Setting

THE IMPACT OF RECOVERY

Unevenness in economic development and strains in the social structure resulting from such unevenness, have their impact on the political process and the political culture of any country. In the case of France it is no longer necessary to argue whether or not in economic terms the country is a perenially retarded developer. She was regarded as such when for nearly eighty years her economic growth was the slowest of all developed countries (about 1.1 per cent annually). But the economic vitality manifest during much of the Fourth Republic and consolidated since then has put France into the ranks of the highly industrialized countries of Western Europe. There is little likelihood that she will lose that position.

Explanations for the massive recovery and rapid modernization vary as greatly as did those for the earlier sluggishness. For this and other reasons a valid political analysis of present-day France cannot dispense with a discussion of the setting in which the resurgence of the economy has taken place. It is especially necessary to determine, however summarily, the respective roles which changes in attitude and transformations of the institutional setup have played; what have been the impulses coming from the international environment and which have been domestic in origin. That such mutations as have occurred are not uniform and that therefore the modernization process remains uneven, is not peculiar to France. As elsewhere, but probably more than elsewhere, the behavior of Frenchmen as producers and consumers is intimately related to their general value and belief system. Hence it is useful to analyze at which point traditional attitudes prevail or are replaced, and where such attitudes are likely to spill over into political behavior.

In terms of per capita gross national product, France at present ranks among the wealthiest nations of Western Europe (in 1967: $2,324, compared with $4,037 in the U.S.), ahead of West-Germany and of the United Kingdom, and nearly twice as prosperous as Italy. Every year since 1950, the annual rate of economic growth has been between 5 and 6 per cent. Equally satisfactory and steady has been the average annual increase in productivity since 1950 — 4.5 per cent.[1]

What should not be forgotten is that in large part such growth is merely a catching up on past retardation. Although the record of the interwar years had been altogether undistinguished, the decade preceding the outbreak of hostilities in 1939 was catastrophic for economic development; the German occupation brought new disaster. Statistically, economic development profited from a low starting point. When 1958 is taken as a base, industrial production in France has advanced more than in Great Britain (an increase of 59 per cent against 41 per cent in Britain). But the gain is only mediocre when compared with West Germany (75 per cent), Holland (108 per cent), or Italy (139 per cent). Hence French progress, while respectable, has hardly reached the proportions of an "economic miracle."[2]

Economists and demographers will continue to argue about the respective significance of population trends and economic growth at various stages of economic development. For France there is no doubt that the slow growth of her population since 1850, a declining birth rate and a net reproduction rate below the level of replacement, had not only an adverse economic

[1] These and most of the following statistical data are from Bernard Mueller, *A Statistical Handbook of the North Atlantic Area* (New York: The Twentieth Century Fund, 1965); or the U.N. Statistical Yearbook, 1968 (New York: United Nations, 1969).

[2] This point is made in what I consider the most careful study of French economic development, A. Cotta, "La Croissance de l'économie française, 1945–1975," *Analyse et Prévision*, II:1–2 (1966), pp. 519–560, at p. 533.

FIGURE I. *Age Structure of French Population
(Estimates as of January 1, 1965)*

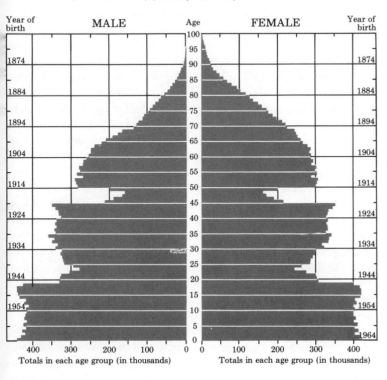

At date:	Number of:			
	Young 0-19 years	Adults 20-59 years	Old 60 years and over	Totals
January 1, 1946	295	545	160	1,000
January 1, 1959	318	516	166	1,000
January 1, 1965	339	487	174	1,000

Source: *Population,* XX:6 (1965), pp. 1118, 1120.

but, even worse, a disastrous psychological effect. Widely publicized pictures of the age pyramid showed quite dramatically the direct and indirect effect of the First World War: the total population deficit (the dead and the children that were not born because of the war) amounted to over three million people, i.e., 7–8 per cent of the prewar population. (The population pyramid, Figure I, illustrates quite dramatically the losses which France sustained through the two World Wars.) Until recently, conversations about the future of France turned frequently to the consequences of this tragic loss for the country's vitality, labor force, and leadership. And, the losses that had been sustained were not made up during the interwar period. The population grew at a rate less than half that of Germany, becoming almost stagnant with the depression. The continuation of interwar trends would have meant a population of 39 million by 1960 and 36.9 million by 1970. Instead, and in spite of substantial new losses caused by the Second World War, the population reached the 50 million mark in 1968 (at about the same time the United States population rose to 200 million). Within the age pyramid, the proportion of those under twenty years of age expands so fast that France today is one of the "youngest" nations of Europe.

Part of this upswing is undoubtedly due to a systematic policy of material inducements, such as family allowances and other devices. Since 1939, with unusual consistency every successive regime enacted measures favorable to population growth. There is, however, ample evidence to show that the drastic upward swing in the size of families is due principally to a change in attitudes towards procreation. Demographic malthusianism was particularly widespread among the bourgeoisie and the peasants. To them too numerous a progeny meant the dividing up of land, of business property, and of inheritance. By limiting the possibilities for a better education, it might destroy class status or upward mobility. Worse yet, it might upset the carefully preserved equilibrium of society at large. If former restraints are being overcome now and a new view of family life prevails, this seems to indicate a "more trustful and future-oriented view of the human condition." [3] It is true that since 1965 births

[3] Crozier, *op. cit.*, p. 307, and Charles P. Kindleberger, "The Postwar Resurgence of the French Economy," in *In Search of France,* pp. 131–135.

have again been declining steadily throughout France. From 18 per 1,000 in 1963 the birth rate fell to 16.6 per 1,000 in 1967. The fertility rate — live births per couple — has dropped considerably since 1965. If this trend which so far has remained unexplained were to continue, by 1985 the reproduction of the population would be barely assured.

France remains lowest in population density among the six Common Market countries. In the "garden that is France" (and French children are commonly taught to think of their country in this way) there live only 238 persons per square mile, as compared with 606 in West Germany and 814 in Belgium. If France had the same population density as other major European powers, there should be more than 125 million Frenchmen.

The country has left its gates relatively wide open for immigration. During the decade of the sixties, every year between 110,000 and 150,000 workers from abroad and members of their families have settled permanently in France. Another 100,000 to 130,000 seasonal workers joined the labor force year by year.

Apart from the population increase itself, the most remarkable demographic development since the war has been the mobility of this growing population. Geographical and professional mobility have supported each other; while both have been an important stimulus to modernization, they also have unavoidably generated certain tensions contingent upon it. Many developments which other Western societies have been undergoing since the end of the last century have been taking place in France only since the last war. Some of them, such as the exodus from the countryside, have occurred with such rapidity that census figures have surprised even the best informed.

On the eve of the last war, the proportion of the population gainfully employed in agriculture was still at a high 37 per cent; twenty-five years later it was 19 per cent. Industry employed in 1964 41 per cent as against 30 per cent, while employment in the tertiary sector (commerce, services, and administration) had risen from 33 to 40 per cent. (This distribution still does not correspond to that prevalent in the most highly developed industrial nations such as the United States, West Germany, and Great Britain.) At the same time, the proportion within the total labor force of employers, self-employed, and unpaid family workers is steadily declining, while that of wage and salary earners rises to figures that are average for Western Europe — a striking development for a country that traditionally has been one of small enterprises and of independent farmers.

Before the war 48 per cent of the population lived in rural communities of fewer than 2,000 inhabitants; only 30 per cent do so at present. Villages of less than 1,000 population are being deserted, especially by the young, at such a rate that in certain parts of the country this movement is toppling local social and economic structures. At the other end of the scale the development is almost as striking: in 1936, there were in the entire country only 16 cities with a population of more than 100,000. According to the census of 1968, there are now 37 such cities, and almost one Frenchman in five lives in one of these metropolitan areas. In fact, the population of these urban centers has risen by more than 2 million or roughly 11 per cent between 1962 and 1969. But only ten cities have more than 200,000 inhabitants (as against 26 cities of this size in West Germany and 20 in Great Britain).

If — compared with other industrialized countries of Western Europe — French urbanization appears to be slow, it has already had an important impact on French mentality and living habits — all the more so as the growth of big and middle-sized cities has brought many people still living in rural communities into professional and social contact with urban life and preoccupations. A recent national sample reveals that geographical mobility has reached proportions that are quite novel for France: at present 20 per cent live in a region different from that in which they were born; 15 per cent have moved from another community within the last five years, and 15 per cent expect not to stay for the rest of their lives in their present place of residence.

Population shifts and a corresponding redistribution of national wealth have, on the whole, accented rather than mitigated traditional differences. The increase in population has profited only one-third of the country; more than two-thirds of the ninety-five departments into which the country is divided now have a lower population than in 1950. As early as the seventeenth and eighteenth centuries, royal edicts tried to put a stop to the growth of Paris; present-day attempts are similarly unsuccessful. In 1968, 9.2 million people, i.e., close to one-fifth of the entire French nation and more than one-fourth of its total urban population, lived in the metropolitan region of Paris. This creates, as in other metropolitan areas of the world, staggering problems on every level. But in a country with centuries-old traditions of administrative, economic, and cultural centralization, it has also produced a dramatic gap in human and material resources between Paris and the rest of the country. The Paris region accounts for more than one fourth of total industrial production; only two other regions, one in the North, the other in the Rhône Valley, contribute ten per cent each to the national industrial product. (See map, page 122.) This explains why the per capita of individuals in the Paris region is about 60 per cent higher than the national average; the regions that rank next in wealth are barely reaching that average. The difference between them and the capital is about twice as great as that between them and the poorest region of France. "Paris and the French desert," was the alarming catchphrase used to describe the imbalance that had developed. However, vigorous economic growth and the progressive development of other urban centers have alleviated the situation somewhat.

Another economic division of the country, dating back at least to the Second Empire, also continues to exist. So far, efforts to overcome it have proven hardly more fruitful than the attempts to halt the population influx into the Paris region. France west of a line that runs from Le Havre to Grenoble and thence to Marseilles is, in comparison to the rest of the country, as underdeveloped as is the south of Italy. The western part of the country comprises 56 per cent of its territory and 37 per cent of its total population. But 80 per cent of the country's industrial production and 76 per cent of industrial employment are located east of the line. In the East where farming is intensive, only 15 per cent are employed in agriculture. Sixty-five per cent or two-thirds of the entire agricultural population live in the West. Here the massive flight from the countryside can be expected to continue.

Traditionally and, as we will see, politically, the division of the country north and south of the Loire River has been a

salient factor. Now, growing differences and tensions, breaking occasionally into open revolts, arise between the rapidly
developing regions northeast of the Le Havre–Marseilles line
and the regions which are losing population and are lagging in
investment, productivity, and, with some exceptions, new industries. The demands of the dynamic and the static parts of the
country are in conflict, and governmental intervention cannot
easily reconcile them without slowing down overall growth.[4]

"FRANCE WITHOUT PEASANTS?"[5]

As we have seen, by comparison with other highly developed
industrial countries, the agricultural sector of France remains
both economically and politically important. Cultivated acre-
age amounts to about half of that of the six Common Market
countries combined; agriculture furnishes still about 9.2 per
cent of the gross domestic product (as against 3.1 per cent in
the United States). Between 1954 and 1965, almost 3 million
people left agricultural employment, and the movement is expected to continue at an annual rate of at least 120,000 — about
every ten minutes a farm closes down as an independent unit of
production. Nonetheless, agricultural production does not decline,
and the increase of productivity in farming is far higher than in
the rest of the economy.

Yet, in spite of modernization and intensified cultivation, the
average net income of the drastically reduced agricultural population is just about half that of the rest of the nation. In fact,
because specialization and productivity progress at very different
rates in different regions, such averages distort reality even more
than usual. An executive of the most important farmers' organization told his constituents that in the country as a whole one out
of every three farms, i.e., a total of almost 800,000 farms, are too
small to be economically viable.

Even those who rightly refuse to explain the unimpressive performance of the French economy in the past by single facts agree

[4] See François Goguel, "Six Authors in Search of a National Character,"
in *In Search of France,* pp. 380 ff.
[5] This is the suggestive title of a useful book which discusses the agricultural situation, past and present, with a great amount of data —
Michel Gervais, Claude Servolin, Jean Weil, *Une France sans paysans*
(Paris: Éditions du Seuil, 1965).

that the survival of the marginal family farm played an important role in the economic backwardness of the country. "The peasant destroyed the feudal regime [at the time of the Revolution]," it has been said, "but he consolidated the agrarian structure of France." [6] When, towards the end of the last century, the multi-crop, nonintensive production methods of the small family farm had become obsolete, the French peasants were not driven off the land as was the case in Great Britain. The republican government and its Minister of Agriculture, Jules Méline, came to their aid with massive measures of protectionism. Behind sheltering tariff walls French farmers (as well as small businessmen) were able to cling to established routines.[7] In a sense, France never repealed its Corn Laws.

Although French agriculture was favored by soil and climate, it fell behind other European countries. Schoolbooks as well as eminent writers exalted the peasantry as the mainstay of a harmoniously balanced economy and society. In fact, a web of protective regulations, including exorbitant tariffs and other privileges, isolated the rural sector of the economy from the mainstream of national life. At different periods protectionism took on different forms. But the mentality which originated in the Méline era has not everywhere run its course.

Modernization, underway since the last war, has brought a "silent revolution" to the countryside. The Planning Commissariate gave it its impetus (see below); now the European Common Market offers certain sectors of French agriculture expanded possibilities for export. Where this is true the rural sector can overcome its previous isolation from other parts of the French economy and from other countries. In many places even the most stubborn individualism seems to be waning; new habits of cooperation are observed which are unlikely to turn, as they have in the past, into restrictive corporatist practices. The rural interest groups have brought to some key posts men that represent the younger generation and the poor regions of mixed agriculture.

---

[6] Georges Lefebvre, "La Révolution Française et les paysans," *Études sur la Révolution Française* (Paris: Presses Universitaires, 1954), p. 256.

[7] For background and details of this politically all-important legislation, see Gordon Wright, *France in Modern Times* (Chicago: Rand McNally, 1960), pp. 346 ff.

(For details see Chap. VII.) Together with a number of influential civil servants and backed by the government, the younger peasant leaders have drafted legislation which seeks a new solution to the old problems of ensuring parity between the farmers and other sectors of the economy. While price guarantees and market supports have by no means disappeared, more attention is paid to "group agriculture" — for instance the joint exploitation of adjoining family farms, or the cooperative processing and marketing of products. The consolidation of marginal holdings, the improvement of a particularly inadequate technical education, and further mechanization and experimentation are used as avenues for long-range structural reforms. As yet, the success of these ambitious reforms is in doubt. Continuing subsidies to the agricultural sector cost the government almost as much as its total revenue from taxes on income.

What might prove most important and in the end decisive is a change in mentality, observed by some, doubted by others. Instead of an inheritance and a property title, farming is considered by many members of the young generation a profession for which proficiency can and must be acquired. When a leased farm promises more certain gain than the family farm, the latter should be abandoned. If such concepts spread, the silent revolution is likely to transform much of rural France. "The great mass of precapitalist peasants [would be replaced] by a smaller, more coherent, more prosperous stratum of independent farmers, rather like those of Britain or the American Middle West." [8]

For the time being, many of the technologically backward farmers, especially in Brittany, in other western areas, and in the center of France, who have been unable or unwilling either to modernize or to abandon their holdings, feel that prosperity has passed them by and that neither the government nor the rest of the country understands their problems. [9] For a few years protest

[8] Gordon Wright, *Rural Revolution in France. The Peasantry in the Twentieth Century* (Stanford: Stanford University Press, 1964), p. 179. For the best up-to-date account of the development of French agriculture in the Fifth Republic and some less optimistic prognostics, see H. Mendras and Y. Tavernier, *Terre, paysans et politique* (Paris: S.E.D.E.I.S., 1969).

[9] See findings of a public opinion poll undertaken for the Ministry of Agriculture in *Sondages*, XXVI:1 (1964), pp. 13 ff. and the article by Lawrence Collins and Dominique Lapierre, "France's Small Farmers Never Had It So Bad," *New York Times Magazine*, December 24, 1967.

movements abated when the government claimed that it was rising constantly to the defense of French producers in hard bargaining with the country's Common Market partners. But it turned out that benefits from the Common Market accrued only to the most efficient producers and that the lowering of the protecting walls spelled new disaster for the marginal farms. Frequent and often violent protest movements have been the consequence. In certain regions, agricultural interest groups are coming anew under the influence of communist front organizations and of other extremists. (For details, see Chaps. VII and VIII.) Anti-European feelings and latent xenophobia are easily aroused.

THE ENTREPRENEURIAL SYSTEM

The complement of the family farm is the French family firm. More than half of the 770,000 industrial enterprises belong to individuals; another third are classified as *"entreprises artisanales"* (craftsmen). Close to 80 per cent of the commercial firms do not employ a single salaried employee, only 17 per cent of them employ more than fifty. In industry 90 per cent of the firms employ less than 10 workers; over one-third of all wage earners work in firms employing from 1 to 50, another third in firms employing between 51 and 500. Although the number of joint stock and limited liability corporations has more than doubled during the last ten years, the family firms and partnerships still claim a considerable share of total business transactions. Large concerns are not lacking, and in several sectors (automobiles, chemicals, electricity) they dominate. But firms doing a yearly business of $2 million amount to less than 2 per cent of the total number of firms (up from 0.14 per cent ten years ago) and are practically nonexistent in many sectors which in other countries are controlled by large concerns. The annual sales of the largest French corporation ranks fifty-fifth among American firms, eighteenth among European firms. General Motors and Standard Oil combined do an annual business equal to the total business of the 500 largest French firms.[10]

But size, dispersion, and concentration are not the only factors

[10] The consequences of such differences for the gap in technology are discussed by Robert Gilpin, *France in the Age of the Scientific State* (Princeton: Princeton University Press, 1968).

that determine the efficiency of an economy. Past discussions have emphasized the obstacles which the mentality of the patrimonial employer, his extreme individualism, and his concern for secretiveness and stability have put in the way of economic development. On the whole, and brilliant exceptions notwithstanding, the performance of the family firm has been found mediocre both in terms of technical innovation and of support given to economic growth. Fears of glutting the market were stronger than willingness to expand. Vigorous competition was considered inadvisable since bankruptcies might upset the social status of other bourgeois families. Business associations, though never as strong as in fully developed capitalistic countries, had usually enough authority to enforce a price level which permitted inefficient high-cost producers to stay in business.[11] (Even today, the average age of industrial firms is about four times that of concerns in other developed countries.) These attitudes limited domestic demand and closed foreign markets to firms that were never export minded to begin with.

While a scarcity of investment capital might in part have been caused by such practices of "economic malthusianism" (a term quite common in France), the continuing scarcity also perpetuated these practices since savings were either hoarded or placed abroad. The outcome was that the country was saddled with many of the problems of industrialism without fully enjoying its material benefits.

Until recently, society did not fully reward success in business ventures, though it regarded failure as justification for the relatively low esteem in which the business community was held. Much of this was due to a belief, not uncommon in Catholic and Latin cultures, that moneymaking lacked nobility. Hence the most talented sons of the bourgeoisie sought careers in the professions or in the civil service. Only as a last resort might they turn to running the family enterprise.[12]

Since prerevolutionary times, entrepreneurial timidity was partly compensated for by the role which the French state

[11] For a detailed treatment see Henry W. Ehrmann, *Organized Business in France* (Princeton: Princeton University Press, 1957), *passim*.

[12] See Cotta, *op. cit.*, p. 534. The abundant literature, mostly American, on this subject has recently been ably summarized and criticized by Crozier, *op. cit.*, pp. 272 ff. See also Kindleberger, *loc. cit.*

played in technological innovation and economic development. The royal *fermiers,* Colbert's mercantilism, and the way in which Napoleon III's entourage interpreted the doctrines of Saint-Simon created traditions which considered government the motor, not a parasite, of the national economy. In terms of Max Weber, a "politically oriented capitalism" emerged and was accepted with the same ambivalence which characterizes French attitudes towards authority in general: protection and promotion by the state were at the same time expected and dreaded. The tradition bound patrimonial employer, producing or distributing for a local or at best regional market, felt harmed, not benefited, by governmental intervention and regulation. On the other hand, the managers of modern and larger enterprises have long accepted the positive role of government, notwithstanding certain flamboyant pronouncements to the contrary.

At present the situation in industry is not unlike that in agriculture. The old structures, many of them essentially precapitalistic, have by no means disappeared and are evolving only gradually; pressures for change are emerging from the modernized sectors of the economy, both public and private, from the new European institutions, and from the younger generations in business and the bureaucracy; the respective values of stability and of competition, of privilege and of innovation, of individual achievement and of cooperation, are in conflict.

As often in French history, a major crisis was needed to set an overrigid system in motion. The Second World War and its aftermath provided the crisis. It compelled the communities which make up French society finally to accept the conditions of a modern welfare economy, even where these conditions run counter to long established traditions.

A MODERN WELFARE ECONOMY

The French economy of today has been characterized as being "less capitalistic and more socialistic than the economies of other European nations." [13] While essentially true, such a

[13] Raymond Aron, *France, Steadfast and Changing.* (Cambridge: Harvard University Press, 1960), p. 62.

diagnosis needs elaboration and refinement before its political implications can be understood.

Government operated business enterprises have existed in France since before the Revolution in widely diversified fields — fields that in other countries of Western Europe are under private ownership. For centuries France has illustrated the proposition that the relationship of public to private enterprise in a society is more a function of a country's cultural heritage than of its level of development. Contingencies of politics and of leadership rather than the degree of modernity determine the way in which public regulation of enterprise is exercised.[14]

The strongest impulses for a wider public sector arose during the periods of the Popular Front (1936–37) and after the Liberation (1944–45). For mixed reasons, economic, political, and ideological, the legislature enacted a great number of nationalizations.

At present, the government operates all or part of the following: railroading; almost all energy production (mining, electricity, etc.) and telecommunication (radio and television); most air and maritime transport; most of the aeronautic industry; 60 per cent of bank deposits; 40 per cent of insurance premiums; one-third of the automobile industry; one-third of the housing industry — in addition to the old state monopolies of post, telephone, telegraph, tobacco and match manufacture, and sundry less important activities. Public concerns account for more than 10 per cent of the gross national product; their investments represent more than one-third of the gross capital formation of all enterprises. Fifteen per cent of the total active population, or 27 per cent of all salary and wage earners (agricultural labor not included), are paid directly by the state either as civil servants or on a contractual basis. Their income comes close to one-third of the total sum of wages and salaries.

It is impossible to generalize on the ways in which so large a public sector is run. There exist substantial differences in legal structure, control, and management personnel among the

[14] C. E. Black, *The Dynamics of Modernization* (New York: Harper & Row, 1966), pp. 17–18. For a general view of government control of French industry since the war, see John Sheahan, *Promotion and Control of Industry in Post-War France* (Cambridge: Harvard University Press, 1963).

various enterprises. After difficult beginnings during the immediate postwar period, political influence in the newly nationalized industries has all but vanished. In terms of productivity and modernization, the record of the nationalized firms is far more favorable than in Great Britain. Massive investments have helped to make many nationalized concerns pacesetters for an entire industry or branch of industry, and governmental banking institutions are playing an important role in the otherwise still limited financial market.

Most important is the fact that the public sector is now thoroughly integrated with the economy as a whole. Private business, especially corporate management, has abandoned its initial hostility and clearly settled for cooperation. In the most optimistic view (not shared by all) the symbiosis that has taken place has reduced both bourgeois and bureaucratic traditions and has furthered the emergence of a new managerial spirit in both elite groups.

The effect which the comprehensive social security system has had on the redistribution of wealth is controversial. Its total expenditure, in comparison with the gross national product, is slightly higher than in Great Britain and Sweden but lower than in West Germany and Belgium. Because of the piecemeal fashion in which many of the reforms have been introduced, parts of the social security system have strengthened rather than overcome economic disparities among different categories of the population — especially among the various regions. Its beneficial effect on population growth and on the health of families is undeniable. Many of its weaknesses stem from an overly bureaucratic structure which, with time, has only increased in weight.[15] Yet public opinion polls show that after twenty years of operation 73 per cent of the population believe that the system has worked well; only 20 per cent are outrightly critical. Given the French temper, this is a remarkably favorable judgment passed on a governmental institution which must necessarily hurt the interests of some.

Since much is expected from the government and since its own objectives are ambitious, public expenditures are, in pro-

[15] Cf. the overall evaluation in Pierre Laroque *et al., Succès et faiblesses de l'effort social français* (Paris: Armand Colin, 1961), pp. 345–49.

portion to the Gross National Product, the highest of all countries
in the North Atlantic area. In 1967, they amounted to 35.5
per cent, and this percentage has been rising steadily since 1950.
Investment in private industry has remained unsatisfactory and
lower than in any other Common Market country. The structure
and the habits of the family firm, the urgency of public investments, and the financial needs of the state weigh heavily on a
capital market with antiquated structures. Under such conditions, the reluctance of the distrustful domestic investor has not
been overcome, and a profit margin that in comparison with
other countries of similar development remains rather small
limits the possibilities for self-financing by business concerns.

In spite of some assertions to the contrary, it is not true that in
the economy as a whole French firms have to carry a significantly
heavier burden of social costs, of fringe benefits for their workers,
and of taxation than their competitors in other lands. Since
Tocqueville's classical description of the devious ways by which
the French peasant, under the Old Regime, evaded the "arbitrary, not to say ferocious, methods of taxation," [16] the legacy of
a peasant mentality has been blamed for the low tax morale of
Frenchmen. Insufficient tax revenue and a tax structure fit to
protect the unproductive are often held responsible for the nar-
rowness of the capital market. Also blamed is a dearth of civic
virtue. There is little doubt that the survival of so many small
units in industry and agriculture which universally, not only in
France, are able to conceal part of their earnings, magnifies the
problem of evasion. French sources have estimated that fraud is
practiced by more than one-third of those with taxable incomes,
a far higher figure than in the United States and Great Britain.

Yet, as a percentage of gross national income, taxes collected
in France (1965) amounted to almost 39 per cent — a tax
burden somewhat higher than that of England or West Germany.
Because of the high rate of evasion practiced by some, this burden
must fall heavily, and sometimes too heavily, on the individual
wage earner and on the modern firms which have only limited, if
any, possibilities for evasion. In all modern countries, industry
contributes most to income from taxes. Since in France the industrial sector is still considerably narrower than for instance in

[16] Tocqueville, *op. cit.,* p. 127.

England or Germany, it has to carry a proportionately heavier weight than in other countries. Indirect taxes, often inequitable and likely to drive up prices, constitute a far greater share of total tax income than in other countries of similar development: 46.6 per cent compared with 38.8 per cent in Germany and 34.5 per cent in the United States.

Since the inauguration of the Fifth Republic the number of tax declarations has soared and the rate of revenue has risen; the broadening of the base of some taxes has put an end to the previous penalization of some of the most productive enterprises. Nonetheless, because of resistance from many sides, the government has been unable to introduce a reform which would attack the basis of the uneven tax burden. The problem of how to combat systematic tax evasion and how to devise a more productive system of taxation is undoubtedly one of the foremost problems not only of economic but also of social and political development in France.

Economic planning in postwar France has extended to most branches of the economy and to many regions. When in 1945 General de Gaulle, then President of the Provisional Government of the Fourth Republic, entrusted to Jean Monnet, a former businessman, the task of preparing a Plan of Modernization and Equipment, he accepted the alternative that Monnet had put before him: "modernization or decadence." Since then the General Commissariat for the Plan has elaborated a series of four-year plans; the Sixth Plan covers the period from 1971–1975. From an era of shortages and rigid regulation, through alternating periods of inflation and deflationary stagnation, and now amidst prosperity, the numerous governments of the two Republics have allowed the Commissariat to carry on.

During his Presidency, General de Gaulle occasionally spoke about the Plan as an "ardent obligation" and praised its achievements in extravagant terms. How to assess the actual impact of the planning enterprise on the economic development of postwar France is a matter of considerable controversy. Each Plan has set goals for overall production and productivity as well as for the development of the various branches of the economy. Numerous modernization commissions made up of members of the planning staff and representatives of the interests concerned prepare the Plan. To check the inconsistencies which unavoid-ably result from such decentralized procedures, the projections of the commissions are fitted into national-income accounts, previously unknown in France. As the French are committed to a flexible process of planning, the objectives laid down in the Plan are merely an indication of what is deemed desirable and possible. No individual firm or trade association faces sanction if it fails to reach the goals which it had originally accepted. Even the Plan's program of public investments is only indicative; binding decisions concerning investments are made by the Ministries concerned.

Nonetheless, it is erroneous to liken the activities of the Plan-ning Commissariat to "revivalist prayer meetings," just because its proposals and projections lack binding force.[17] The role which the planning staff has played in propagating information to all public and private centers of economic decision-making is considerable and has had far-reaching effects: before the war, the absence of such information and in many fields the lack of reliable statistics were a severe handicap to economic develop-ment. In addition, the planning staff and its working methods have established communication between sectors of the economy that previously were rigorously separate and hence ignorant of each other's production and investment plans. In many instances, such confrontation as has taken place has led to the mediation of claims, has brought present-day rationality into historically frozen positions, and clarified the options to be incorporated into the Plan. Such communication, to be sure, does not by itself propa-gate economic growth. But it is its precondition.

The institutionalized contacts afforded by the planning process between public officials and the world of business and agriculture are in many respects a departure from the traditional political style. There is no commitment to a definite ideology of either comprehensive planning or economic liberalism. Carefully elab-orated but easily modified compromises on means — an empiri-

---

[17] This is the view expressed by Kindleberger, *op. cit.*, p. 155. A far more positive appreciation, which I share, is that of Michel Crozier, "Pour une analyse sociologique de la planification française," *Revue Française de sociologie,* VI (1965), pp. 147–163, and by François Bloch-Lainé, "Réflexions sur les explosifs," *Esprit,* XXX:308 (1962), pp. 59–64.

cism which takes full cognizance of changing market conditions and psychological imponderables — are different from the political "deal" of the past in two respects: they are not considered a betrayal of previously proclaimed principles because such principles are not involved; they have none of the onus of a secret bargain since they have been reached in the give-and-take of open discussions, witnessed by third parties.

Novel also is the relationship between the Commissariat and other sectors of public administration. Contrary to bureaucratic traditions, the number of staff members in the Commissariat has been kept deliberately small. Placed under the immediate responsibility of the Prime Minister, the staff members rely for expertise and technical knowledge on their colleagues in the amply staffed administrative bureaus. The outlook and working methods of the planning staff enjoy the esteem of at least the younger generation of ranking civil servants. In their judgment, the Commissariat may provide the model for overcoming some of the gravest shortcomings of the traditional administrative style (to be discussed below, Chap. VI).

If the Plan has had an undeniable effect on administrative methods and mentality, it is now generally admitted that there have been periods when goals and policies set by the Plan had to be abandoned altogether. Sometimes this became necessary because the expanding economy was overheating, and inflationary increases in prices (considerably higher than in neighboring countries) were threatening the needed level of stability. At other times, the very success of the European Common Market and the gradual disappearance of customs barriers limited the reliability of forecasts elaborated for only one of the participating countries. Over the years such experiences were bound to discredit the faith in the success of national planning. The *mystique* which General de Gaulle wanted to attach to the planning enterprise has by now largely evaporated.[18]

The current (Sixth) Plan hopes to see the GNP increase annually by 6.1 per cent, while the rise in prices should be held

---

[18] See the articles by Alain Vernholes and others, "Le Plan à l'heure du désenchantement," *Le Monde,* March 19 and 20, 1970. R. B. du Boff, "The Decline of Economic Planning in France," *Western Political Quarterly,* XXI:2 (1968), pp. 98–109 concludes: "Much of the praise accorded indicative French planning has been premature and undeserved."

to about 3 per cent. Yet only a short time before the French parliament endorsed these objectives, its members had heard their new Prime Minister, Jacques Chaban-Delmas, characterize the French economy as "fragile" and lacking important characteristics of a "modern industrial power." [19] This was at least an implicit admission that the picture which General de Gaulle had drawn in his speeches and press conferences during more than ten years had been far too bright. Obviously, the Fifth Republic has inherited many of the limiting conditions under which it operates. Many of the barriers to modernization must be attributed to traditional strains rather than to failings of the new regime. Conversely, it is true, much of the vitality and many of the mutations for which General de Gaulle claimed credit resulted from attitudes that took root and from reforms that were accomplished or well on the way before he returned to power.

The government that took over after George Pompidou's election to the Presidency has promised to achieve the goals of further industrialization and modernization by a liberalization of economic policies. It gave assurances that what M. Chaban-Delmas called the "tentacles of the state" would be loosened. Nationalized enterprises are to be given more autonomy and broader managerial responsibilities. An Institute for Industrial Development may purchase stock options in private firms to encourage mergers as well as the expansion of regional industries to a national scale. Private initiative and investment are to be encouraged in such fields as highway construction, telecommunications, and housing. But, the Prime Minister also promised that the government was determined to attack some of the deeper-lying causes of the "fragility." In many instances, he said, a craving for protection and an insistence on formal equality of treatment are in fact consolidating social injustice and preventing the elimination of anachronistic barriers. Hence, both state subsidies to firms and farms and certain features of the social security system need overhauling.

---

[19] *Le Monde*, September 18, 1969. In Paris this speech is sometimes referred to as the "Khrushchev speech" of the Pompidou regime, since it criticized, albeit implicitly, many of the shortcomings of the policies of the preceding ten years, just as Khrushchev had denounced the era of Stalin's rule.

Such a realistic analysis of the difficulties that continue to hamper French modernization is by no means novel. But during the years of Gaullist rule, government authorities avoided a frank discussion of these difficulties. In order to claim for France a foremost rank in the concert of nations, General de Gaulle emphasized the steady growth of the economy and ignored perennial obstructions and tensions. Incapable of altering the structures which were largely responsible for the high cost of production, the government imposed immediate sacrifices on those ill-prepared or ill-equipped to defend their share of the national wealth. Social and economic inequalities were aggravated by rapid economic development even though the psychological effect of this phenomenon was mitigated by a general upward movement. Since earnings rose faster than prices, total purchasing power increased markedly. Yet while the purchasing power of the German worker increased between 1958 and 1967 by 75 per cent, that of the French worker rose by only 35 per cent. Real wages of the average French worker are estimated to be at least one-fourth below those of the average German worker. Within France, the increases that have been won have varied greatly for different categories. At the bottom of the ladder, earnings barely kept pace with the cost of living; the earnings of skilled workers rose eight times as fast as those of unskilled labor; and workers in private industry fared far better than the millions employed in public enterprises, since the government wanted to keep public outlays down. The earnings of both farmers and unskilled workers have risen less than has national wealth, and their relative position has therefore deteriorated.

Established priorities have prevented the government from dealing with some problems of long standing, among them the dissatisfaction with available housing conditions. In the past, the low rate of construction, particularly striking in comparison with neighboring countries, and the continued overcrowding of obsolete, substandard housing, helped to maintain extremist parties and movements. The country, which in number of passenger cars per inhabitant outranks all European countries except Sweden, ranks thirteenth in number of new lodgings built (here West Germany occupies the first place). In fact, France's position is even worse than these relative figures seem to indicate:

one third of the dwellings constructed since the war have replaced those abandoned because of age or lack of repairs. At present, about 20 per cent of existing housing is considered overcrowded by any standard.

From appearances the construction paralysis seems to have ended; in many towns and around every larger city, modern dwellings are rising. However, official figures indicate that until recently the increase in housing from year to year just about kept pace with the growth of the GNP. Since 1958, the share of housing in total investments actually has diminished substantially, year after year. In order to cut the dreaded budgetary deficit, low-rent, subsidized housing, for which the need is greatest, has continued to lag behind demand and often behind plans. Such lags are greatest in densely populated regions with antiquated housing; construction activity is liveliest in places that are attractive to tourists and the rich. In part this is due to real estate speculation which the government in spite of its vaunted vigor has been unable to stop, and which has been denounced as "the scandal of the Gaullist regime." At the present rate of construction, it would take a quarter of a century to fill the reasonable needs of a growing population no longer content to live in overage dwellings. By many, and among them members of the government, the dearth of housing is considered the open wound of the French social fabric.

During the decade of Gaullist rule, such inequities as existed were the consequence of a policy that sought to postpone the solution of urgent problems in the hope that progress and modernization would alleviate seemingly unavoidable but hopefully temporary maladjustments. The social explosions of May, 1968, proved that such hopes had been in vain. (For details, see below, especially Chap. VII). After an unexpected rebellion almost toppled the regime, the government had to satisfy urgent demands and lay aside objectives of the Modernization Plan and of stabilization policies. Shortly thereafter, currency and trade balance had to be defended by drastic measures.

In the sober spirit characteristic of General de Gaulle's successors, the government has called for a reordering of priorities in the field of economic and social policies. Prime Minister Chaban-Delmas admitted that in the past France has never been able to advance except by major crises (of which that of 1968 was only the most recent). Whether his appeal to strive for modernization by the orderly ways of fundamental reforms will be heeded, remains to be seen. (For a discussion of the political problems involved, see below, especially Chap. XI).

CHAPTER III

Political Socialization

POLITICAL SOCIALIZATION AND POLITICAL CULTURE

This volume, like others in the Comparative Politics Country Series, attempts to explain the significance of the political attitudes and political behavior of its citizens for a country's politics. Such an emphasis does not exclude an analysis of governmental institutions (see Chaps. IX, X), nor that of the political infrastructure — formed mainly by interest groups and parties (Chaps. VII, VIII). Yet, we assume that the way people act within the political system is of foremost importance both for the functioning of the system and for an adequate explanation of how it functions.

Like all human beings, Frenchmen of all ages play many roles, not all of them relevant to the political system. Which roles they play and how they perform depends on a variety of objective factors, as well as on their values, beliefs, and emotions. Many social scientists, dissatisfied with a narrow and legalistic interpretation of politics, have studied the basic values existing in a society to explain political behavior and through it the political system. These studies, however, have sometimes led to erroneous generalizations [1] or to high-level abstractions with little explanatory force.

To understand the particularities of the political realm, we need not be concerned with all the ideas that swirl around in

[1] Cf. the trenchant remarks by the French author François Goguel, in *In Search of France,* pp. 374 ff., commenting on such generalizations by two American social scientists, appearing in the same volume.

a society, nor with all the patterns which mold the individual and determine his conduct. What matters is the individual's political socialization — his attitudes towards the political system, towards the institutions through which the system functions, and towards the values by which it lives.[2]

Every political system, at all its levels, allocates authoritatively the resources at its disposal. Attitudes towards the political system are therefore concerned with specific orientations towards authority and the forms in which authority manifests itself. How Frenchmen view authoritative decisions — how they accept or resist them, and how they distinguish between those to be obeyed and those to be circumvented.

Socialization is a learning process which proceeds by observing and experiencing authority. But authority patterns, i.e., the way people look at those giving them orders, do not only exist in the political life of a nation. They are observed and experienced first and, at least in a democracy, foremost in the family and other primary groups, in the church and the schools, on the job and in associations. Participation in social activities often provides training for roles assumed in political life. The subsequent sections of this chapter will therefore deal with various social settings.

Like any learning process political socialization passes on from one generation to the next a "mixture of attitudes developed in a mixture of historical periods."[3] Centuries ago Montesquieu spoke of the composite of values, emotions, and beliefs as "the general spirit, the morals of a nation." More recently several authors have defined this composite as political culture.[4] It is important to consider this not merely a residual concept ("What one cannot adequately define nor describe is political culture") but to understand the relationship between political culture and political socialization.

[2] This line of thought owes much to Gabriel A. Almond and Sidney Verba, *The Civic Culture* (Boston: Little, Brown and Company, 1965), esp. Chaps. I and XII, as well as to the other writings by these two authors quoted therein.

[3] Sidney Verba, "Comparative Political Culture," in Pye and Verba (eds.), *Political Culture and Political Development* (Princeton: Princeton University Press, 1965), pp. 512 ff.

[4] See the writings by Almond and Verba, but also the important discussion by Samuel H. Beer, *Patterns of Government* (New York: Random House, 1958), esp. pp. 32 ff.

Any political culture provides the link between what happens in the mind of the individual (and in the primary groups to which he belongs) and politics. Its study is equally important to the student of micropolitics focusing on the individual and his attitude, and to the student of macropolitics, mostly concerned (as we are here) with the structure and function of a political system as a whole. There is constant interaction between a country's political culture and its citizens' political socialization. If one thinks of political culture as an alphabet, then the process of arranging the letters into words is determined by the process of socialization which the citizen has undergone. The way a Frenchman looks at political events, especially at the decisions of his own government, has much to do with the attitudes he has observed and learned in the social and in the political realm. Conversely, the capabilities of the political system, whether it can act forcefully or must temporize and maneuver, often depends on the behavior of the citizens. Their actual or presumed reactions to specific events or general policies may condition the content and style of political decisions.

An understanding of the limitations which an inherited political culture imposes on political development is of particular importance in studying an old country such as France. More than a century ago Tocqueville spoke of his compatriots as "a people so unalterable in its *primary instincts* that it is recognizable in its portraits drawn 2,000 or 3,000 years ago . . ." [5] Political institutions, even if they are seemingly created *de novo,* are shaped by the political culture. Hence change and mutation cannot adequately be understood without accounting for the influence which values and beliefs bring to bear on any attempted reform.

The Frenchmen who after the Second World War gave a new constitutional framework to the Fourth Republic had the mandate to establish a regime totally different from that which led the country to the disaster of 1940. Most of them honestly believed that this was what they were doing. Yet, in spite of past

[5] Tocqueville, *op. cit.,* pp. 210–11. Emphasis supplied: what Tocqueville called "primary instincts" overlaps the two present-day terms, "socialization" and "political culture." A somewhat strange if interesting present-day "portrait" is provided by Nathan Leites, *The Rules of the Game in Paris* (Chicago: University of Chicago Press, 1966).

experiences and of great differences in the *texts* of the constitutional laws, it soon turned out that the Fourth Republic was unable to avoid the pitfalls of the Third. The attitudes and beliefs not only of the political actors inside and outside parliament but also of the French citizens as voters, as members of interest groups, etc., frustrated the intended change.

Yet Tocqueville himself went on to ascribe unforeseen changes in the country's destiny to the changeability of the "moods (and) . . . tastes" of Frenchmen. Today, the contrast between politics in the Fourth and Fifth Republics shows that constitutional texts are not necessarily devoid of political effect. The experiences accumulated since the war and the acute crisis precipitated by the fighting in Algeria opened the way for changes which were manifestly impossible twelve years before. Yet, as will be shown (see Chaps. IX and X), also the constitution of 1958 was altered by the impact of the political culture.

The style in which political roles are acted out is another illustration of the intimate relationship between the socialization of the individual citizen and the political culture. It is true that at various periods the style of the political actors, and more generally of a country's elites, may be quite different from that of its citizens, either as individuals or as members of groups. There is, for instance, serious doubt as to whether the orientation of a majority of French voters towards politics is any more ideological than that of the American voter (see Chap. IV). Public opinion polls are an important source of information for a political profile of a nation by indicating the major groups which make up the nation. But in any public opinion sampling the number of intellectuals and political leaders is obviously too small to be statistically relevant. The style of a community (as an expression of the political culture) can neither be deduced solely from answers to a questionnaire, nor from the mere pronouncements of the elite. This is one of the major difficulties in any attempt to make the findings of micro- and macropolitics mutually relevant.[6]

If one sets out to construct a model of basic values which will presumably explain the major manifestations of political

[6] A number of intensive elite surveys, conducted by both French and American specialists and due for publication in the early seventies, should do much to fill these gaps in our knowledge.

life, one should guard against giving undue weight to the ideological orientation of one stratum of society. In fact, in each country, and even under a dictatorship, there is a pluralism of values, a plurality of cultures and styles. This is particularly true of France, a country of divided elites. It is therefore necessary to investigate as concretely as possible the socialization process of citizens and of leaders alike. Only by looking subsequently at the political process, as it unfolds at a particular historical moment, will it be possible to determine what values and beliefs (or, to draw once more on Tocqueville, what "sentiments" and what "principles") are dominant.

RELIGIOUS AND ANTIRELIGIOUS TRADITIONS

France is at once a Catholic country — at least 92% of Frenchmen now living are baptized in the Catholic faith — and a country which the Church itself considers as "dechristianized." Until well into the present century, the opposition between believers and nonbelievers has been one of the main determinants of the political culture. Since the Revolution, it has divided society and political life at all levels.

In 1789, very few people started with the idea of making war on religion. But a series of historical accidents achieved an early split between the Revolution and the Church. The forces of counterrevolution based their legitimacy on a religious faith for which unquestionable authority and ecclesiastic discipline were more central than in some other countries, while the double revolt against King and Church gave to the democratic creed a rationalist basis whose purest French expression was voltairianism. (It has been said of Voltaire that only a Catholic country could produce him.) Just as for Catholic Frenchmen the Revolution was the work not just of erring or evil men but of Satan, antireligious beliefs took the form of a militant faith. The Jacobin-inspired cult of reason was indeed a "cult," which lives on in spirit though no longer in form. This explains why the secularized state and its institutions have never been given sacral dignity: there is no reference to God in any of the republican constitutions, no prayer at official functions, no "In God we trust" on the coins, no religious oath for office holders. Such practices, quite common in many countries that respect the separation of church and state, would have been sacrilegious to both camps in France.

Whether the evolution of French society under the Orleanist monarchy and the Second Empire might have offered chances for a religious reconciliation is a moot question. For with the establishment of the Third Republic in 1870, the gulf between the political cultures of Catholicism and anticlericalism reopened and deepened further. After a few years the errors of its enemies permitted militant anticlericalism to take over the Republic.

Parliament rescinded the centuries-old concordat with the Vatican, expelled most Catholic orders, and severed all ties between Church and state, so that "the moral unity of the country could be reestablished." There was a time when the hostility between Catholicism and anticlericalism almost broke out into generalized violence. In those rural regions where Catholic observance had already become an expression of habit rather than of genuine faith, dechristianization spread when the new legislation deprived the Church of all official prestige.[7] From the rostrum of parliament Viviani, Premier at the outbreak of the First World War, boasted that his generation had extinguished forever in the minds of the oppressed classes all hopes for salvation by divine providence. At the same time, representatives of the small town bourgeoisie which had replaced the *haute bourgeoisie* as political leaders, swelled the membership of the organized "antichurch" — the Freemasonry.

French Freemasonry, like that of other Latin countries, had broken earlier with the religious and political conservatism, and even the deism, of Anglo-Saxon Masonry. During the formative years of the Third Republic, its agnosticism turned into fervid anticlericalism. Its lodges, especially those of the influential Great Orient, functioned as the nurseries of much of the political and the administrative personnel of the Republic. The views of the membership on political and economic problems varied widely and evolved over time. But the commitment of every Freemason to an unrelenting fight against the Catholic creed and the Church as an institution proved a strong cement. To the Freemasons and their middle-class sympathizers, religion was a vehicle of political oppression, just as to the majority of the working class it was an

[7] Wright, *France in Modern Times,* p. 332.

instrument in the service of economic exploitation. The number of Freemasons was estimated never to have exceeded 50,000. But since they were intentionally distributed over many organizations, both public and private, they exercised, at least until 1914, a greater influence on the minds of republican Frenchmen than their number would suggest.

The intransigeance of the republican regime was matched by that of the Pope who excommunicated every deputy who had voted the separation laws. Faithful Catholics were driven into a political ghetto. Regular attendance at mass by army officers (reported by Freemasons converted into amateur spies) became a hindrance to promotion. A feeling of being besieged from outside the walls of their faith was given expression in many Catholic publications of the period. The faithful saw no other way than the overthrow of the existing political regime to overcome their isolation.

The Catholic subsystem existing within the republic drew its strength from a well-developed network of private education and associations (see this chapter and Chap. VII). The mass-pilgrimages to cathedrals or shrines were not ordinary church services but rites of communion: the sermon-speeches held at such occasions stressed the distinctiveness of those assembled and denounced the sins of those outside the community of faith.

A keen observer of the prewar political stage maintained that he could distinguish between political conventions held in the same region by devout Catholics and by anticlerical republicans merely by looking at the features of the participants: the faces of the former resembled wooden sculptures of the thirteenth and portraits of the fourteenth and fifteenth centuries; the others had stepped out of nineteenth-century paintings, many could have been Daumier's models.[8] Such visual impressions indeed confirmed that there were then two French nations rather than one.

The opposition between the political Right and Left was frequently determined by attitudes towards the Catholic Church. In rural regions where religious practice continued to be lively and where the advice of the local clergy counted on election day, conservative candidates carried the vote. But even govern-

[8] Thibaudet, *op. cit.*, pp. 36–37.

ments of the center usually did not invite the support of conservative deputies whose anticlerical lineage was dubious. For a total of sixty years (1879 to 1939), with rare exceptions no practicing Catholic obtained cabinet rank in any of the numerous Ministries. The political isolation of the Catholics has correctly been compared to that of the communists since 1947, when every government left of center has found it necessary to disclaim communist support even though offered.[9] The existence of such political ghettos of whatever kind necessarily narrows the basis of representation.

The experiences of national unity during the First World War and the reconciliation of believers and nonbelievers in the resistance movement of the Second World War were bound to erase many of the political differences which religious divisions created. Today the interaction of religious and political forces has been transformed in many respects, yet past alignments still determine, in many cases, the role which religious beliefs or agnostic convictions play in the socialization of the individual.

Indifference towards religious practices continues to be fairly widespread among Frenchmen baptized in the Catholic faith. Although 62 per cent consider themselves "practicing Catholics," only 38 per cent of them attend religious services at least every Sunday, 36 per cent go to church occasionally, and 26 per cent never attend church services. A comparable inquiry among young people between sixteen and twenty-four years of age shows some but not very significant differences, here the figures are 37 per cent, 42 per cent, and 20 per cent.[10] But these national averages hide enormous geographical and social disparateness as well as differences between the sexes. In rural France, parts of Flanders, Alsace-Lorraine, and those regions which for geographic, administrative, or economic reasons have been relatively isolated (the Northwest, especially Brittany, some of the Alps, and some

---

[9] See François Goguel and Alfred Grosser, *La Politique en France,* 4th edition (Paris: Colin, 1970), p. 30.

[10] For these and all other statistical data on religious attitudes see "L'Église Catholique et les Prêtres," *Sondages,* XXIX:1 (1962), pp. 23 ff.; "Religion et Politique," *ibid.,* XXIX:2 (1967), pp. 7 ff.; Jacques Duquesne, *Les 16–24 Ans* (Paris: Le Centurion, 1963), pp. 202–231, and the comments by A. Coutrot and F. Dreyfus, *Les Forces Religieuses dans la société française* (Paris: Colin, 1965), *passim.*

of the countryside south of the *Massif Central*), have withstood dechristianization. Where social hierarchies have remained strong, religious practices are more firmly rooted: this is true in the border regions of the North where family life is close and in the West where nobility and clergy have long been a determining factor in village life.[11] Everywhere the wealthier farmers attend church service far more assiduously than the owners or tenants of marginal farms, sharecroppers, or laborers.

The rapid progress of urbanization might soon deprive these data of all but historical interest. However, it is as yet impossible to predict what mass emigration will do to the religious practices of the newly urbanized population, especially if it were to come from such regions as the underdeveloped West where the Church still has a strong hold.

In the Middle Ages, Christianity was propagated from the urban agglomeration. Now the large cities and the lines of communication between them seem to contribute most to dechristianization. From a survey of young people, it appears that the attitudes in city and country will continue to differ: 59 per cent of those living in large urban centers believe that for their generation religion is less important than for their parents; only 42 per cent of those living in communities of less than 2,000 population think so. For the cities, regional variations remain important: in Strasbourg there are more than 33 per cent practicing Catholics, in the Mediterranean harbor of Marseilles less than 11 per cent go to church with any regularity.

Most telling are the differences among the social classes in big cities. In the Paris region, which the clergy considers as "mission territory" because of low church attendance, 19 per cent of the managerial group but only 1.7 per cent of workers go to mass. In less dechristianized cities such as Lille, 3 per cent of the unskilled, 8 per cent of the skilled workers, but 60 per cent of the professional group are churchgoers. On a national level, almost half of all Frenchmen who have severed church ties belong to the working class. The estrangement between the working class and the Church, in spite of the renewed vitality of Catholic

---

[11] Edward R. Tannenbaum, *The New France* (Chicago: The University of Chicago Press, 1961), p. 41, and his entire chapter on Catholic practices, significantly entitled "Children of the Past."

workers' organizations, remains a central fact of religious and cultural life.

The urban bourgeoisie continues to be traditionally divided: at various historical periods, especially the nineteenth century, contradictory experiences have deposited here a layer of devout Catholicism, there an unrepentant voltairianism. Sometimes the divisions run within the same family. But by and large, church services in the urban centers are mostly attended by the upper and middle classes, with a definite predominance of women and young girls.

The difference between the religious attitudes of men and women is far more pronounced in France than in other countries of similar development. A far higher proportion of men have severed all church ties, a far greater number of women attend church with regularity. Among those who find the church an institution that deserves "outright criticism," 64 per cent are men and only 36 per cent women. Only 47 per cent of the men, but 62 per cent of the women who believe that the church still has considerable political influence in France approve of this situation. Such differences, even though to a varying degree, are common to all classes, all regions, to the rural as well as to the urban milieu.

Of course, church attendance is only one manifestation of religious or agnostic feelings. Other factors, more difficult to gauge and less suited to generalization, must be considered. According to a detailed study of a village community situated in a region of about average religious practices and considered in many respects typical, mass, religious weddings, and funerals have little religious significance. Those who do attend these rites are there mostly from habit and for social reasons. They look upon the priest as they look upon the mayor: each fulfills different public functions.[12] Religious faith is regarded as something beyond the reach of the uninitiated: it is the clergy's business.

In a representative national panel, only 38 per cent of regular churchgoers conceive the role of the church in exclusively spiritual and evangelical terms, to 35 per cent of them the func-

[12] Lucien Bernot and René Blancard, *Nouville, un village français* (Paris: Institut d'Ethnologie, 1953), pp. 239, 299.

tions of the church are predominantly mundane: it defends the established order, inculcates respect for morality, etc.

When young Frenchmen in all parts of the country were asked to list the values they cherished most and whose loss they would most regret, there were no significant differences between the first three preferences of religious youth and of nonreligious youth. Both groups listed health, money, and love, though not quite in the same order. For those who attended church regularly, religious faith occupied fourth place, while it appeared at the bottom of everybody else's list. On the basis of these and other answers to similarly critical questions concerning public and private morality, a study has concluded that less than 12 per cent of the youth can be classified as convinced Catholics — far less than the number of churchgoers in the total population. On the other hand, it is significant that on many problems the current thinking of the faithful and of the faithless coincides rather than diverges. Two-thirds of the students in Catholic schools approve of divorce "in certain cases," as against three-quarters of students in public institutions.

There are also indications that the separation of church and state is losing some of the rigidities which have so far characterized the secular character of a republican regime in France. While the constitution of the Fifth Republic was being written, a public opinion poll asked whether the electorate would be in favor of inserting into its preamble a reference to "God the Creator and the Father of all mankind": 37 per cent approved, 33 per cent disapproved, 22 per cent declared to be indifferent to the question. (No such reference was included in the actual text of the constitution, which simply affirms that the republic is *laïque*.) The classical Left, composed of communists, socialists, and radicals, still disapproved of the proposition in far greater numbers than other voters. Yet, with the exception of the communists, even here the percentage of those who declared to be "indifferent" to the question appears astonishingly high to those who remember the passionate fights at the beginning of the present century. How fundamentally feelings have changed is well illustrated by the results of a poll, conducted during the presidential election campaign of 1969: 38 per cent preferred a church-going President of the Republic, only 10 per cent frowned on one, while 43 per cent were indifferent.

There are no more walls built around the religiously devout; he is no longer barred from careers; he may be different but he is no longer estranged from the world that lies beyond his own community of faith. Finally, lines of political division are not drawn primarily according to religious orientations. Believers and nonbelievers are to be found in many political camps, their values and interests are represented by a variety of organizations which no longer appear invariably on the Right or Left of the political spectrum. In a recent public opinion poll 51 per cent of the respondents classified politically active Catholics with the Right, 14 per cent with the Left, while a significant 35 per cent declined to answer. In the presidential election of 1969, Catholics and agnostics were to be found in the camps of the two main candidates, Georges Pompidou and Alain Poher, while four years earlier religious affiliation was still of some importance for the identification with the various candidates who then ran for the Presidency.

The changes that have thus occurred are a consequence both of shifts in the general environment and of mutations in French Catholicism. The groundwork for the latter had been prepared during the interwar years. In fact, traditions of a nonauthoritarian, democratic, and socially conscious Catholicism which had been quite lively during the middle of the nineteenth century dried up during the Second Empire and the struggles with the anticlerical republic.

After the Second World War the diverse Catholic movements and the Church hierarchies changed outlook and methods of action and did much to accomplish the rehabilitation of Catholicism. In a pluralistic society, Catholic organizations, publications, and teachings became themselves pluralistic and gave expression to a wider range of social and political choices.[13] A new style and better defined role assigned to lay members enabled Catholic action groups to become more effective as innovators in a variety of fields.

In the organization of farmers, workers, and employers and among intellectuals, in certain administrative bureaus (such as that of the Plan), there now exists a novel (and entirely informal)

---

[13] See the interesting remarks by Otto Kirchheimer, "Private Man and Society," *Political Science Quarterly,* LXXXI:1 (1966), p. 21; as well as Pitts, *op cit.,* pp. 279–288; Hoffman, *ibid.,* pp. 36–37.

"freemasonry" of those who have been active in the various branches of the Catholic youth movements. (For details see Chap. VII.) It is estimated that more than 3,000 (of a total of 38,000) mayors of local communities have such a background. The use which the Church, Church-affiliated educational institutions, and the multiple Catholic organizations make of the mass media shows little of the sectarianism of earlier days.[14]

After the war, the experience of the worker-priests holding mass in factories and slum dwellings was the most widely noted and most dramatic sign of a novel orientation. Yet upon orders of the Vatican this form of missionary work had to be abandoned, at least temporarily, when it turned out that when placed in a working class milieu many of the priests admitted that they were overwhelmed by the justifications of communist ideology. (Manual workers are still little inclined to attend church services or to participate in any religious activities.)[15] Of late, causes and organizations which place themselves to the left of the Communist party have attracted a relatively large number of faithful young Catholics of all origins. This is not only the consequence of changes in the attitudes of the Catholic hierarchy, but another sign that what was previously a rather sharply defined subsystem has now overcome much of its former isolation. Young Catholics move with the trends prevalent in their generation.

Simultaneously Freemasonry has no longer to be reckoned with as an important influence in political life. The vanishing significance of the unifying fight against clericalism has brought out the weakening fissures in the Masonic lodges. From time to time in the public at large, specific issues can still activate anticlerical feelings which then erupt volcano-like. In 1960, presumably 11 million signatures were gathered within a short time and especially in rural regions to oppose new legislation generalizing public subsidies to parochial schools. It was the first, and for a

[14] See Coutrot and Dreyfus, *op. cit.,* pp. 292–305, and William Bosworth, *Catholicism and Crisis in Modern France* (Princeton: Princeton University Press, 1962), esp. Chaps. IV–VII.

[15] For a careful inquiry into the present relationship between the church and the working class, see Gérard Adam and Marc Maurice "L'Église catholique et le monde ouvrier," in Société Française de Sociologie, *Tendances et Volontés de la Société Française* (Paris: S.E.D.E.I.S., 1966), pp. 285–321.

long time the only, interruption of the lethargy that has characterized political life under the Fifth Republic. Subsequent events, especially the rather smooth working of the new legislation, seem to indicate that the protests drew on a body of traditions which has in fact lost political and even ideological vitality.

French Jews (numbering since the recent exodus from North Africa about 500,000 most of whom live in urban centers) were politically so integrated that they did not need to be discussed as a separate element of the political culture. This has, at least, temporarily, changed because of General de Gaulle's policy towards Israel. In the referendum of April, 1969, which resulted in de Gaulle's resignation, there emerged for the first time, a "Jewish vote." It is widely believed that the entire Jewish community voted "no" independently of social status and might thereby have contributed substantially to the result. Whether such an event will reawaken the latent anti-Semitism which exists among certain groups of the population remains to be seen.

By contrast to the traditional attitude of the Jewish population the Protestants (800,000 or 1.6% of the total population) have, at least until recently, lived somewhat apart — a heavy concentration in Alsace, in the Paris region, and in some regions of the center and of the southeast of France has been characteristic of this small religious minority. About two-thirds of its members belong to the upper bourgeoisie — business, banking, the civil service, journalism, and the professions are heavily represented — so that Protestant sermons are frequently of a much higher intellectual level than those in Catholic churches. Socially and even economically a clannishness and a rather deliberate style of life mark the Protestant milieu. Politically, until recently the separateness of the French Protestants was expressed by the fact that they usually voted much further to the left than others in the social milieu to which they belonged or the regions in which they resided. They identified themselves with the advanced opinions of republicanism, not because of an explicit political influence of their churches which has been minimal, but because of the corresponding identification of Catholicism with the political Right and antirepublican movements. If the Protestants were faithful, even though culturally different, republicans, the republic did not confine them to a ghetto: on the contrary, the number of

Protestants in high public positions was and remains very large in proportion to their number in the country.

The new alignments which the recent mutations of French Catholicism have made possible, have had a corresponding impact on the beliefs and attitudes of Protestants. Since the Liberation it can no longer be said that Protestants vote "Left" with any consistency. Their electoral behavior, like their activities in cultural and economic associations, is now determined by other factors than religious affiliation. They too, and for the first time in almost 300 years, have been fully integrated in the mainstream of French political culture.

FAMILY AND CLASS

For Frenchmen who view their neighbors and their fellow citizens with distrust and the institutions around them with considerable cynicism, the family group is a safe haven. Balzac's novels, among others, illustrate how the immediate family (parents-children) was embedded in the larger extended family, how both supported each other and might be ruthless in assuring family well-being. To the outsider, French or foreign, the Frenchman was always sociable, especially when met on neutral ground such as restaurants and other people's salons for the purposes of stimulating conversation. But otherwise distance was maintained and intimacy rarely granted: people had a tendency of barricading themselves in their homes as if they were fortresses.[16] Concern for stability, safe income, property, and continuity (including rational calculations as to matrimony and conception) were the characteristics common to bourgeois and peasant families: the urban and rural proletariat were excluded from this pattern which was sanctioned by legislation and highly valued as a generalized standard.

The belief that the family must remain the foremost training ground for acculturation was matched by a resolve of all competent family members — parents, older siblings, and others — to contribute to the training of the child. Close supervision, incessant correction, threatened and applied sanctions (though usu-

---

[16] André Siegfried, *France. A Study in Nationality* (New Haven: Yale University Press, 1930), pp. 12–13. In what respects Siegfried's "classic" is now outdated, see below.

ally little physical punishment), and a rather authoritarian style were characteristic of family life. "No use discussing," "that's how it is," etc. were accepted formulae. But the great difference from authoritarian family life elsewhere, e.g., in Germany, was that in general little more than outwardly conforming behavior was required. The child and adolescent were free to withdraw emotionally and intellectually into their own thoughts and build, if they were so inclined, their own value system.[17] The fear of face-to-face relationships which characterizes the French administrative and political style was and remains prevalent in many families before it is reproduced and strengthened by the educational system.

The structure of the family has recently undergone a number of important changes. Patriarchy was always mitigated by the fact that in France both lines of kinship — the father's and the mother's — were considered important for the nuclear family and its protection. Although their actual effect is controversial, a variety of factors seemed to have weakened the authority of the French father. Family allowances paid to each family with two or more children and the special compensations for nonworking mothers are quite normally considered to be the wife's rewards — they might be higher than the husband's wages. In the rapidly urbanizing society of higher mobility which France has become, prolonged absences of the father from home are more frequent. Because of better training and new experiences, the sons of farmers or of small businessmen no longer accept unquestioningly the outmoded working methods of their fathers.

These factors have shaken seriously, and in quite different milieus, the patriarchal authority of the head of the family. There is a corresponding inclination of the young of both sexes to feel that they have far better personal relations with their mothers than with their fathers, even though outright and permanent conflicts with the latter are not too frequent. The desire on the part of young people to assert their independence by leaving the family residence altogether is on the increase. In part, this is an aspect of the rural exodus but happens also in the large cities.

[17] These processes within a family of the upper bourgeoisie are masterfully described in Roger Martin du Gard's great novel *The Thibaults* (New York: The Viking Press, 1939).

What is most striking is a general change in atmosphere. In a dynamic society, family members, including children, bring into the family circle the results of their varied experiences, instead of merely passing on and receiving traditions. Leisure time activities, especially travel by parents and children, have influenced the style of family living and often the relationship of the family with the world outside. The search by the family group for equilibrium and balance is, of course, not abandoned. But to enable the family to continue its role as one of the molders of individual motivations, a fresh equilibrium is sought to take into account the new forces pressing from the outside. André Siegfried's characterization of the French family as fundamentally "anti-social," stated some 40 years ago, is no longer a valid generalization.[18]

To what extent the French family subjects its members to political socialization in a narrower sense is altogether uncertain. A number of investigations,[19] though not strictly comparable, agree that in most families political (and religious) discussions are extremely rare. This seems to be less symptomatic of a general lack of interest in political questions than of a desire to avoid possible controversy and of an unwillingness to impose parental opinion in such matters (as distinguished from rules concerning behavior). Only 29 per cent of French voters knew anything at all about the political orientation of their fathers, as compared with 91 per cent of American voters. This enormous difference can be explained in part by the complications of the French party system. Secretiveness, another mark of individualism, is not only practiced by the family cell (and the family firm) in its relations with the outside world, it also colors intrafamily relations.[20]

[18] See above, n. 15.

[19] Duquesne *op. cit.,* Philip E. Converse and Georges Dupeux, "Politicization of the Electorate in France and the United States," *The Public Opinion Quarterly,* XXVI:1 (1962), 89–90; and an inquiry among children in the Grenoble region: C. Roig and F. Billon-Grand, *La Socialization Politique des enfants: Contribution à l'étude de la formation des attitudes politiques en France* (Paris: Colin, 1968). The Grenoble study has now been critically reviewed in light of comparative findings by Fred I. Greenstein and Sidney G. Tarrow, "The Study of French Political Socialization. Towards the Revocation of Paradox," *World Politics,* XII:1 (1969), pp. 95–137.

[20] Some of these earlier findings, especially those reported by Converse and Dupeux, *op. cit.,* are now questioned by more recent (as yet unpublished) studies (esp. one by Mark Kesselman) which suggest a far higher level of political socialization within the family.

It is more difficult to explain the rather surprising results of the inquiry conducted among children in the Grenoble region. Although they came from widely varying family backgrounds, the children's outlook on important historical events and personalities was fairly uniform, a finding one would expect from a society high in consensus. It hardly reflected the divisiveness which historical memories and issues are known to provoke in the adult world. Yet a very high percentage of the children reported that they had frequently listened to political conversations among adults; hence "muteness" does not offer an explanation. Could it be that today's children are simply not highly impressed by the disputes reflected in their parents' beliefs or even that, at least outside of certain elite groups, these beliefs are no longer expressed with a great deal of vehemence?

In the adult world the degree of and feelings about class stratification produce different attitudes towards authority. These attitudes shape a society's authority pattern and have thereby a direct impact on the style in which authority is actually exercised in both the social and the political realm.

Frenchmen, like Englishmen, are very conscious of living in a society that is divided into classes. But since in France equality is valued more highly than in England, deference towards the upper classes — an important element of the British political culture — is far less developed and indeed a resentful antagonism is widespread. The number of those who are conscious of belonging to a class remains high, the solidarity within the same group intense. In a 1964 public opinion poll, 59 per cent declared that they belonged to a class, 29 per cent denied it, the rest gave no answer. But 82 per cent of those who classified themselves as workers felt solidarity with other members of that group; 89 per cent of the peasantry and 73 per cent of the "middle classes" expressed similar feelings.[21]

When asked whether in their opinion "class struggle" was still a reality, 44 per cent of all respondents answered in the affirmative, 37 per cent denied it, and 19 per cent gave no answer. Re-

---

[21] See an (unpublished) poll by the French Institute of Public Opinion of July 1964. Different data on class identification and mobility have been discussed by Natalie Rogof, "Social Stratification in France and the United States," *American Journal of Sociology,* VIII:4 (1953), pp. 347–57, but they have been widely criticized on various grounds.

markably enough, the answers did not vary greatly according to political preferences, except that avowed communists were somewhat more likely to believe in an ongoing class struggle. The respondents to a careful inquiry conducted in the Grenoble region in 1967 and 1968 observed that while class conflict may have declined, class has undoubtedly remained the fundamental political unit.[22]

The sense of belonging and being loyal to a class is matched by a generalized lack of communication between the classes. Sensibility to social precedence, rather than deference, and a spontaneously produced particularism of collective behavior lead to far greater differences in the style of living than the disparity in financial means would warrant. Eating places, cafés, weddings, dances, sports, and funerals cater to different classes and have different rites. They are manifestations of separateness, rarely of common folklore.

The nation's elites continue to be recruited from an extremely small sector of the society.[23] Upward social mobility exists but is frequently awkward and slow, especially into the ranks of the upper bourgeoisie. In general, it is not enough for an individual to cross the barrier; not only he but his entire immediate family must gain entry and must adopt the standards and style of the class to which access is sought. In general this will take more than one generation, especially since money is not the only deciding factor. According to a recent testimony: "The bourgeoisie accepts in its ranks only those whom it considers worthy, those who resemble its own sons and who have the same mentality." [24] An examination of successful careers reveals very few self-made men. Just as in Tocqueville's time, social promotion by marriage out of the class remains infrequent, which is a testimony to the continuing solidity of the bourgeois family.

It is true that partly because of the prevalent egalitarian ideology classes have the function not only of serving as barriers but

[22] See Suzanne Berger and others, "The Problem of Reform in France: The Political Ideas of Local Elites," *Political Science Quarterly,* LXXXIV:3 (1969), p. 443 and *passim.*

[23] See the valuable study, rich in empirical data, by Alain Girard, *La Réussite Sociale en France. Ses caractères — ses lois — ses effets* (Paris: Presses Universitaires de France, 1961), p. 350.

[24] J. Gagliardi and P. Rossillon, *Survivre à de Gaulle* (Paris: Plon, 1959), p. 107.

also of leveling.[25] Once an individual has overcome the obstacles that barred his access to a higher class, his humble origin will be forgiven and forgotten. He will usually find that he has obtained more than mere legal equality. The peer group not only exercises pressure to obtain a degree of outward conformity, it also grants protection by insisting that its members, new or old, be accorded that *considération* (esteem) which creates the desired barriers against lower classes. Although this particular pattern of stratification was initiated by the elite group of a bourgeois society, it has shaped relations between other social classes and categories.

The deep fissure between bourgeoisie and working class has molded the social history of the country for more than a century. Such problems as church-state relations have invited temporary political alignments between part of the middle classes and the proletariat. Nonetheless the struggle between the classes is the more permanent fact and has resulted in antagonistic values and beliefs, i.e., a divided political culture with different symbols, flags, and holidays. The legislation and policies of the Third Republic evoked rather than compensated for the memories of the working class massacre in 1848 and especially of the bloody and revengeful suppression of the Paris *Commune* in 1871. In both houses of parliament, a majority, made up of the defenders of small business and the family farms, delayed social legislation for so long that the much decried reforms of the Popular Front in 1936 did little more than catch up with developments in other industrialized countries. Protectionism, slow economic growth, and the resulting difficulties in obtaining credit were not propitious for the social promotion of workers. Nor were they apt to instill in the worker an esteem for the functioning of the capitalist system.[26]

As a reaction, the industrial working class, numerically weak by comparison with other countries, opposed to the bourgeois

[25] The phenomenon is described in these terms and with interesting, though partially dated details, by Edmond Goblot, *La Barrière et le niveau, étude sociologique de la bourgeoisie française moderne* (Paris: Alcan, 1925), see esp. pp. 4, 6, 16. For a recent inquiry into these questions, see Claude Durand, "Mobilité sociale et conscience de classe," in Darras (ed.), *Le Partage des bénéfices* (Paris: Éditions de Minuit, 1966), pp. 275–293.

[26] See, also for the following, Val Lorwin, "Reflections on the History of the French and American Labor Movement," *Journal of Economic History*, XVII: 1 (1957), pp. 25–44.

society a counterfaith appropriately called *ouvriérisme:* workers should never entrust their defense to members of the bourgeoisie, not even to those who in parliament mouthed the cause of socialism; to send workers into parliament was acting the part of a mother who sold her daughters into a house of prostitution. Deprived of expectations of individual social promotion, the proletariat was reduced to harboring apocolyptic dreams of collective emancipation. At the end of the last century, the ugly working-class suburbs of Paris and the elegant *beaux quartiers* of the capital had become symbols of two hostile civilizations facing each other.

When it turned out that the hopes aroused by the Popular Front and later by the Liberation had been vain, the old traditions of an almost instinctive *ouvriérisme* were revived. These experiences, because they were interpreted as a chance for revolution that had been missed, gave to the political style of the postwar years a superficially revolutionary tone.

Afterwards, when prosperity spread, fairly large groups of wage-earners saw their real income sufficiently increased so as to live in a style that was previously unobtainable and was therefore taunted as "bourgeois." The availability of durable consumer goods and the development of consumer credit, the "motorization" of almost everybody, the multiplication of television sets, the high value placed on leisure time activities — and the correspondingly high budget for the month-long paid vacation — all have produced attitudes which have upset the ingrained habits of individuals and groups. As class distinctions lose some of their former sharpness, a new egalitarianism no longer stops at class borders. The common patterns of a mass culture are changing at last — even the style of celebrations and of sports events.

Nonetheless, as careful observers have pointed out, it is necessary (and in France probably more so than in other modern industrial societies) to distinguish between the spheres of consumption and of production.[27] As a consumer, the worker has ceased to live apart or in a class ghetto; once he leaves the factory he may no longer regard himself as a worker. But as a

[27] Serge Mallet, *La Nouvelle Classe Ouvrière* (Paris: Éditions du Seuil, 1963), pp. 9, 31, and 32; Andrée Andrieux and Jean Lignon, *L'Ouvrier d'aujourd'hui* (Paris: Rivière, 1960), p. 189 and *passim*. For a comparative discussion see also T. B. Bottomore, *Classes in Modern Society* (New York: Pantheon, 1966).

producer, the fundamental characteristics which have always distinguished the working class from other social strata have remained unchanged, or at any rate are perceived as unchanged: hierarchism, inequality, and an authoritarian style are resented as before. However, until the Events of May, 1968, it appeared as if the vast majority had resigned itself to an acceptance of industrial work and its conditions, interrupted by a protest vote for the communist ticket on election day.

When, in 1968, strikes began to spread after the students' street fights had acted as a detonator, it was not just the extent of the work stoppages that came as a surprise. True, the work stoppages engulfed at times between 6 and 7½ million workers out of a total labor force of 17 million; [28] the demands for higher wages and better working conditions were unusually bold. But what was most unexpected were the radically anticapitalist slogans, the unconcealed hostility against many employers just stopping short of physical violence but expressing anger and contempt. It is true that in many instances young workers set the style for the sit-in strikes and remained militant even after the communist trade-union leaders did their best to direct the movement into more customary channels. But these were workers belonging to a generation that in an extensive survey conducted a few years earlier — had been described as sharing none of the antiestablishment bias of historic *ouvriérisme*.[29] The Events of 1968 will be described below (see Chap. VII) as having been in some way a classical expression of age-old forms of French rebellion. The strike movement and especially the way in which workers, young and old, acted out their roles demonstrated how close to the surface feelings of class identification and class antagonism have remained.

ASSOCIATIONS

Many observers, the French sociologist Durkheim among them, have deplored that France is weak in secondary groups standing

[28] This is the figure which the careful article by Gérard Adam, "Étude Statistique des grèves de mai-juin 1968," *Revue Française de Science Politique* (abbreviated hereafter as *RFSP*) XX:1 (1970), pp. 105–118 arrives at. Newspaper figures and estimates by the trade unions published during the Events had been as high as 9 million.

[29] See Duquesne, *op. cit.*, pp. 140–41, and the results of other inquiries quoted there.

between the state and the individual and able "to drag them [the citizens] into the general current of social life." [30] It is no longer true, if it ever was, that the system lacks interest groups articulating and defending innumerable material and immaterial interests and values. (For details see Chap. VII.) But it remains correct that neither interest groups nor other associations, numerous though they are, play as significant a role in the socialization of the citizen as they do in other countries.

A negative bias against authority might have encouraged association if the egalitarian thrust and the competition between individuals did not cast suspicion on those who recommended that efforts be combined. The ambivalence towards participation in group life is not merely negativistic apathy, but a lack of belief in the value of cooperation.

Nonetheless, there exists now a fairly dense network of organizations concerned not only with interest representation but also with leisure time activities, social life, and the like, and membership in these associations is quite widespread and frequent, even though it reaches nowhere near American levels. For example, a not entirely reliable survey undertaken in 1951 concluded that only 41 per cent of French adults belonged to any kind of association. But although, on the one hand, this included political parties, on the other, it did not account for multiple memberships.[31] A more recent inquiry concerned respectively, with the sixteen to twenty-four and the fifteen to twenty age group, found that only between 28 per cent and 35 per cent belonged to any association open to either young or adult, of these a good half to sports clubs.[32] Even such numbers are considered inflated by some observers.

[30] Émile Durkheim, *The Division of Labor in Society* (New York: The Macmillan Company, 1933, originally published in 1893), p. 28.

[31] Arnold M. Rose, "Voluntary Associations in France" in Arnold M. Rose (ed.), *Theory and Method in the Social Sciences* (Minneapolis: University of Minnesota Press, 1954), pp. 74–75. Professor Rose's findings have been criticized on the basis of empirical research by Orvell R. Gallagher, "Voluntary Associations in France," *Social Forces*, XXXVI:2 (1957), pp. 153 ff. Duncan MacRae, Jr., *Parliament, Parties and Society in France, 1946–1958* (New York: St. Martin's Press, 1967), p. 30 presents an interesting table comparing associational membership in the United States and France. One only wished that his basic data were more reliable and more comparable.

[32] Duquesne, *op. cit.,* pp. 216 ff., and pp. 138–41, Rapport d'enquête

However, these and similar data are not too meaningful if one wishes to assess the importance of associations in the life of the individual. It is not enough to count associations or membership affiliations. They play a role in the socialization process only when they determine activities and emotions of the citizens. Some observers seem to confirm that membership in French organizations involves less actual participation than in American or British organizations and hence has less impact upon social and political attitudes.[33] It is true that here, as to a lesser extent in the United States, social class makes a difference. The upper urban bourgeoisie appears to have the most active associational life in a style that frequently imitates the mores of the nobility. But various community studies that have been undertaken agree that outside that limited circle formally organized associations have little importance and cut very little into the lives of their members. The need for human fellowship is satisfied either within the family or, depending on class and environment, in such unstructured gatherings as the *salon,* the café, or, for the young, the *bande* (not to be confused with a gang). The individual's reluctance to get involved finds justification in the fact that in a highly centralized political system grass roots associations are generally ineffectual. Neither the promotion of reforms nor the defense of established situations seem to be the proper domain of community action — influence has to be exercised at the seat of power. This has encouraged and facilitated the politization of a wide range of associational activities (for details, see Chap. VII).

Of late there are indications that associative life is becoming denser and more rewarding. Its value is no longer assessed merely in terms of the associations' success in the interest group arena. Modern mass media (see Chap. V) have encouraged a flowering of cultural clubs, mostly but not only among the young; they have often swept aside the traditional barriers of class, of denomination, and of political conviction. The organizations of young farmers already mentioned have usually preserved their twofold function as interest groups and organs of cooperation. Their fairly wide ac-

de ministère de la jeunesse et des sports, *Jeunes d'aujourd'hui* (Paris: La Documentation Française, 1967) pp. 179 and *passim.*

[33] See Eric Nordlinger, "Democratic Stability and Instability. The French Case," *World Politics,* XVIII:1 (1965), pp. 127–157.

ceptance is all the more remarkable as they are the outgrowth of a Catholic movement. In other milieus similar activities are noted. "What characterizes all these organizations," a French sociologist has written in a statement which, it is true, some would consider too sweepingly optimistic, "is the need to make contact between category and category, between spiritual family and spiritual family, the horror of a priori formulas and systems, the passion for reform and the ideology of participation." [34]

Young workers and white-collar employees, young farmers, young businessmen and students, express their intention of affiliating with their professional associations, trade unions, etc., in significantly greater numbers than their elders. Most of them are also convinced that their contemporaries are more interested in such associations and in their future role than is the older generation. At the same time, it appears that this role is viewed differently now than in the past: associations are regarded as necessary and normal elements of modern society rather than as "movements" or standard bearers of a cause.

If such attitudes were to be accepted widely, associational life might furnish a far more important contribution than heretofore to the learning process of elites and of common man.

EDUCATION

"All national educational systems indoctrinate the coming generations with the basic outlooks and values of their political order." [35] Education is the foremost process by which a community preserves and transmits its physical and intellectual characteristics. At a dramatic moment of its history, France was ruled by a man who recognized the central significance of education for the perpetuation of his values. Well into the second half of the twentieth century, the French educational system has remained an imposing historical monument — in the unmistakable style of the First Empire.

The edifice that Napoleon I erected integrated education at all levels, from primary school to postgraduate professional train-

---

[34] Michel Crozier, "The Cultural Revolution: Notes on the Changes in the Intellectual Climate of France," in Stephen R. Graubard (ed.), *The New Europe* (Boston: Houghton Mifflin, 1964), p. 624.

[35] V. O. Key, *Public Opinion and American Democracy* (New York: Knopf, 1961), p. 316.

ing, both public and private, into one centralized and strictly structured corporation: *the* imperial university. Its function was to teach the "national doctrine"; the teachers were to have, according to Napoleon, the Jesuit mentality, but that of secularized Jesuits free from Rome and devoted solely to defending the public interest. A "Grand Master" presided over the entire institution; he ensured the uniformity of programs at the various levels and the conformism of students and teachers at all levels. The development of secondary education and the training of its teachers became a particular and personal concern of Napoleon. The lycées and collèges, selecting their pupils at an early age, were invaluable in recruiting the elites for a regime unwilling to rely solely on privilege or birth. Both an egalitarian temper and the need to develop rapidly a nontraditional loyalty shaped the structure and the program of these training grounds for the future servants of civil and military society. Enforced by strict military discipline, enlivened only by vulgar patriotism, an otherwise deliberately abstract instruction used Latin, rhetoric, logic, and mathematics as vehicles for molding what was called the "cultivated" mind.[36]

Succeeding regimes have loosened disciplines; the outwardly military style has disappeared; the tides of clerical and anticlerical influence have advanced and receded. But whether imperial, royal, or republican, all regimes discovered that the machinery created by Napoleon was an admirably convenient and coherent instrument for dispensing both changing and permanent values of French civilization. Hence the centralized imperial university has never been dismantled. The "Grand Master" — commanding through government appointed rectors, the twenty-three academies into which the country is divided for purposes of educational administration — is nowadays the Minister of National Education.

Habits of centralization and devotion to a special kind of egali-

---

[36] For the description of the napoleonic origins of the system and of its later development see Hippolyte Taine, *Les Origines de la France contemporaine. Le Régime Moderne,* II (Paris: Hachette, 1894), pp. 153 ff. It is true that the legislation which determined the actual organization of the universities dates only from the end of the nineteenth century. See Antoine Prost, *L'Enseignement en France, 1800–1967* (Paris: Colin, 1968), pp. 235 ff.

tarian ideology feed on each other and mark many teachers of all ranks in the public education system. The curriculum and teaching methods, the criteria for the selection and the advancement of pupils and teachers, the content of examinations, and the perpetual changes of all of the foregoing continue to be centrally imposed, usually by the Ministry in Paris. It may no longer be true as it once was that the Minister can determine merely by looking at his watch which verse of Vergil is being translated in all third-year Latin classes of the realm. But in the Fifth Republic, to give a present-day example, the songs used to recruit voice teachers in all public schools are still designated annually by ministerial ordinance. Such authoritarian practices, even when they are devoted to the propagation of emphatically nonauthoritarian concepts, leave little room for administrative or pedagogic initiative at any level. Local authorities, educational associations, parent-teachers organizations, and teachers unions have become rather active as legitimate interest groups. But until the most recent reforms they left the discussion and determination of educational policies to the administrative hierarchy. When a new field of academic concern was added, on whatever level, standards of uniformity demanded that it be introduced almost everywhere without consideration for needs or resources.

The practice of making the individual's advancement at every step dependent on an appropriate examination is not peculiar to France. But nowhere has there developed such a widespread cult of competitive examinations, a cult which draws its strength from an obsessive and quite unrealistic belief that everybody is equal before an examination. In one important respect there is little difference between the certificate of studies delivered at the county seat to the 14-year-old upon leaving school, the *baccalauréat* sanctioning secondary studies, the senselessly specialized *aggrégation* needed for a professorship, or the various *concours* by which the administrative elite of the nation is selected: success or failure in the examination shake not only the candidate and his family but the entire milieu to which he belongs. The walls of many cathedrals are hung with votive tablets imploring or thanking the Virgin Mary for assistance in examinations. French society is strewn with individuals to which failure or a lower than expected rank have inflicted irreparable psychological damage. Some rigidities of earlier times may have been overcome, but a voluntarily centralized and anonymous system still offers little opportunity to judge candidates by any other performance than their oral or written answers in an examination and the jury's appreciation of them.

On the other hand, there is no mechanism to ensure or control a continuing high performance once the prize is won. This may result in increased bureaucratic rigidity and, in the educational system, intellectual sclerosis. Moreover, the seemingly egalitarian process of selection frequently hides outright corporatist practices, such as the co-optation of university professors by secret faculty ballot.

Altogether it would be wrong to assume that the educational system is tyrannical because it is so vastly different from the schools and universities that train for the "civic culture" in England and the United States. Beginning with Napoleon's times, the centralization of authority in a far-removed national government has often resulted in a wholesome weakening of controls and in a lessening of community pressures which because of their closeness might have become offensive. Since the demise of the Empire, there has developed within the framework of uniform rules considerable freedom of expression in the classrooms and lecture halls. Such freedom was backed early by tenure rules which satisfied both libertarian and egalitarian conventions. Education as an effective weapon for emancipation and social betterment has been more than an official ideology — farmers' and workers' families regard the instruction of their children (and a better instruction than they had) as an important weapon for fighting "them," which includes the authorities organizing the instruction. In the past, the moving of rural youth into the ranks of elementary school teachers has been of great importance for the two-step social promotion discussed earlier.

The French child and adolescent is trained primarily in those arts of living which profit the critical and civilized individual who is an island unto himself. A vivid and sometimes quite ruthless competitiveness isolates him from his fellow students. The generally authoritarian stance of his instructors is not conducive to warmth in the teacher-pupil relationship, and the mutual fear of the face-to-face relationship determines the climate of most classrooms. Rote learning rather than insight into the learning process, a minimum of oral discussion and hence passivity on the part of the students, in the secondary schools, at least, an almost undiminished emphasis on rhetoric and logical presentation, are still widely accepted pedagogic methods. A curriculum which prides itself on being abstract and nonpractical bears the distinct marks of the Jesuit pedagogy which was Napoleon's paradigm.

A French social psychologist has described the causes and consequences of these educational and intellectual traditions in revealing terms:

> [The Frenchman's] love of clarity results simultaneously from a certain laziness which turns him away from a deeper search and complications; from a desire never to be fooled and from the example set by an elite group which has been trained for two millennia by the exercises of composition and by dialectics. The love for order is in the classical tradition: the Romans have imparted it to the Gauls, the lasting influence of the rhetors, the Justinian and Aristotelian renaissance, humanism, the Jesuit program, and later the [Napoleonic] University have reinforced ancient traditions. The qualities of the French mind are a precious gift for the entire world. . . . The risk is that taken altogether, a certain superficiality neglecting the shadowy zones of thought simplifies decisions excessively or complicates them by an excess of abstract logic. It sometimes resolves a difficulty with an elegant sally.[37]

Until recently, the prominent place given Latin in the curriculum of secondary education and the other requirements of the *baccalauréat* were designed as barriers between the bourgeoisie and the other classes.[38] The *baccalauréat* however has remained almost the sole means, and until recently also a guarantee, of access to higher education. Although various lycées offer some alternate curricula, traditional educational goals have not been abandoned. After the child has reached the age of fourteen, any attention to pedagogical methods is deliberately discarded as being alien to secondary and higher education.

[37] Gabriel Le Bras, "Psychologie de la France," *Revue de psychologie des peuples* (1952), quoted here from Michel Beaujour and Jacques Ehrmann, *La France Contemporaine* (New York: Macmillan, 1965), p. 70.

[38] Although the book by Goblot (see above n. 25) is now outdated in many respects, it remains entirely and significantly up to date in its description of the role which the *baccalauréat* plays in the bourgeois family.

But with forty to fifty students in each of the many terminal classes of the secondary schools and hundreds in the lecture halls of the universities, such a system suits and profits only that self-motivated individualist for whom it was designed originally. It even works to the disadvantage of the gifted child who comes from other than the bourgeois milieu. The distance between teacher and pupil, the absence of pedagogy, and the emphasis on the cultivated use of language widen the cultural gap further. The obstacles which children of various milieus face after they have gained admission to a lycée are illustrated by the findings of a recent inquiry: 86 per cent of the children of bouregois families stay in school for the entire six years of secondary school and are therefore entitled to take the final examinations, but only 55 per cent of those with a lower middle class background, 35 per cent of farmers' and 21 per cent of workers' children are similarly successful.[39] The others had fallen by the wayside, although all of them had proven talented enough to transfer to the secondary level.

His singular success in an educational system which is uniquely suited to the milieu from which he comes convinces the young bourgeois that his position in society is due to an inborn talent. In his opinion, few others will be able to acquire the necessary knowledge, or the privileges which his knowledge affords. Postwar reforms have tried to counter such class snobbery by facilitating the transition between the various branches of the educational system and by moving the teaching personnel more freely from one to the other. Hence a certain amalgamation of methods and outlook could be on the way.

Yet even before the raising of the compulsory school age from fourteen to sixteen years — a reform constantly delayed for budgetary reasons — the proportion of French youth pursuing studies at various levels is higher than elsewhere in Europe. At age seventeen, close to 17 per cent of the population is engaged in studies which correspond to the academic curriculum in an American high school. If one adds technical instruction and the like, more than one-third of this age group in France are full-time students, more than twice as many as in Germany or in England, even though substantially fewer than in the United

[39] See Raymond Poignant, *L'Enseignement dans les pays du Marché Commun* (Paris: Institut Pédagogique National, 1965), p. 105.

States. For the age group between twenty and twenty-four, France ranks equally high among its European neighbors. In 1956, close to 6 per cent were enrolled in institutions of higher education and now this figure reaches probably more than 7 per cent (as compared with about 4 per cent in England and Germany and 27.2 per cent for the United States). In 1965 close to 10 per cent of young men and women, 21 years of age, were full time students.[40] On the other hand the dropout rate of students is particularly high in France, so that the number of comparable diplomas might not be higher than in Great Britain.

These data indicate that in spite of the difficulties which have been discussed education in France more than elsewhere in Europe remains a vehicle of social promotion, even though it is far from providing the social mobility that might be desirable. Table I illustrates the wide disparities in the class composition of the student body. In some schools that are strategically important for the training of the country's political and administrative elites, the students are now more exclusively of bourgeois origin than they were during the immediate postwar years.

The role of the schools in that particular form of socialization which trains either directly or indirectly for citizenship has varied over time. In the early days of the Third Republic, and especially during its period of virulent anticlericalism, the government had no difficulty in relying on the teacher for the propagation of the rationalistic, positivistic faith. In all classrooms, but particularly in those of the countryside, such teaching was also imbued with an emotional patriotism that drew its strength from anti-German feelings, and from the belief that France remained the epitome of civilized humanity. Objectively, the revered history textbooks of the period were almost disarmingly ethnocentric. For many a young Frenchman they provided an early introduction to the dichotomy of an abstract, ideal *patrie* and a frequently despised government, of a country in whose defense one was willing to die but whose political institutions were considered badly suited to daily life.

[40] *Ibid.,* pp. 146, 155; Ministère de l'Éducation Nationale, *Informations Statistiques,* No. 74–75 (1965), p. 414 and *Tableaux de l'Éducation nationale, Édit. 1966* (Paris: S.C.S.C., 1967), p. 215; and J. F. Dewhurst (ed.), *Europe's Needs and Resources* (New York: The Twentieth Century Fund, 1961), p. 315.

TABLE I. *Social Origin of Students* (*in percentages*)

	Farmers	Agricultural workers	Employers industry	Employers trade	Craftsmen	Professions, management, and high civil service	Lower civil service and middle management	White collar workers	Manual workers	Service personnel	Diverse other categories	Total
Enrolled in secondary schools preparing for higher education	6.5	1.3	1.9	8.0	5.1	15.1	15.0	16.5	20.3	1.3	9.0	100.0
Enrolled in institutions of higher education	5.4	0.5	3.0	8.5	3.8	29.5	17.7	8.6	7.7	1.0	14.3	100.0
Percentage in the total labor force	15.7	4.3	0.4	6.6	3.2	4.0	7.8	12.6	36.7	5.4	3.3	100.0

Compiled from *Informations statistiques du Ministère de l'Éducation Nationale*, Nos. 74–75 (1965), p. 435, and *Annuaire Statistique de la France 1963* (Paris: Imprimerie Nationale, 1964), p. VIII.

After the First World War the teachers in the public schools turned from patriotism to internationalism and pacifism. An entire generation, especially of rural youth, bore the impact of such convictions imparted to them. It appears that at present school children share what might best be described as a "quiet patriotism." [41] For them their country remains not only an object of national affection. A large majority among them also believes, on the basis of the instruction they receive and from the messages conveyed to them by the mass media, that France still has a foremost mission in the modern world: that of spreading intellectual and moral values. But if such traditional trust in the values of "French civilization" (see above Chap. I) is still strong, young Frenchmen also "feel" European. Most of them wish to see their country incorporated into a larger European community even at the price of some loss of sovereignty for their *patrie*. (What price they would be willing to pay remains vague, however.)

In the classical curriculum of the secondary schools, citizenship training has always been as alien as any empirical social science. History instruction usually combines stress on humanistic values with resigned determinism. "Civic instruction," as prescribed by ministerial directives, has generally been turned into a farce.[42] Most decisive, however, is the fact that, as least in the lycées, the human climate and the educational atmosphere are isolating and therefore in essence anticivic.

While the number of students in nonpublic institutions of higher learning is insignificantly small, private schools continue to play a definite if constantly declining role on the primary and secondary levels. Most of them are Catholic. As could be expected from what has been said earlier about the well-defined regionalization of religious practice and of dechristianization, Catholic schools are very unevenly distributed throughout the country.

The times when Catholic schools were "ghetto" schools, highly valued as transmitters of a threatened tradition or bitterly fought as an alien body within the republic, are over. Since the war, the

---

[41] According to several surveys and polls as summarized by Alain Duhamel, "Les Français et l'Europe," *Le Monde,* July 8, 1970.

[42] For a general but still too favorable picture see "L'Éducation du citoyen," *Cahiers Pédagogiques,* XIV: 12 (1959), pp. 1–148.

usual issue at stake was the allocation of public funds to the parochial institutions which the Catholic community was unwilling to rescue from financial starvation. Even in such terms the controversy quickly took an ideological turn. Reopening old wounds, the fight over subsidies, transmitted to parliament by the feuding organized interests was one of the reasons for governmental instability under the Fourth Republic. In the Fifth Republic, presidential authority was needed to accredit a compromise solution which might not have displeased Napoleon: to receive financial assistance parochial schools must submit to the administrative authority of the state. If the compromise works, another ideological conflict of long standing will be liquidated.

Discussions about a thorough reform of all education, but especially of secondary and of higher education, have never abated since the end of the Second World War. It was widely recognized that the mere pressure of numbers was bound to explode the old structures, to modify methods and to transform the style of education. A secondary school system that in 1970 was expected to provide instruction for four million adolescents and to certify many of them for access to higher education could not remain identical to one which at the beginning of the century trained two hundred thousand. Between 1958 and 1968 the number of students in higher education rose from 170,000 to more than 600,000 (of which 130,000 sought accommodation in the Paris region).

But the troubles besetting the system were not only due to quantitative pressures. The teaching methods practiced at the lycées proved entirely inappropriate for the socialization of the lower middle classes which were winning entry into secondary education. Increased social mobility and the modernization of the country resulted in a situation in which "the university and the economy have grown out of phase." [43] Because the univer-

---

[43] See, also, for the following, Stephen S. Cohen, *Modern Capitalist Planning: The French Model* (Cambridge: Harvard University Press, 1969), pp. 239 ff. An equally perspicacious analysis, provided long before the Events of 1968 is to be found in Raymond Aron's "La Crise de l'université," *Preuves*, No. 159 (1964), pp. 10–22. For an excellent discussion of the problems of higher education from the perspective of social promotion, see P. Bourdieu and J. C. Passeron, *Les Héritiers. les étudiants et la culture* (Paris: Éditions de Minuit, 1964).

sities failed to respond to the demands of mass education, the students' dissatisfaction with the content and methods of their education was frequently combined with anxieties about their professional career. For others, a minority, the haphazard efforts of the system to serve the needs of the society by providing training for skills were distasteful because, in their eyes, such as design subjected higher education to the demands of technocratic capitalism. The conjunction of these two discontented strata produced the spark of rebellion which from Nanterre (a new university in a joyless suburb of Paris) spread to all universities and to many secondary schools as well.[44]

In its attempts to reform the educational system the Fifth Republic was no more successful than its less efficient predecessor. Nine Ministers of National Education succeeded each other in ten years. Numerous conferences, sometimes involving the President of the Republic, produced an abundance of contradictory paper reforms. Both the exorbitant centralization of the system and the leverage of vested interests (professors, teachers and administrators) frustrated the reformers time and again. Substantial increases in budgetary allocations for educational buildings, equipment and personnel never kept pace with the needs and often appeared wasted, not only because of bureaucratic delays but also because weighty problems of substance remained unsolved. In more than one way the campus at Nanterre reflected the errors inherent in authoritarian and yet heedless planning undertaken without consulting those affected.

In May, 1968, at the very time when students and police were battling in the streets 61 per cent of Paris respondents to an

[44] For a sociological and psychological analysis of student unrest leading to the explosion, see Alain Touraine, *Le Mouvement de mai ou le Communisme utopique* (Paris: Éditions du Seuil. 1968), especially the chapters on the crisis of the university, pp. 63–125. The author was a professor at Nanterre. Raymond Aron's (an ex-professor at the Sorbonne) critical articles on the university situation published in *Le Figaro* during May and June 1968 are an important complement by a more conservative observer. They are now available in an appendix to Raymond Aron, *The Elusive Revolution. Anatomy of a Student Revolt* (New York: Praeger, 1969). The richly documented article by Philippe Bénéton and Jean Touchard, "Les Interprétations de la Crise de mai-juin 1968," *RFSP* XX:3 (1970), pp. 503–543, provides most valuable data on the reasons for the crisis of the French universities.

opinion poll believed that the students' demands for educational reforms were justified; only 16 per cent thought otherwise. When later in the month President de Gaulle launched the most ineffective televised appeal of his career, he attributed the crisis of the university to the inability of those in charge "to adapt themselves to the modern necessities of the nation"; he pledged that the system of higher education would be "reconstructed not according to centuries-old habits, but in line with the actual needs of the country's development." [45]

Backed by the President yet another Minister of National Education, Edgar Faure, elaborated after the 1968 elections over opposition from many quarters and in record time a comprehensive reform law. Not a single member of parliament dared oppose it and only a few abstained, although it was well known that the forthrightness of the reform ran counter to the preferences of many members of the Gaullist majority. After General de Gaulle's departure from the scene, M. Faure was dismissed and a less controversial minister took over the task of operating the new law.

By giving to all institutions of higher learning a considerable degree of administrative, financial and pedagogic autonomy, the laws sets out to destroy the Napoleonic structure.[46] By introducing at the local, regional and national levels faculty-student committees with seemingly broad decision-making powers for all concerned, it seeks to legitimize practices of democratic cooperation. Excluded from the committees' prerogatives are, however, all questions of faculty appointments and promotion. The sometimes monstruously large *Facultés,* which were an administrative impediment to closer student-faculty relations and to intra-disciplinary collaboration as well, are to be replaced by smaller units, resembling American-style academic departments and which are free to regroup in universities of manageable size.

It is as yet too early to evaluate the overall success of the reform and altogether impossible to gauge its impact on the socialization

[45] For the address of May 24, see *Année Politique* (abbreviated hereafter *AP*) *1968* (Paris: 1969), pp. 379–80.
[46] For a good summary of the complicated law, see *ibid.* pp. 367 ff. The author of the law has furnished an interesting explanation of its motivation, in Edgar Faure, "Loi d'orientation: les idées derrière les textes," *Preuves* (3ᵉ Trimestre 1970), pp. 92–99.

process. In a legislative text of audacious ambitions, much had to be left vague. Innumerable administrative regulations had to fill in the gaps and did so often in a confusing way. To impose details by ministerial fiat was deemed contrary to the spirit of the reform. But not to do so gave to conservative forces the possibility of returning to old ways even if the accustomed structures were given new labels. There will be a total of 60 to 70 universities in the country. Some of them are too small or too specialized to permit the desired interdisciplinary cooperation. Others (especially some designed to serve the Paris region) will remain paper creations for a long time.

Student participation in the prescribed election has been uneven at best: many students have refrained from casting a ballot, either out of indifference or because they followed the instructions of the Extreme Left, desirous to see the experiment fail. But where student participation in the elections falls below a specified level, the law provides that student representation on the committees is decreased accordingly so that presently the faculty dominates many committees. Delays in setting up some of the governing boards, and elsewhere confusion over their composition, has offered another opportunity to postpone if not altogether to elude the reforms. Should confusion and anarchy spread, the law empowers the Minister of Education to take emergency measures, in some ways similar to those which the French constitution reserves for the President of the Republic in a situation of national distress (art. 16, see below, Chap. IX). But this would be tantamount to a return to excessive centralization.

In many universities, though by no means all, an earlier ardor for pedagogical reforms seems to have evaporated. The financial means available are insufficient to shift from the large lecture courses (which remain unpopular) to other forms of instruction. Altogether the continuing control of university finances by the Ministry of Finance frequently turns the desired autonomy into a sham. The widely known fact that President Pompidou, himself an *agrégé* and one-time professor of Greek, is a staunch conservative in most education matters, has slowed the reformers. The need for and the appropriateness of examinations at various stages of academic studies is ardently debated, and even more so the question of entrance requirements. Officially there is still no quota on admissions; the elimination of unqualified students has to be effected surreptitiously. There are earnest discussions of — but so far no solution to — the problem of providing at the university level a greater amount of general education rather than immediate specialization. With the mass influx into the secondary schools, this question can no longer be avoided as it could be when the secondary schools served mainly the training of elites.

No comprehensive law has as yet reformed the secondary schools. Many of them were engulfed in the strike movement of 1968, not only for political reasons but because they too suffered from students' dissatisfaction with methods, curriculum, and atmosphere. Newly created councils, composed of teachers, parents, and students, advise — somewhat in the manner of the local Boards of Education in the United States — the school principal (previously subject only to ministerial directives). Complaints that this has brought about an intolerable politization of secondary education are heard from many sides. In near despair the Minister of Education remarked in 1970 that controversies over the curriculum (such as the proper place of Latin) or over mundane questions of school administration still have a tendency to turn into wars of religion.

Will the lag between the traditional style of authority and the needs of a modern society in development finally be breached? [47] Will the struggle between the conservatives, reformers, and revolutionary radicals from within and without the educational system permit the new legislation to bring about what it set out to do: to transform the "centuries-old-habits" about which General de Gaulle had spoken? The question may remain open for years.

CONCLUSION

From our discussion of the ongoing socialization of Frenchmen, it has become clear why an often noted contradiction in the behavior of Frenchmen is more apparent than real. Why, it is frequently asked, is a nation whose history has frequently

---

[47] On this problem, see Hoffmann, *op. cit.,* p. 73, and in a strikingly similar vein more than half a century earlier, Émile Durkheim, *Education and Sociology* (Glencoe: The Free Press, 1956; originally published between 1903 and 1911), pp. 135 ff.

been an inspiration to free peoples everywhere and which is made up of self-reliant, rational, and mature individuals, unable to establish a stable democracy? The answer to this question may be found in the fact that the values which the individual Frenchman has learned to accept as normal and which many of them cherish are often in conflict with the needs of a political system combining freedom and authority.

Tensions between the desire to assert the "uniqueness" of the individual and centuries-old experiences with a centralized bureaucratic control of society have produced ambiguous attitudes towards authority. They request that strict rulings treat everybody and everything alike in order to minimize possibilities for capricious discretion and discrimination. Since one suspects that the "others" — the authorities or the peers — will flout these rules in the interest of privilege, not willing obedience but only a minimum of commitment, of outward compliance with community rules, can be expected. Hence, again in the words of Michel Crozier, "the disproportion between the authority which seems to us indispensable to govern a human group and the authority that we can accept as members of a group." [48]

The distrust of others as a threat to individual self-fulfillment demands the distrust of, indeed wherever possible rebellion against, conventions and beliefs established by others.[49] As another French sociologist has remarked: whereas many Americans believe that self-fulfillment consists in adjustment to a society whose basic values are not challenged. Frenchmen think that man is himself only when he rebels.[50] "I revolt, therefore

[48] "La France, terre de commandement," *Esprit,* XXV:12 (December 1957), pp. 779–97. Recent empirical studies, as yet incomplete and unpublished by John S. Ambler, Sidney Tarrow, and others, cast some doubt on the general validity of Michel Crozier's often cited theses. The "ambivalence" of attitudes and the "paradoxes" many writers on France have discussed will certainly need further investigation.

[49] The table published under the heading "Trust in Others" by Eckstein, *Division and Cohesion in Democracy. A Study of Norway* (Princeton: Princeton University Press, 1966), p. 222, makes it appear as if a higher percentage of Frenchmen than of Americans trust their fellow-citizens. It rather points to the dubious value of such comparative polling data.

[50] Raymond Aron, as quoted by Stanley Hoffmann, "Protest in Modern France," in M. A. Kaplan, (ed.), *The Revolution in World Politics* (New York: John Wiley, 1962), pp. 69 ff.

we are," Albert Camus has written to dramatize the universality of protest. Since such protest is raised in the name of principle, since it is seen as a phase in the struggle against the forces of evil, it is usually highly moralistic — which is again fundamentally different from what has been described as the "unmoralistic" character of most Americans.[51]

The insistence on authoritatively enforced rules and the simultaneous distrust of established authority and of the peer group produce a political culture that expects little from cooperation or a broad-based participation in decision-making. The individual is self-confident enough not to expect strength from cooperation with others. Face-to-face relationships without which no cooperative form of action is possible are avoided as a possible source of friction. Intransigeant insistence on one's own position is regarded as more promising to conflict solution than bargaining. Typically enough, French dictionary definitions of the equivalent of bargaining and of compromise are all slightly pejorative. Only the arbiter who forces the conflicting parties to accept his verdict for a binding *compromis* earns prestige. The field of industrial relations is one of many where all partners show a preference for the imposed rather than the mutually agreed balance of interests.[52]

It is obvious that such reservations against direct negotiations are likely to perpetuate the estrangement between groups and classes. "Every fraction of the social body," complains a progressive employers' organization, "has the — frequently justified — feeling that it is not understood by all the others. No group has the monopoly of this obsessional fever which one sometimes diagnoses solely among the working class. . . ."[53]

The overall result of such mental attitudes has frequently been *incivisme,* that lack of solidarity and of civic sense which many Frenchmen deplore even while they are practicing it. When

[51] Cf. Robert E. Lane, *Political Ideology* (New York: The Free Press, 1962), p. 344.

[52] This too is a statement which more recent public opinion polls do not seem to confirm. There might be a difference here between the feelings of the wage earners and those of the leaders who are in charge of conducting the negotiations.

[53] Association des Cadres Dirigeants de l'Industrie pour le Progrès Social et Économique. "Rapport sur l'activité de l'Association en 1953," *Bulletin,* No. 78 (March 1954), p. 86.

it results in a stalemate which stalls overdue changes, the nation is likely to turn to an authoritarian pacifier to solve the crisis. To accredit the solution which he imposes, he will frequently resort to a heroic style which in such a situation appears far more acceptable than the humdrum of laborious bargaining.

In spite of superficial similarities, this setting is not identical with the one in which a people try to be saved from themselves by a totalitarian rule which they are unable to control. Since the confidence which Frenchmen have in themselves as individuals is not impaired, they do not see the need for totalitarian manipulation of their minds. They still distrust their government as well as their neighbors and want to voice their distrust. The freedom left for such criticism and the unwillingness to enforce conformity distinguish the authoritarian from the totalitarian regime. The Fifth Republic, both under de Gaulle and since his retirement, has been as little totalitarian as the liberal phase of the Second Empire to which it has been correctly compared. But the Events of 1968 demonstrated that, like the French authoritarian governments of the past, the Gaullist regime was also unable to get to the roots of the citizens' perennial ambivalence towards authority.

From the perspective of this study, the search for the "perfect" institution is vain. What matters most is whether the transformation of the political culture, especially as transmitted in the process of formal and informal education, will overcome those traditions in the socialization of Frenchmen that have proven an obstacle to political modernization and to a mature democracy.

CHAPTER IV

Political Participation

IN A DEMOCRATIC SOCIETY the citizen's participation in the process by which political decisions are made influences both his political socialization and his political recruitment. When he takes part, directly or indirectly, in the selection of candidates for political office, when he votes in local or national elections, he experiences at first hand manifestations of the political system to which he belongs and he thereby undergoes further socialization. The process started in the family, the school, associations, and the like continues, but by getting involved in this kind of elementary political activity, the citizen also performs a political role and is therefore recruited into the system.

Hence socialization (discussed in the preceding chapter), political participation discussed in the present chapter, and the recruitment into active decision-making positions (to be treated in Chap. VI) are tied together by the role which the citizen might play in any or all of these processes.

THE CITIZEN IN LOCAL POLITICS

The concept of "grass-roots democracy" is not peculiar to Anglo-American political systems. The notion that a viable democratic society must have a solid grounding in democratic institutions at the local level is widespread and generally realistic, even though occasionally tinged with romanticism. "The strength of free nations is rooted in their local governments," Tocqueville has written. When after the last world war the Allied Powers were responsible for the rebuilding of democratic institutions in Germany and Japan, they soon entrusted local officials with the discharge of public functions and authorized local elections as the first manifestations of a renascent political will.

In France, as elsewhere, politics at the local level play a multiple role in the socialization of the citizen. They continue the process of civic education which home and school have begun, at least interstitially. They offer possibilities for political participation beyond but including casting a ballot for local officials. They are a vantage point from which the political process can be watched at first hand and without some of the distortions which the observation of distant national politics entails. In many countries, and France among them, the local scene also provides the training ground for the political activist, for those who seek and find fulfillment in local government as well as for those who move on to a wider stage. All of these functions are interconnected. Whether and how effectively local politics can discharge them depends on the place of local government in the institutional framework of the total political system, and on the political culture surrounding both.

A marked characteristic of the French system is the extreme diffusion of local government units.[1] There are close to 38,000 communes (the basic area of local administration), or about as many as in the other five Common Market countries and Great Britain together. For comparison: there are fewer than 35,000 local school boards in the United States! But more than 35,000 French communes have less than 2,000 inhabitants, or an average of 450. The average population of all communes, including the large cities, is 1,300. This administrative structure is inherited from the Revolution and Napoleon, and in part goes back to the parishes of the *Ancien Régime*. It has survived stubbornly the economic and social transformations which an erstwhile agricultural country has undergone since then. In merely quantitative terms, it offers unrivaled opportunities for political socialization

[1] The best, nonlegalistic descriptions of local government has come from the pen of British authors: Brian Chapman, *Introduction to French Local Government* (London: Allen and Unwin, 1953), and F. Ridley and J. Blondel, *Public Administration in France* (New York: Barnes and Noble, 1969), pp. 85–122.

and participation. Since every commune is administered by a municipal council elected by universal suffrage and composed of between nine and thirty-seven [2] members, there are a total of more than 470,000 municipal councilors in France — 1.8 per cent of the electorate. This is not much less than the dues-paying membership of all political parties taken together. It has been estimated that three-fourths of the members of the Radical party and at least one half of the dues-paying members of the Socialist party have at one time been municipal councilors!

The communes are combined into ninety-five departments, an upper-tier unit of local government, created during the Revolution from a desire to give France a uniform and rational structure that would eliminate the dangers of a centrifugal pull by the old provinces. The elective body presiding over the department, the *Conseil Général,* wields less power than does many municipal councils in its area, but the higher body opens additional avenues of elective office.

The formal equality bestowed on the local government units recognizes no legal difference between a metropolis and a mountain hamlet, between a department of over two million or one of 77,000 inhabitants. As could be expected, discrepancies have increased considerably since 1789. Yet if there was artificiality when the structure was created, its very age has lent legitimacy to the established units. Whether communes and departments are, under present conditions, still efficient entities of local government, whether their legal equality is more than a hampering fiction, will be discussed below (see Chap. IX). But for citizens' identification, departments and communes have become natural, because traditional, entities of local government upon which to center political attention.

Another characteristic of French local government differs sharply from American and British practice; it also affects fundamentally the roles of all of the main actors on the local political scene. Because of governmental centralization, municipal government possesses no constitutional autonomy beyond the right of

[2] Only the city councils of Paris, Marseilles, and Lyons are larger. But in order to forestall any such autonomy as the Paris Commune assumed in the bloody uprising of 1871, neither Paris nor its twenty boroughs have a mayor.

existence. All the powers exercised by the local government units
are granted by the national government. Such decentralization
as is practiced means merely that local officials have the legal
right to exercise "their" powers. What these powers actually
consist of is determined by the central government.[3] And the
manner in which such centrally decreed decentralization is made
operational is of great importance. Bureaucratic and representative institutions function side by side; every individual operating on the level of either the department or the commune acts in
a dual capacity. Whether they are elected by the citizens, as are
the mayors of the communes, or appointed by the Minister of
Interior in Paris as are the administrative heads (the prefects) of
the ninety-five departments, their every act is both that of a local
government official and of an agent of the national government.
(Whenever the mayor acts in an official capacity, such as marry-
ing the couples appearing before him, he dons the tricolor sash,
symbolizing state authority.)

The instrumentality tying together bureaucratic and representative institutions is the "tutelage" (*tutelle*), in principle,
and largely also in practice, quite different from the hierarchical supervision within a governmental administration. Political
tutelage is exercised in two directions: control over the personnel
of the decentralized authorities and control over their decisions.
The elected local authorities are chosen by the electorate without
the intervention of the state; yet under certain conditions they
can be dismissed, and, more importantly, their decisions can be
annulled as illegal by the prefects to whom they must be submitted for approval.

The level of local taxation is determined by the local councils; but for fear of incompetence and dishonesty local taxes
are collected by the central government which permits, among
other things, the complete audit of local finances by the national
administration. In the total budget of local finances, grants-in-aid
by the national government are of increasing importance, especially for all long-range investments. A commune which wants

---

[3] See Mark Kesselman, *The Ambiguous Consensus: A Study of Local
Government in France* (New York: Knopf, 1967), pp. 171 ff. This work
is largely based on excellent direct observation, but its material is mostly
drawn from small villages and towns.

to float a loan will in general turn to one of the institutions controlled by the state, since, except for the very large cities, the market for municipal bonds is extremely limited. Even more restricting is the fact that local government authorities are not even expected to finance expenditures of certain local operations. The budgets of all French local government units amount to 13 per cent of total public expenditures; in West Germany, the corresponding figure is 24 per cent. Neither education (except for the buildings and for janitorial help) nor the police forces (except for the *garde champêtre*) are financed out of the local budget. This means that local government authorities have no control over these services. It might well be argued that such control is the test of local autonomy.

There are frequent and generally justified complaints about the tutelage as an instrument of archaic paternalism and of centralization; the prevailing system of finances is criticized as obsolete and inimical to economic growth and modernization.[4] Nonetheless, the present setup is far from being entirely inefficient, it profits from being a local adaptation of the traditional pattern of authority.

The established centralization does not regularly result in a slow and impersonal process. For the partner of the local authorities is not some ministerial bureau in Paris but the prefect and even more frequently the subprefect presiding over one of the 317 *arrondissements* into which the 95 departments are divided. If the entire system of local government is characterized by strong executive power, both the elected mayor, and the appointed prefect are strong executives. It is quite true that many initiatives for change come from above (in rural regions mostly from the subprefect), and that all initiatives starting from below become effective only with prefectoral approval. But this does not condemn the mayor to passivity. It rather means that the mayor and his immediate assistants are expected to bargain incessantly with the authorities of the state for such approval.

The tone of prefectural directives may often be harshly author-

---

[4] Cf. Roger Aubin, *Communes et Démocratie, I: Tâches et moyens de la commune* (Paris: Editions Ouvrières, 1965), pp. 221 f. The two volumes of this handbook are a mine of information on local government and politics. Even more up-to-date is Paul Bernard, *Le grand tournant des communes de France,* (Paris, Armand Colin, 1969).

itarian, and the mayor will never cease complaining about the lack of understanding shown by the representatives of the state, but more often than not relations between local authorities and their partners representing the central government are quite close and cordial. Within the commune an effective mayor emerges as the powerful executive which law and custom permit him to be. But at the same time the tutelage authorities value him as the link between the myriad of human problems within every commune and the abstract power of the state.[5] This is not less true of the communist mayors than of others. (In 1960, of the 150 largest cities and towns, 25 were administered by communists.)

In public opinion polls the mayor or the persons to whom he delegates functions, such as an assistant and especially the town clerk, are usually singled out as the "most important" or the "most useful figure around here," outranking deputies to the national parliament and civil servants. It is true that in most cases the other members of the municipal council, though they have elected the mayor from their own midst, do not amount to much. For all the informality of proceedings, the mayor resembles a local potentate in the midst of his council of elders and vassals.

In many cases the authority of the mayor does not depend on his skill. He rather corresponds to the image of a traditional and often quite authoritarian father figure, acting out on the stage of local politics the role not only of the paterfamilias but also that of the head of family firm and family farm. This explains why conservative methods, or an acknowledged conservative, are successful even in those communes which otherwise feel and vote to the left. It also explains why, barring a scandal, an incumbent mayor gets reelected as long as he wishes to serve. There are municipalities where the office of the mayor has remained in the same family for many generations.

As that of an elected notable in the commune, the mayor's

---

[5] See Kesselman, *op. cit.*, pp. 66 ff., and pp. 38–52 for an excellent composite "portrait of mayor." In a carefully documented article, the same author has concluded: "The closeness of the relationship (between the mayor and the Prefect) stems from a host of common goals and interests. Each wants the kind of legitimacy that the other has the power to grant . . ." See "Over-Institutionalization and Political Constraint: The Case of France," *Comparative Politics* III:1 (1970), p. 32.

authority has increased with the decline in influence of the public school teacher and of ascriptive local notables, especially of the land-owning gentry. Many a *châtelain,* in the past often a mayor himself, has no longer the means to keep up his château and has consequently lost his interest in the welfare of the community.[6] Modern mass communication and the pull of urbanization have uprooted the teacher — formerly wedded to his rural school, acting as adviser to the families of his pupils, and frequently indispensable as town clerk. Quite apart from the feminization of the teaching profession, the duties of the town clerk have become too arduous to be handled by the teacher. But a full-time clerk, without an independent basis of authority, is nothing else but the mayor's agent, however indispensable his clerical services might become to the citizen enmeshed in the intricacies of a bureaucratized existence.

The prestige of local office is enhanced by the fact that the *cursus honorum* for a political career on the national scene starts usually in the commune and in the *Conseil Général* of the department. If in fact local government does not always provide a suitable training ground, it serves nevertheless as jumping-off point for the ambitious. To be taken seriously in Paris, a politician must have the credentials of local success. Whenever a new political regime is established, such as the Fourth Republic in 1945 and the Fifth in 1958, attempts may be made to cut such close ties in order to facilitate the access to national prominence for persons who had neither the time nor inclination to climb the ladder of local politics. But it never takes long before some of the normal career requirements are reestablished even if that means that the new men of power sink local roots *post hoc.*

Traditionally the combining of the functions of a deputy or a senator with those of a mayor has been one of the goals of a political career. More than two-thirds of all deputies elected between 1900 and 1940 had been elected to local office before becoming representatives of the nation.[7] Vincent Auriol, fre-

---

[6] For a typical case see Wylie, *op. cit.,* p. 186.

[7] In 1955, 176 *députés-maires* and 123 *sénateurs-maires* sat in the two houses of parliament. Although the first elections in the Fifth Republic (1958) brought many new men into the national arena, the number of *députés-maires* increased to 221.

quently Minister and finally President of the Republic, claimed that none of the offices he held gave him as much satisfaction as did that of Mayor of the town of Muret (pop. 6,800 and close to his birthplace), "our little *patrie*." The first public election in which the present President, Georges Pompidou, was a candidate was a local contest in a town of 1,049 people. His competitor in the Presidential election of 1969, Alain Poher, has been a mayor of a small community, Ablon-sur-Seine, since the end of the Second World War. Undoubtedly, such interlacing of national and local elective office has had a stabilizing influence on both levels. Flash political movements whose activists had no local ties have usually lost momentum after a short time. Municipal affairs are not seriously disrupted by sudden upheavals: in the local elections that took place one year after General de Gaulle's return to power, three-fourths of the mayors that had been in office under the defunct regime were reelected.

But so close a relationship is also unsettling. The deputy or senator who knows that he will be judged on the basis of his success in commune or department will frequently spend much of his energy in obtaining satisfaction for local demands. Prime Minister Chaban-Delmas, long-time Deputy and Mayor of Bordeaux, boasted long ago that he would find the millions which Bordeaux needed for housing — but not in the pocketbooks of the people of Bordeaux. In this way the national representative, "ambassador" of his commune to Paris, brings constant local pressures into the national scene. Parish pump politics and centrifugal interests complicate further the working of the system. Another consequence has been that because of their strong local basis, political personnel become immovable and stability turns into stagnation. Needed reforms of structure and finances of local government, placed before the national legislature, are likely to be defeated by those representatives whose position benefits from the *status quo*.

French and foreign observers alike are uncertain in their evaluation of the French citizen's interest in local politics. A British author concludes that although local authorities possess greater power in his country, there is more interest in local matters and more vitality in local government in France. French political scientists believe that, among other symptoms, a high level of abstentions in local elections indicates that at present local politics fulfill very inadequately the function of inducing citizen participation.[8] In part such divergences result, of course, from the difficulty of generalizing about experiences in more than 38,000 local units which are different in everything but their legal structure — even average election figures are not too meaningful, the less so as the electoral system varies with the size of the communes. In rural communities participation is sometimes considerably higher in municipal than in national elections. In the large urban centers the situation is reversed. Just as the citizens of large American cities know that they must turn to the Federal Government rather than to the State Houses, French urban voters realize that the elective bodies of local government (either the municipal councils or the *Conseils Généraux*), conceived for the administration of an agricultural society, are inadequate for the solution of present-day problems.

However, electoral participation is not the only yardstick by which to measure political interest. Bonds of sympathy between the elected local authorities and their constituents are quite strong. In an opinion poll held shortly before the municipal elections of 1965, only 23 per cent of the voters wished to see their council members replaced by others, although the six years since the preceding elections had brought important changes to the entire nation. As we will see, there was during the Fourth Republic no circuit of confidence between the voters and an omnipotent National Assembly. Yet in local government despite its limited powers, there was such a circuit between representatives and people.[9]

The confidence that exists is based mostly on a record of efficient and capable administration, independent of the political color of the incumbent. But it is enhanced by the fact that municipal administration is the natural symbol for a community of local interests which are forever threatened by the central govern-

[8] Cf. Chapman, *op. cit.,* p. 221, with Goguel and Grosser, *op. cit.,* p. 66. The question of the turnout in local elections is treated in detail by Kesselman, *Consensus, op. cit.,* pp. 19 ff.

[9] See "L'Opinion Publique au début de l'année 1965," *RFSP,* XV:3 (1965), pp. 534–36, and Philip M. Williams, *Crisis and Compromise: Politics in the Fourth Republic* (1966 ed., Garden City: Doubleday and Company, Inc., 1966), p. 332.

ment — and frequently also by a neighboring town. The commune thus becomes a bastion manned by the mayor and his "team." Because of the narrow limits within which it must move, the achievements of local government often fall short of expectations. The central government will regularly be blamed for this, and in the next national election the citizen might react by casting a vote of protest against the regime. Hence the interest of the citizenry in the affairs of local government can sometimes be as disturbing for the stability of the system as the strong local roots of the representatives. Where civic involvement is exclusively determined by a parochial commitment, it might in the end produce effects which are inimical to a cohesive civic culture. "There exists," French observers have noted, "a local society far richer and more lively than Parisians generally imagine. If its capacity to innovate has been extremely weak, its capacity to resist changes remains extremely strong."[10]

Since the local government is regarded above all as a dispenser of effective administration and as the focus of communal solidarity, a nonpartisan stance is fairly widespread both in elections and in the behavior of the elected. In the smaller communities the political labels which the candidates wear are quite meaningless. Sometimes the opposing candidates represent mere local factions. Often lists "For the Defense of Local Interests" are considered more attractive than party lists. They resemble frequently the "balanced ticket" of an American municipality: representatives of various economic interests and social groups, local notables, sometimes representatives of minority groups are all given a place. When an incumbent mayor stands for reelection, he enjoys an almost complete freedom from the institutional restraints which well organized political parties might place on the selection of candidates and the determination of programs. The mayor, aided by his assistants, fulfills the party's function all by himself, which is, however, quite different from being the boss of a local machine.

In cities over 30,000 the political label of the mayor, especially

[10] Pierre Grémion and Jean-Pierre Worms, "La Concertation régionale, innovation ou tradition?" Institut d'Études Politiques de Grenoble, *Aménagement du territoire et développement régional,* vol. I (Paris: Waltz et Puget, 1968), p. 59.

when he runs for the office for the first time, is usually somewhat more distinct. But even when the mayor is a national political figure, the local election campaign will deemphasize as far as possible his party affiliation. The Gaullist Mayor of Bordeaux weathered in his city administration the years during which the Gaullist movement touched rock bottom. Gaston Defferre, leader of the socialist group in parliament and for a time prospective candidate in the presidential elections, sought to distance himself from his own party when he campaigned for reelection as mayor of Marseilles. "Things are different from parliamentary elections," he declared. Candidates would not behave in this way if the voters did not approve of keeping party politics out of municipal affairs. Recently, 46 per cent of the voters declared that the attitude of local candidates towards General de Gaulle's policies was of no concern to them. Significantly, the proportion of those who were unconcerned was highest among farmers (57 per cent) and in rural communities generally, while in the big cities and especially in Paris the political orientation of the respective municipal councilors became a somewhat weightier factor.

By and large not only the elected representatives but also the "tutelage" authorities take the nonpartisan character of local government at its face value. This explains in part the success of communist-administered communes flourishing under regimes which have for twenty years pushed communism to the outer reaches of the political system. If communist mayors complain more frequently that the prefects suspend their decisions and interfere with their projects, this merely indicates that their administrations are trying to break out somewhat more boldly from the narrow confines of French local government.

The price that has to be paid for nonpartisan harmony on the municipal level is, at least in the small rural communities, frequently quite high. A constantly renewed effort not to destroy the consensus often discourages dynamic action and indicates more interest in equilibrium than in progress. Political activity and problem solving are not carried to the market place where opposition would have to be faced and where bargaining would have to take place in public. Instead, success and failure depend on personal relations, many of which are hierarchically ordained.

Such arrangements have, in turn, their effect on the participatory attitudes of the citizens. Once the elections are over, the citizenry in many communes pays scant attention to the activities of their local representatives. The meetings of the city council are hardly ever attended by the public. Nothing of importance seems to happen there since most mayors prefer to make decisions and take action behind closed doors. If citizens feel aggrieved they will assemble to protest in front of the buildings housing the prefect or subprefect rather than lay their case before the city council. In fact, local government is "representative" government in the strict sense which does not permit the electorate to interfere in any way with its work. A municipal code for all of France, enacted in the dying days of the Fourth Republic and not modified by the new regime, forbids all referenda on local matters or even straw voting. This suits most mayors who, once elected, wish to behave like little monarchs ruling both their constituents and the city council with a strong hand.

The rules set by the council, most of whose members are quite inactive, are accepted as rulings coming from above, i.e., from the conjunction of the two strong executives: the mayor and the prefect. Such a system is hardly suited to teach citizens the art of solving problems together. Here again generalizations are hazardous, especially since traditional attitudes seem to be giving way in more than a few localities. There are municipal councils that organize themselves so as to give a hearing before appropriate subcommittees to a variety of interests. Citizen groups are invited to cooperate with the local authorities either on a functional or geographical basis.

Of late, local politics are sometimes becoming the battleground for the struggle between generations. For many members of the younger generation, political activity means entering the municipal council and aspiring to be elected mayor. To overcome isolation, they will establish contact with like-minded elements in other communes. With the flatness of the political landscape in a regime where political prominence is reserved to the Presidency, the office of mayor remains one of the few places where authority and ability are still visible.[11]

---

[11] See Philip Williams, "Party, Presidency and Parish Pump in France," *Parliamentary Affairs,* XVIII:3 (1965), p. 257.

The style and behavior of these new local leaders is often incompatible with traditional attitudes. Where the "old" mayor sought distinction by living within a limited budget, the "new notables" do not shy away from imposing new tax burdens on their constituents. In cities and towns with an expanding economy the electorate approves of such efforts and is willing to shoulder additional obligations. Another characteristic of such municipalities is that their candidates for local government office shun party commitment even more emphatically than others.

VOTING IN PARLIAMENTARY ELECTIONS

Writing in 1910 Alain, philosopher-preceptor of classical French republicanism, stated that election day had only one significance: the citizen designated the deputy best suited to resist the ever-encroaching power of the central government. Parliament was not there to launch reforms which in the end would only result in more infringements upon the rights of the individual. Its mandate was rather to submit to the authorities, like the States-General on the eve of the French Revolution, the citizens' complaints against unending arbitrariness.[12]

As in most of his writings, Alain when giving such advice did not prescribe novel attitudes but admonished his fellow Frenchmen not to forget old, established traditions. All through the Third and Fourth Republics, with the exception of a short interlude between 1945 and 1947 when a modern party system seemed to be in the making, the French voter looked upon his representative in parliament as his personal "ambassador" in Paris. By his vote he entrusted him with the defense of constituency interests, caring little as to how a coherent national policy could emerge when the cleavages of society were faithfully reproduced in parliament. France remained the classical example of an atomistic representative system, conceived for another age. In this sense, a deputy who harassed every government until he could finally destroy it by a vote of censure was carrying out the assignment which his constituents had given him.

In other Western parliamentary systems, the emergence of structured and disciplined parties has modified (in the age of

[12] Alain, *Politique* (Paris: Presses Universitaires, 1952), pp. 2, 7.

mass democracy), the earlier system of representation. Binding instructions from party or parliamentary groups leave to the representatives little room for independent decisions based on constituency considerations, but determine instead the course of action for government or opposition. In the United States, where the parties do not wield such power, not the congressional but the presidential elections give to the electorate a voice in deciding who should govern and who should be replaced at the helm of the government. In republican France, neither disciplined parties nor popular elections of the executive allowed that involvement of the electorate which has elsewhere given strength and legitimacy to representative institutions.[13]

In the words of an astute and close observer of French parliamentarianism:

> They [the French voters] were not consulted on concrete problems, as might have been the case if elections had been able to establish a clear sanction for durable and coherent government administration and a choice between specific programs. They were not even consulted on the way the Parliamentary "game" was played between elections. . . . The weakness of the political parties and their narrow oligarchical organization was such that it was impossible to assume that they represented the opinion of most Frenchman.[14]

This explains the long-standing ambivalence of the French voter towards the parliamentary system. As the guardians of constituency interests, deputies and senators still commanded respect. Either as an individual or as the member of an interest group, the voter would lay his grievances before "his" deputy either in writing or during the deputy's frequent tours of his constituency. But when the deputies engaged in what de Gaulle used to call the "games, poisons and delights" of the system, when they made and unmade governments, seemingly and in fact without any regard for the "popular verdict" of the preceding elections, popular contempt engulfed both the representatives and the system. The electorate felt that it was "absent," kept away from mean-

[13] For more details, see Henry W. Ehrmann, *Direct Democracy,* pp. 885 f., and the authors there quoted.
[14] Goguel, in *In Search of France,* p. 396. The author is the Secretary General of the French Senate.

ingful participation and outside the centers where policy alternatives were decided. Such feelings were at the root of a basic
antiparliamentary bias on the part of many regular voters, a bias
that was noted even at a time when cabinet instability was not
yet disturbing the basic equilibrium of a "stalemate society." [15]

When contrary to expectations the Fourth Republic was as unable as its predecessor to make elections meaningful for determining the policies of rapidly shifting majorities, the circuit of confidence between the electorate and its representatives was totally
interrupted. Electoral participation did not flag, but shortly before the last elections of the Fourth Republic, 33 per cent of the
voters were convinced that their vote would have no influence
whatsoever on future political developments. At that time not
more than 2 per cent designated the premier who assumed office
after the election as their choice for that post. Only 11 per cent
were in favor of retaining the prevailing system under which the
deputies were at liberty to overthrow the government at will without themselves being threatened by a dissolution of parliament.
If 39 per cent were unable or unwilling to express any preference
for either the existing setup or proposed alternatives, 31 per
cent were, even then, in favor of a direct election of the chief
executive.[16]

Popular attitudes towards the proper functions of parliamentary elections underwent a rather drastic change during the postwar years; they remained, however, as contradictory as they had
always been. In 1944, shortly after the Liberation, 72 per cent of
the voters were of the opinion that votes should be cast on the
basis of programs put forward by the political parties: only 16
per cent said that they would vote "for a man." In January 1958,
shortly before General de Gaulle reentered the political scene,
only 27 per cent of the voters (overwhelmingly communists)
wished to decide on the basis of sympathies for a party, for 52
per cent the "man" would determine their vote.[17] (To which kind

---

[15] The term was coined by Stanley Hoffmann, *ibid., passim.*
[16] See *Sondages,* XVII:4 (1955), pp. 11, 18, and XVIII:3 (1956), p.
54. According to experienced French observers these as well as the public
opinion data which follow should be evaluated with caution, since both
questions and answers were often ambiguous.
[17] *Ibid.,* XX:3 (1958), pp. 56–57.

of "man" their sympathies went in national elections will be discussed below, Chap. VI.)

After the fall of the Fourth Republic, the insistence of the new
leadership that the old parties were unrepresentative was widely
accepted by the citizens whenever an electoral contest pitted the
traditional parties against the new regime. In the opinion of the
voters this did not mean that a democratic system could do without parties: only 26 per cent thought so in 1962 and 20 per cent
in 1965, after the Fifth Republic had been in power for seven
years.[18] Yet in the same opinion poll the respondents showed little
inclination for a disciplined party system: only 18 per cent believed that a deputy should vote with his party; 50 per cent
wished to see him reach his own individual decisions in each case;
for 21 per cent the answer would vary according to the question
to be voted upon. Whether those who answered in this way were
conscious of it or not, their preferences indicated how deeply
rooted were the traditions of a system of atomistic representation.
To them parties and elections were to disperse power rather than
to gather its segments and to yield them as one.

It has often been argued, by Frenchmen and foreigners alike,
that the electoral systems as practiced in France have been responsible for the weakness of the party system, for cabinet instability, and thereby ultimately for the voters' ambivalence towards
parliamentary elections and representative institutions. It is true
that since direct and general manhood suffrage was introduced
in 1848 (women won the franchise only in 1945), French men
have never voted under the system practiced in both the United
States and Great Britain. In these two countries single member
constituencies in which the leading candidate is elected, whether
or not he has won an absolute majority, have apparently been an
important factor for the emergence of a two-party system. Could
one not have expected the same development in France, if a
similar voting system had been adopted in time?

Ever since parliamentary institutions were introduced in France,
the electoral system "has been treated as a weapon in the struggle
between different political camps and between different political

---

[18] *Ibid.*, XXVIII:1 (1966), p. 37 and for an overall evaluation of political parties in public life, *ibid.*, XXXI: 1, 2 (1969), p. 32.

forces for the control of State and society." [19] Since the establishment of the Third Republic in 1871, about a dozen different electoral laws governing national elections have been adopted and tried; in between, a number of abortive reform proposals have given rise to passionate debates in parliament. The mode of local elections has also frequently been tampered with. Only once has a national electoral system survived for thirty years (1889–1919); none of the others was used for as long as ten years before being considerably changed or completely discarded. Obviously, such constant modifications have not lent to any system that legitimacy which comes from permanence. Instead these modifications have fostered the voters' cynicism and their feeling of being used for the ends of a "political class" over which they had no control.

Nonetheless, the proposition that a single-ballot, simple-majority system would have bestowed greater stability to French politics is untenable. If such a solution has not been adopted by now it is largely due to the fact that the two camps which must be formed to make such a system work never had sufficient cohesion. The divisions which have existed within the Right and the Left were not created by the electoral systems. Rather, the electoral systems which were tried appeared unavoidable because of existing divisions. In order to reduce the vote of the people to a simple alternative, their representatives should have been able to reduce their differences to simpler terms — such a simplification has never appeared to be within reach.[20]

The two major electoral systems that have governed all parliamentary elections, albeit with innumerable variations, have mirrored rather faithfully a divided body politic. During the Fourth Republic proportional representation was practiced, a system which in the Scandinavian countries and now in the Federal Republic of Germany has not prevented strong parties and stable government coalitions. In France it was soon in need of modification because if the extremist parties on the Right and

[19] See Peter Campbell, *French Electoral Systems* (Hamdon: Archon Books, 1965), p. 17. For the general problem of the relationship between electoral systems, representation, and political stability, see A. J. Milnor, *Elections and Political Stability* (Boston: Little, Brown, 1969).

[20] See Raymond Aron, "Électeurs, Partis et Élus," *RFSP*, V:2 (1955), p. 252.

the Left had been represented in accordance with their electoral strength, no government whatsoever would have been possible. Most elections in the Third Republic were held under a system in which run-off elections were necessary unless one of the candidates obtained an absolute majority of the votes cast. Because of the multiplicity of groups and factions few seats were won in the first ballot. Since in the second ballot a plurality of votes was sufficient to win, the less successful candidates withdrew in favor of their competitors, which gave to the earlier ballot some of the characteristics of an American primary. But political results were different. The coalition of factions or parties which obtained between the two ballots in order to reach agreement on the most promising candidate, never persisted for long in parliament: fundamental divisions reappeared. Except on the Extreme Left, there were no organized parties that could exact voting discipline from the representatives.

If under the present regime greater stability has prevailed, this cannot be attributed to the method by which the deputies to the National Assembly are elected. For in essence it is the same system, slightly modified, which was in force during the most troubled years of the Third Republic, and which had been discarded after the war for its parochial and "log rolling" effects.[21] When in 1958 General de Gaulle designated it as his personal preference, to the surprise of many of his closest collaborators, he did so in the tradition of all electoral reformers in France: he wished to promote short-range goals, in this instance to prevent the strong expression of any one current of opinion in parliament, which he preferred to keep divided. As has happened before, the outcome was quite different from what had been expected, for politics are shaped by factors other than the electoral system.

In both the Third and the Fourth Republics general disenchantment with parliamentary institutions never prevented a high turnout at national elections. Since the consolidation of republican institutions in 1885 (and with the one exception of the somewhat abnormal post–World War I election of 1919), electoral partici-

---

[21] The main difference between the prewar and the present system consists in the rule that only candidates who in the first ballot obtained at least 10 per cent of the votes can run in the second ballot. This has narrowed the field somewhat but not much. Previously, a candidate who had proved to be that low in voters' appeal was inclined to give up.

pation never fell to less than 71 per cent of registered voters. In most elections participation was much higher; in the last election of the Third Republic (1936) it rose to 84 per cent and, twenty years later, in the last election of the Fourth Republic it stood at 83 per cent. Actually, voting by the male population since the Second World War must be considerably more intense than before. For women now account for about two-thirds of the nonvoters, and yet overall electoral participation did not substantially decline after the introduction of woman suffrage.[22]

Altogether, the frustrating results of most elections notwithstanding, the political mobilization of the citizenry by the election process remained strong all through the lives of the now defunct republics. Constituency interests and an individualized appeal to the voters kept tension and hence interest high.

At first sight it appears as if voting participation in the parliamentary elections of the Fifth Republic has undergone a significant change and at any rate fluctuated more than before. (For details, see below Table VI.) It is true that in the elections of 1958 and of 1962 only 77 and 69 per cent of eligible voters went to the polls. But these two elections took place within weeks of a national referendum of great importance. Both in 1958 and in 1962 the electorate had accepted by referendum the constitutional proposals put before it by General de Gaulle. After this many voters were known to have felt that the die was already cast and that in an election all they could do was to corroborate their earlier "yes" or "no" vote. Such an act of confirmation obviously elicited less interest, hence the high rate of abstentions which was of about equal proportion for all parties.

In 1967 and then again the following year in the aftermath of the Events of 1968, the number of abstentions was down to the normal — below 20 per cent. In both these elections, the one held in an unusually normal, the other in an acute emergency situation, the electorate was basically asked to decide between the government in power and the forces opposed to it. This was undoubtedly a different decision than that which the voters in the Third and Fourth Republics had faced. But in terms of electoral participa-

[22] For estimates of women voters' behaviour see Mattei Dogan and Jacques Narbonne, *Les Françaises face à la politique* (Paris: Colin, 1955), esp. pp. 85–87 and the inquiries therein cited.

tion, their response was similar and so, it appears, was the pattern of abstention.[23]

As in other countries, social class, age, and education were and remain important factors in determining the degree of electoral participation: the least educated, the lowest income groups, and the youngest and the oldest age groups voted less. Among women, those employed voted more frequently than those at home.

What makes for the higher rate of abstention among the younger voters is difficult to decide. Does the socialization into the citizen's voting role take a certain time beyond the date at which he reaches the legal voting age? Are the preoccupations of the young with private concerns so paramount that they pay as yet little attention to their voting obligations? Or have parliamentary elections, for the politically more conscious youth, lost some of their significance?

More pronounced than in other countries has been the difference involving behavior between rural and urban constituencies. Quite generally, voting has been heavier in the countryside than in the cities to the point of offsetting other determinants, such as education and income. This is generally attributed to the greater personal intensity experienced by the rural voter during the campaign and afterward in his relation with his deputy. During an electoral campaign, the smaller the district the more fascinating become the personal confrontations of the candidates, their mutual accusations in the election literature, and the equally vehement discussions among their followers. Local antagonisms usually have the effect of mobilizing voter interest.

If one measures political participation simply in terms of voting alone, a regional difference appears to exist: south of the Loire River abstention is generally higher than in the North. But if in the past one also took into account other "participatory" factors, such as attendance at electoral meetings, reading of the posters, political discussions, then the rural voters in the South as well as elsewhere appeared far more involved than the urban population.[24]

---

[23] This pattern is investigated through a wealth of materials and ingenious extrapolation for the period from 1876 to 1967 by Alain Lancelot, *L'Abstentionnisme électoral en France* (Paris: Armand Colin, 1968). The Preface by Réné Rémond (pp. ix-xiv) advances hypotheses which lend themselves to comparative investigations.

[24] For details see Georges Dupeux, "Citizen Participation in Political

In the parliamentary elections held in the Fifth Republic the style of the campaigns and the citizens' reactions to them strike one as a somewhat baroque mixture of the old and the new. Campaigning and political propaganda have acquired a national dimension which they often lacked in the past. Modern communications and an apparent simplification of issues have brought this about. The national and regional press, radio and television, and uniform tracts and posters for the entire nation, the latter only slightly altered to fit local needs, put candidates and issues before the voter. The professionalization of campaigning has made rapid progress: the use of public opinion polls and of public relations experts, and the systematic observation of electioneering in other countries have become widespread. Candidates still make public a traditional "confession of faith," i.e., a statement of their program (in rather vague terms to be sure). But for the Gaullists as well as for the communists, the pronouncements have become stereotyped. For the majority, the slogans were variations on the theme: "Onward with President de Gaulle." For the opposition forces the theme crowding out all others was a defiance of "personal power." (The last parliamentary elections were held in 1968 with General de Gaulle still in the Presidency; the next one is due only in 1973 unless the National Assembly is dissolved beforehand.)

This does not mean that local electioneering has lost its individuality. The electoral system with its small constituencies and its two ballots invites a multiplicity and variety of candidacies and ensures thereby a considerable amount of decentralization and parochialism. In many ways the elections of June, 1968, had a distinctly plebiscitarian character suggesting, after a grave crisis, a "yes" or "no" for de Gaulle (see below). Yet for the first ballot, an average of more than five candidates presented themselves in each of the 487 electoral districts.[25] Even though attendance at electoral meetings is no longer large, candidates cannot afford to

---

Life, France," *International Social Science Journal*, XII:1 (1960), pp. 41 ff.

[25] For a fascinating account of political life before and during the 1968 election in a small rural constituency, quite typical of many others, see Georges Chaffard, *Les Orages de mai. Histoire exemplaire d'une élection* (Paris: Calmann-Lévy, 1968).

neglect them. It is true that rather than addressing themselves to individual voters, they now seek out local notables, foremost among them the mayors, which is additional evidence of the political vitality of local government. Candidates grant interviews to interest group representatives in their districts and see to it that such talks are publicized.

If on the second ballot usually only two candidates are facing each other (as was frequently the case in the preceding Republics also), it is not always a foregone conclusion which candidate will withdraw after the first ballot and in favor of whom. This ensures to the end of the contest liveliness and political tension and in turn explains the normally low rate of abstention. It also seems to indicate that neither the recent simplification of the party system (see below Chap. VIII) nor the continuing ambivalence towards parliament as an institution, nor even the great fascination with other forms of voting (to be discussed now) have deprived parliamentary elections of their function in the socialization process of the French citizen.

VOTING IN PLEBISCITARIAN CONTESTS: REFERENDUM AND PRESIDENTIAL ELECTIONS

During the seventy years of the Third Republic, proposals for the direct appeal to the electorate were weapons in the arsenal of antirepublican and bonapartist critics of the regime (see Chap. I). It came therefore as a surprise when shortly after the Liberation of the country, in a climate of democratic frenzy, General de Gaulle proposed to consult the electorate on the problem of the new constitution.

However, the political atmosphere in which the three referendums were held in 1945 and 1946 seemed to clear them of plebiscitarian or bonapartist suspicions. Only later did General de Gaulle interpret the first ballot which Frenchmen were invited to cast after the war as a mark of confidence in his person and as a condemnation of "party omnipotence." [26] In the midst of the material harshness of the post-Liberation period, 80 per cent of the voters cast their ballots in the first two direct consultations of the electorate since the declining days of the Second Empire.

[26] *War Memoirs, III,* p. 270.

Massive abstentions in the third referendum, when only a minority of registered voters adopted the constitution of the Fourth Republic, were not due to a lack of interest. Rather, conflicting pressures resulted in hesitations to cast either a negative or an affirmative vote.

There were many indications that an electorate for which constituency concerns had long blotted out the symbolic value of elections as manifestations of a national political will, approved of nation-wide consultations, at least in time of crisis. In a public opinion poll held in 1945 only one-fifth of the electorate criticized the use of the referendum for the proposed ends. Nonetheless, the Fourth Republic returned to the undiluted representative traditions cherished by deputies, senators, and local notables. When de Gaulle founded his own party in 1947 to combat the regime and to question its very legitimacy (see Chap. VIII), the new party soon called for the extensive use of the referendum on constitutional amendments, major legislation, and international treaties. In a press conference held by General de Gaulle in 1948, at the height of his ephemeral role as a party leader, he stated that "in France the best Supreme Court is the people." In case of constitutional deadlock or when parliament lacked a majority, one should "ask the people to decide. That would be a truly functioning democracy." [27]

The constitution of the Fifth Republic, as enacted in 1958, was far more modest in its departures from a classical representative regime. It is true that the constitution itself was submitted to the electorate for approval. But the direct appeal to the voters which it permitted under carefully circumscribed conditions (art. 11 and art. 89 of the constitution) was hedged by parliamentary controls. The government gave official assurances that the referendum would never be used by the executive as a means of arousing popular opinion against the elected assemblies. Moreover, parliament remained the sole, directly elected trustee of the sovereign nation. The popular election of the President of the Republic was explicitly rejected as being "too political" in favor of his des-

[27] Quoted here from Jean Gicquel, *Essai sur la pratique de la Ve République* (Paris: Librairie Générale de Droit et de Jurisprudence, 1968), p. 359.

ignation by an electoral college of some 80,000 local government officials.

In fact, the attraction which the referendum held for General de Gaulle, the introduction of direct popular suffrage for presidential elections, and the attitude of the electorate towards such novel modes of consulting the voters, permitted the thorough transformation of political institutions.

Between 1793 and 1969 the French electorate has been convened sixteen times to vote in a national referendum. (As mentioned earlier, there exist no local referendums.) It has been said correctly that all but the two consultations in 1946, when subsequent drafts of a constitutional text were submitted to the voters, have in fact been not referendums but plebiscites.[28] A referendum (such as practiced in the American states and the Swiss cantons), is a device, handled with more or less political felicity, but always inviting the voters to decide between equally available solutions. By contrast, a plebiscite usually requests the voters to endorse an already established policy from which the return to the *status quo ante* either is impossible or can be obtained only at a seemingly exorbitant price. At the very least, a providential leader (such as the two Bonapartes or General de Gaulle) demands an act of faith from the electorate by declaring that he could not continue at the helm without a massive vote of confidence. He thus raises the specter of political or social chaos as the alternative to his continued rule. In the eighteenth century, Jean-Jacques Rousseau asigned to the leader the task of formulating correctly the few questions which were to be put before the people in such a way that the general will would "see things as they are (and) sometimes as they ought to appear to it." With the approach of mass democracy, the nineteenth-century Swiss historian Jacob Burckhardt had stated that the "future belongs to the masses and to the men that can explain things simply to them." Since in fact political problems have become immensely more intricate rather than simpler, this means that issues may be simplified to the point of distortion. Moreover, by wrapping sev-

---

[28] See Gilbert Bortoli, *Sociologie du Référendum dans la France Moderne* (Paris: Librarie Générale de Droit et Jurisprudence, 1965), pp. 2 ff. There is *ibid.*, p. 9, a useful table of all referendums held in France between 1793 and the present.

eral propositions into one, the plebiscite not only maximizes chances for approval but also usually ties the sanction of an irretrievable past to the acceptance of dimly specified future policies.[29]

On some or all of these grounds the five referendums organized since 1958 qualify as plebiscites. (For the results, see Table II.) In 1958, a vote against the new constitution might in fact have brought the country back to the civil war which it had narrowly escaped a few months earlier. Forty per cent of the general electorate declared they reached their decision on the constitutional project on the basis of its intrinsic values, 41 per cent because of the personality of General de Gaulle. However, for the floating voter (corresponding roughly to the "independent voter" in the United States), the figures were 39 per cent and 47 per cent respectively.[30] The two following referendums prepared or endorsed in highly ambiguous terms the peace settlement of the unending Algerian war, isolating successfully the diehards who by their rebellion threatened both order and prosperity. When — only six months after the second referendum on peace in Algeria — the President asked the electorate to endorse once more his policy by direct vote, the majority of those casting an affirmative vote declined to 46 per cent of the registered voters; the proposition was approved by only 62 per cent of the votes cast as against 91 per cent in favor of the preceding referendum. For General de Gaulle these results were extremely painful: less than half of the electorate had stood by him this time, too slim a margin for a leader seeking popular confirmation of his rule.[31] Even though supported by a diminished majority, the referendum did alter the constitution, accepted merely two years before, in one decisive point: the President of the Republic was no longer to

[29] For the difference betwen a true referendum and a plebiscite, see Otto Kirchheimer, "France from the Fourth to the Fifth Republic," *Social Research,* XXVI:4 (1958), p. 403.

[30] See *Sondages,* XXII:4 (1960), p. 44. The French Institute of Public Opinion classifies as floating voters all those who declare that in the next elections they would vote for another party than in the last.

[31] Presumably he considered resigning already at that time, but decided to carry on in order to pursue his foreign and atomic policies, see J.-R. Tournoux, *La Tragédie du Général* (Paris: Plon, 1967), p. 439, like all writings by this author, a highly interesting though probably not always reliable account.

TABLE II. *French Referendums (R), 1958–1969, and Second Ballot of Presidential Elections (E), 1965 and 1969* (Voting in Metropolitan France)*

Date	Registered voters (In millions)	Abstentions		Yes-votes and votes for de Gaulle or Pompidou as President			No-votes and votes for Mitterand or Poher for President		
		(In millions)	% of registered voters	(In millions)	% of registered voters	% of votes cast	(In millions)	% of registered voters	% of votes cast
9/28/58(R)	26.61	4.01	15.1	17.67	66.4	79.2	4.62	17.4	20.7
1/8/61(R)	27.18	6.39	23.5	15.20	55.9	75.3	5.00	18.4	24.7
4/8/62(R)	26.99	6.59	24.4	17.51	64.9	90.7	1.79	6.6	9.3
10/28/62(R)	27.58	6.28	22.7	12.81	46.4	61.7	7.93	28.8	38.2
12/19/65(E)	28.22	4.36	15.4	12.64	44.8	54.5	10.55	37.4	45.5
4/28/69(R)	28.66	5.56	19.4	10.52	36.7	46.7	11.94	41.6	53.2
6/15/69(E)	28.75	8.90	30.9	10.69	37.2	57.5	7.87	27.4	42.4

* For further details on the vote in the presidential elections, see Table V, p. 118.

be elected by an electoral college of notables but by direct popular suffrage (art. 7).

Such a way of electing the Head of State had been suspect to true French republicans since Napoleon III had risen to imperial power through a popular majority in presidential elections. In both the Third and the Fourth Republics, the President was, therefore, elected by the two houses of parliament, convening as one body for the occasion. Shortly after the war, in 1945, a public opinion poll revealed that, at least at that time, a majority of the electorate was quite willing to see the executive strengthened, even at the price of relinquishing the institutional preferences of French republican traditions. Fifty per cent declared in favor of a popularly elected president, only 40 per cent wished to see him designated by parliament.[32]

Neither the constitution of the Fourth Republic nor, in its original form, that of the Fifth Republic selected the solution preferred earlier by the voters. In October, 1962, all of the non-Gaullist parties objected to the constitutional novelty of electing the President by direct suffrage; they also had no difficulty in denouncing as illegal the form in which the amendment was submitted: the amendment procedures of the constitution permitted a call for a referendum only after a concordant vote of the two houses of parliament, which the government had neither sought nor obtained. (For details, see Chap. X.)

This explains why the new referendum aroused more resistance than the previous consultations. However, a comparison of Tables II and V shows that in the parliamentary elections of 1958, the parties that campaigned for the "no" in 1962 had obtained not less than 82 per cent of the votes two years earlier, while the actual "no" vote in the referendum amounted to only 38 per cent. Hence in his contest with the "intermediaries," such as parties, the President had been quite successful.

Once General de Gaulle considered the results of the referendum sufficient to continue in office, the introduced reform, the popular election of the President, enjoyed ever-increasing favor with the electorate. De Gaulle also affirmed his resolve that he

---

[32] Michel Brulé et J. Piret, *Les Transformations Sociales de la France contemporaine. Réflexions sur 20 années de sondages politiques de l'I.F.O.P.* [Institut Français d'Opinion Publique] (mimeographed n.d.), p. 9.

would continue to use the referendum as an appropriate method of letting the electorate "determine directly such problems as are considered essential." [33]

De Gaulle's preference for the referendum as an instrument of direct democracy was shared by an important segment of public opinion. In 1962 and again in 1969, only a few weeks before a majority of "no" votes in another referendum was to bring about General de Gaulle's resignation, 51 per cent of respondents in a public opinion poll favored the direct consultation of the electorate. Only 24 per cent in 1962 and 27 per cent in 1969 were opposed to it.[34] (See Table III for the evolving opinion of the electorate.)

Undoubtedly the frustrations of the voters, who in the past had felt that parliamentary elections provided no leverage for major policy directives, accounted in large part for the popularity of the referendum. The political participation which the plebiscites invite is at best fleeting and frequently a sham, since the decisions on which the electorate is ostensibly consulted have been reached beforehand. But where the confiscation of power by the members of parliament had been resented, a similar confiscation by the providential leader was accepted as commensurate with the prevalent style of authority. In a society where face-to-face relationships have been traditionally disliked, the referendums freed the citizens from active participation in bargaining practices required of group decisions. The concentration of power in the hands of the leader was tolerable because the distance between him and his followers was far greater than that between the voter and his deputy. Except for a few dramatic occurrences, General de Gaulle was intentionally keeping public opinion at arm's length. He provided what has been called a "counter-pedagogy." This ambiguity of deceptively simple questions put before the electorate in the referendums and leaving no choice

[33] Address of November 7, 1962. French Embassy, Press and Information Division, *Major Addresses, Statements and Press Conferences of General Charles de Gaulle.*

[34] *Sondages,* XXXI:3 (1969), p. 7. This approval was shared by followers of parties left of center. According to another poll taken in March, 1969, the rate of approval was as high as 56 per cent, with only 22 per cent demuring. See the article, most important for what follows in the text, by Alain Lancelot and Pierre Weill, "L'Évolution Politique des électeurs français de février à juin 1969," *RFSP,* XX:2 (1970), pp. 252 ff.

between passive approval or total rejection was only one example.[35]

TABLE III.   *Public Opinion Regarding Institutions of the Fifth Republic*

%	Nov. 1945	Nov. 1961	Dec. 1962	May 1964	Nov. 1965	May 1969
A. The Election of the President by Popular Suffrage:						
For	50	52	46	74	78	81
Against	40	17	23	10	6	8
No opinion	10	31	31	16	16	11

%	July 1945	Sept. 1962	Oct. 1962	March 1969
B. The Use of the Referendum for Important Decisions:				
For	66	51	45	51
Against	20	24	32	27
No opinion	14	25	23	22

Adapted from Jean Charlot, *Le Phénomène Gaulliste* (Paris: Fayard, 1970), p. 57, and *Sondages*, XXXI:3 (1969), p. 7.

When in May, 1968, the country was shaken by one of the most violent crises in its history, it was quite natural for General de Gaulle to seek a way out by promising another referendum. While there was fighting in the streets of the capital, while all over France factories and public buildings were occupied by workers and students in revolt, the President of the Republic explained in a televised speech that he "needed, indeed needed, once more an expression from the people to tell him what they wanted." [36] A referendum would be submitted to the electorate spelling out what the "renovation" would amount to in all the domains where dissatisfaction with past policies of his regime had led to rebellion. "Of course," he concluded, in the case of a negative vote, he would have to relinquish his office.

The appeal fell flat. With participatory democracy being acted out throughout the country, de Gaulle's version of direct democ-

---

[35] On this point see Georges Lavau, "Réflexions sur le régime politique de la France," *RFSP*, XII:5 (1962), p. 820, and Hoffmann, *op. cit.*, p. 101.
[36] In the address of May 24, quoted above, Ch. III, n. 45.

racy proclaimed from the Élysée Palace had lost its leverage. "Imagination and eloquence had changed sides." [37] While government bureaus busied themselves with preparing the text of the promised referendum which was never to see the light of day, the legitimacy of the Fifth Republic was wearing as thin as that of the Fourth in 1958 and as that of the Third Republic in 1940. But this time neither a colonial war nor a foreign invasion could provide an excuse.

Then, only a week after the earlier address and probably upon the advice of his Prime Minister, Georges Pompidou, General de Gaulle in another speech announced that the government was abandoning the plans for a referendum and instead was dissolving the National Assembly and calling for new elections, hence using art. 12 rather than art. 11 of the constitution.[38] This turned out to be a masterful tactical stroke. Instead of crystallizing opposition against a referendum to which de Gaulle had once more and willfully given all the characteristics of a plebiscite, the regime forced the major political forces to muster their strength in a traditional electoral contest. Circumstances, it is true, were bound to give to the elections the significance of a plebiscite. By promising law and order and brandishing the threat of "totalitarian communism," the Gaullist party and its allies won their greatest electoral victory yet (see below, Chap. VIII).

Nonetheless, the outcome was unsatisfactory for General de Gaulle. To him, parliamentary elections confirmed only indirectly and temporarily what he liked to call his own "profound legitimacy." They did little to strengthen the "privileged" bond that united the leader and the people who had elected him. Moreover, and this was possibly most important to him, a concern for his own historical image drove him on to new ventures. In his assumed role of a "revolutionary" [39] he was concerned that a con-

---

[37] Jean Lacouture, *De Gaulle* (Paris: Seuil, 2nd ed. 1969), p. 10. This small essay remains the best and most judicious biography of de Gaulle. The English translation (New York: New American Library, 1966) is that of the first edition (1965) with only a few additions.

[38] For conjectures on what really had happened during the critical days, see J.-R. Tournoux, *Le Mois de mai du Général* (Paris: Plon, 1969), *passim*. For more details on the Events of May, see below, Chap. VII.

[39] "I am not at all embarassed to be the kind of revolutionary which I have been so frequently," he declared in a radio-interview; see *A. P. 1968*, p. 384. For an excellent interpretation of General de Gaulle's initia-

servative parliament would want to forget the lessons of May. It was therefore incumbent upon him to lead the way to fundamental reforms, playing once more the "legislator" of Rousseau's *Social Contract* and soliciting an expression of the general will through another referendum.

After considerable hesitations, General de Gaulle decided that two questions that had preoccupied him for some time were best suited to overcome the conservatism of structures and habits: the reform of the upper house of parliament, the Senate, and a strengthening of the administrative structure of the twenty-one regions into which the country had been divided for some time (for a discussion of the substance of these proposals, see below, Chaps. X and IX). In regard to the Senate reform, the constitutional lawyers and the highest administrative court — the Council of State — were quick to point out (as they had done at the time of the referendum of October, 1962) that the attempt to enact a constitutional amendment by way of referendum violated the terms of the Constitution of 1968. The administrative reform of the regions could have been effected through ordinary legislative channels.

For General de Gaulle the proposed reforms were attractive precisely because, as in 1962, they were bound to arouse the resistance of those holding "vested rights" such as most Senators, local notables, legal experts, and party and interest group leaders. From other quarters the reforms were criticized as not going far enough. To appeal directly for popular support over an agglomerate of oppositions was to provide the test he sought: "By this law I ask them [the people] to give to the state *and, in the first place to its leader,* a mandate for renewal" (emphasis supplied).

Differently from the law enacted by the referendum of 1962, the sixty-nine articles of the new proposal, covering fourteen closely printed pages never aroused strong popular interest. A strenuous and costly campaign organized by the authorities was

tives between the Events of May and the referendum of 1969, see Alain Lancelot, "Comment ont voté les Français le 27 avril et les 1er et 15 juin 1969," *Projet*, No. 38 (1969), esp. p. 929; and Frédéric Bon, "Le Référendum du 27 avril 1969. Suicide politique ou nécessité stratégique?" *RFSP*, XX:2 (1970), esp. pp. 219 f.

unable to change such indifference.[40] From the very beginning it appeared that the regional reform met with a fair amount of sympathy because it held promise of economic development, while the attack on a long-established republican institution such as the Senate was viewed with a suspicion feeding on the accusation of illegality. To separate the two propositions would of course have been possible, but it might have resulted in a mixture of victory and defeat which was incompatible with General de Gaulle's intentions. An artificial agglomeration of issues has at all times been the characteristic of a plebiscite.

The nature of either proposition would have lent itself for once to a true referendum: acceptance or rejection by the electorate would have had the ordinary effect of legislation either enacted or defeated. But since he wished to see his position sanctioned not just by a referendum but by a plebiscite, de Gaulle once more declared explicitly midway during the campaign, that he would resign if there were no majority of "yes" votes. Public opinion polls showed that this announcement met with widespread disapproval and that, instead of mobilizing support for the referendum, it hastened the voters' disaffection. It turned out that if General de Gaulle's appeal was as plebiscitarian as it had been previously, the situation no longer was. There was widespread dissatisfaction with the record of governmental performance, but there was no immediate emergency on the horizon. The voters were far from being happy, but they as well as their representatives in parliament were quite willing to forget the shock of the previous year while the referendum wished to remind them of the unfinished business which the Events of 1968 had left.

In the field of foreign affairs, it appeared that people were becoming tired of de Gaulle's ambitions and visions which international and monetary developments had come to belie. There was also, for the first time in the history of the Fifth Republic, an alternative other than chaos to General de Gaulle's rule: Georges Pompidou, former Prime Minister under de Gaulle, had made it known, well before the referendum campaign, that he was a can-

---

[40] For an account of the referendum campaign in addition to the articles quoted in the preceding footnote, see J. E. S. Hayward, "Presidential Suicide by Plebiscite: de Gaulle's Exit, April 1969," *Parliamentary Affairs,* XXII: (1969), pp. 289–319. For the polling data below, see *Sondages,* XXXI:3 (1969), pp. 7–341.

didate in case of a presidential vacancy. For what reasons General de Gaulle had suggested Pompidou's resignation immediately after the 1968 elections will remain controversial for some time to come. A vast majority of Frenchmen were convinced that this was done to prepare M. Pompidou for the presidential succession, and in the months that followed they continued to view the eventuality of such a succession with equanimity.[41] Hence, General de Gaulle's threat of resignation did not conjure previous anxieties; the proposals contained in the referendum were judged on their merits and in such terms they did not command majority approval. Once more, as in May, 1968, but for different reasons, the formula of direct democracy as understood by the founder of the Fifth Republic was found wanting. Nothing in the constitution compelled General de Gaulle to resign in the aftermath of an unsuccessful referendum. It was only the highly personal concept he held of his role that urged him to resign.[42] But that concept was no longer accepted by a majority of the electorate once the voters had discovered a way of replacing the charismatic hero figure through constitutional processes.

An analysis of the no votes in the referendum (53 per cent of the total votes cast, almost 42 per cent of the registered electorate), shows that it was spread heavily throughout the country but more concentrated in Paris and in many towns than in the countryside. When compared with the results of the 1962 referendum, (see Table IV), the greatest swing from "yes" to "no" occurred in the younger (20 to 34) age group, among senior executives and professionals and among workers. Regionally those districts which in the past had voted left were casting a negative vote. But this would not have been sufficient to defeat the refer-

---

[41] *Ibid.,* pp. 48 f.

[42] The most passionate defense of General de Gaulle's step was offered in an interview by the staunchest Rousseauan among his advisers, the late Professor René Capitant, at one time his Minister of Justice; see *Der Spiegel,* May 26, 1959: "The people is sovereign. It wanted de Gaulle's departure [sic!]; he has accepted the verdict. He could not do otherwise." In an article in the Paris daily, *Le Figaro,* May 9, 1969, a French historian (Georgette Elgey, "Pratique de la démocratie") has quoted a passage from the first edition of this book (p. 254) to show that by resigning de Gaulle had met the test for democracy set by the "American expert." The careful reader will notice that, writing in 1968, I was hypothesizing an entirely different situation, namely that of a conflict between a parliamentary majority and the President.

TABLE IV.   *Comparison of Results in the Referendums of 1969
             and 1962 (per cent of those expressing an opinion)*

	"Yes" April 1969 %	"Yes" Oct. 1962 %
Total	48	63
Men	43	57
Women	53	70
Ages:		
Voters between 20 and 34	43	65
Voters between 35 and 49	44	60
Voters between 50 and 64	48	63
Voters 65 and over	60	66
Occupations:		
Farmers	58	71
Businessmen	46	47
Executives and professionals		62
White collar, lower civil servants, etc.	47	56
Workers	38	61
Retired and without profession	59	65
Places of Residence		
Rural communities	56	69
Towns of less than 20,000 population	44	72
Towns of 20,000 to 100,000 population	46	57
Towns of more than 100,000 population	47	60
Region of Paris	39	55

(Note: "Businessmen" and "Executives and professionals" share the bracketed 1969 figure of 46.)

According to polls conducted before the actual referendums. (*Sondages,* XXXI:3 (1969), p. 33.). Note that actual results were slightly different: 1969 Referendum: "Yes": 47%; 1962 Referendum: "Yes": 62%.

endum, had not many voters of the Center joined the opposition. This included some of the leaders and followers of the Independent Republicans the party which had been a coalition partner of the Gaullists since 1962. The newly emerging coalition of the "No's" disparate though it was, awakened hopes that it would be possible to beat the Gaullist candidate in the presidential elections to follow. As it turned out, a referendum that had amounted to regicide was followed by elections that crowned the king's dauphin.

The presidential elections of 1965 (the first such elections since 1849) had already shown how popular this new mode of political participation had become. The voters' behaviour throughout the campaign showed that they derived great satisfaction from knowing that, unlike in past parliamentary elections, national and not parochial alignments were at stake and that they were invited to pronounce themselves effectively on such issues. The traditional and at one time deeply rooted attitude that the only useful vote was a vote against the government no longer made sense when almost everybody knew that the task at hand was to elect the head of an executive endowed constitutionally with strong powers, for a normal term of seven years.

In 1965 the great surprise had been that in the first ballot General de Gaulle was short of a majority of votes cast so that run-off elections between the two top candidates became necessary. Prior to the first ballot de Gaulle had refused to present himself as a political candidate, let alone as the leader of the majority which had controlled the government during the preceding years. The electorate saw it otherwise, with the result that de Gaulle fell into the trap of the institution which he himself had created. Instead of merely confirming the powers of a President, the voters judged him on his past record, including his personality, and subjected the promises and the personalities of his competitors to the same test. When in the end a majority of the total electorate decided for de Gaulle's reelection, this amounted to a lack of confidence in the anticipated performance of his opponent, François Mitterand, a candidate without definite party commitment but in 1965 endorsed by all parties left of center, including the communists.[43] After the election General de Gaulle was once more representing the nation, and he, like the American President, did so because a majority of the voters approved of his past record as a political leader. That there was from then on a gap between his self-image and the role which the electorate assigned to him is quite possible, and such a gap as did exist might have contributed to the crises of confidence which shook the country during his second term.

[43] For an analysis of the election results, see Philip Williams, "The French Presidential Elections of 1965," *Parliamentary Affairs*, XIX:1 (1965–66), pp. 14–30, and François Goguel, "L'Élection présidentielle française de décembre 1965," *RFSP*, XVI:2 (1966), esp. pp. 242–44. A highly sophisticated attempt to explain voters' attitudes in the 1965 election, on the basis of public opinion data, grouping the voters according to traditional political orientations is made by Emeric Deutsch, Denis Lindon and Pierre Weill, *Les Familles politiques aujourd'hui en France* (Paris: Éditions de Minuit, 1966), pp. 55–77.

On the other hand it became quite clear that the institution of a popularly elected president, functioning both as the head of state and the chief political executive was steadily gaining support. On the eve of the elections of 1969, more than four-fifths of the voters approved of the institution, with only 8 per cent opposed, while in 1962, 38 per cent had voted "no" on the constitutional amendment introducing reform. (See also Table III)

The nomination procedure for presidential candidates, as stipulated in 1962, reflected General de Gaulle's dislike for political parties. Officially parties were not to play any role: the signatures of one hundred easily accessible notables from ten different departments were sufficient to put a candidate on the first ballot, providing him thereby with free time on national television and contributions to his campaign out of public funds. This explains why in both the 1965 and the 1969 elections some previously unknown candidates emerged shortly only to disappear again after the first ballot. But all serious candidates in both elections were indeed backed by political parties or by a coalition of such parties, the provisions of the law notwithstanding.

Within two days after General de Gaulle's resignation Georges Pompidou declared his candidacy without, it is true, waiting for the official designation by the Gaullist party of which he had remained the leader in parliament. He thereby left little choice to his own party which, stunned by the loss of General de Gaulle's stewardship, might have been in danger of losing cohesion. By his forthrightness he also brought back to the fold the coalition partner of the Gaullist government who during the referendum campaign had strayed into the camp of the No's. By contrast, the forces of opposition were in utter confusion.[44]

It now turned out how disastrous the Events of May 1968 and their aftermath had been for the fragile cohesion of the Left (for details see below, Chaps. VII and VIII). The Events and their aftermath also had discredited François Mitterand who less than four years earlier had run a strong campaign against

---

[44] A detailed history of the period, patterned after the classical accounts of American presidential campaigns is provided by R.-G. Schwartzenberg, *La Guerre de succession* (Paris: Presses Universitaires, 1969). See also, in addition to the articles cited in footnotes 34 and 39, Goldey, "The Events of May and The French General Election of June 1968," *Parliamentary Affairs,* XXII: 2 (1969), pp. 116–33.

General de Gaulle.[45] This made it possible for the leadership of the Socialist party, itself in full disintegration, to prevent an alliance between the noncommunist Left and the Communist party so that the latter had to run their own candidate. The Independent Socialists (P.S.U.) and the Trotskyites were happy to put forward candidates of their own merely for the purpose of exhibiting their doctrines to the wider audience which they are badly lacking at other times.

In the Center there emerged, almost by constitutional prestidigitation, Alain Poher, a politician previously almost unknown to the public. He had been elected as speaker of the Senate a few months earlier. Quite naturally he moved into the foreground of the fight against the referendum which sought to transform thoroughly the traditional upper house over which he presided. According to article 4 of the constitution, General de Gaulle's resignation made him the interim President.[46]

M. Poher's elevated position exposed him to public scrutiny, and for a moment it appeared that Frenchmen liked what they saw, were it only because he seemed to represent the very opposite of the leader who had disowned them. According to the first public opinion poll organized after the interim President had announced his candidacy, it seemed likely that Pompidou would be ahead in the first ballot without however winning the required majority (43 per cent for Pompidou, 35 per cent for Poher), but that in the second ballot when presumably all non-Gaullist forces would unite behind Poher, the latter would beat the Gaullist candidate with 55 per cent as against 45 per cent for Pompidou. (This would have been the exact reversal of the 1965 results for General de Gaulle and Mitterand.)

Actual results in both ballots differed vastly from such forecasts (see Table V) and for reasons that are significant for the attitude of the electorate towards the institutions of the Fifth

---

[45] His, *Ma Part de vérité* (Paris: Fayard, 1969) provides insight into the desperate difficulties (and intrigues) plaguing the leadership of the Left.

[46] If the referendum had passed, that provision too would have been altered and in case of a presidential vacancy the Prime Minister would have been in charge, another step towards recognizing the essentially political function of the presidency. General de Gaulle had refused at all times to provide for a Vice-Presidency since the holder of that office would have been not only heir presumptive but also an alternative to de Gaulle.

Table V.   *Comparison of Results in the Presidential Elections of 1969 and 1965*

	1969	1965
First Ballot		
Total Voting (in millions)	22.5	24.0
Abstentions (% of registered voters)	21.8	14.9
	% of Votes Cast	*% of Votes Cast*
Pompidou ('69)—de Gaulle ('65)	43.9	43.7
Poher ('69)—Mitterand ('65)	23.4	32.2
Duclos ('69) (Communist)	21.5	
Lecanuet ('65) (Center)		15.8
Tixier-Vignancour ('65) (Extreme Right)		5.3
Defferre ('69) (Socialist)	5.1	
Rocard ('69) (Left Wing Socialist)	3.7	
Ducatel ('69)—Marcilhacy ('65) (Conservative)	1.3	1.7
Krivine ('69) (Trotzkyite)	1.1	

Second Ballot. Breakdown of Vote[a]	*Pompidou–Poher*		*de Gaulle–Mitterand*	
Men	56	44	49	51
Women	60	40	61	39
Ages:				
Voters between 21 and 34	53	47	49	51
Voters between 35 and 49	58	42	55	45
Voters between 50 and 64	58	42	55	45
Voters 65 and older	66	34	65	35
Occupations:				
Farmers	61	39	59	41
Businessmen, Executives, Professionals	59	41		[b]
White collar, lower civil servants, etc.	57	43	55	45
Workers	50	50	45	55
Retired, without profession	66	34	60	40
Places of Residence:				
Rural communities	62	38	57	43
Towns of less than 20,000	57	43	53	47
Towns of 20,000 to 100,000	64	36	47	53
Towns of more than 100,000	54	46	57	43
Paris Region	53	47	51	49
By party preference as expressed in parliamentary elections of 1968				
Communist party	12	88		
Federation of the Left	20	80		[b]
Center	43	57		
Independent Republicans	79	21		
Gaullists	85	15		
Abstentions or no opinion	41	59		

[a] According to polls conducted between the two ballots and forecasting accurately actual election results (see *Sondages*, XXVII:4 (1965), pp. 36–37, and XXX:3 (1969), p. 72). For total voting and results, see Table II, p. 106.
[b] No comparable data.

Republic as well as indicative of important trends in political alignments. The opposition forces wished to understand the results of the referendum as a rejection by the electorate of the plebiscitarian features of the regime. Their candidates, especially Alain Poher (but in the campaign for the first ballot, also the socialist Gaston Defferre who went down to a crushing defeat) projected the image of a President who, instead of being a strong political executive, would at most play the role of an arbiter reconciling, if need be, the feuding factions in government and parliament. This awakened fears of a return to the disorders of past republics — especially because a candidate elected on an anti-Gaullist platform would have to face the strong Gaullist majority which dominated the parliament elected in 1968. The conflict would be even graver than that between a White House and Congress controlled by different parties, since the French system, halfway between a presidential and a parliamentary regime, still required that the government be supported by a majority in parliament. The perspective of the President-elect dissolving parliament in order to secure a majority favorable to his views was unattractive to voters who wished to return to normalcy rather than to new electoral contests. Moreover the difficulties accompanying the nomination of the opposition candidates had shown clearly how little unity there was on the side of the opposition.

Under such circumstances the election of Poher would have deprived the voters of that leverage which the designation of the President by popular vote had finally entrusted to them: the direct designation of the Chief Executive who would be able to transform electoral preferences for policy and personnel into political reality. The posture and the arguments of the opposition created doubt that it was willing to play the game by the rules essential for making the system work. It is true that there was much and fairly widespread dissatisfaction with governmental performance in the Fifth Republic. But the procedures involved in the election and the powers of the President had won wide acceptance, with the result that Georges Pompidou profited from his opponents lack of credibility.[47]

[47] This motivation of electoral behavior emerges clearly from the public opinion polls conducted by the two major polling organizations, IFOP and SOFRES.

Pompidou's remoteness from the conduct of government during the preceding months facilitated a campaign that steered a middle-course between faithfulness to the Gaullist past and promises of a new deal. The programs, or rather platforms, published by the two main candidates excelled by their vagueness. They also showed, as did the tone of their campaigns, that in most bipolar contests, the contenders, as they do in the United States and in Great Britain, move towards the center to touch the broadest possible audience. Even though the programs resembled each other, interest in the campaign remained nonetheless high throughout. Differences in personality were judged as a projection of future performance in office. Television and radio appearances commanded much attention, but the candidates found it impossible to dispense with the more classical forms of campaigning and with mass meetings which both of them had hoped to avoid. In spite of the secondary role which parties played in the nomination and although the candidates found it prudent to avoid too close an identification with any party, it became clear that in the age of mass communication, party organization has become indispensable for an effective campaign. But only the Gaullist and the communist candidates had such an organization at their disposal; all others, including Alain Poher, were handicapped rather than helped by the amateurish efforts on their behalf. In a country of traditionally weak party organizations this experience holds an important lesson for the future of presidential elections.

The surprising success of the communist candidate, Jacques Duclos, a 72-year old leadership veteran, was however due not only to assistance by the party apparatus. From a support by a mere 10 per cent of the electorate expressed in opinion polls at the beginning of the campaign, Duclos doubled this figure on the first ballot so that he, the candidate of a single party, trailed by but little the vote for Poher who hoped to draw a large coalition of opposition forces. Such a result showed that in spite of its criticized role in the May Events and in spite of the Soviet invasion of Czechoslovakia, the party had not lost its attractiveness.[48] For the second ballot the Communist party admonished its

[48] It did better than in the preceding parliamentary elections although in a presidential election a party of the Extreme Left (or Right) is always

followers to stay home rather than to vote for the candidate of the Center whom the communist posters depicted as being identical with and hence just as unacceptable as Pompidou. Two-thirds of the Duclos voters seemed to have followed the directive supported also by the communist-oriented trade unions. This was additional evidence of the extent of party influence. If it brought the overall abstention rate to unheard of heights (31 per cent), such an attitude was once more not due to a lack of interest but to a well-determined political decision. The communist leadership well knew that by issuing these directives they were sealing Poher's fate and ensuring Pompidou's victory. The Gaullist candidate was more acceptable to them not only because they put greater trust into his foreign policy orientation; they also feared that a left-of-center government, trying to do without their support, would once more isolate them, while under a Gaullist government, they could become the core of a broader opposition (see also below, Chap. VIII).

That in each ballot the vote for Alain Poher remained several millions below the "no" vote in the referendum held only a few weeks earlier, demonstrated how wrong the calculations of the opposition had been. The four candidates to the left of Poher made a poorer showing in the first ballot than M. Mitterand in the first ballot of the 1965 elections. At least on the basis of these elections it appears that millions of voters, traditionally in the camp of the Left and the Extreme Left, did not, as had sometimes been expected, return to the fold after General de Gaulle's disappearance from the scene. In the second ballot Georges Pompidou did slightly better than the "yes" votes in the referendum. Even though he obtained about 2 million fewer votes than General de Gaulle in 1965, he did somewhat better than his illustrious predecessor in percentages of votes cast because of the lower overall participation.

The distribution of second-ballot votes for Pompidou shows (see in addition to Table V, also the map, p. 123)[49] that his

---

likely to be handicapped since voters know that their candidate cannot win.

[49] Because of the high rate of abstentions the map shows percentages of registered votes rather than of votes cast. This gives a better picture of actual support.

Distribution of Employment and the New Regional Organization of France

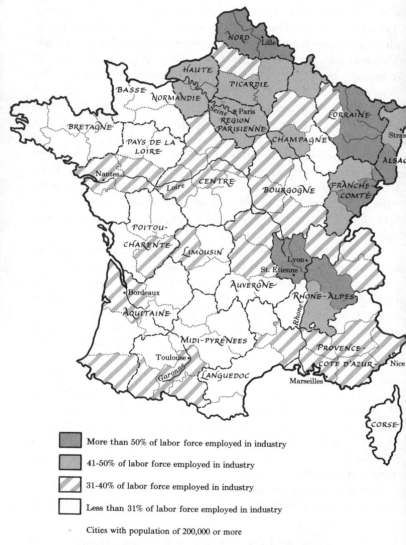

More than 50% of labor force employed in industry

41-50% of labor force employed in industry

31-40% of labor force employed in industry

Less than 31% of labor force employed in industry

Cities with population of 200,000 or more

Adapted from *Atlas Historique de la France Contemporaire 1800-1965*
(Paris: Colin, 1966), pp. 38, 47

Geographical Distribution of the Pompidou Vote in the Second Ballot of the Presidential Elections, June 15, 1969

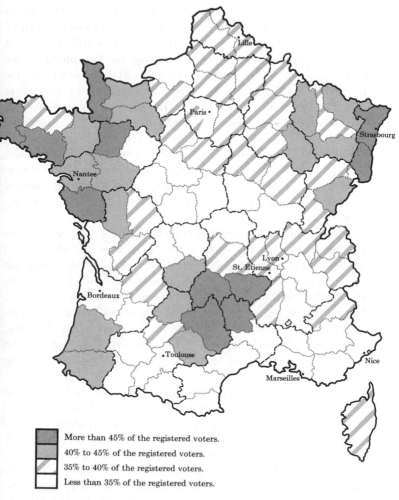

More than 45% of the registered voters.

40% to 45% of the registered voters.

35% to 40% of the registered voters.

Less than 35% of the registered voters.

Adapted from *Revue Française de Science Politique,* XX:2 (1970), p. 325.

vote was more evenly distributed throughout the country than the Gaullist vote prior to 1968. While he has kept former strongholds in the northeast and northwest, corresponding to long-established conservative traditions, the countryside south of the Loire is no longer the fief of the Left, as it still was in the preceding presidential elections. The vote for Pompidou in the Massif Central, where he hails from, might have been one for the native son. But elsewhere also, at least half of the voters traditionally left of center seem to have joined the majority. A comparison of the two maps (on pages 122 and 123) also shows that there is little correlation between economic structure and vote. It is no longer true, if it has ever been, that Gaullism owes its majority to the economically dynamic sections of the country, while the opposition recruits its following primarily in "under-developed" regions of a stagnant economy and a declining population.[50]

Among farmers and in rural communities the vote for Pompidou was proportionally even higher than that for General de Gaulle, who always did particularly well there. Even though the working class vote now appears to be equally divided between the Gaullist candidate and his opponent (which has never been the case before), one must not forget that abstention was particularly high among workers because of the communist directive. On the other hand Pompidou did better than Poher among the younger voters who had been reluctant followers of the aging General.

The voters have obviously accepted the logic of presidential elections and have welcomed the role assigned to them as a valuable experience in the process of their own political socialization. As a consequence the succession crisis against which de Gaulle had warned time and again when he sought plebiscitarian reaffirmation did not occur. That the new President will wield soon again the weapon of a referendum is unlikely. As in the United States, presidential elections might by themselves provide the needed balance should parliamentary elections once more have an atomistic effect and thereby disperse power rather than organize it.

[50] This conclusion is also reached in the careful study by François Goguel, *Modernisation économique et comportement politique* (Paris: Colin, 1969).

CHAPTER V

Political Socialization
Through the Mass Media

THE FLOW OF COMMUNICATIONS

"All of the functions performed in the political system — political socialization and recruitment, interest articulation, interest aggregation, rule-making, rule application, and rule adjudication — are performed *by means* of communication."[1] Some of these processes have been described in previous chapters, others will be discussed in subsequent parts of this study. The present chapter explaining the role of the mass media in France tries to find out, in the words of Harold Lasswell: "Who Says What, In Which Channel, To Whom, With What Effect,"[2] a paradigm which directs us towards many important political problems, only a few of them involving the mass media.

There are as many "channels" of information and communication as there are political learning processes — families and classrooms, playing fields and meeting halls, interest groups and parties. The mass media of modern society "do not simply displace or supersede other channels; rather, they link existing networks while giving rise to a host of dependent nets which service, disseminate, and frequently transform their product."[3]

[1] Gabriel Almond, "Introduction" in Gabriel Almond and James Coleman (ed.), *The Politics of the Developing Areas* (Princeton: Princeton University Press, 1960), p. 45.

[2] Quoted here from Richard R. Fagen, *Politics and Communication* (Boston: Little, Brown and Company, 1966), pp. 4, 5.

[3] *Ibid.*, p. 45.

In an established polity such as France, the potentialities and the limitations of the communications process as used by the mass media, are often determined by the way in which Frenchmen appraise the integrity of this process. Indeed their appraisal will be one of several factors indicating their faith in or their cynicism about the political system.[4]

In many of the political crises of the past, the French press played a dramatic role. During major campaigns, and great scandals or *"affaires,"* newspapers politicized the elites and mobilized the masses. They were used, and often subsidized, by the antagonists. In the absence of strong political parties and of sufficient revenue from advertising, business firms, tycoons, and governments (both French and foreign), habitually backed major newspapers. The widespread and largely justified belief that much of the press was run by "occult forces" seriously impaired its function as a channel of political communication.

When during the Second World War the resistance movement developed blueprints for the future, quite naturally much attention was given to the future status of press and radio. As a matter of course, the newspapers which had continued to publish in France during the German occupation were to be replaced by the organs of the resistance movement. In addition, a nationalized enterprise was to allocate printing presses and other resources to all existing political forces; the sources of information were to be kept clean and lean. For as the spokesmen for the resistance movement declared solemnly: "The press is free only when it depends neither on the government nor on the moneyed powers, but solely on the consciences of journalists and readers."

The realities of postwar politics soon did away with such aspirations. Today, the press operates under the same conditions as it does in other Western democracies, except that revenue from advertising remains comparatively low. In becoming more like newspapers elsewhere in the West, the French press has departed in many respects from its prewar structure and approach. Most important among such departures are the fusion of many newspapers and the deemphasis of their political commitment.

[4] See Lucian W. Pye, *Communications and Political Development* (Princeton: Princeton University Press, 1963), p. 8.

In spite of a growth in population the circulation of daily newspapers in France declined between 1946 and 1959 from 15.1 to 9.6 million a day. Since then there has been a slow, steady, and possibly significant, increase (12.8 million in 1966).[5] The decline in readership, a common phenomenon in most Western democracies, may be partly the result of a decline in the number of newspapers. In 1964 Paris had only 14 dailies as against 28 in 1946 and 57 before the First World War. Outside the capital, their number has decreased in the years since the last war from 175 to 93. According to public opinion polls, 75 per cent of Frenchmen are regular readers of the daily press; 12 per cent admit that they never look at it. In a representative youth panel, the corresponding figures are 45 per cent and 21 per cent. Among the farming population nonreaders make up 22 per cent, and in the least developed regions 39 per cent of the total adults.

The most striking difference from prewar days is the emaciation of the party press. The communist *Humanité,* the national newspaper of a party which had five million voters in the 1967 elections, has a circulation of little over 200,000 copies, as against close to one million copies for the two communists dailies after the Liberation. Only the far less politically and more culturally oriented Sunday edition of the *Humanité* still holds close to the half-million mark. The Socialist party had to abandon altogether its once highly respected daily. The U.D.R. — the government party which since 1962 has attracted a larger percentage of votes than any French party in history — publishes its daily, *La Nation,* in just a few thousand copies, mainly so that its editorials can be quoted on radio and television. But during the fifties and early sixties the two foremost nonpartisan Paris newspapers which shun an editorial opinion on many issues, the *Parisien Libéré* and *France-Soir,* have skyrocketed to a total of 2.1 million copies, or almost 45 per cent of all papers presently published in the capital. The two papers that come next in reader appeal, even

[5] Bruce M. Russett, et. al., *World Handbook of Political and Social Indicators* (New Haven: Yale University Press, 1964), p. 108, ranks France nineteenth in circulation of daily newspapers, behind most other countries of similar development. Unfortunately, at least for France, the figures do not correspond to the data given here and gained from reliable sources, see *A.P.,* 1966, pp. 393 ff.

though at a considerable distance, *Le Figaro* and *L'Aurore* (between 400,000 and 500,000 copies each) have a somewhat more definite political orientation; both are conservative, but they too shun all party affiliations.

The provincial press has the same characteristics. Unlike England, the newspapers in the various regions of France have stood the competition from the capital quite well. There are seventeen provincial newspapers that print more than 150,000 copies each; one of them, *Ouest-France,* is the third most important daily in the country. Others hold a quasi-monopoly in their respective regions, after having absorbed many of the strictly local papers. But while before the war some of the regional papers, especially in the South, were the mainstay of political parties, such ties are now cut. Their appeal is clearly directed to the reading public in its entirety. Hence it is not astonishing that their readership, and that of the two most successful Parisian dailies as well, reflects faithfully the social composition of the adult population at large. Half of the readers of the *Parisien Libéré* are workers who were obviously not unduly disturbed about the bias their daily paper showed when it expressed sympathy for the rebellious generals in Algeria. Other Paris newspapers appeal, by their presentation and style, to one social group over others.[6] But their audience is differentiated according to socio-economic status, not by political opinion.

A possibly significant departure from such a pattern occurred in 1970 during a by-election in the Lorraine region. The respected daily *L'Est Républicain* decided to back by vigorous editorializing an independent candidate, Jacques Servan-Schreiber who at the outset seemed to have no chance of winning a seat long held by the Gaullists (see also below, Chap. VIII). It is generally believed that the newspaper had no small role in M. Servan-Schreiber's surprise victory. It remains to be seen what influence this episode might have on other regional newspapers.

As long as most dailies feel compelled to offer to a politically undifferentiated clientele a product which antagonizes none, they tone down information that might prove divisive and avoid, as

[6] See *A.P.,* 1963, p. 382, to compare changes that have occurred in the distribution of readers with data from 1949 in *Sondages,* XVII:3 (1955), p. 59.

far as possible, controversial comments. Pressure from the reading public as perceived by circulation figures results in conformism of the newspapers, and such conformism reinforces the political indifference of their readers.[7] Responsible journalists complain about the "self-censorship" which their papers exercise; they acknowledge that present trends were underway long before the present regime was installed. Where before the war the financial backers expected most newspapers to be sympathetic to their own political preferences or economic interests, the concern now is for general innocuousness. The earlier policy aroused frequent opposition, the present invites indifference and at worst boredom. "Letters to the Editor" on any but trivial issues remain rare — one of many indications that politics is still regarded as a spectator sport. Typically, a provincial paper will print side by side national and international news and items of local or regional interest. What is generally missing, in striking contrast with corresponding American newspapers, are references to political activities taking place at the various levels; efforts of local authorities on the national scene, cooperation between local and national interest groups, etc. Such activities are going on, but are seldom considered newsworthy.

There are no reliable data as to the proportion of readers that turn to their dailies in search of political information. Twenty-one per cent of all readers, 37 per cent of women, and 45 per cent of the farmers admit that they never pay attention to political news in the dailies.[8] It is doubtful whether for this group radio and television have become the sources of political information or whether they simply do not seek such information.

Two Parisian dailies occupy a special place as communication media: *La Croix* (circulation 115,000) and *Le Monde* (about 500,000). The former, issued by an important Catholic publishing house which also circulates about twenty other periodicals with a much wider reader appeal than the daily, was founded to combat the institutions of the Third Republic with all the violence it could muster. Today its columns give limited space to

[7] Goguel and Grosser, *op. cit.,* pp. 155 ff.
[8] See Philip E. Converse and Georges Dupeux, *op. cit.,* p. 6. Their comparative data, which indicate a much greater political interest on the part of the American newspaper reader, are noteworthy but not quite convincing.

religious information as such. Not committed to any party and open to divergent opinions, it seeks nonetheless to develop a coherent stand on major political and social issues and to represent and possibly develop a dominant trend in modern French Catholicism.

The influence of *Le Monde* is far wider than its circulation and is still on the increase. It recruits readers and enjoys respect in many political camps, and it provides food for daily reflection, a basis for discussions, and a working tool for intellectuals, professionals, students, and especially the political and economic elite. Its editorial and reportorial staff are of unusually high quality; the covering of such events as political elections is unequaled by any American paper. Its editorial policy is as critical of the present regime as it was of the defunct Fourth Republic, yet it has no sympathy for political radicalism of any kind. Its *Tribune Libre* solicits divergent opinions. There is wide agreement that — compared with the prewar press — daily newspapers have lost much of the political interest and tension they used to convey, but it is also conceded that none of the prewar dailies enjoyed the independence of *Le Monde*.

Some of the needs for political controversy and partisan information are filled by certain weeklies, representing all shades of opinion. Their audience is fairly small, but they function as an important channel of communication for information not otherwise available, even though their information is not always reliable. While there is no lack of thoroughly cause-oriented weeklies, nor of periodical publications with wide mass appeal, such publications as the British *Economist* and the *Observer,* the German *Zeit,* or the Sunday supplements of certain American newspapers devoted to political information and discussion but devoid of shrill partisanship, do not exist as yet.

As to the publications destined for the broad public, France is now as well provided as other countries and with the same wares. Circulation figures increase steadily even if they do not yet reach the density in coverage of similar American periodicals. Noteworthy is the fact that in "dechristianized" France *L'Écho de Notre Temps,* a monthly which addresses Catholic women in an unsectarian style, leads (with 1.6 million copies) the circulation record of all periodical publications, with the exception of a weekly listing the television programs (2 million copies).

As we have seen, the press had lost much of its political coloring before the advent of the Fifth Republic. Nonetheless, the institutions and the style of the new regime have changed the role of the government in the communication process rather drastically. The flow of information from the centers of decision-making to the printed media has been redirected, its substance altered. In the past, parliamentary debates and even more the communiqués and intentional leaks of committee members and other representatives furnished a great deal of political information to the peripheral public. A deputy or senator who had become a cabinet minister did not break off his cordial "working" relationship with journalists. Discreetness was expected to a far lesser extent from him than, for instance, from a member of the British Cabinet.

Parliament is no longer a center of decision-making and has therefore lost most of its importance as a source of information. Deputies that belong to a seemingly solid majority no longer need the press to further their political or personal ends. During General de Gaulle's presidency, the ministers, even those with a political rather than administrative background, were chary of confidences. As a result, newspapermen had to prod the immediate collaborators of the Minister and certain members of the bureaucracy to piece together the details of conflicts and political struggles that underlie decision-making. But always, the rumors gathered in such a way by even the most responsible newspaperman were spotty and often misleading. As a result, the level of political information declined further. "Finally one wonders," an outstanding journalist has written, "whether . . . one does not hear anything because nobody says anything, whether one does not know anything because nothing happens, or whether the regime is able to mask everything, to mute everybody." [9] Remarkably enough, such dilution of information occurred at a time when the press enjoyed, at least since the end of the Algerian war, almost complete freedom from interference and censorship — except for the self-censorship that has been mentioned.

Dissatisfaction of the general public with the amount of

[9] Pierre Viansson-Ponté (leading political columnist of *Le Monde*), "Vingt ans d'information politique (1946–1966)," *La Nef,* XXII:27 (1966), p. 50. The entire issue of this magazine is devoted to a discussion of political information in present-day France.

information it receives about governmental decisions and policies is relatively widespread. In 1964, 43 per cent of all respondents and 62 per cent of men with a college education complained about a lack of information. More than five years later, after General de Gaulle had left the Presidency, the complaints were hardly less emphatic: 38 per cent considered themselves badly informed about economic and international affairs, 44 per cent about governmental activities. Each time the younger age group was dissatisfied to an even higher degree with the news it was able to obtain.[10]

During his Presidency, General de Gaulle used each of his carefully timed and staged biannual press conferences as an important occasion to spell out his world views and to communicate major decisions ranging over a broad field. The content and form of such communications were determined unilaterally, since questions addressed to the Chief of State were usually prearranged. Under de Gaulle's successor presidential press conferences are less formalized without approaching the give-and-take of White House conferences. It appears that since 1969 the government is less parsimonious with official information. In his first message, spelling out the government's agenda for reform, the new Prime Minister gave high priority to a better informed citizenry. He thereby admitted that socialization by the mass media had been unsatisfactory.

At present the newspapers are hardly a sufficient source of information for a government that wishes to gauge public attitudes. To a certain extent, the elected representatives, especially the deputies of the majority, still serve as transmission belts between their constituents and the authorities. The routine contacts between high-ranking civil servants and the representatives of organized interests fulfill the same function and are particularly valuable in a country where, until recently, the cult of secrecy has obscured official statistics.

Public opinion polls are important means of filling the gap in information. Considered with diffidence for a long time, polling has now become a major and generally accepted operation; its

---

[10] *Sondages,* XXVI:3 (1964), pp. 38–39 and SOFRES, *Polls of October-November 1969 and January 1970* (generously communicated to me for which I wish to express my gratitude).

results are widely publicized by the press. Most of the polling operations are private and competitive but live to a considerable extent on government contracts. As in the United States, popularity curves exist for the President and his principal collaborators. During all electoral contests, but especially during referendum campaigns and presidential elections, opinion polls and the publication of their results by the press have become an important factor in the decision ultimately reached by the voter.

But in addition there are searching inquiries into attitudes, opinions, and habits which, traditionally, Frenchmen have carefully concealed even from members of their families. If French society is becoming less opaque, this is to a considerable extent due to the vogue for opinion polling. Altogether polling enables the government and numerous public administrations to gather data without the help of the intermediaries who serve as channels of information in a classical parliamentary democracy. Hence the pattern of a more direct democracy, which the Fifth Republic has sought to establish, is well served by the wide use of public opinion polls; just as in commercial polling, they are based on the plebiscitarian assumptions of "one citizen, one vote, one value." [11]

As to the communication flow in the opposite direction, the modern mass media such as radio and television were particularly appropriate to the style of the regime during its Gaullist phase. Neither de Gaulle nor Castro created the mass media channels which they both used to widen and continue the bases of their charismatic relationship with the masses. [12] But in France the popularity of television and the techniques employed by the government in handling the new medium became so outstanding that the regime was sometimes spoken of as a "Telecracy." Those who described the Fifth Republic as "de Gaulle plus Television" wished to point to the institutional shapelessness which prevailed during much of General de Gaulle's rule.

Most characteristic were de Gaulle's appeals to the nation (in

[11] On this point see Stein Rokkan, "Comparative Cross-National Research: The Context of Current Efforts," in Richard L. Merritt and Stein Rokkan, *Comparing Nations: The Use of Quantitative Data in Cross-National Research* (New Haven: Yale University Press, 1966), p. 16, and the authors there quoted.

[12] See the pertinent remarks on Cuba in Fagen, *op. cit.*, p. 68.

General's uniform rather than in a double-breasted suit) when mutinous settlers or officers threatened the republic from Algeria. On these occasions, the hero invited the citizens to share with him not only the experience of exciting events but also the responsibility of resolving the crisis. In fact, twice rebellions collapsed shortly after almost the entire population watched a television appearance by de Gaulle. The effective use of modern communications made the rebels realize that the national community was intact, and proved far more decisive than the *post hoc* utilization of presidential emergency powers (see Chap. IX). On the other hand, each time when for whatever reason de Gaulle's performance on the "little screen" was unsatisfactory — such as during the elections of 1965, the May Events, or during the last of his referendum campaigns — public attitudes towards the regime were directly affected.

Almost all households possess a radio. TV is estimated to reach at present between twenty-one and twenty-three million people. In the villages, television has frequently and drastically transformed leisure time habits and social life. At least a partial socialization of the village population into the broader national or regional community is taking place all the more easily because the diffident French farmer has always trusted what he can "see" more than what he reads or is told.

All existing television chains (two national and twenty-two regional relays) are a public monopoly. Since the war, there are no private radio stations broadcasting from French territory. But the so-called peripheral stations, covering all of French territory from border zones and until recently privately controlled, have a far more recognized status than the "pirate" stations in Great Britain. On the other hand, the official French radio had to wage a long up-hill fight to acquire prestige for its newscasts. "Listening to the news" meant for many distrustful Frenchmen tuning in on the newscasts of the privately rather than the publicly owned stations. As far as radio was concerned, this was still true during the referendum campaign of 1969.[13] This seems to indicate that Frenchmen still have the same doubts about the

[13] See *Sondages,* **XXXI**:3 (1969), p. 19. The voters who were to cast a "yes" ballot expressed far more confidence in the official radio than those who were to vote in the negative.

integrity of the communications process which made them widely critical of the prewar press. It is true that by now television has become for most households the single most important source of political information and there exists no alternative to the televised newscasts by the government-controlled network.

For this reason, the problem of governmental control of the mass media has been at all times one of the most ardently discussed questions in the public life of the Fifth Republic. "The regulation of broadcasting and television," a moderate deputy of the opposition has written, "becomes more important than the articles of the Constitution."

GOVERNMENTAL CONTROL OF INFORMATION

The regulation of information is by no means peculiar to the present regime; it antedates the wide diffusion of television. In Great Britain, parliamentary inquiries into the operations of the B.B.C. have concerned themselves with the quality of its radio and television operations; there never was any doubt that the network was free from governmental interference. By contrast, whenever the annual budget of the information services was debated in the parliament of the Fourth Republic, bitter and justified complaints were voiced about the manner in which each of the short-lived cabinets was using the government controlled communications systems to further its political ends. To conceive of the mass media as a public service, which was to be put at the disposal of all political forces, remained a difficult concept for a political community in which government and opposition contested each other's legitimacy. Each majority, however ephemeral, claimed to speak in the name of all and therefore saw no virtue in permitting dissonant voices to be heard over the publicly owned air waves. Such practices rapidly created a body of precedents which every government used when it wished to interfere with the presentation of political and, often, of general information.

An additional obstacle to objectivity is the habit common to all French journalism of fusing news report and editorial comment. To present the news without coloring it with the opinion of the reporter is considered dull and would probably by now be rejected as uninteresting by the reading and listening public.

With the advent of the Fifth Republic the situation worsened.

There was never any competition to the government monopoly in the field of television. The government was also known to have acquired shares, and in some cases a controlling majority, in the private radio stations. Moreover, there was no longer that cascade of rapidly succeeding governments which in the past had checked the one-sidedness of information, at least over time.

Protests against the one-sided use of the mass media by the government during the campaigns of 1962 and at other occasions led in 1964 to the creation of a new agency, the *Office de Radio-diffusion-Télévision Française* (O.R.T.F.) soon to employ a total of 12,000 people. At the time the new law was enacted, it appeared as if it offered at least a framework for a liberalized policy.[14] The Minister of Information supervised but no longer administered O.R.T.F.; a Board of Directors was given seemingly broad powers to direct general policy and to supervise the general standards of programs. It was empowered to check on the accuracy and objectivity of information and to insist on a balanced presentation which should give to "the principal trends of thought and the important currents of opinion" access to the mass media. As a matter of fact greater objectivity of the news media obtained during the presidential elections of 1965 to which a specially appointed National Control Commission and the government itself wanted to give a maximum guarantee of fairness and respectability. But the improvement was temporary. From many sides new complaints were heard that on the national and on the regional networks of both radio and television information of great public interest was being omitted when it was considered inappropriate by the authorities. In fact, an interministerial committee made frequent suggestions as to which topics should be treated lightly; entire programs were known to have been deleted. Since many in the management of the O.R.T.F. are very close to the centers of decision-making, no binding directives were needed to ensure a large measure of conformism.

By April, 1968, indignation against the government's high-handed information policy had become so intense that a motion

[14] For a detailed analysis of the legislation and its history, see P. M. Gaudement, "Le régime de la radiodiffusion et de la télévision en France" (with an extensive summary in English), *International Review of Administrative Science,* XXXI: 1 (1965), pp. 15–23; IV–VI.

of censure, specifically directed against the political control of the mass media, lost in parliament by only eight votes. The Events of May brought the "battle of the O.R.T.F." to a dramatic head.[15]

When television and radio crews wished to report first on the student manifestations, then on the fighting in the streets, on police methods, and on factories on strike, when they insisted on presenting a debate about General de Gaulle's televised speech, the government, constantly interceded with the management of the O.R.T.F. and sought sanctions against individual employees. A general strike by many employees was the answer, paralyzing the operations of the O.R.T.F. during the height of the crisis. The strikers were not satisfied when the government offered improved pay and working conditions; they demanded a complete overhaul of the structure of the O.R.T.F. which in their eyes had remained a decisive instrument for the manipulation of public opinion. In typical language the Office became another "Bastille," which had to be stormed if freedom of expression was to prevail.

Because it was so clearly political in character the strike outlasted other strike and protest movements by several weeks. After work was resumed, those most active in opposition to the government were dismissed. A reorganization of the O.R.T.F. gave a somewhat broader representation on various advisory boards to outsiders but no effective guarantees for a true autonomy of the operations from governmental interference. In the referendum campaign of the following year the O.R.T.F. was used to the fullest extent to familiarize its audience with the regional reform plans and thereby to promote "yes" votes. Its efforts were of no avail. It is not impossible that in 1969, as well as on previous occasions, all too zealous efforts by the government may have had a boomerang effect.[16]

Typically enough, when M. Poher was installed as interim

[15] For a well-informed if passionate account of the crisis, see *AP 1968, op. cit.,* pp. 369–74.

[16] Whether the official radio and TV propaganda influenced the voters in previous campaigns has always been controversial. For the 1962 elections, cf. René Rémond and Claude Neuschwander, "Télévision et comportement politique," *RFSP,* XIII:2 (1963), esp. pp. 345–46, and Guy Michelat, "Télévision, moyens d'information et comportement électoral," *ibid.,* XIV:5 (1964), pp. 877–905. For the presidential elections of 1965, cf. *Sondages,* XXVII:4 (1965), p. 19 and Williams, "The French Presidential Elections," esp. p. 28.

President, one of his first actions, taken without the advice of the Prime Minister, were orders to the director of the O.R.T.F. to observe strict neutrality in the weeks ahead.[17]

The new regime has given renewed assurances of relaxing political controls over radio and TV.[18] An avowed anti-Gaullist has been appointed to an important staff position in the news section of the first television chain. But, many of the best talents have already been driven away from the O.R.T.F., and resignations in protest over governmental interference are still occurring.

[17] See Dominique Pado, *Les 50 Jours d'Alain Poher* (Paris: Denoël, 1969), pp. 149 ff. This directive seemed to have earned him widespread approval.

[18] New directives, issued by the O.R.T.F. in November, 1969, promise to give guarantees of more objective reporting. For their text, see Goguel and Grosser, *op. cit.*, p. 210–12.

CHAPTER VI

Recruitment and Style
of Decision-Makers

THE "POLITICAL CLASS"

A study seeking to explain the facts of political life must determine not only who the leading actors on the political scene are, how they got there and where they came from, but also how they wield their power. Therefore, an analysis of their own socialization and recruitment, of their background, and of their style of action is needed. Besides the decision-makers' origin many other factors, particularly the milieu in which the politicians act and interact, explain their particular style.

How to reconcile the existence of a political elite, comprising both those who live for politics and those who live off politics,[1] with the original assumptions underlying a democratic polity is a ubiquitous problem. Many modern critics of representative regimes, especially Mosca, Pareto, and Michels, have questioned the realism of democratic theory by pointing to the existence of an elite holding a near-monopoly of decision-making. In their writings they both scorn and praise the "political class," usually in the same moralizing tone in which Jean-Jacques Rousseau denounced the dangers inherent in all political representation. Because of their polemic use of the term, the designation of the political decision-makers in a democratic society as a "political

[1] The distinction is made by Max Weber in "Politics as a Vocation," in *Essays in Sociology* (New York: Oxford University Press, 1958), p. 84.

class," has generally become the earmark of an antidemocratic bias.

However, in modern France, and especially since the beginning of the constitutional crisis of the 1930s, not only the "elitist" enemies of the representative regime speak of a "political class" when they wish to criticize those who in their opinion have succeeded in "confiscating the theoretical sovereignty of the people as expressed in universal suffrage." [2] Even before the First World War, Robert de Jouvenel in a still widely quoted statement, referred to a few thousand political decision-makers who use their monopoly of political power not to control each other, which they are supposed to do, but to further each other's ends.[3]

Then as today (or at least until the advent of the Fifth Republic), members of parliament were the basic nucleus of this decision-making group. For in France it was less possible than in some other Western democracies to make a significant political career outside the national legislature. Besides members of parliament the holders of elective offices in municipalities or departments, some local party leaders, and perhaps some journalists of national renown were counted among the political class — which altogether totaled not more than fifteen or twenty thousand persons. All of them, whether already elected to parliament or not, gravitated towards the halls of the lower or the upper house, the National Assembly or the Senate. Hence, when analyzing the recruitment and the style of this group of decision-makers, it is justified to center attention on the elected representatives.[4]

It has been described above (see Chap. IV) how loosely organized parties, voting habits, and electoral laws combined to cut the deputies loose from any expression of political will on

[2] As quite typical see François Goguel, in *In Search of France,* p. 395. The term is also widely used by intellectual spokesmen for the political Left, such as Professor Duverger, and by liberal newspapers and periodicals, such as *Le Monde* and *Esprit.*

[3] Robert de Jouvenel, *La République des camarades* (Paris: Grasset, 1914), p. 262. For an excellent more recent description of the French parliamentary system and its mores, see Roger Priouret, *La République des députés* (Paris: Grasset, 1959).

[4] For reasons of space this discussion is limited to the deputies, i.e., the members of the lower house. *Mutatis mutandis* much of what is said here applies also to the upper house, the Senate. Some of the institutional problems of the Senate will be discussed below, Chap. X.

the part of the electorate. Isolated in their legislative chambers ("the house without windows" a scornful comment on the, perhaps symbolic, architecture of the parliamentary building), the deputies exercised a seemingly limitless power. Their ritualistic style has been criticized from within no less than from the outside. Decades before General de Gaulle denounced it, the socialist leader Léon Blum, shortly before he himself became a deputy, spoke about the depressing, shut-in atmosphere of parliament and linked it to the monotonous quarrels of married couples. "If only we had in France political parties," he sighed, "and if these parties had an organization and a doctrine!" And he concluded (as early as 1917!) that the understandable reactions of the electorate towards the mores of parliament were rapidly becoming a "public danger." [5]

In the closed circuit to which it was confined, the incessant struggle for political power in parliament was actually little more than a reshuffling of cards.

The style in which this game was played — the rules according to which the roles were distributed — was sometimes criticized as overly dogmatic and ideological, sometimes as recklessly opportunistic. In fact they were both.[6] Without clear mandates from either the electorate or political parties, but with the traditional mission of rebelling against authority, decisions were postponed by the endless debates on matters of principle rather than bargaining realities. But when, periodically, circumstances would tolerate no further delay, then last minute compromises required turnabouts without any reference to previously announced metaphysical convictions. The professed egalitarianism resulted in a passion for anonymity and made it difficult to build a stable leadership. Yet there developed here another dichotomy between an egalitarian style and reality. Those likely to qualify for a cabinet

[5] "Lettres sur la réforme gouvernementale," *Revue de Paris,* VI (December 1, 1917), pp. 453–54.

[6] Jacques Fauvet (editor-in-chief of *Le Monde*) in *The Cockpit of France* (London: Harvill, 1960) stresses the ideological character of French politics; an American observer, Nathan Leites, in his *On the Game of Politics in France* (Stanford: Stanford University Press, 1959) sees the political class committed to "games" rather than to doctrines. Both books make a convincing case and both are one-sided, the work by Mr. Leites outrageously so.

post, especially those who had already been members of a government, formed a group quite distinct from the ordinary deputies or senators. Only if they violated the unwritten rules by too forthright an exercise of authority would they incur sanctions, such as their elimination from further ministerial office. Responsibility was further diluted by the fact that constantly shifting majorities gave most deputies the impression that they were simultaneously in power and in opposition.

Before the First World War, the esoteric games played by the representatives were not considered incongruous by the outside world since politics itself was believed to be a game and not a condition shaping men's lives. But when the crisis of the thirties changed this, the behavior of its representatives became meaningless and irritating to the French nation outside the restricted circle of an all but autonomous political class.

For the political culture of a democracy it is crucial that there be confidence in the persons and the role of the political actors. Such confidence, commanding loyalty not only to the men but also to the system, was lacking, and therefore the nation was estranged from its own affairs as transacted in parliament. A natural affinity between the participating actors exists also in the American Senate and in the British House of Commons. But in France it became suspect, as evidence of collusion. In an age when for various reasons political power becomes more and more personalized and when therefore utmost visibility is expected, the French representatives' emphasis on anonymity further increased the suspicion that their highly stylized practices hid malfeasance. As a matter of fact, anonymity or at least restraint in behavior was demanded from the successful member of parliament. Time and again outstanding men were resented by the public as well as by their peers. At least the appearance of mediocrity was the preferred style.

Yet the frequently heard stereotype contrasting a stable country with its instable parliamentary system was likely to conceal the fact that talent, skill, and character were by no means lacking among the parliamentary personnel. In all countries, professional politicians develop special characteristics which amount to their personal equation. But because the activities in which French politicians had to engage were energy consuming and paralyzing, the mores of parliament "tended to magnify the occupational traits into an absurd caricature." [7]

It has already been noted (see Chap. IV) that the normal *cursus honorum* of the French deputy (and senator as well) begins in elective offices on the local or departmental level. During the last forty years of the Third Republic, more than two-thirds (two-fifths in the Fourth Republic) of the deputies held such offices before their own election to the Chamber.[8] At least 160 out of the 283 senators presently serving in the upper house are also members of a departmental *Conseil Général*. Even in the crisis elections of 1958, which swept many newcomers into parliament, less than one-fourth of the deputies had never held local or departmental office. Because of their structural weakness, most political parties do not provide a sufficiently large and solid base for the recruitment of aspirants to a parliamentary seat. Hence a career in local government serves as the selection process, and the local implantation of deputies and senators is far stronger than in Great Britain or Germany.

The local notables, however, not only furnish a reservoir for the political class, they also function as the necessary, desirable link between the social and the political cadres. Where, under special circumstances, a candidate has been "parachuted" into a constituency from the outside, he will hasten to sink solid roots into local political life after his election to national office. The consequences of such a strong commitment by the representative to local and departmental affairs have been described earlier.

This is not to deny that the parties have a role in the recruitment or formal nomination process. Especially for the socialist and communist candidates previous party activity is a condition of endorsement, although even for them local notoriety is a strong recommendation. But if the Fourth Republic had intended to replace a republic of local leaders by one of party activists, it soon turned out that it had failed. Party endorsement of those seeking election to parliament was necessary, especially under the then prevailing list system of proportional representation. In gen-

[7] Raymond Aron, *France Steadfast and Changing* (Cambridge: Harvard University Press, 1960), p. 23.

[8] For data on the local implantation of members of parliament in the Fifth Republic, see Philip M. Williams, *The French Parliament. Politics in the Fifth Republic* (New York: Praeger, 1968), pp. 32 ff.

eral, however, such endorsement was given to those who had proven their worth on the local scene. The political weight of party leaders who for whatever reason were not deputies or senators was and continues to be insignificant. Socialists and communists excepted, very few deputies have started their political career in party office.[9]

The regular career of the political class may be modified in times of crisis. In the immediate postwar elections of 1945 and 1946, the very small group of people that had been active in the resistance movement against the German occupiers and the Vichy regime furnished 80 per cent of the deputies; it is true that some of them had already been politically active before the war but at lower party echelons. Their sudden rise to prominence was in part an indication that political parties identified with the resistance movement exercised temporarily a stronger influence on the selection and recruitment process. Even in later elections, including those of 1958, resistance activists represented about two-thirds óf the membership of the lower House. But because their chances for reelection increased in proportion to their activities in local government, this group that had started outside the normal *cursus honorum* joined it afterwards.

The first elections in the Fifth Republic also occurred in a crisis situation. But in terms of the normal political antecedents of a parliamentary career they hardly amounted to an upheaval. Of the total 202 deputies which a new party, the Gaullist U.N.R., elected in 1958, less than 30 had never held some political office beforehand. A majority of the U.N.R. deputies who were new to parliament had been mayors or members of municipal and departmental councils.[10]

If there is a political class, an inherited political career is very rare. There are increasingly fewer families for which elective office is a tradition as it is still in Great Britain. The chronological age of the deputies reflects, as is to be expected, the breaks that

[9] See the data in Aubin, *op. cit.,* II, p. 206, and Léo Hamon, "Members of the French Parliament," *International Social Science Journal,* XIII:4 (1961), pp. 547 ff. In my opinion this author attributes too great an importance to the role of parties in the nomination of candidates.

[10] See Mattei Dogan, "Changement de régime et changement de personnel," in *Le Référendum de septembre et les élections de novembre 1958* (Paris: Colin, 1960), esp. pp. 260–62.

occur when one regime succeeds the other. In 1936, after the last elections of the Third Republic, 120 deputies were younger than forty, and 250 older than fifty. In the first parliament of de Gaulle's Republic, the under-forty outnumbered the over-fifty. But the average age of the deputies, while lower than in the last elections of the Fourth Republic, was still higher than after the war in 1946. The average age of the deputies elected to the National Assembly in 1968 was 50 years, with little difference between the various parties.

Political longevity, however, is of greater significance than chronological age. For a successful political career it is not sufficient to be elected a deputy; it is necessary to remain one.[11] Between 1877 and 1932, the classical era of the French representative system, two-fifths of all deputies were reelected for four-year terms between three and ten times. Three per cent of the deputies were in at least seven legislatures and typically kept their seats for about a third of a century. Certain deputies were seated, without interruption, from their first election to the end of their last mandate. Paul Reynaud, who lost his seat in 1962 when he led the fight against General de Gaulle's constitutional referendum, had been a deputy since 1919, with only short breaks after temporary defeats.

Comparisons with the Fourth Republic are misleading since there were five legislative elections during a period of thirteen years. But relative longevity persisted: almost half of all deputies were elected three to five times. It was typical of the French party system that the group of deputies who could not be classified politically because they really did not belong to any party made up, also in the Fourth Republic, the highest percentage of those who were constantly reelected, with the communists next in political longevity.

Continuity in time and fixity of locale were intimately linked. An incumbent who sought reelection in his constituency could hardly ever be dislodged. This, together with the particular can-

[11] See, also for the data following in the text, Mattei Dogan "Political Ascent in a Class Society: French Deputies, 1870–1958" in Dwaine Marvick (ed.), *Political Decision-makers* (New York: The Free Press, 1961), pp. 57–90 and the same author's "Le personnel politique et la personnalité charismatique," *Revue Française de sociologie,* VI:3 (1965), pp. 305–24.

didate's activity and experience in local affairs, usually provided great familiarity with constituency interests and competence in defending them. But, especially in times of crisis, such longevity as prevailed reinforced the voters' distrust for the political class as a self-perpetuating clique. The French version of "throw the rascals out" (*Sortez les Sortants*) was thus heard at least at each change of regime, and frequently between.

In 1958, 406 incumbent deputies were not reelected, but 62 of them had chosen not to run. Such a hecatomb of politicians had not occurred since the beginning of the Third Republic. On the benches of the new parliament, less than one-third had been deputies in the previous Assembly. However, as has been explained, only a small fraction of those new to parliament were also new to a political career. In the elections of 1962 half of the deputies who won a seat were not incumbents. If this indicates a new trend in parliamentary turnover, the recruitment pattern is but little modified. Only slightly over one-fourth of the non-incumbents were truly new to elective office. The others had belonged to parliament in the past, or, most frequently, had held posts in local government. In the elections of 1968 the number of freshmen deputies rose to 139 because of the heavy influx of Gaullists.

The professional and especially the social origin of members of parliament has changed significantly since the establishment of the Third Republic in 1871. Then the nobility and the upper bourgeoisie had furnished respectively 34 and 36 per cent of the deputies; in the first elections after the First World War, only 10 per cent and 30 per cent of the deputies could be assigned to these social categories. The middle and the small bourgeoisie were now represented by 35 per cent and 15 per cent respectively of the deputies.[12] Since then the same trends have continued. Compared with the British House of Commons, the membership of the lower house of the French parliament has been of more modest social origin. From about 1879 on, the representatives of the middle bourgeoisie dominated parliament and cabinets but later began to be edged out of this dominant role by men of yet lower middle-class origin. Since then, an amalgam of these two groups

[12] See Georges Dupeux, *La Société Française 1789–1960* (Paris: Colin, 1964), p. 188, and Wright, *Modern France, op. cit.*, pp. 356 ff.

has become dominant, before the First World War furnishing about one-third of the deputies, during the interwar period one-half, and in the Fourth Republic about 70 per cent. The upper bourgeoisie, which in England until recently formed the backbone of the Conservative party, exercised political influence in France only indirectly: through interest groups and the bureaucracy. On the other hand, the number of deputies with working-class background is smaller than in the House of Commons. It has never risen to more than 15 per cent, partly because the syndicalist tradition of the French labor movement frowned upon the assumption of parliamentary seats by trade-union leaders. In more recent times, the number of deputies with a working class background has depended on the number of communists elected to parliament. This in turn has fluctuated not so much with the voters' sympathies but with the electoral tactics of the communists and their neighboring parties.

Among the political actors inside and outside of parliament, the number of intellectuals has always been greater in France than in other countries, their political activities more visible than elsewhere. Perhaps one should call Voltaire the first French "intellectual in politics." In the nineteenth century such traditions continued. In the short-lived Second Republic, a poet (Lamartine) and a scientist (Raspail) were candidates for the Presidency of the Republic. Subsequently, Victor Hugo and Émile Zola participated actively in politics. More recently, a number of outstanding writers (Gide, Barrès, Malraux, Sartre, and Mauriac) have let their voices be heard in the political market place both on the Right and on the Left.

In parliament, the number of "intellectuals" (in a broad sense) — teachers and professors, journalists, doctors, high civil servants, etc. — has usually been higher than in other countries: about 31 per cent before the Second World War, 35 per cent in the Fourth and 40 per cent so far in the Fifth Republic. One account of the political regime spoke in 1927 of the "Republic of the Professors." [13] The highly revered *École Normale Supérieure* in Paris, training ground for many university professors, especially in the humanities and in the social sciences, also functioned for many

[13] Albert Thibaudet, *La République des professeurs* (Paris: Grasset, 1927). In France secondary school teachers are also usually "professeur."

generations as a "political seminar." Many parliamentary leaders, predominantly those of the Left, discovered and sharpened their political ambitions while they were students at the school. Undoubtedly, the ideological style characteristic of political life inside and outside parliament must in part be ascribed to the high proportion of intellectuals in the political class.

> In France, at least, it was the intellectuals who were most impassioned in political debates in the Assembly under the Fourth Republic as under the Third. They were often the most intransigent ideologues. . . . they were apt to pose problems abstractly, with more or less sincerity, and often to expound them with ability. But this aptitude meant that they often proposed unrealistic solutions; and that they fixed upon subtleties and neglected essentials, thus uselessly complicating and prolonging parliamentary debates by inventing false problems and disagreeing among themselves.[14]

That lawyers have always made up the largest single professional group in parliament is a fact that is common to France and other representative regimes. Before the Second World War, the legal profession supplied one-fourth of all deputies, many of them prominent, so that lawyers actually accounted for more than one-third of the cabinet posts. There were some brilliant members of the Paris bar among them. But the vast majority were local notables, trained in law and experienced in local administration. Rural constituencies, seldom represented in parliament by farmers, usually preferred lawyers over other candidates.[15] Frequently not less competent than the heads of administrative bureaus, these lawyers imposed their style on the regime and formed the backbone of a parliament which considered the exercise of the tightest possible control over the cabinet and the bureaucracy to be its foremost mission.

Since the Second World War, the number of lawyer-deputies has decreased rather drastically, a trend that has continued in the Fifth Republic. In the parliament elected in 1968, the single largest group is now made up of top civil servants on leave (56, or 7 per cent of the total) followed by members of the teaching

[14] Dogan in Marvick, *op. cit.*, p. 67.

[15] Figures indicating that in the Fourth Republic 12 per cent and in the Fifth Republic between 8 and 10 per cent of the deputies are *agriculteurs* are misleading since most of these are not farmers but the owners of large estates and often absentee owners at that.

profession at various levels (55) and by heads of enterprises and other businessmen (52). The number of lawyers is reduced to 28 (or 5 per cent of total), a record low. An outstanding new development in the social composition of parliament is the large number of high civil servants who have decided to run for elective office, usually on the Gaullist ticket.[16] This corresponds to a political sensitization of the younger bureaucrats, which will be discussed below and in Chap. IX. There also is a relatively large increase of businessmen, engineers, and industrial managers. But quite apart from the fact that this group is not as homogenous as for instance the teaching profession, a merely quantitative approach to this question is misleading. Many of those classified as businessmen, sales representatives, and the like play a very minor role in the halls of parliament, while most of the lawyers and members of other professions are prominent and active.

With the new institutional arrangements of the Fifth Republic radically reducing the powers of parliament (see Chap. X), the decline in parliamentary prestige and influence has turned some of the best talents towards other political or administrative activities. The new regime has increased the remuneration of the deputies and, at the same time has reduced their powers. But this has not made up for the frustrations (and still considerable cost) of a deputy's seat in Paris.

The ties between national and local political careers, far from being broken, have probably been reinforced. The traditional local leaders may lose their footing, yet they are replaced on both the local and the regional level by younger activists. The new notables soon discover that as before their achievements will remain precarious without assistance from the national government. To obtain such assistance, a seat in parliament still offers the best access and leverage.

As under previous regimes, in such cases a parliamentary career becomes the consecration of notoriety obtained elsewhere. Should this traditional amalgamation continue, parliament will remain or would become again an important means for the identification and further development of the most talented, if not of primary

---

[16] For interesting data on this phenomenon, see Charles Debbasch, *L'Administration au pouvoir. Fonctionnaires et politique sous la Ve République* (Paris: Calmann-Lévy, 1969), pp. 58–61.

recruitment. This in turn would return to parliament some of its lost prestige and its attractiveness to a revived political class.

There also exists one rather disparate group — one might best characterize it as a milieu — which is highly involved in political issues but as yet little in politics, and which so far has shunned parliamentary career. These "aspirants" [17] to the political class are usually between thirty-five and forty-five years of age; their political orientation might vary widely. Many of them have been active in the resistance movement, or if too young for that, in contact with it through their families. Others became known to each other during the few months when the government of Pierre Mendès-France seemed to give a new style to the politics of the Fourth Republic. At first their political activities were confined to the local level, to various interest groups and political clubs — a phenomenon largely of the Fifth Republic. (See Chaps. VII and VIII.) Whether or not they actually participated in the earlier resistance movement, they are in many respects the intellectual heirs of the resistance. A passion for reform and for intensive thinking about the correct strategy for achieving reform in France is common to them. In a country of divided elites, communication between elites is the contribution they wish to make to modernization. They hope to guard against the temptations of technocratic ambition by a commitment to an ideology of democratic participation, which they seek to submit to the test of practicality.

Some of these aspirants have already entered parliament through regular or by-elections. Most of them are found on the benches of the government coalition, others are aligned with the opposition but usually out of sympathy with the traditional parties. Yet others have entered the personal staffs of the Ministers in the government appointed by President Pompidou.

THE BUREAUCRACY

More than a century ago, Tocqueville remarked that "since 1789 the administrative system has always stood firm among the debacles of political systems." [18] He personally had known top

---

[17] The term was coined by Roy Macridis, in Karl W. Deutsch et al., *France, Germany and the Western Alliance* (New York: Scribner's, 1967), pp. 31 ff.

[18] *The Old Regime,* p. 202.

administrators who had entered the ranks of the bureaucracy before the storming of the Bastille and who retired at the end of an uninterrupted career long after the Bourbons had been restored to power. Since Tocqueville wrote, it has become axiomatic that the vagaries of the actors on the political stage have been balanced and thereby rendered largely innocuous by a stable bureaucracy. It is quite true that some of the anarchic and demagogic tendencies of the political system could be indulged in only behind the protective shield of a seemingly regular pattern of administrative behavior. But the latter never did neatly balance the former so that a satisfactory equilibrium could be established. Indeed, since they relied on each other, there was symbiosis as much as opposition between the two systems.

In the judgment of a recent French observer, in many ways a latter-day Tocqueville, "the bureaucratic system of organization of French public administration is certainly one of the most entrenched of such closed systems of social action that has existed in the modern world."[19] This came about not only because an administration, burdened as it was with tasks which it shares in other representative regimes with the political leadership, sought strength in isolation. An intense dislike for all outsiders of whatever social origin had been a characteristic of the civil service under the *Ancien Régime*. Later, both the elected representatives, the "political class," and the bureaucrats waxed intolerant of individuals and associations who wished to take independent action, removed from the aegis of either administration or parliament. The decision-makers' aversion to a participatory political culture was deepened by the citizens' ingrained and "learned" incapacity for cooperation and participation. Hence there was in the end congruence between French society and its administrative style. Such congruence goes far to explain the singular success of French bureaucracy in the political system, as well as its shortcomings. A comparison of the pattern of French administration and of its success with that of other countries highlights not only a difference in techniques, in recruitment, and in style. It permits comparing different political cultures on an all-important level.[20]

There are between 3,000 and 10,000 high civil servants in France whose functions correspond by and large to those of the

[19] Crozier, *The Bureaucratic Phenomenon, op. cit.,* p. 308.
[20] The work by Ridley and Blondel, *op. cit.,* is implicitly comparative.

administrative class of the British civil service. (For the total number of civil servants, see Chap. IX.) Among the high civil servants a few hundred can be singled out as active and often daily participants in the process of political decision-making. In French they are sometimes called the *grands fonctionnaires,* while their next-ranking colleagues are merely high (*hauts*) administrators.

The selection of even the highest (as well as of the lowest) civil servants takes place by rigorous competitive entrance examinations, in which elaborate rites guard against all favoritism, and give the appearance of upholding the passion for equality. When Napoleon I founded the *École Polytechnique,* which still produces the top administrators with an engineering background, and when after the Second World War Michel Debré (who in 1959 was to become the first Prime Minister of the Fifth Republic), established the *École Nationale d'Administration,* the training ground of most of the other prestige corps of the bureaucracy, they both wanted to open the civil service to "talent," whatever its economic standing or family background. In 1945, the demands for infusing the political and administrative elites with new blood had been particularly strident. In order to democratize the ranks of the high civil service, it seemed opportune to break the *de facto* monopoly which the *École Libre des Sciences Politiques* had held over the preparation for entrance examinations to the top positions. That school, founded in 1871, in the aftermath of another floundering political regime, recruited its successful students almost entirely from among the uppermost Parisian bourgeoisie, with an admixture of aristocratic elements. This led to a recruitment for the top level of the bureaucracy which was vastly different from that of the American civil service. By and large it can be said that even today in the United States the bureaucracy, both federal and state, represents a cross section of society and is therefore likely to reflect its values. This never has been the case in France. In order to democratize recruitment without abandoning the customary high standards of performance, the new School of Administration (known as the E.N.A.) was to open its training facilities not only to all qualified students, but in equal number to those already serving in the less exalted echelons of the civil service. By their admission to the school they could prepare for advancement to the apex of the bureaucratic pyramid.

Undoubtedly the new school has had some impact on administrative developments.[21] But as an instrument of social promotion it has largely failed. Today, between 60 and 65 per cent of the school's trainees and 68 per cent of the most successful among them are the children of high civil servants or come from families with a professional or managerial background (a group which in the total population amounts to 3.1 per cent). The middle and lower middle classes furnish less than another third — a slow increase in their number is the only transformation that has taken place. Farmers and working-class families are hardly represented at all. During a four-year period (1961-64) there were on the average one student from a working-class background and three from farmers' families in a class of about 85 graduates a year.[22] Most striking is the fact that the number of candidates from inside the civil service has constantly declined. Moreover, many of those who now enter in this way usually stem from almost the same milieu as the other trainees. The predominance of candidates of Parisian origin has somewhat diminished. But 93 per cent of the students admitted in a recent year had previously attended the Paris School of Political Science, and that school enrolls once again more upper middle class students than it did in the immediate postwar years.

If the social composition of the student body preparing for the highest administrative positions at the E. N. A. is even more "upper-class" than that of the rest of the student population, this is due only to a small extent to the absence of a solid

---

[21] A good if incomplete analysis of the E.N.A. is provided by François Gazier, "The National School of Administration: Semblance and Reality," *International Review of Administrative Sciences,* XXXI:1, 1965, pp. 31–34; VIII–IX.

[22] The interesting comparative table established by V. Subramaniam in "Representative Bureaucracy: A Reassessment," *American Political Science Review,* LXI:4 (1967), p. 1016, shows that the social origin of high civil servants in France is far different from that found in developed Western democracies, but resembles that of Turkey and India. Slightly differing data are provided by Girard, *op. cit.,* p. 308; Club Jean Moulin, *L'État et le citoyen* (Paris: Seuil, 1961), p. 138; and the very informative article by F. F. Ridley, "French Technocracy and Comparative Government," *Political Studies,* XIV:1 (1966), pp. 34 ff.

system of grants and fellowships. Far more important is the fact that the entrance examinations like most other academic tests in France put a far higher premium on traditional knowledge, elegance of exposition, familiarity with and adjustment to the dominant humanistic culture, than on original thinking and on "raw" native ability.

The one, possibly significant, change which has occurred in recent years is the decrease in the number of candidates by one-third for the same number of openings in the administration. Such decline in interest is generally taken as an indication that the milieu from which the aspirants to these positions have come no longer values the *mandarinat,* as the top level of the bureaucracy is significantly called, as highly as it did in the era of a stagnant economy.

Since its establishment, the E. N. A. has furnished some 1,800 men and a few women to the highest echelons of the bureaucracy. Others in this category have, as before, come from the renowned *Grandes Écoles,* such as the *École Polytechnique,* the School of Agronomy, etc., which prepare the state engineers in various specializations not only for technical but also for leading administrative careers. The most brilliant of the state engineers exercise controlling functions in the manifold nationalized enterprises. Many others change relatively early to positions in private industry. The phenomenon of transferring from public to private employment (in administrative circles called *pantouflage* — one puts on the "soft slippers" of jobs outside the civil service) has traditionally deprived the French civil service of some of its best and most experienced personnel. For about a decade it was relatively rare among the graduates of the E.N.A. but is now again practiced widely.

More than 40 per cent of those who have graduated from the E.N.A. are attached to and dominate the services of the Ministry of Finance and Economic Affairs, 20 per cent are in the Foreign Service. Among the latter and among other graduates who are distributed over many administrations, a sizable number is concerned with economic matters.[23] Whether this indicates that the

---

[23] See the comprehensive account in Jean-François Kesler, "Les Anciens Élèves de l'École Nationale d'Administration," *RFSP,* XIV:2 (1964), pp. 258 and *passim;* and the same author's "L'Influence de l'École Nationale d'Administration sur la rénovation de l'administration et ses limites," in *Tendances et Volontés, op. cit.,* pp. 257–67.

new School and the training it affords furnishes the bureaucracy, and thereby society at large, with something like a "freemasonry" specializing in economic change and modernization is a highly controversial question. Their common training and especially a common and acute feeling of superiority provides for all E.N.A. graduates a bond of which the publications of their alumni association are one expression. But the traditional particularism which has divided the high bureaucracy and has created elites within the administrative elite has in no way been overcome.

Besides the Foreign Service, the *Corps* of the Inspectors of Finance, of the Council of State, and of the Court of Accounts offer the most coveted civil service positions to the few hundred who have graduated at the top of their classes.[24] Even during their training period there develops an intense rivalry between members of the same class, which might be normal under extremely competitive conditions, but which also develops a stark snobbery among those who have reason to believe that they will end up in exalted positions. Their classmates will often be assigned to the less "noble" administrations, for ministries are invariably graded according to the quality of their services and their personnel. Sometimes graduates who are not members of the elite corps are recruited for a highly rated administration, but theirs may be a routine function which makes little use of their previous training and intellectual ability. Little by little their identification with the ministries to which they are assigned tends to outweigh their affinity to their fellow-graduates of the E.N.A. About two-thirds of the graduates fill the ranks of the so-called "civil administrators." It was hoped that these men would provide greater mobility and freedom from the sometimes pronounced snobbery to the upper strata of the administration. But it appears that they are known mostly by a low morale, since they do not feel that their talents and their training are used adequately. Typically, the low-prestige administrations (among them the Ministries of Agriculture, of Public Health, and of National Education) recruit their top personnel from graduates with a middle-class background rather than from the ranks of the high bourgeoisie.

[24] Prior to the establishment of the E.N.A., candidates for the *Grands Corps* prepared individually for exacting entrance examinations, different for each *Corps.* Of late the Foreign Service has become a less coveted career than the *Corps,* probably a reflection of the country's diminished position in international affairs.

By contrast, the members of the *Grands Corps* are ubiquitous and mobile. Considered the reservoir for highest talent, they serve not only the administrations to which they are formally attached, but are sent on a virtually unlimited number of exacting assignments. They occupy top positions — the coveted places of *directeur* — in the important ministries. They frequently head up the personal staff of a Minister or of the President of the Republic (on the overall functions of these staffs or *cabinets* see Chap. IX). They are in charge of the numerous interministerial committees entrusted with laying the groundwork for the preparation of important decisions. Though they do not always have direct control over decision-making, they consider themselves, and with much justification, the "intellectuals" in the administrative machinery.

If the members of the *Grands Corps* are a somewhat self-conscious caste within the larger group of the high civil servants, the different *corps* are also divided among themselves. Every *corps* is both a fortress and a prison for its members whose rivalries and controversies stem from a different perspective on what needs to be done. Here decisions are fought over in a passionate and often almost chauvinistic style. This kind of particularism tends to interfere with overall effectiveness and adds instability to the system. Contrary to original expectations, the common training at the E.N.A. has been unable to overcome either the particularism which separates the *corps* from each other, nor the sort of "feudalism" which divides them from the rest of the administrative class (in the British sense of the word). In many situations, and especially in times of crisis, the *Grands Corps,* together with certain other top civil servants, have provided the personalities that are capable of imposing the necessary reforms on the administration. They have become the agents of change for the entire system.[25] Hence their mentality and the way in which they view their own role in the process of change need to be considered here.

The education and training which future high civil servants receive both before and after their admission to the E.N.A. is in many ways different from that of prewar times. Many still earn a law degree, but there is in their course of study less emphasis on the formalities of civil law. Although, according to the opinion of many

[25] See, also for what follows, Crozier, *The Bureaucratic Phenomenon,* pp. 197, 309. But see also his more recent article, quoted below n. 32.

close observers, training in economic science is still inferior to that afforded in Great Britain and the United States, the principles and refinements of Keynesian economics occupy more time than previously and less attention is given to a more narrowly circumscribed fiscal and accountant's knowledge. The hold which the tenets of economic laissez-faire once had has given way, as has much of the passion for system-building based on abstractions. The discourse between instructors and trainees and among the trainees themselves is pragmatic and deliberately unideological. A modified case method and an attempt to provide an integrated social science knowledge are characteristics of the instruction. While the training shies away from providing much "administrative science," it includes a good deal of administrative practice. Altogether, it is probably true to say that it is now more managerial and less upper class.[26] Much of this is new and, in the opinion of old practitioners, adds significantly to the abilities which their future colleagues must demonstrate before gaining admission to the E.N.A.

Other aspects of training and mentality remain more traditional. They characteristically correspond to the values of the rather homogeneous milieu from which the top civil servants and the members of the examining boards are recruited. The brilliant and well balanced exposé, product of that "solitary preparation for mastery" which has been described earlier as an educational ideal (see Chap. III), often hides the fact that the trainees are insufficiently informed about available alternatives for action. The abstract cult of humanist values is seldom matched by a sensitivity for human relations, so that the civil servant is oftentimes an inept interlocutor of his partners outside the bureaucratic universe. An exclusive commitment to economic and administrative efficiency might lead to unjust solutions. If the administrator has confidence in what he calls the scientific approach, his confidence is frequently based less on technical knowledge than on logical analysis.

Criticism of the school's curriculum and of the mentality it produces have led to searching investigations of its future. A committee investigating the problems involved in the training of the administrative elite has proposed a series of partial reforms, all

[26] See Ridley, *op. cit.*, p. 38, and T. B. Bottomore, *Elites and Society* (London: C. A. Watts and Co., Ltd., 1964), p. 82.

designed to bring the candidates into closer touch with the realities and the tensions in the society surrounding them. But the committee also concluded that only the thorough overhauling of the system of higher education as well as of administration would be able to get at the roots of the deficiencies for which the E.N.A. has often been made responsible.[27] The particularism of its graduates appears unavoidable in an administrative system that continuously reproduces the divisions created by divergent functions and by an exaggerated centralization.

The ethos of the top-ranking bureaucrat has always included the strong conviction that he is the principal if not the sole defender of the public interest. One aspect of this ethos is the absence of corruption. There are hardly any scandals involving the financial integrity of a high civil servant. But, on the other hand, he might easily believe that he alone is virtuous. His latent or open hostility towards parliament might not be more virulent than that of the ordinary citizen, but it is more focused. He resents parliamentary institutions and their personnel as disintegrating forces because, under the assault of special interest and of particularism, they are apt to dismantle the reform proposals hatched in the administrative bureaus. In the eyes of the bureaucracy, the intermediaries between the state and society become the enemies of a rational society. Administrative centralization, even if excessive, is regarded as a necessity since only at the top can enough sense of the public interest be generated to resist successfully arbitrariness and the pressure for privilege. An intended, if seldom achieved, remoteness from such pressures has given to the bureaucrats a somewhat abstract perception of a mission entrusted to them by the state, rather than the feeling of being the servants of a concrete community. Planning and "prospecting" for 1985 they are sometimes apt to overlook the needs and troubles of their contemporaries.

For all his desire to see problems of public policy taken out of the realm of "politics," the French public servant is frequently politically less neutral than his British colleague. The "colonization" of certain ministries by political parties which occurred after the Liberation was a short-lived phenomenon. With the advent of

---

[27] See François Bloch-Lainé, "Réflexions sur l'avenir de l'E. N. A.," *Preuves* (1st Trim., 1970), pp. 113–20.

the Fifth Republic, no large-scale takeover of the administration by proven Gaullists has taken place. But past and present civil servants have run for elective office and have identified themselves with certain outstanding politicians without being prevented from resuming afterwards their administrative careers. It has been said with some justification that in both the Fourth and the Fifth Republics the most promising students at the E.N.A. considered their training a preparation for high political posts, including that of Prime Minister, rather than for a purely administrative career.

It has also frequently been assumed that the Fifth Republic with its frank emphasis on the prestige and procedures of the administrative state would promote the image of the high bureaucracy as a powerful and self-sufficient caste. Certainly, many of the pronouncements of one of the most articulate spokesmen of the regime, Michel Debré, have exalted technical expertise and depreciated politics. They betray a mentality reminiscent of Claude-Henri Saint-Simon, would-be reformer of the carly nineteenth century, who has long been the apostle of many civil servants. Debré himself, before entering politics, belonged to the *Corps* of the Council of State, as did the socialist leader Léon Blum. Both the last Prime Minister under de Gaulle (M. Couve de Murville) and the first under Pompidou (M. Chaban-Delmas) belong to that most illustrious *Corps* of them all, the Inspectorate of Finance.

Yet, if it has amplified existing tendencies, the new republic has hardly made the high bureaucracy into an autonomous and unified technocracy. The fragmentation of the top civil service into splinter bureaucracies, described previously, is only one reason why diversity rather than uniformity has prevailed. The great problems which the national collectivity had and continues to face (the Algerian problem and decolonization; European integration; foreign and defense policies; desirable priorities in economic and social policies) have divided the bureaucracy as they have other elites. Before long, seemingly technical conflicts turn into political disagreements, themselves the result of polarizations concerning fundamentals or personalities. The greater pragmatism that prevails generally has in fact led many civil servants to take a less exalted view of their role as infallible arbiters. In their contacts with interest groups they seeks to conform to a new image of a representative bureaucracy which reflects better than hitherto the society within which they act.[28] What emerges is a managerial elite which tends to assume leading positions in the state and, after their *pantouflage,* in the economy as well, but certainly not a unified technocracy.

Whereas in other countries the administration frequently reacts to innovating impulses originating elsewhere,[29] the French bureaucracy continues to be the main originator of innovation. A close and astute observer of the administrative scene in France has distinguished two different role conceptions which prevail among present-day civil servants. One group firmly believes that the state and its administrative machinery should bring about, by persuasion if possible, by force if necessary, needed structural reforms. "The state can do everything it wants to do," they argue — it can overcome all obstacles that stand in the way of progress. Many of them are almost fanatic about "prospective" thinking: long-range vision and planning appear as remedies for all temporary setbacks. A second group sees as its foremost mission the protection of the equilibrium between contending forces and values. While they are in no way averse to progress, they are anxious to see the necessary mutations proceed in orderly fashion. At all times the state must be able to control the forces which the dynamics of group pressure might let loose.

Both groups are distributed, even though not evenly, throughout all the administrative *corps* and are represented among different age groups in the administration. What they have in common is a decidedly apolitical bent. "For one group among the highest civil servants, the state is the carrier of progress, for the other an important arbiter, but in the eyes of both the state is authoritarian and paternal and free from all political ferment." [30]

Whatever their personal outlook, the traditional structures within which bureaucrats have to operate and the administrative style which emphasizes impersonal and hierarchical relations often

[28] For details, see Henry W. Ehrmann, "French Bureaucracy and Organized Interests." *Administrative Science Quarterly,* V:4 (1961), pp. 534–55, and "Bureaucracy and Interest Groups in the Decision-Making Process of the Fifth Republic," *Faktoren der politischen Entscheidung, Festgabe für Ernst Fraenkel* (Berlin: Gruyter, 1963), pp. 273–93.

[29] See Almond and Powell, *op. cit.,* p. 158.

[30] Bernard Gournay, "Un Groupe Dirigeant de la société française: les grands fonctionnaires," *RFSP,* XIV:2 (1964), pp. 229–31. The entire article deserves close study.

impede the role of the bureaucrats as agents of change; a role both self-assigned and publicly imposed. Because of the high degree of centralization general policy making continues to be characterized by a constant transfer of decision-making to the highest administrative echelons. Control of all operations, large and small, and especially of the overall budget by the Ministry of Finance, is particularly cumbersome and throttles initiative. While the Ministry is generally known, from the geographical location of its headquarters, as the *Rue de Rivoli,* its agents are practically the masters of all administrations in the capital as well as the provinces.[31]

It is significant that a growing number of civil servants admittedly are losing faith in the classical French bureaucratic model. They are conscious that their knowledge of economics, domestic and international, and their insight into human and group relationships are far greater than that of their predecessors. But they are dubious as to whether such knowledge can really be made fruitful as long as the old style prevails and excessive compartmentalization is continued.

Typically, the complaints about the structure and the working methods of the bureaucracy have become more strident ever since the explosions of May 1968 expressed the need for drastic reforms of French society. These voices warn that as long as the administrative elite remains divided and isolated ("It governs but it governs a desert," one of its most qualified observers has concluded),[32] it will also remain impotent to effect the indispensable changes. From inside and outside the administration the present stage of administrative decision-making is described despairingly as sheer "anarchy" or as "leading to the destruction of the state." [33]

Inasmuch as French judges are without exception civil servants,

[31] See the informative book by Gabriel Mignot and Philippe d'Orsay, *La Machine Administrative* (Paris: Editions du Seuil, 1968), esp. pp. 103 ff.

[32] Michael Crozier, "Pourquoi la France est bloquée," *L'Express* (May 4–10, 1970). See also the same author's *La Société Bloquée* (Paris: Éditions du Seuil, 1970). In his earlier writings the author had been more optimistic about the self-regeneration of the bureaucracy by the methods which the Planning Office and some others had developed.

[33] Typical is a special issue on administrative problems of the respected magazine *Esprit,* XXXVIII:1 (1970) where (on 200 pages!) a variety of writers, among them highly placed administrators and judges, discuss the crisis of the system.

their role and outlook should be considered here briefly. Training, mentality, and again tradition isolate them to a high degree from the political milieu, including the local politicians, from the business world, and even from administrative circles. A recently established National Center of Juridical Studies, fashioned somewhat after the E.N.A. and preparing law school graduates for positions in the higher judicial echelons, may help in bringing judges closer to present-day problems. Traditionally, a strong adherence to legalism meant that adjudication, as the judges see it, should be based exclusively on legislative texts and on other statutory enactments. There is supposedly little, if any, room for considering the intentions of the legislators, the social context, or immutable or changing principles. Nonetheless, like any judiciary, the French judges by the decisions they render cannot help playing a political role. "Judges are not 'sold to the bourgeoisie,'" a high judge, writing anonymously, has stated, "they are part and parcel of it." [34] But their role is far more *sub rosa* than elsewhere, with the possible exception of the administrative judges who by training and prestige are closer to the high bureaucracy than are the judges sitting on civil or criminal courts. The latters' appointments and promotions are seemingly safeguarded from political influence by constitutional guarantees (see Title VIII of the constitution) and by appropriate legislation. Yet to give judgments "in conformity" with those placed higher up in the judicial hierarchy and to "obey without receiving orders" is described by the judge, already quoted, as a fairly common attitude at least of those hoping for promotion. [35]

In the past, the higher ranks of the judiciary came usually from the same social milieu as top civil servants. The main difference was regional: together with the upper bourgeoisie of the capital,

---

[34] Casamayor, *Les Juges* (Paris: Éditions du Seuil, 1959), p. 143. For interesting details on the relationship between political authority and the judiciary see Georges Lavau, "Le Juge et le pouvoir politique," in Louis Trotabas (ed.), *La Justice* (Paris: Presses Universitaires, 1961), pp. 59 ff.

[35] Casamayor, "Justice et politique" *La Nef*, XXVII: 39 (1970), pp. 35 ff. Everybody in Paris knows who the judge is who "hides" behind the pseudonym of a vehement critic of the judicial system without incurring sanctions. This of course is in itself a tribute to the survival of French liberal traditions and to the independence of the judiciary. The entire issue of *La Nef* is devoted to a serious discussion of the judiciary and the problems of judicial reform.

a few other urban centers — mostly south of the Loire River and often situated in regions of mediocre economic development — contributed to judicial recruitment. A slow but fairly steady lowering of prestige has resulted in a greater number of high judges from the middle classes and, above all, in the "feminization" of the profession. Today about two-thirds of the Paris candidates for judicial posts are women.

Such a development is due, at least in part, to the utter impoverishment of the judicial apparatus. The number of judges today is lower than before the First World War and equals about that of a century and a half ago. Many judges hold forth in crowded and partly dilapidated buildings and amidst antiquated equipment. Delays and insufficient time for orderly proceedings are common complaints. The environment in which they have to work is necessarily cramping the style of all except the highest judges.

It is quite characteristic that for years the professional journals of the judiciary were full of complaints about the career chances and working conditions of the judges and critical of their place in society. But, especially in comparison with the higher bureaucracy, the will for change was slow in emerging. The Events of May 1968 have altered this too. Almost one-third of the judges throughout the country have joined an active organization which hammers at the doors of the Ministry of Justice to obtain at least a minimum of overdue reforms.[36]

[36] See Louis Joinet, "L'Avenir du syndicalisme judiciaire," *ibid.,* pp. 117–28.

CHAPTER VII

Interests—Secured and Frustrated

INTEREST REPRESENTATION IN
A FRAGMENTED SOCIETY

In every polity means exist to bring the demands and desires prevalent in the society to the attention of the decision-makers.[1] In France, as elsewhere, this function is served by a variety of structures. As in all modern states, the associational interest or pressure groups which specialize in the articulation of values and interests through a more or less permanent organization, occupy the foreground of the political stage. But other structures have by no means lost all importance. What have been called nonassociational groups, distinguished families, local or regional notables, prominent religious leaders, and especially the modern business firms or "industrial empires," exercise in France an influence which, although it is intermittent, often outweighs that of trade associations, trade unions, or other groups. In addition, interests are generated and articulated within governmental structures themselves. In France, the bureaucracy, both civil and military, does not simply react to pressures from the outside; its cleavages and the frequent absence of political directives have made it quite frequently into an autonomous force of interest representation.

For a truly realistic appraisal of the role of groups in the policy process one must investigate the actual and relative influence of

[1] See Almond and Powell, *op. cit.*, pp. 73 f. The discussion that follows adopts the framework established by these authors in Chap. IV of their book.

the various organized and unorganized interests, the effectiveness of alliances and the impact of countervailing forces, both organizational and ideological.[2] Interest articulation by associational and nonassociational groups takes place at the boundary line between society and the political system. It is, therefore, entirely embedded in the political culture of the country. The political culture described in previous chapters, shapes, limits, and guides the pattern of group demands and activities. In turn, the groups influence the political culture in its evolution.

Discussions about the legitimacy of group activities do not only reflect constitutional and philosophical traditions. They are also determined by past experiences. Frequently, and not without reason, organized interests in France are held responsible for the fact that a society with egalitarian traditions has so often reproduced and aggravated existing inequalities. In other countries too the defense of the *status quo* might be the dominant concern of interest groups. But in the stalemate society that France has been for so long, such a position has had a special significance for retarding economic, social, and political development. Moreover, the ideological fragmentation of political life has determined the way in which demands are formulated and interest groups are organized. Once formed, the groups have done much to harden ideological divisions.

". . . if the general will is to be able to express itself, it is essential that there should be no partial society within the State and that each citizen should think only his own thought." This categorical condemnation by Rousseau of all intermediate groups has occupied an important place in French political theory and has been a factor in shaping legislation for more than a century. The individualism it expresses was shared by most of the philosophers of the French Enlightenment and fed on the observation of oppressive guild practices under the *Ancien Régime*. This attitude triumphed in the legislative enactments of the Revolution, especially the famous Le Chapelier law which outlawed all associations. The statute was rescinded only after more than a century (by a law in

[2] This point is made by Roy C. Macridis, "Interest Groups in Comparative Analysis," *The Journal of Politics*, XXII:1 (1961), pp. 25–45, and particularly in regard to the French situation by Jean Meynaud, *Nouvelles Études sur les groupes de pression en France* (Paris: Colin, 1962), pp. 384 ff. — an indispensable work for the student of French interest groups.

1901), and even then with some reservations. However, the legal obstacles were frequently ignored; many categories of Frenchmen did not wait for the change in legislation to form groups and to constitute in fact the "partial societies" condemned by Rousseau.[3] But the necessity of achieving this by subterfuge was nevertheless bound to shape group practice and to spread doubts about the legitimacy of group activities.

Groups which seek to influence political decisions continue to incur public opprobrium. An outstanding public lawyer, member of the Council of State who became a cabinet member in the Fifth Republic, has not long ago characterized interest representation of whatever kind as a violation of the "still valid principles of 1789." [4] Until a few years ago, "pressure groups" (*groupes de pression*) and "lobbies" were political scare words, partly because public attention was focused on the showy activities of disreputable or unpopular groups. The first "modern" lobby in France, made up of many kinds of organizations and manipulating both parliament and bureaucracy almost at will, was the colonial lobby. Formed at the turn of the century, it was responsible for many of the colonial ventures of the Third Republic, and prolonged the costly wars of the Fourth. Other well-known lobbies were those of the munitions makers, the "merchants of death," and those of the interests which spread disease and vice by liquor or prostitution.

In reality, there has never been anything particularly scandalous about the defense of organized interests in France, nor has the pressure been truly irresistible. Indeed the structure and the organizational means of most associational interest groups are less solid than in many other countries. This is only partly caused by the legal and ideological obstacles that have been mentioned; more important is the general aversion to associational life (see Chap. III). In addition in a society which has never been as hierarchically organized as the state, industrialization was slow and the agricultural sector isolated — "Rather than a national market

---

[3] See Georges Lavau, "Political Pressures by Interest Groups in France," in Henry W. Ehrmann (ed.), *Interest Groups on Four Continents* (Pittsburgh: Pittsburgh University Press, 1958, 1964), p. 60.

[4] Bernard Chenot, *Organisation économique de l'État* (Paris: Dalloz, 1951), p. 184.

there was a conglomeration of small ones." [5] Accordingly, pressure groups were often more coherent on a local than on a national or regional scale. Yet their effectiveness on that level was limited by the centralization of governmental decision-making. This explains in part the difficulties encountered by interest confederations (the so-called *Spitzenverbände*), which in other countries have grouped quite effectively all of agriculture, labor, business, etc. These confederations must always mediate between and align for common action the naturally divergent interests of their member organizations. In France they have only been intermittently successful; even after organizational unity has been established, it is always likely to disintegrate again.

Weakness also results from the "cult of the small" which many groups, especially in business and farming, practice in order to establish their contested legitimacy. Internal cohesion must then be paid for by the defense of the least productive members and an alignment based on their requirements for survival. Moreover, the small and inefficient producers are usually most given to an "atomism" averse to all organization.

During the crisis-ridden last years of the Fourth Republic, the Union for the Defense of Shopkeepers and Artisans, launched by Pierre Poujade, mobilized the small businessmen threatened by the consequences of modernization and rationalization. Desirous as they were to resist authority, if need be by violence, they felt insufficiently protected by the existing interest groups, even though the latter were prepared to shield the marginal units in the economy. For a time Poujade succeeded in transforming the revolt of the injured interests into a political movement which won 2.5 million votes in the 1956 elections. But the eventual failure of this and other flash parties demonstrates that there are boundary lines which group activities cannot transgress without risk either to themselves or to the society in which they operate.[6]

In more normal times, actual membership in almost all associations amounts to only a fraction of potential membership. At present, trade unions organize at most 17-20 per cent of eligible wage

[5] See Hoffmann, in *In Search of France,* p. 11.
[6] For more details on the Poujade Movement, see H. W. Ehrmann, *Organized Business,* pp. 183 ff., and Stanley Hoffman, *Le Mouvement Poujade* (Paris: Colin, 1956).

earners, and probably as little as 15 per cent. Only 17 per cent of the young have joined youth organizations. A somewhat higher percentage of the farmers belong to one of the numerous agricultural interest groups. There never has been a steady, if slow, progression of membership. Many of the important groups have known a mass influx of new members at dramatic moments of the country's social or political history, such as at the time of the Popular Front victories or the post-Liberation era. But as soon as conditions become normal, "normal" individualism reasserts itself and leaves the associations with too small a membership to justify their claims of representativeness. The treasuries of many groups are often so depleted that they are unable to employ a competent staff. The modern pressure group official is a fairly recent phenomenon to be found only in certain sectors of the group system, such as business associations. The few organizations that count their members by the millions are likely to serve small interests or broad ideas: the home distillers of liquor, the friends or foes of the parochial schools, including the parent-teachers associations of the private and the public schools.

Political and ideological divisions add further to the fragmentation of group activities and augment the obstacles that stand in the way of effective articulation and defense of the interests. The trade-union movement and the agricultural organizations exemplify the difficulties which exist almost everywhere.

The French labor movement has never looked upon itself as an interest group "like the others," nor has it been regarded as such by outsiders.[7] Whatever their political or philosophical persuasion, all of the major labor confederations want to rebuild society and polity on new foundations. Their pervasive anticapitalism feeds on many sources (forcefully expressed in the preamble of their respective bylaws): on Marxist concepts of the class struggle, on Christian or personalist indignation about the iniquities of the existing system, and even on preindustrial reflexes and resentments.

Most European trade unions have aspired to combine demands

[7] For the French trade-union movement see Henry W. Ehrmann, *French Labor from Popular Front to Liberation* (New York: Oxford University Press, 1947); Val Lorwin, *The French Labor Movement* (Cambridge: Harvard University Press, 1954); and the up-to-date account on both labor and business organizations in Jean-Daniel Reynaud, *Les Syndicats en France* (Paris: Colin, 1963).

for the material betterment of their constituents with the fight for broader ideals of emancipation. But the heavy ideological baggage of French labor has encumbered normal trade-union activities. Not infrequently, ideological commitment appears to serve as a compensation for weakness of organization and for the ensuing ineffectiveness of a divided labor movement. One attacks the existing economic system when one is unable to obtain limited reforms. On the other hand, union members are well aware that such lasting reforms as have been obtained are either due to legislation or to the intervention of the labor inspectors, the administrative field representatives of the state. Hence the relationship between improvements and union activities, especially as carried on by union members, appears tenuous at best.

From its beginning, the labor movement has suffered from particularly extreme membership fluctuations. The largest confederation, the communist-controlled *Confédération Générale du Travail* (C.G.T.), admits that its membership has dwindled from more than 6 million in 1945–46 to 1.7 million members in 1961, and that the number of union locals has been about halved. That the C.G.T. still attracts the largest number of wage earners and especially of industrial workers is largely due to the same reasons that explain the continuing electoral strength of the Communist party (see Chap. VIII). But the C.G.T. has also fallen heir to the cherished traditions of the "heroic age" of French syndicalism. Its larger following and a capable staff enable it to provide the services which the membership expects.

Altogether it must be realized that membership figures published by labor are notoriously unreliable. In 1963 estimates of 800,000 for the C.G.T., 450,000 for the Catholic oriented *Confédération Française des Travailleurs Chrétiens* (C.F.T.C.), and at most 380,000 for the anticommunist *Force Ouvrière* (F.O.), appeared fairly realistic.[8] Since then there might have been a slight increase in the membership of the various organizations; their relative strength has remained about the same. But by now, most, though not all, of the unions formerly affiliated with the Catholic labor confederation have broken off and formed yet another organization, the *Confédération Française et Démocratique du Travail* (C.F.D.T.). From the outset they wished to

[8] Reynaud, *op. cit.,* p .127.

assert their complete independence from the Catholic outlook, yet rejected a fusion with the somewhat discredited F.O. In 1969, the C.F.D.T. declared its commitment to a staunchly anti-capitalist socialism, accepting the notion of class struggle as an ineluctable fact. Its unions prove attractive to young workers, especially since they took a more radical posture than other labor organizations during the Events of May-June 1968.

The competition between different and often antagonistic trade-union movements necessitates a special pattern of action. At places of work, this fragmentation leads to what is euphemistically called trade-union "pluralism." Such pluralism determines bargaining procedures, as well as the relationship between the unions, the authorities, and the political parties. Existing legislation sanctions the fact that the same group of wage earners might be represented by different organizations. While this eliminates certain kinds of jurisdictional disputes, it also impairs the representativeness of the multiple trade-union movements.

A corresponding and long-standing division between agricultural organizations was more clearly political, although ideological overtones were not absent. Towards the end of the Second Empire, conservative and Catholic elements had formed one organization of farmers, including the large estate owners; after the establishment of the Third Republic, freemasons and republicans founded another. For a time both associations recruited in those regions to which they were politically attuned, both establishing credit institutions, insurance companies, producer- and consumer-cooperatives. For a time both had access to the Ministry of Agriculture, but when the Ministry came under the all but permanent control of radical-socialist ministers, the freethinkers were given a decided edge over their competitors. In addition, there also existed socialist and communist farming organizations and the fascist oriented "Green Shirts."

After the Second World War, it seemed for a moment that the time had come to form a large confederation grouping all rural interests. Founded upon the aspiration of a socialist Minister of Agriculture who hoped to emulate Vichy's peasant corporation in a climate of freedom, the confederation claimed to group 80 per cent of those eligible. But before long subsidiary groups reasserted their autonomy and the peak association lost all importance.

Some of the earlier political differences have been overcome. But the diversity of interests, the individualism and occasionally the sectarianism of their constituents explain the existence of close to five hundred rural defense organizations on the national level alone. This is an expensive structure, made possible only because many of the groups live in one way or the other on public subsidies.

The most prominent rural defense organization is now the *Fédération Nationale des Syndicats d'Exploitants Agricoles* (F.N.S.E.A.). While politically neutral, it is frequently shaken by internal controversies about the proper future course of agricultural development. By and large its rejuvenated leadership accepts the necessity of thoroughgoing structural changes for French agriculture and the reforms initiated by the governments of the Fifth Republic. But there has grown up on its left another farmers' organization, the so-called M.O.D.E.F., which capitalizes on the grievances of the smallest family farms. It is openly inspired by the Communist party and pursues a fairly demagogic line of anticapitalism and simultaneous defense of property owners, bitterly opposing the exodus from the countryside. Starting its efforts in the most backward agricultural regions, it has of late spread elsewhere and is holding now close to one third of the seats in the semiofficial Chambers of Agriculture.[9]

Within several interest groups young members form an organization apart. But, characteristically, this is not primarily a functional division, catering to the special needs of an age group, but rather another ideological alignment. The best known among these groups are the Young Farmers and the Young Employers. They attempt to elaborate a well-defined doctrine about new forms of capitalist enterprise and competition or about rural organization. The thinking of their most active members, like that of some of the leaders in the Christian trade-union move-

[9] On the M.O.D.E.F., see "Le Mouvement de coordination et de défenses des exploitations agricoles familiales," *RFSP,* XVIII:3 (1968), pp. 542–563. For a good account of present-day agricultural interest organization, see Yves Tavernier, "Le Syndicalisme Paysan et la Cinquième République," *ibid,* XVI:5 (1966), pp. 869–912, and Claude Servolin and Yves Tavernier, "La France. Réforme de structures ou politique des prix?" in H. Mendras et Y. Tavernier, *op. cit.,* esp. pp. 68–216.

ment, has often been stimulated by an updated and dynamic social Catholicism (see also Chap. III). Inside the larger interest organizations the activities of these groups meet with varied fates. Sometimes they are resented because their ideological commitment creates additional conflicts. Prominent members of the *Jeunes Agriculteurs* have won leadership positions in the F.N.S.E.A. and are now accused both from inside the organization and from without of having become too moderate. The *Jeunes Patrons* have withdrawn from the representative and exceptionally well-staffed confederation, the *Conseil National du Patronat Français* (C.N.P.F.). But under a new leadership, the C.N.P.F. itself proceeded (it is true not for the first time in its history) to an overhauling of its structure and pledged its total commitment to an accelerated industrialization of the country.[10]

In all countries there is usually some overlapping between groups organizing the special interests of the various economic and social sections into which the population is divided and those groups promoting shared attitudes and common causes. But in France the mixing of both in the same organization has been carried very far, and such fusion has given special characteristics to the defense of all interests.

In addition to management, labor, and agriculture also such interest organizations as the students' associations, the ex-servicemen's, pensioners, and taxpayers' groups are riddled by ideological and political dissensions. The result is a form of interest articulation which is frequently far less satisfactory than one which is primarily pragmatic and instrumental.[11]

Given the ideological style of the country's political culture, it is not astonishing that there is a luxuriant growth of groups devoted solely to the promotion of causes. Some of them, such as the League for the Rights of Men, are centuries old. As already mentioned, the vigorous associations which, since the beginning of the Third Republic, are aligned on the issue of public versus parochial education are still able to mobilize mass support. Other groups spring up and disappear in major or minor crisis situations. At times their impact on public opinion has been consider

---

[10] For details, see, CNPF, *Patronat,* No. 300 (Nov.-Dec., 1969).

[11] Almond and Powell, *op. cit.,* p. 89, point to the special difficultie that arise from this form of interest articulation.

able; their emotional appeal is well-suited for many audiences. Since many of them demand only a temporary commitment, they rarely need the permanent and qualified staff which only few French interest groups can assemble. On the other hand, civic groups demanding a sustained, cooperative effort from their members have only lately acquired prestige.

It has often been observed, in the United States and elsewhere, that multiple group membership has a moderating influence on the articulation and defense of interests. The leaders of one association have to take some account of the fact that their proposals must be acceptable to members who also belong to other groups.[12] No exact data are available on this phenomenon in France. However, there is evidence that in spite of the lower density of associational life multiple and overlapping membership in interest groups is a fairly frequent occurrence. But in France it appears that this escalates rather than moderates demands. For those who belong to different groups usually are also aligned in each of them with a definite ideological, political, or religious persuasion. Whether acting as parent, wage earner, or veteran, they will defend in each of their associations the ideals of the "spiritual family" with which they identify. This makes for more stubbornness and rigidity on the part of the membership and hence of the interest groups to which they belong.

In addition to the modern associational interest group more traditional structures, such as notables of all kinds, are still playing an important role in the articulation and defense of interests. In the past, the "bourgeois dynasties" (as leading families in business and banking used to be called), imposed their advice on the public authorities, controlled elections, and, if necessary, instigated and led revolts. Even today, some of the most important firms pay little attention to their own trade associations. Since they have direct and satisfactory access to the centers of decision-making, they consider the cumbersome associational groups as an unnecessary concession to democracy. The moral, and sometimes political, influence of church leaders is exercised quite regularly outside the channels of the numerous organizations animated and controlled by the Catholic hierarchy. In rural regions, the mayors

[12] See David Truman, *The Governmental Process* (New York: Knopf, 1951), pp. 509 ff.

and other local officials derive their influence from their status as holders of official positions rather than from the associations to which they might belong.

MEANS OF ACCESS AND STYLES OF ACTION

Interest groups are active in all the arenas from which authoritative decisions can be influenced: in the electoral process and in parliament; through contacts with the political executive and with members of the bureaucracy, and through those media which allow them to put their case before the general public or more specialized audiences.[13] By comparison with interest groups in other countries, the majority of the French groups appears less attuned to the intensive use of propaganda and of public relations. With some significant exceptions, few sectional interest groups will use the information media for broad-gauge appeals; cause groups have seldom the means to do so. In part such reluctance stems from the described uncertainties about the legitimacy of group activities. Organized business, for instance, has shunned for a long time all endeavors to create a public image of the community it represents. Partly this was due to the traditional secretiveness of the French businessman, partly to the conviction that, since France has become a business civilization only of late, the accomplishments of business and of its associations would hardly be appreciated by the public.

The setting of parliamentary and local elections have encouraged strenuous group activity during every campaign. The smallness of the constituency under most of the electoral systems that have been used, the personalized relationship between representatives and electorate and, most of all, the flabbiness of party organization and discipline have at all times driven the groups to appeal directly to the candidate. Before the election, groups rather than individual voters put their demands to him. He was requested to pledge, often "on the dotted line," to defend the groups' concerns. His answers to such requests, whether positive or negative, was published in the newsletter which the group circulated among its membership. A candidate who in the first

[13] For a general overview of group activities see Henry W. Ehrmann, "Pressure Groups in France," *Annals of the American Academy of Political and Social Science*, CCCXIX (1958), pp. 148 ff.

ballot had to face several competitors and could at best be elected by only a small margin of votes felt inclined to submit to such pressures. Even if he were not to honor his promises once he was elected, the din of organized groups during the campaign often deafened the candidate's political ears and prevented him from discussing larger issues. In this respect, however, the groups did little more than reinforce the traditional style of atomistic representation.

The role which groups played in financing election campaigns (and thereby in the selection of candidates) was admittedly important but also obscure, except for some widely publicized "scandals." [14] Candidates who obtained a stipulated minimum percentage of the total vote in their constituency were and continue to be reimbursed by the government for certain specific campaign expenses. There is, however, no provision for the high costs of modern campaigning; control of total expenditures has always been lax and could easily be circumvented. In the absence of well-filled party treasuries, many candidates simply had to rely on group support which was likely to limit their freedom of action more than the mere signing of pledges.

In the Fifth Republic the scenario has not changed essentially. During election campaigns, groups still appeal to the candidates, and the candidates show deference or independence according to their temperament and lights. Although party discipline in the Gaullist party is strict, its candidates are nonetheless encouraged by the party leadership to seek communication with and support from organized interests as a means of sinking stronger roots in their constituencies. For similar reasons, many candidates of the opposition continue to cultivate group contacts.

The example of Switzerland and of the American states shows that organized interests are able to play a prominent role also in a referendum campaign. But when the consultation of the electorate by referendum takes on a plebiscitarian character, as it did in France after 1958, groups judged it the better part of wisdom not to take sides in a political contest. The groups formed to "Keep Algeria French" went down to resounding defeats in two of the verdicts of the electorate. Significantly enough this neu-

---

[14] For details on some of them, see H. W. Ehrmann, *Organized Business,* pp. 219 ff.

trality of interest groups during referendum campaigns changed with the consultation organized in 1969. As explained previously (see Chap. IV), the proposed reforms could be assessed independently from the plebiscitarian appeal General de Gaulle chose to give them. Therefore, interest groups came out for or against the referendum according to the possible consequences of the legislation for their clientele. In addition, new groups sprung up to either support or to help defeat the proposals.[15]

Most interest groups also shunned an all too open participation in the presidential elections of 1965, when General de Gaulle was the favored candidate. It has remained controversial whether the pronounced coolness of the largest farmer organization, the F.N.S.E.A., towards the incumbent was one of the factors that forced de Gaulle into run-off elections which he considered humiliating. In the 1969 elections all of the candidates courted the major (and some minor) interest groups in ways not very different from those of any candidate for parliament.[16] In return at least some of the groups openly declared their preference for one of the candidates over his competitors.

In preceding regimes organized interests found parliament the most convenient channel for access to political power. When he wanted to inaugurate a policy of free trade, Napoleon III felt compelled to divest the elected representatives of all influence in the setting of tariffs since parliament was all too inclined to give in to the protectionist wishes of business. In the Third and Fourth Republics the highly specialized and powerful committees of both houses of parliament became often little more than institutional façades for pressure groups.[17] Open committee hearings, as they take place in Congress, were unknown. Instead, "study groups" brought deputies and group representatives together behind closed doors but in the very halls of the National Assembly. Under the influence of groups desiring to profit from their electoral support, deputies, irrespective of party affiliation, joined "friendly societies" (*amicales*) expressly formed to discuss the concerns of various lobbies. For the associations and their leadership the *amicales* became convenient "super-parties." Quite frequently,

---

[15] For details, see Hayward, *op. cit.*, pp. 292 ff.
[16] Details are given in Schwartzenberg, *op. cit.*, pp. 174–185.
[17] See Williams, *Crisis*, pp. 374–77.

by means of the *amicales,* groups were able to substitute bills of their own design for those submitted by the government. There have also been episodes when at the moment of important votes lobbyists filled the galleries of parliament in order to remind the people's representatives of the obligations they had incurred.

All this added to the climate of confusion and irresponsibility. There was no clear boundary line between the function of interest groups and that of parties. It seems, however, that more often than not the actual impact of the penetration by the groups into the parliamentary arena was more apparent than real. Many of the bills and amendments which deputies moved on behalf of the lobbies lost out because of the general inefficiency of parliamentary proceedings. While in the election campaigns the absence of a valid party system increased the leverage of the groups, the situation was to some extent reversed in parliament. Since parties did not provide a shield behind which the deputies could transact business on behalf of groups, the identification of individual representatives as spokesmen for special interests was generally easy to make and became soon detrimental to their effectiveness. Some carefully concerted but discrediting lobbying by powerful groups resulted occasionally in resounding defeats for the causes defended by organized interests; the ratification by parliament of the Schuman Plan for the European coal and steel industries over strenuous opposition by the business lobby is one example.[18]

It is true that interest groups gained considerable leverage by the myth they had created about themselves in the minds of deputies and senators. Pressures from organized groups were believed to be irresistible. Not to oppose them was considered a legacy of political wisdom handed down, lazily as it were, from generation to generation.

General de Gaulle and his closest collaborators, such as Michel Debré, have frequently lumped interest groups and political parties together in the category of "intermediaries" from which the state would not tolerate interference. The foremost reason for reforming and "rationalizing" parliament was the desire to reduce the role of parliament in the making and unmaking of govern-

---

[18] For details on the defeat of the opponents of the Schuman Plan, see Henry W. Ehrmann, "The French Trade Associations and the Ratification of the Schuman Plan," *World Politics,* VI (1954), pp. 453 ff.

ments. But many of the new rules, established by constitution and legislation (for details see Chap. X), also had the effect of diminishing the role of organized interests in the legislative process. By and large this has been accomplished, but it does not mean that interest groups have lost all influence on rule-making and policy formation.

The new arrangements have forced a change in tactics and, where such a change was not possible, lessened the status of those groups which in the past had concentrated their activities on parliament and on individual representatives. To be effective, all groups must now use the channels which the best equipped among them have long found most rewarding, channels which give them access to the administration. Here, as in most modern democracies, both institutionalized procedures and the network of personal relations remain important.

The indispensable collaboration between organized private interests and the state is institutionalized in advisory committees, attached to most if not all administrations. They are composed mainly of group representatives who have thereby acquired the right to be consulted on administrative decisions affecting their constituents. Some of these committees have functioned since the Revolution, but their growth has been made particularly luxuriant through legislation enacted since the two World Wars. On the national level alone, there exist now no less than five hundred "Councils," twelve hundred "Committees," and three thousand "Commissions," all bringing together group representatives and members of the bureaucracy. Contrary to what has occasionally been promised, in the Fifth Republic few of the advisory boards have been abolished, and many more have been added. One of the few advisory councils that has disappeared is the Superior Council for the Plan, another indication of the general decline of the planning enterprise (discussed above, Chap. II).

Frequently, the advisory bodies are simply additional channels of influence and often, from the perspective of the groups, not the most important ones. It is controversial whether the consultation which takes place here leads to a democratization and humanization of administrative procedures or instead to an undesirable fragmentation of authority. Much seems to depend or the way in which bureaucracy uses these instruments of what in France is called "administrative pluralism." Where the civil servants merely take into account the opinions and the documentation presented to them before they reach an autonomous decision, the effect is beneficial. But there are also many cases where the authoritative decision bows entirely to the group's suggestions, so that in effect administrative functions are parceled out to socioeconomic forces. Often administrators no longer dare to make decisions unless the groups are willing to assume responsibility for them. In certain situations, where an administration has belatedly resisted their wishes, groups have chosen the tactic of resigning noisily from the advisory boards in order to alarm their constituents and to arouse public opinion.

Although such occurrences were most frequent in the declining days of the Fourth Republic, they are not unknown at present. The courage of the administrator, just as that of the elected representative, is a more effective check on group pressures than the ostentatious style of a regime.

The routine contacts between group representatives and the bureaucracy offer to organized interests the most numerous and most valuable points of access. There is nothing scandalous about such contacts. From the perspective of the bureaucracy, interest groups are audience, advisors, and clients, foremost participants in the process of bargaining over governmental policy, and instrumentalities for the enforcement of its rulings. From the perspective of pressure politics, the administrative bureaus are a decisive center of power.

Since administrative decision-making in France is widely dispersed in spite of its formal centralization, interest groups must intervene in a great number of bureaus and agencies, even when concerned with just one decision. To be effective, a group needs more than a bilateral relationship with a single administration — it must play on an extensive keyboard in order to touch all the points where its interests or values are affected. No generalizations are possible as to whether in these daily encounters the public interest emerges unscathed or whether the groups "colonize" parts of the administrative machinery to such an extent that organs of state are transformed into institutionalized pressure groups. Both extremes as well as a great many intermediate situations obtain.[19] The so-called vertical agencies, which like the clientele administration or the regulatory agencies in the United States are concerned with a single if sometimes composite interest, are most easily permeated by the views defended by the groups.

An official committee instituted in the early days of the Fifth Republic to investigate reasons for uneven economic development concluded:

> Under present conditions, characterized by vertical and watertight compartmentalization of administrators, a great number of civil servants . . . have become accustomed to regard in good faith the defense of the interests which they are called upon to control a natural and essential aspect of their function, an aspect which for them tends to eclipse or to falsify their vision of the general interest.[20]

In the years that have elapsed since this report was published, little has changed. Hardly any of the recommendations offered by the committee have been acted upon.

It is quite natural that some interests have easier access to governmental bureaus than others. An affinity of views between group representatives and public administrators might be based on common outlook, common social origin, or education. The official of an important trade association who is not content with presenting the raw demands of his constituents but has already sorted them out and submits them in rational fashion gets easily a more sympathetic hearing in the bureaus than an organization which seeks to defend atomistic interests by mobilizing latent resentment.

Since it is now far more advantageous to impress two well-placed administrators than twenty deputies, the weight of the best organized interests, equipped with qualified staff and useful documentation, has undoubtedly increased. This also holds true of such nonassociational interests as business firms or some prominent families.

[19] For details, see H. W. Ehrmann, "French Bureaucracy and Organized Interests," pp. 541–43.

[20] *Rapport sur les obstacles à l'expansion économique* (Paris: Imprimerie Nationale, 1960), p. 24.

Too complete a symbiosis between the public authorities and certain interests, to the exclusion of others, might result in that "quasi-corporatism" which is prevalent in Great Britain.[21] Periodic criticism of the civil servant as an unscrupulous technocrat originates often with spokesmen for interests which feel that they no longer get an adequate hearing.

At all times organized interests have also brought pressure directly on the political executive. For a long time and for many groups the ministerial *cabinets,* the circle of personal collaborators of every French Minister, have been an important target. For reasons to be explained (see Chap. IX), the functions and importance of these *cabinets* have, somewhat surprisingly, increased in the Fifth Republic. Hence qualified groups still seek and generally find access to the members of a *cabinet* and through them to certain Ministers. Inasmuch as the present regime has strengthened the position of the political executive, it has also enabled both the Prime Minister and the President of the Republic to function somewhat more effectively as arbiters between competing claims and to exercise stricter intra-administrative control over many agencies and ministries.

Since generally the failure of the party system was held responsible for the downfall of the Fourth Republic, in 1958 many hopes turned towards the interest groups, less affected by public opprobrium than were the parties. From many sides associations of various kinds were hailed as the *forces vives* of politics, while the parties were regarded as moribund. Those wishing to engage in political activities as well as the "aspirants" to political power (see Chap. VI) often found participation in interest group life more rewarding than membership in a political party. The new emphasis on groups has emboldened a French observer to liken present-day France to Tocqueville's America.[22]

Groups took on functions, such as civic and political education, which the parties no longer fulfilled. Already during the

---

[21] The term was coined by Samuel H. Beer, "Group Representation in Great Britain and the United States," *The Annals of the American Academy of Political and Social Science,* CCCXIX (1958), p. 136.

[22] André Philip, as quoted by Hoffmann, in *In Search of France,* p. 70. In order to highlight the contrast between France and the United States, Tocqueville laid much stress on the merits of the "civil associations" he found in America.

early years of the Fifth Republic, the student movement, no longer satisfied with the mere corporative interests of its constituents, spoke out on questions of general policy, such as the war in Algeria, the defense of civil liberties, and the place of the rising generation in the nation.[23] Drawing on a tradition that reaches back to the *sociétés de pensée* of prerevolutionary times, the "clubs" emerged, at least temporarily, as a new form of public interest organization. (For details, see Chap. VIII.)

In the past regularized contacts between certain associations and the administration had often been fruitless — at least insofar as trade unions were concerned — because of the groups' principled opposition to the existing economic and social order. Now such tensions seemed to lessen. Younger trade-union leaders felt that their best interlocutors were neither the politicians nor the liberal intellectuals but the "uneasy technocrats" in the top bureaucracy. Even the C.G.T. was invited and found it possible to participate in the official committees and boards concerned with economic planning.[24] The government took the initiative in attributing to organized interest groups a fairly large share in the new regional institutions. The legislation which the electorate rejected in the referendum of 1969 would have broadened such opportunities.

Even before the multifold crises of 1968 and 1969 were to rock the political system, the widespread fascination with the new look which many interest groups took on during the first years of the Fifth Republic had already been shaken by political realities. Though sometimes preceded by a dialogue with the groups, the decision-making process of the regime remained deliberately authoritarian and thereby limited the groups' participation in the process. When economic and social policies prolonged or aggra-

[23]For an excellent description of the student movement during the early years of the Fifth Republic, see Meynaud, *op. cit.*, pp. 64 ff. For a general appraisal of interest group operations in the Fifth Republic see also the same author's, "Les Groupes de pression sous la Ve République," *RFSP,* XII:3 (1962), pp. 672–97.

[24] See the discussion by Alfred Grosser, in Robert A. Dahl (ed.), *Political Opposition in Western Democracies* (New Haven: Yale University Press, 1966), pp. 299 ff. Nicholas Wahl, "The Fifth Republic: From Last Word to Afterthought," in Elke Frank (ed.), *Lawmakers in a Changing World* (Englewood Cliffs: Prentice Hall, 1966) speaks, pp. 62 ff., about an "imposing array of intermediaries."

vated social iniquities and created new tensions, they discredited those group leaders who had hoped to demonstrate that a strategy transcending narrowly conceived special interests would yield results. Faced by such difficulties interest groups and their membership reverted quite naturally to those methods which had been traditional in France.

In any system the style of group action is largely determined by the means of access to power open to the group and by the group's position in society. Their organizational frailty, as well as certain historical memories, imposed on French interest groups a seemingly contradictory pattern of action.

On the one hand, most interest associations rely quite extensively on the state for some kind of support. Even at the height of their anarcho-syndicalist opposition to the state, labor unions carried on most of their business in publicly subsidized buildings, the *Bourses de Travail;* to a large extent this is still the case. At all times the Chambers of Commerce and the Chambers of Agriculture have received ample if indirect governmental subsidies in recognition of the fact that besides articulating the interests of their constituents they also fulfill a number of official functions such as training of apprentices, controlling weights and measures, gathering statistical information, etc. By having one foot in society and the other inside the governmental structure, these organizations form an institutional link between the state and the groups. The full-grown corporatist experiment of the Vichy regime sought to generalize such practices. It gave to entire sectors of economic and social life an organizational structure which the country had never known before because the ties established by voluntary associations had been too tenuous. When after the Liberation freedom of association was reestablished, many interest groups were not averse to a preservation of the framework which Vichy had created. Employers' associations, trade unions, and rural groups are enmeshed in the administration of the comprehensive social security system, public insurance boards, and the like.

On the other hand, the same interest group system exhibits occasionally a radicalism which has become rare in countries of similar development and is more generally found in an early industrial era. In part one is the consequence of the other. Groups want to demonstrate that their participation in administrative tasks and the public support they derive therefrom does not sap their militancy. To make this clear is particularly necessary when the plurality of ideologically divided organizations forces each of them to compete for the same clientele. In particular, trade unions and farmers' associations suffering from membership fluctuations try to mobilize potential members and marginal groups by inflated demands and by boldness of action. For groups that lack the means of using the information media such tactics also become a way to put their case before the public at large.

In a radical context even the defense of purely economic, social, or cultural interests takes on a political color. Here the poor boundary maintenance between the society and the political system[25] has even broader significance than it has for the functioning of parliament. In order to intensify their political effectiveness, interest groups and parties, both too weak to act singly, organize alliances of more or less temporary duration but always adept in using a combative style. French history of the last decades is rich in episodes where a merger of lobbies and political movements has shaken the system. Their emphasis has usually been on protest rather than on demands for constructive action. Honored traditions facilitate the transition from protest movements to militant organizations inclined to transcend the limits of legality.

The dramatic events of the great Revolution, the recurrent significance of street fighting and barricades in the upheavals of the nineteenth century, and other romantically embellished reminiscences have made "violence into a sort of second nature of the French political temperament." [26] For the labor movement the myth of the revolutionary strike seemed at one time the only means of mobilizing workers for some kind of participation.[27]

---

[25] The phenomenon has been described in general terms by Almond and Coleman, *op. cit.,* pp. 37–38.

[26] Rémond, *op. cit.,* I, p. 378.

[27] See Crozier, *The Bureaucratic Phenomenon,* pp. 259–60. It was undoubtedly the organizational weakness of the French labor movement which led Georges Sorel, an intellectual without trade-union connections, to conceive of the myth of the general strike as an instrument of mobiliz-

For groups and individuals lawless action has remained an outlet for frustrations imposed by the dominant style of authority. Such action also betrays a pervasive distrust in the satisfactory processing of demands by the political system. In addition, the use of violence is an attempt to obtain by blackmail what one despairs of obtaining by moderate and concrete demands.

Even though the Fifth Republic was committed to the strengthening of governmental authority in every domain, rebellions and political protest movements organized for the defense of interests have increased considerably in number and intensity since 1958. First in 1961, and periodically since then, agitation in various parts of rural France reached the pitch of an extensive and violent *Jacquerie,* with loss of property and lives. It forced the government to retreat on some fundamental issues.[28]

Of course, the continuing unrest in the countryside was largely due to the painful adaptation of many agricultural regions and sectors to the needs of a modernizing economy. Periods of despair alternated with hopes that either the incorporation of French agriculture into the Common Market or structural reforms would at least alleviate the most acute difficulties. Such alternation itself created tensions which led to spontaneous outbursts whenever hopes were disappointed. Rival groups felt that they risked losing all control over their membership if they did not take the lead in organizing rebellions and, if possible, in fomenting further trouble. As a consequence, the protest movements became steadily more political and more radical.

The labor movement, divided though it was, resorted several times to strikes which were avowedly motivated by political opposition to the government and which succeeded in paralyzing, even if only for a limited time, most economic activities affected by the strikes. A prolonged strike in the national coal mines in 1963 drove the popularity curve of President de Gaulle to a lower level than it ever was before or after. His efforts to terminate the strike by military requisition failed, as did, for a time, the attempts

---

ing for class warfare. On the general significance of "anomie" see Eckstein, *op. cit.,* pp. 254 f. His brilliant analysis applied in every way to the French situation, even before the Events of 1968 furnished new evidence.

[28] For more details on the background and the setting of the 1961 movement, see Wright, *Rural Revolution,* pp. 167 ff.

by the unions to persuade the workers to return to work. With
hindsight this episode was the first of several to acquire some of
the characteristics of the mass strikes in 1968. But also in the
intervening years, there occurred in cities and countryside spontaneous outbursts of dissatisfaction whose importance interest
group leaders tried to minimize to themselves and to the public
in order not to lose further prestige.

In the past the Senate and the National Assembly had been the
most valuable channels of influence for a variety of defense
groups. Because of the declining role of parliament in the policy
process, such channels were now blocked. Especially for groups
with a large membership, contacts between their leaders and the
bureaucracy could not replace the leverage which these groups
used to boast of in parliament. Their "taking to the streets" was
a natural consequence.

Under the Fourth Republic the unruliness of group action was
often due to the fact that the government lacked either the stability and strength to mobilize opinion behind the solution which
it proposed or the ability to explain its actions. Under General
de Gaulle, the government pursued its policy of holding the public at arm's length and disdained to provide such information.
More than once the authorities expressed surprise at the bitterness of public reactions to official policies. But there had never
been a greater surprise — and consequently never a greater lack
of preparedness on the part of the government — than in the
spring of 1968 when pent-up frustrations burst into violence.

THE EXPLOSIONS OF 1968 AND THEIR AFTERMATH

That the fuse blew in the university system was not particularly
surprising. The reasons for a profound malaise have been explained above (See Chap. III) : the rapid increase in the number
of students; dissatisfaction with haphazardly organized new facilities; but also doubts about the goals of education and the
adequacy of traditional structures and methods. Events abroad
had a considerable impact. Student rebellions elsewhere, but
especially in the Federal Republic of Germany, provided encour-
agement and a desire to emulate. In both the French secondary
schools and the universities the groups that were to become most
active in the revolt derived part of their membership from orga-

nizations that had opposed the war in Vietnam and were desirous of turning their energies elsewhere when they thought that the Paris negotiations would lead to an end of American intervention. The activities by the political Left of the student youth resulted in a recrudescence of activities by the Extreme Right. More than once the panicky moves by university authorities to reestablish order were motivated by the fear of a campus "civil war."

The absence of any valid interlocutor between students and authorities and the complete breakdown of communications between them after the first disturbances had occurred, enabled small groups of activists to heighten the combativeness of all. The government had long been unwilling to attribute useful functions to a valid student organization. General de Gaulle himself had rebuked the National Student Association (U.N.E.F.), when it had taken a forthright stand against the continuing of the war in Algeria.

Partly as a consequence of this lack of recognition, the U.N.E.F. had been torn for years by internal dissensions; its leadership was inexperienced and enjoyed little authority over its constituents. Five or more small groups represented various ideological tendencies which corresponded *grosso modo* to the New Left in the United States and in other countries. All were vigorously opposed to the communists and their student organization — which after constant purges was leading a shadowy existence. When student unrest swelled and when it turned out that the university was the most vulnerable of all existing structures, the activist minorities found in battle a unity which debate and organizational efforts had denied them. They mobilized an army of sympathizers who were growing steadily more numerous and more radical in their demands. What had started as protests about overcrowded facilities and antiquated methods of examination led step by step to a revolt against the entire system until lock-outs and sit-down strikes had swept most of the French universities and many of the Paris high schools. The manning of barricades and bitter street fighting in Paris, Lyons, Nantes, and Bordeaux was to follow.

To a small number of radical student leaders, the assault on the university was only a tactical means for bringing down the government and destroying the bourgeois society. The mood which developed among the students in the streets of Paris and in the buildings they occupied throughout the country was far less political in motivation. But it gave to the rebellion the cohesion which was needed to defy the authorities. What was acted out by them was a psychodrama[29] rather than a cultural, let alone a political, revolution. The traditional dread of any face-to-face relationship dissolved into a feast of soul-baring. A collective shedding of inhibitions, a determination to overcome alienation and isolation, a liberating psychological release, a surge of spontaneity and a search for human dignity, and finally a denial of all authority — that of the bourgeois father and teacher, of the clergy and of party leadership — were shouted, sung, and inscribed on the walls. For the first time girls participated actively in a student movement. If the protest against capitalism and its democracy was prevalent, language and ideas were far more those of the utopian socialists of the nineteenth century than of Marxism or even Leninism. To be practical seemed irrelevant. "Be realistic, ask for the impossible," might well have been the most typical of the innumerable slogans intoxicating mildly or wildly tens of thousands of students — rebels all, but neither revolutionaries nor reformers.

"I have something to say, but I do not know what," was another of the characteristic graffiti.[30] And when Cohn-Bendit, the torrentially eloquent student leader, was asked what he and his followers would have done with their barricades, had the police not stormed them on the fateful night, he replied: "La fête . . . we would have organized a festival!" [31]

[29] So Stanley Hoffman in an excellent article, "The French Psychodrama," *The New Republic,* CLIX (August 31, 1968), pp. 15 ff.

[30] Two collections of slogans have been published; both are helpful for an understanding of the stormy weeks: Julien Besançon, (ed.), *"Les Murs ont la parole"* (Paris: Tchou, 1968) and Alain Ayache, (ed.), *Les Citations de la révolution de mai* (Paris: J. J. Pauvert, 1968).

[31] For all its liveliness the book authored by the brothers Cohn-Bendit does not contribute much to an understanding of the Events, see Daniel and Gabriel Cohn-Bendit, *Obsolete Communism. The Left-Wing Alternative* (New York: McGraw-Hill, 1968). The number of books and articles dealing with the crisis is by now staggering. In addition to the searching analysis by Touraine, *op. cit.,* the best accounts in English are the book by Patrick Seale and Maureen McConville, *Red Flag/Black Flag: French Revolution 1968* (New York: Putnam's, 1968), the pamphlet by Bernard E. Brown, *The French Revolt: May 1968* (New York: McCaleb-Seiler,

By the middle of May the student revolts had sparked another explosion far more threatening to the government than the rage of the young bourgeois. When the workers discovered that under pressure the government was willing to promise sweeping university reforms, a long accumulated resentment about social injustices broke into the open. The feeling of having been denied a fair share in an expanding economy, the abnormally low rate of minimum wages, the longest working hours in Europe, unpopular reforms, especially those of the social security system, and also a widely felt need for recognition of trade-union activities at places of work, motivated the workers' demands in private and public enterprises.[32]

In many plants industrial relations were indeed unsatisfactory and had reached the low which had led to the massive strikes under the Popular Front Government in 1936.[33] By and large the core of the general strike lay less in the traditional than in the new industries, especially the automotive-electrical-chemical complex.

The government had long ignored the discontent of the working class because it counted on the notorious weakness of the trade-union movement. Now the workers astonished employers, government, and trade-union officials alike by their radical stubbornness and their unwillingness to abandon the fight for partial concessions. In a number of occupied factories the young workers were joined by students, an alliance which had never occurred previously, and which, at least for a moment, fused class struggle and generation clash. When in some instances both workers and

1970) and the article by Aristide and Vera Zolberg, "The Meanings of May (Paris, 1968)," *Midway* (Winter, 1969), pp. 91–109. An extreme (Trotskyite) perspective is provided by Daniel Bensaïd and Henri Weber, *Mai 1969: une répétition générale* (Paris: Maspero, 1968), which the reader in search of a "balanced truth" may wish to supplement with Raymond Marcellin, *L'Ordre Public et les groupes révolutionnaires* (Paris: Plon, 1969). The author became Minister of Interior during the Events, and as such was in charge of the national police force. A most helpful survey of the enormous literature on the Events will be found in the article by Bénéton and Touchard, *op. cit.* For an interesting collection of (translated) statements by French participant-observers, see Ch. Posner, (ed.), *Reflections on the Revolution in France: 1968* (Baltimore: Penguin Books, 1970).

[32] For an impressive list of the workers' "bread and butter grievances," see Cohen, *op. cit.,* pp. 248 ff.

[33] For an example in a reputedly "quiet" provincial region, see Chaffard, *op. cit.,* esp. p. 211.

students were savagely attacked by the police such experiences strengthened the newly established bonds. What the students and the strikers had in common were not only the symbols of the red and black flags hanging from occupied buildings and factories, but the determination to challenge all authority at the very place where it could be challenged most effectively.

The violent explosions that shook the country had surprised the organized political forces opposed to the regime not less than the government. They were far too weak and too divided to have caused any of the outbreaks, except indirectly by their very frailty. Their lack of contact with the young, their primary concern with combinations in parliament and with paper-programs lacking reality had made them completely insensitive to the anxieties and aspirations of the students. Trade unions had long become aware how little hold they had on the young workers, especially on those who had only recently emigrated from the countryside. Often living by themselves like foreign labor, the young workers had been prone to wildcat strikes suggesting that their socialization had not yet been achieved by traditional factory society.

For the Communist party and the party-controlled trade-union movement, the C.G.T., the threat which arose from the events was as much a threat to their very existence as it was for the government. The break between the communists and the student movement occurred early. The more the students denounced the bureaucracy of party and C.G.T. as being deliberately moderate in demands and tactics and as traitors to the objectives of the upheaval, the more they in turn were accused by the communists of anarchism and disorderly radicalism. In an increasing number of factories, the C.G.T. leadership was outflanked from the left by the young workers, and soon not by them alone. Members of the dissident Socialist party, the P.S.U., and unions affiliated with the C.F.D.T. were doing all they could to carry out such a maneuver against the communists.

In order to channel the spontaneous outbreaks, the Communist party and C.G.T. organized a one-day general strike and several street demonstrations, always seeing to it that they were able to control them. After the sit-in strikes became widespread, the C.G.T. pressed the government to solve the conflicts as rapidly as possible by initiating on the national level an agreement between employers' associations and trade unions. But when the spokesmen for the C.G.T. returned to the factories to recommend the acceptance of the considerable gains in wages and benefits which the agreements had brought, they were received with catcalls and had to stiffen their demands.

Whether the C.G.T. and possibly the Communist party maintained discreet contacts with the government throughout the crisis is controversial, but not unlikely.[34] But there is no doubt that a careful and conservative commentator was right in his overall evaluation: "Not at any moment did the Communist party and the C.G.T. further an uprising. Not at any moment did they wish to torpedo the Gaullist government whose foreign policy corresponds to their fondest wishes and which permits their progressive integration into French society. Obviously they would have taken care of the state if it had been handed to them. But their constant objective was not to 'make a revolution,' but not to let themselves be outflanked on their left by the students, by the Maoists, by the young workers . . ."[35]

After a few critical days, General de Gaulle recovered by turning the situation into a defense of "order" against "red totalitarian revolution" — a calculated historical injustice toward the communists but a show of superior political strategy.[36] During the short time when a vacuum of power seemed to exist, a lack of credibility prevented the opposition from filling it, just as its candidate was to lack credibility in the presidential elections of the following year. By losing the initiative de Gaulle's foes permitted him to regain it. Not only the failure of the communists but the very character of the rebellion reduced whatever chances

[34] François Mitterrand, *op. cit.,* p. 107, believes that there is evidence for this but is not entirely convincing in substantiating his claim.

[35] Raymond Aron, "Après la tempête," *Le Figaro,* June 4, 1968. The official, and very defensive, defense of the party's actions during the Events is provided by its Secretary-General, Waldeck Rochet, *Les Enseignements de mai-juin 1968* (Paris: Éditions Sociales, 1968).

[36] Too much reliable evidence is missing to write the history of the circumstances surrounding the solution of the crisis. Attempts at explanation are made by Tournoux, *Le Mai . . . , op. cit.,* and by Philippe Alexandre, *L'Élysée en péril* (Paris: Fayard, 1969). In addition, see for what follows in the text, the interesting evaluation by E. J. Hobsbawm, "Birthday Party: Why France's May Revolt Failed," *The New York Review of Books,* XII:10 (1969), pp. 4–12.

of overthrowing the regime might have existed. The absence of effective organization was not an accident due to the inexperience of an ephemeral leadership. The mass movement had a political phraseology which dramatically articulated passions and dreams, interests and values, long submerged or ignored. What the movement lacked were both political aims and strategy; hence, it was bound to disperse its considerable energies.

By provoking a crisis which held panic for some and fascination for others, Frenchmen enacted the scenario, described by Tocqueville more than a century earlier: "At one moment he [the Frenchman] is up in arms against authority and the next we find him serving the powers-that-be with a zeal such as the most servile races never display. So long as no one thinks of resisting, you can lead him on a thread, but once a revolutionary movement is afoot nothing can restrain him from taking part in it. That is why our rulers are so often taken by surprise; they fear the nation either too much or not enough . . ." [37]

The Events of May, surprising a prosperous and rapidly modernizing country, once more demonstrated the perennial obstacles to a self-reform of the political and social system. The outcome of the crisis was the customary one: it was left to the state, itself intact, to introduce overdue reforms.

The Events of 1968 had a traumatic effect for all. For interest groups and the authorities they also have remained a "reference point" for what to do and what to avoid. The groups, newly aware of the danger of being outflanked, are attentive to the grievances of their constituents and hesitate to determine beforehand the limits of acceptable civil disobedience. The government does not want to repeat mistakes; it is therefore inclined to rush police to places where encounters with legitimate group demands are taking place. On the other hand, General de Gaulle's successors seek broad agreements with trade unions, farming groups, and others, as a new and more concrete form of the earlier idea of "participation." Yet, frequently it turns out that when such agreements are put to a vote or to some other tests, workers, farmers, and citizens are distrustful of procedures and promises.

[37] See Tocqueville, *The Old Regime . . . op. cit.*, p. 211.

"Every interest group in this country," a moderate observer has written in an article entitled *The French Malaise,* "has a lengthy list of unfulfilled promises and of more or less fraudulent maneuvers of which the administration has been guilty for many years. Hence the anger, and even worse, the contempt." [38]

Such anger breaks out time and again into activities seldom organized but tolerated by the groups: assaults on tax collectors, sequestration of government officials, the blocking of highways, burning of filling stations, wildcat strikes. There is continuing concern that the kind of minor guerilla warfare spreading to various parts of the country will provoke a backlash, invite violent clashes between antagonistic factions, and eventually lead to authoritarian measures by the government.

At the same time, while disorder threatens on some fronts, collaboration between some of the established interest groups and between them and the administration is developing. What is termed a "contractual policy" has made considerable headway. Since early 1969 a number of important agreements have been concluded benefitting either particular categories of wage earners, individual concerns in the private or public sector, or the entire labor force. [39] This development is greatly furthered by the pronounced moderation of the communist trade unions and by the ascendancy of reform-minded leaders in the employers' movement. Yet it still remains true that where projected and ambitious reforms can be made effective only by the active cooperation of those the reforms are designed to serve, an attitude of diffidence — if not outright hostility — hampers lasting progress.

The difficulties besetting the new educational legislation because of a lack of collaboration by those concerned, have already been described (see above, Chap. III). Because confusion and doubts about the validity of the contemplated changes prevail, a small number of radical students may still have a leverage out of proportion with their number. Here, too, the communist students are on the side of "order"; but the leadership of the official student organization, the U.N.E.F., remains in the hands of the

---

[38] J.-M. Domenach, "Le Malaise Français," *Le Monde Hebdomadaire,* Nov. 13–19, 1969.

[39] For a rather impressive list, see *Le Monde,* July 14, 1970.

left wing socialists.[40] It was quite characteristic of the prevailing climate that since 1968 even the students at the E.N.A. who are being trained for the top positions in the bureaucracy engaged in a protest movement against governmental policies.

At the same time public opinion data reveal that a majority of respondents is convinced of the futility of strikes and protest movements to ameliorate social and economic conditions. Even many workers, and communists among them, tend to think that temporary gains will always be wiped out and that little can be expected from any cooperative effort.[41]

[40] For an account of the history of the organization, see A. Belden Fields, *Student Politics in France. A Study of the Union Nationale des Étudiants de France* (New York: Basic Books, 1970).

[41] See *Sondages,* XXXI:1–2 (1969), pp. 78 ff. and SOFRES, *Poll of December, 1969* esp. pp. 21 ff. Repeated inquiries revealed that about one-third of the respondents think that another outbreak like that of 1968 might well occur "within the next two or three months," something like a barometer of a continuing malaise.

CHAPTER VIII

Political Parties

THE TRADITIONAL PARTY SYSTEM

"The character and number of the political parties seeking to represent the various groups in a country are perhaps the chief determinants of how far the government acts through a stable system of interchanges between the key solidary groups and the political elite." [1] There is general agreement that French political parties have regularly prevented the functioning of such a stable system. Except for short and atypical periods they were "equally unable to make commitments in the name of their voters or to obtain legitimacy through transforming the voters' opinions and attitudes into impulses converted into governmental action." [2]

There are, however, divergent explanations of such inability. Should one conclude with General de Gaulle that the parties are merely a mirror of the perpetual French "political effervescence" and an expression of a "Gallic propensity towards divisions and quarrels"? Is it the number of parties or their characteristics which are most to blame? Has the socio-economic structure of the country caused both the plurality and the characteristics of the parties? Or is the party chaos more apparent than real, hiding as

[1] Seymour M. Lipset, "Party Systems and the Representation of Social Groups," *European Journal of Sociology,* I:1 (1960), p. 53.

[2] Otto Kirchheimer, "The Transformation of the Western European Party Systems," in Joseph La Palombara and Myron Weiner (eds.), *Political Parties and Political Development* (Princeton: Princeton University Press, 1966), p. 180.

it were behind opprobrious forms a basically stable division in the body politic? [3]

Answers to these questions are not only essential to an understanding of the perennial difficulties of democratic politics in France. They of necessity also determine the choice of remedies and of possible alternatives to the unsatisfactory functioning of the party system.

Some of the most knowledgeable analysts of election data have been struck by a chronic and seemingly unalterable division of Frenchmen into two camps, two large political "families," each motivated by a different political mood or temperament. Whether one wishes to identify these camps with the "Right" and the "Left" or christen them the "party of order" and the "party of movement" [4] is of less importance than the fact that if one views elections from this perspective, political alignments have remained surprisingly stable over long periods of history.

The party distribution in the first election held under general manhood suffrage (1849) shows that the proportions of votes going to the Right and to the Left were about the same as in the last elections of the Third Republic (1936) which led the Popular Front to victory. The conservative forces which backed General MacMahon in 1877 came from the same regions that supported the authoritarian-minded Poincaré in 1928. As late as 1962, the opposition to General de Gaulle was strongest where for more than a century republican traditions had had a solid foundation. Neither domestic upheavals nor international cataclysms have upset the geographical distribution or the proportional strength of the two sides. An electoral system such as that of the Third

[3] The possible influence of the electoral system has been discussed above, Chap. IV.

[4] The classical study of the party system in the Third Republic, François Goguel, *La Politique des Partis sous la IIIe République* (2 vols.; Paris: Éditions de Seuil, 1946), tries to reduce party orientations to "order" and "movement." But in his conclusion, especially vol. II, p. 338, the author is inclined to soften the dichotomy which his work emphasizes so much. The same author's *Géographie des élections françaises sous la Troisième et la Quatrième République* (Paris: Colin, 1970) offers ample historical documentation and cartography. For the present alignments, the study of Deutsch, Lindon and Weill, *op. cit.*, provides an interesting analysis.

and the Fifth Republics has apparently favored this simplification of political alignments. In the majority of constituencies the run-off elections have resulted in the confrontation of two candidates, each representing roughly one of the two camps.

All this is not without significance but does not explain the malfunctioning of the party system. For a simple and stable division could have resulted in a pattern of two parties, or coalition of parties, alternating in power and opposition and hence giving valid expression to the voters' options. However, to discover simplicity and stability one must view French "political effervescence" from a distance sufficiently great so that the tensions between and within social groups and categories, between and within the coalitions and parties, disappear from sight. Yet these tensions and their organizational expressions in fact shape political reality. "France contains two fundamental temperaments — that of the left and that of the right," Jacques Fauvet has stated quite correctly. But he had to add that she also contains "three principal tendencies, if one adds the center; six spiritual families; ten parties, large or small, traversed by multiple currents; fourteen parliamentary groups without much discipline; and forty million opinions." [5]

Any party system normally reflects some of the major characteristics of the political culture within which it functions. Historical circumstances but also constitutional arrangements will usually determine to what extent the party system neutralizes or, possibly, maximizes the difficulties created by a given political culture. In the French republics both traditions and constitutional practices have created or conserved a party system which has considerably aggravated rather than eased the inherent difficulties.

French parties, like parties everywhere, exist to fulfill a variety of functions. Most important among them are the aggregation of interests and demands and their transformation into policy; the mobilization of the citizenry for political participation and the integration of the citizenry into the system; the recruitment and selection of political leaders for executive and other posts; and the control of such leadership, especially the control of the gov-

[5] Quoted here from Wright, *France,* p. 423.

ernment. Finally, parties are "alliances in conflicts over policies and value commitments within the larger body politic." [6] Not all of these functions will be served equally well by all parties or at all times. What must be explained is why French parties have done so badly, over long periods, on almost all counts. Why have their structure, their style, and their orientation, all closely connected factors, been inadequate to their tasks and, in many cases, to their ambitions?

Except for the Extreme Left, French party organizations have remained most of the time as skeletal as were parties in many countries at the time of their nineteenth-century beginnings. They developed in a largely preindustrial and preurban environment, catering at first to upper-middle class and later to middle-class elements. Their foremost, and frequently sole, function consisted in providing the organizational framework for the selection and election of candidates for political office on the local, departmental, and national level. "France was one of the first countries to bring a maximal electorate into the political arena, but the mobilization efforts of the established strata tended to be local and personal." [7]

The slow and irregular industrialization of the country hampered the formation of a disciplined working-class party which would have challenged the bourgeois parties to overhaul their own structure. The electoral system and a powerful upper house of parliament with a heavy overrepresentation of the rural population kept the workers in a position of electoral inferiority.[8] Before 1914, the Socialist party was at best an incipient mass party, weakened not only by doctrinal dissensions in its midst, but by the workers' distrust of all institutions of the bourgeois state. Their distrust extended to the socialist representatives in parliament, most of them of middle-class origin. When after the First World War the communists were able to mount a well-organized party, the split of the working-class vote between two mutually hostile camps attenuated the threat from the Left. Hence the traditional

[6] Seymour M. Lipset and Stein Rokkan, "Cleavage Structures, Party Systems, and Voter Alignments; An Introduction," in Lipset and Rokkan, (eds.), *Party Systems and Voter Alignments: Cross-National Perspectives* (New York: Free Press, 1967), p. 5.

[7] *Ibid.,* p. 51.

[8] See Kirchheimer, "The Transformation," pp. 178 ff.

parties could afford to preserve the loose structure they had previously adopted.

Current typologies of political parties distinguish between organizations that gradually emerge from groupings inside the legislature and those that are created outside the parliament among the voting population.[9] Those French parties which have represented the majority of the electorate throughout long periods belong clearly to the first category, the internally created parties. Their major weight is to be found in their parliamentary representation; all truly important party activities occur inside the legislature. Political organization at the local and constituency level aims mainly at assuring the election or reelection of members belonging to various legislative blocks or factions in parliament. Up to the present, none of these parties can boast of anything like the constituency structure of a large British or continental party, a structure which is, of course, also unknown in the United States.

An internally created party is almost always less disciplined and ideologically less coherent than one that has emerged outside the legislature. Its organizational and hence its financial structure will usually be rudimentary, the very notion of membership in the party remains indeterminate, sometimes to the point of being meaningless. Where constituency parties have existed at all, they have been deferential to their legislative contingents; the elected representatives have usually been far more of an asset to the party than the party to them. For this very reason political leaders that were not socialists or communists have hardly ever emerged from the ranks of a party but from elective positions, either local or national.

During the election campaign the candidates can expect little financial support from the party (and this has remained true even for the socialists). Between elections, those representing the traditional party formations are not amenable to any party directives coming from outside parliament. Even within a parliamentary group or fraction the formal institution of a whip is unknown. Whether the moral authority of a particular parliamentary party chairman is able to overcome the centrifugal trends of divided interests and loyalties depends on the circumstances. In most cases

[9] See Maurice Duverger, *Political Parties* (New York: Wiley, 1955), especially pp. XXIII–XXXVII. For a recent discussion of Duverger's criteria, see La Palombara and Weiner, *op. cit.,* pp. 8 ff.

representatives vote, on important as well as on unimportant matters, solely in accordance with the commands of "career, conscience, and constituency." [10]

Occasionally this has led to the expulsion from the party of a deputy (rarely of a senator) who had defied all too flagrantly a party directive. In a country with a developed party system, such as Great Britain or West Germany, the bolting of a party is usually tantamount to the end of a political career. In France, the party renegade if he chooses to do so, can stand for reelection in the same district which had sent him to parliament before and usually he has kept his seat under a new, and generally meaningless, party label. Some outstanding political leaders, such as Alexandre Millerand and Pierre Laval, have in their long careers moved from the Left to the Extreme Right, always representing the same constituency.

One of the most decisive reasons for the survival of this form of representation and of party organization is undoubtedly the voters' preference for it. An electorate which distrusts authority and wishes to be represented at the seats of power only in order to be protected against an always suspected arbitrariness of government is also suspicious of parties organized for reformatory political action.

An egalitarian radicalism which puts a high valuation on "the people" and on the basic soundness of the public but distrusts the solidarity claimed by any organization in the name of collective interests will not easily propound party discipline. The strength of such radical traditions in France, and that of populism in the United States, is undoubtedly one of the major reasons for party weakness in both France and the United States.[11] In the case of France it is of particular significance that the two prevalent political orientations, the representative and the bonapartist (see Chap. I), have for all their mutual antagonism one thing in com-

---

[10] See Williams, *Crisis and Compromise,* pp. 348 ff. This work remains an indispensable source for party history during the Fourth Republic.

[11] This point is made by Samuel H. Beer, *British Politics in the Collectivist Age* (New York: Knopf, 1965), pp. 42 f., to explain the differences between party organization in Britain and in the United States. It is equally applicable to France, where the teaching of Alain (see above Chap. I) provided an "ultra-democratic" justification for party weakness. See especially his *Éléments d'une doctrine radicale.*

mon: their aversion to well-established and strongly organized parties.

Consequently, party membership, except during short and dramatic situations, has always been low. According to a recent estimate not more than 1.5 per cent of the registered voters are party members. With about 300,000 adherents, the Communist party has a larger membership than all other parties combined, the Gaullists included. Forty years earlier the relation between the electorate and party membership was about the same.[12]

Organizational weakness and its underlying causes will easily result in a multipolar party system. But the primary cause of such division is past conflicts over interests and values, many of them but dimly remembered except for the resentments they caused and which have persisted. Historical traditions have determined whether constituencies are regularly on the right or the left of the political spectrum. Different property laws under the monarchy, clerical or secular administration during the *Ancien Régime,* differences in agricultural crops or in the speed of industrialization, religious affiliation — all these have shaped political alignments which frequently have perpetuated themselves long after the original causes have disappeared.[13]

The violence with which partisans have clashed in the past, the bloodshed that has occurred time and again, has made reconciliation difficult not only on the level of party leadership but among party followers. When during a critical period of the Fourth Republic the headquarters of the socialists and of the M.R.P., a party with a predominantly Catholic clientele, decided that the time had come to forge a closer unity between them, the *militants* (the party activists) in both camps found such collaboration with former enemies distasteful and sabotaged it as best they could.

Historical references provide justification not alone for the

---

[12] Duncan MacRae, Jr., *op. cit.,* p. 49, presents an interesting chart for the ratio between membership and electorate of major parties during the Fourth Republic. One only wishes the membership figures on which he had to base his calculations were more reliable.

[13] On the historical roots of party cleavages, see Mattei Dogan, "Political Cleavage and Social Stratification in France and Italy," in Lipset and Rokkan, *op. cit.,* esp. pp. 182 ff. The entire article provides valuable and comparative data on the social composition of the French parties.

major division between Right and Left, but also for the equally important divisions within the two camps. On the Right one can still
distinguish, among others, traditionalists (not all of them monarchists), "Orleanists," i.e., conservatives with a credo of laissez-
faire, and bonapartists.[14] On the Left, there were the Jacobins and
the socialists before the Russian Revolution added the communists.
In many cases actual party names have long become meaningless
because they too can, in general, be explained only by historical
circumstances, especially by the secessions which gave rise to ever
new factions.

Because of the large number of weakly structured parties, most
of them represent only a small section of the electorate. A party
without risking ridicule, cannot claim to represent the interests of
the entire electorate, or even of a large sector, takes on the characteristics of an interest group, and has little or no autonomy from
the social strata it defends. Instead of aggregating interests and
values, the representatives of such a party merely articulate them.
They thereby transmit to parliament, or, if they have the opportunity, to the government, the undiluted individualism of their
constituents — another instance of poor boundary maintenance.

Every party that operates from a limited base faces a variety of
competitors seeking to draw strength from the same clientele. It
can hope for no more than a marginal increase in bargaining power
for the inevitable deals which it must conclude, in power or in
opposition, with other small parties once the elections are over.[15]
If such parties were to spell out the differences which separate
them from their competitors in realistic and pragmatic terms, the
contest would frequently appear merely as one between interest
groups or between personalities. In order to avoid such a demon-
stration and still score over their competitors, parties will define
even the most narrow political issues in lofty ideological and often
esoteric terms. This is a general phenomenon in multipolar party
systems. ". . . the more the number of parties increases, the more
their identification becomes a problem; and the remedy to which

[14] See René Rémond, *La Droite en France* (Paris: Aubier, 1963), especially pp. 7 ff. He entitles the "prologue" to his work: "One or several
Rights?" Mr. Rémond's excellent study is now available in an English
translation, *The Right Wing in France: From 1815 to De Gaulle* (Phila.:
U. of Penna. Press, 1968).
[15] See Williams, *Crisis and Compromise*, p. 69.

each party has recourse in order to be perceived as distinct is a punctilious ideological and principled rigidity." [16] It is only seemingly paradoxical that many parties have the characteristics of an interest group and yet indulge in ideological language. Since many French interest groups also conduct their propaganda in ideological terms, the style of parties and groups is frequently identical. This is caused by organizational weakness common to both, and by the desire to replace the lack of organization by strong, ultimative, and hence ideological, language.

Although one expects an ideological underpinning from externally created mass parties rather than from those based on atomistic representation, there is no true contradiction here either. After the elections and in the ensuing bargaining between parties, much of the ideological baggage is discarded. The gap between high-sounding principles and the need for pragmatically based coalitions becomes painfully obvious. It makes ideologies appear as subterfuges and convinces the voters that electoral contests are manifestations of sheer irresponsibility.

The inconveniences of the French multi-party system were compounded by the constitutional arrangements and parliamentary practices of the Third and Fourth Republics. To survive and to govern effectively, a cabinet needed more than just the absence of a majority willing to overthrow it, it needed a positive majority in favor of the government's policy and its legislative proposals. This, however, was difficult to obtain where majorities consisted not of disciplined parties or of parliamentary groups kept in line by an effective whip but to a large extent of ephemeral coalitions. Their cohesion or disruption depended on whatever problem was under consideration. As different problems came up, governments toppled or were condemned to immobility.

Neither Right nor Left was able to govern by itself for any length of time because it not only would invariably lose a temporary majority, but it also included at its extremes the groups that contested the legitimacy of the existing political or social order. In order not to risk the badly needed electoral support by these extremes, both right wing and left wing coalitions had to make concessions to their

---

[16] Giovanni Sartori, "European Political Parties: The Case of Polarized Pluralism," in La Palombara and Weiner, *Political Parties*, p. 159.

own radicals and thereby narrowed the scope of possible action to such an extent that immobility ensued.

As a normal consequence of the existing party system, a center coalition has been in control of the government most of the time, no matter what the outcome of the preceding elections may have been. According to some calculations, during the period from 1789 to the advent of the Fifth Republic, France has been ruled by center governments for all but thirty years or for more than 80 per cent of this period. In a two or three party system, it is quite normal that the major parties move towards the political center in order to gain stability and cohesion. But where extreme party plurality prevails, the Center is a "swamp" instead of a cohesive political force.[17] It cannot pursue for long even moderate policies without losing necessary support, for there are no clear lines of division between government and opposition.

An opposition will behave responsibly if it knows that it may have to perform in the foreseeable future and that after taking over power it will have to live up, at least in part, to the promises it has made. French politicians belonging to the Center and temporarily without a cabinet post were free to use every means to weaken the government by steady criticism and eventually to cause its downfall. They knew that if they were to become part of the next shapeless center coalition they would probably never have to assume effective leadership but at most would share some peripheral responsibility behind the smokescreen of shifting coalitions.[18] At the same time, the policies of the Center threw substantial sectors of public opinion into permanent opposition, which strengthened the centrifugal strains on the system.

However unsatisfactory the results of a fragmented party system were, the fragmentation reflected a similar division of the electorate. This explains why from one election to the next the transfer of votes was in general extremely small and why all established parties, whatever their political color, had a fairly stable electoral following.[19] The disaffection from the party system as such was

[17] The problem of the Center as a "swamp" has been analyzed at length by Maurice Duverger, "L'Éternel Marais, essai sur le centrisme français," *RFSP*, XIV : 1 (1964), pp. 33–51.

[18] See Sartori, *op. cit.*, pp. 157 f.

[19] See MacRae, *op. cit.*, pp. 230 ff., on the stability of party strength in the Fourth Republic.

pronounced and often expressed in opinion polls both prior to and after the events of 1958. The voters made both the number of parties and their behavior responsible for the poor functioning of republican institutions. But at election time party loyalties seldom shifted. The strength of traditional alignments, frequently transmitted from one generation to the next, was generally unimpaired.

An exception to such stability was the successes of flash parties or surge movements. They were not unknown during various periods of the Third Republic but occurred with greater regularity in the Fourth.[20] They were reactions against the immobility induced by a party system that was simultaneously too stable and too weak. They mobilized, if only for a short time, dissatisfied voters, drawing millions of them from the established groupings and a far smaller proportion from those who had abstained in the preceding elections. Typically, all these movements saw the need for a better structured and more active constituency organization and demanded a disciplined vote from their parliamentary representatives. But they all failed to bring about the attempted reforms, whereupon their forces dispersed usually as fast as they had assembled.

Only once, after the Liberation of France in 1944, has there existed a serious chance for a thorough overhauling of the party system. The representative regime of which the Third Republic had been the prototype was thoroughly discredited. Three parties, the Communist, the Socialist, and the *Mouvement Républicain Populaire,* emerged in the first elections of the new republic with a combined following of about 75 per cent of the electorate. All were intent on forming disciplined mass parties and on governing the country by an effective coalition government. Yet after a few transitional years, and due to the cold war as well as to domestic pressures, the country reverted to the traditional forms of atavistic and atomistic representation and to the rule by shifting coalitions of the Center which now included the socialists.

During the last eight years of the Fourth Republic none of the parties eligible for a center coalition could claim more than about 15 per cent of the vote, and many of these parties were plagued by

[20] On the surge movements, see *ibid.,* pp. 268 ff., and the interesting table on p. 233.

TABLE VI. First Ballot of French Parliamentary Elections, 1956–1968, and Seats Won in the National Assembly in Both Ballots (Voting in Metropolitan France)[a]

	1956			1958			1962			1967			1968		
	Votes in millions	% of votes cast	Seats in Parliament	Votes in millions	% of votes cast	Seats in Parliament	Votes in millions	% of votes cast	Seats in Parliament	Votes in millions	% of votes cast	Seats in Parliament	Votes in millions	% of votes cast	Seats in Parliament
Registered votes in millions	26.77			27.24			27.53			28.3			28.2		
abstentions, in %		17.3			22.9			31.3			19.1			19.9	
Parties															
Communists (P.C.)	5.53	25.7	150	3.88	18.9	10	3.99	21.8	41	5.0	22.5	73	4.4	20.0	34
Socialists (P.S.U.)	—	—	—	—	—	—	0.4	2.4	0	0.5	2.2	4	0.9	3.0	0
Socialists (S.F.I.O.)	3.18	14.8	94	3.17	15.5	44	2.31	12.6	66	4.2[c]	18.7[c]	116[e]	3.6[c]	16.5[c]	57[h]
Radicals & Allied	2.88	13.4	77	1.71	8.3	33	1.38	7.6	39	}	}	}	}	}	}
M.R.P. and Centre	2.37	11.1	83	2.41	11.2	56	1.63	8.9	55	3.0	13.4	27	2.3	10.3	33[g]
Gaullists	0.95	4.4	21	3.60	20.4	212	5.85	31.9	233	8.4[d]	37.8[d]	244[e]	10.2[d]	46.0[d]	354[f]
Conservatives	3.09	14.4	109	4.74	22.9	118	2.54[b]	13.9[b]	35[b]	0.8	3.7	15	} 0.5	} 2.4	0
Extreme Right	2.86	13.3	52	0.67	3.0	0	0.16	0.9	0	0.2	0.8	0	}	}	0

[a] Unaffiliated deputies and splinter groups not listed.
[b] Both pro- and anti-Gaullist conservatives.
[c] Allied in the Federation of the Left.
[d] Votes cast for lists presenting both Gaullists and its coalition partners, the Independent Republicans.
[e] 200 Gaullists and 44 Independent Republicans.
[f] 293 Gaullists and 61 Independent Republicans.
[g] Including affiliated conservatives.

internal dissensions.[21] In the last elections (1956) before de Gaulle's return to power, an *average* of almost ten candidates contested each available seat in parliament. In the same elections, the parties committed to fundamental opposition, whether from the Left or the Right, obtained 43.4 per cent of the popular vote.

In a heterogeneous society such as France, living through a period of intense internal and external pressures, multiple opinions and attitudes are bound to prevail. As before the war, the political parties did little to integrate and simplify them; instead they rigidified and crystallized existing antagonisms. In 1958 the problems introduced by decolonization and France's entrance into the Common Market culminated in a major political crisis which the party system lacked the resilience to face.

A discussion of the present-day parties will make clear in what way and to what extent the parties, old and new, have responded to the advent of the new regime. (See Table VI for the electoral strength and parliamentary representation of each party.)

PRESENT-DAY PARTIES

The Communists (P.C.). In all democratic countries the communists are a "party not like the others." For many decades their reliance on directives from Moscow was not equaled by whatever loose international ties other parties might have established. Because of the singular importance of France to the international position of the Soviet Union, the French P.C. was ordered time and again, and at most dramatic moments, to alter its course abruptly, but always according to the demands of Russian foreign policy.

Yet a party which for more than twenty years has had an electoral following of between 19 and 25 per cent of the voters at all parliamentary elections and which is represented by more than twenty thousand city and town councilors and more than one thousand mayors throughout France, is also, and simultaneously, "a party like the others." Its very existence constantly impinges

[21] For a comprehensive analysis of the relationship between social class and political parties in the Fourth Republic, see the amply documented study by Maurice Duverger et al., *Partis politiques et classes sociales en France* (Paris: Colin, 1955). For party preferences of different social categories, see also the tables in MacRae, *op. cit.*, pp. 257 f. For more recent data see Alain Duhamel, "La Structure sociologique de l'électorat," *Sondages,* XXVIII: 2 (1966), pp. 4–14.

upon the rules of the political game, and this is as true in the Fifth Republic as it has been in the past.[22]

The P.C. has always been at least as disciplined and centralized as communist parties elsewhere and as no other French party has ever been for any length of time. In the troubled aftermath of the First World War, the French communists succeeded in doing what almost none of the other European communist movements had been able to bring about: the winning over of a substantial majority of the membership of the Socialist party and of its valuable assets, such as the daily *L'Humanité*.[23] However, by the time of the economic depression of the thirties, what was left of the party was not much more than a bureaucratic apparatus and, around it, devoted *militants,* who had at the same time lost most of their foothold in organized labor. After the changed tactics of Stalinist Russia made the formation of the French Popular Front possible, the party membership increased massively, and, when after the Liberation a heroic resistance record had blotted out the bitter memories of the Hitler-Stalin Pact, the party reached a membership of close to a million. Surrounding it were numerous, large front-organizations and the communist-dominated trade unions affiliated with the C.G.T. At present, realistic estimates put the membership at not more than three hundred thousand.

The differences in motivation and mentality of the *militants,* of the merely dues-paying members, and of the communist voters vary considerably, though they may overlap. For the activist, the party, together with its traditions, its symbols, and its doctrine of class struggle, remains a "home," a subculture within which he moves most of his waking hours. His loyalty is affective, probably more so than it is rational. His devotion (and the impulsion coming from the party apparatus) permits the functioning of some seventeen thousand party cells of which less than one-fourth operate at places of work; more than one-third are rural cells; the rest are grouped according to residence.[24]

[22] Goguel and Grosser, *op. cit.,* p. 128.

[23] For the early history of the P.C., see Robert Wohl, *French Communism in the Making* (Stanford: Stanford University Press, 1966).

[24] There is no longer a dearth of scholarly (as distinguished from polemic) studies of the P.C. Of particularly high quality and scope are Fondation Nationale des Sciences Politiques (various authors), *Le Communisme en France* (Paris: Colin, 1969), and Annie Kriegel, *Les com-*

According to party sources, 60 per cent of the 1967 membership are manual workers, 18 per cent white-collar employees, and 9 per cent intellectuals (including engineers and teachers). Forty-two per cent of the members are under 40 years of age; one-fourth are women. Its composition gives the party more of a working-class character than any other French political organization at any time. Yet this "class party" has been able to attract voters from many socio-economic groups, in industrial as well as in rural regions.

For the communist voters, their ballot is above all an expression of protest and discontent. At least emotionally, a fairly large share of the communist vote corresponds to the protest which millions of underprivileged citizens of the United States manifest by never casting a vote. But at the same time, the P.C. appears to many voters to be the legitimate heir of radical movements and radical causes of the past, the only trustworthy defender of the small against the government, the church, the powerful, and the rich.

Georges Lavau has characterized the party as "tribunitial" in its appeal,[25] likening it to that Roman magistrate whose specific function it was to protect the individual plebeian citizen from arbitrary action by patrician officials. Voicing the citizens' wrath, the P.C. seeks to mobilize the social plebeians in present-day France by giving them a feeling of strength and confidence. In all of its programmatic statements, the term "defense" moves into the foreground. There is little if any talk of a communist offensive; most European Social-Democratic parties could subscribe to the P.C.'s mild vision of a "socialist France" in which an opposition would be tolerated. It would be wrong to consider this nothing else but deceptive electioneering. The attitudes and activities in many arenas of public life show clearly that the P.C. has settled within the system and seeks to increase its political weight by catering to

---

munistes français: Essai d'ethnographie politique (Paris: Éditions Seuil, 1968). Slightly dated but still valuable: François Fejtö, *The French Communist Party and the Crisis of International Communism* (Cambridge: M.I.T. Press, 1967). On the reasons for the earlier success of the P.C. in attracting members of the intellectual as well as the working-class elite, see Raymond Aron, *L'Opium des intellectuels* (Paris: Calmann-Lévy, 1955) and Gabriel Almond, *The Appeals of Communism* (Princeton: Princeton University Press, 1954).

[25] "Le Parti Communiste dans le système politique français," in *Fondation Nationale, op. cit.,* esp. pp. 25–37.

the bread-and-butter interests of its constituents. In many cases, and especially in the countryside, this means opposition to modernization and praise for some of the most outdated political and administrative institutions. Such an orientation explains the party's unmitigated hostility toward all movements that appear on its own left, especially during and since the Events of May 1968. The students' revolt was unacceptable since it appeared to question the monopoly of the working class as the leader of all valid revolutions. But it also sinned by evoking the "spectre" of revolution at a time when the P.C. had little taste for or faith in any revolution.

In electoral terms the party's nonsectarian line has proven profitable ever since it was inaugurated in 1936. Although there have been ups and downs in the attractiveness of the party for the electorate since the advent of the Fifth Republic, these usually have been reflections of more general reactions of the electorate towards the regime and hence additional evidence that the P.C. has become an opposition party "like others." [26] The ascendancy of the Gaullist party has cost not alone the communist, but the entire opposition, a segment of its customary support. After rather heavy electoral losses in 1958 drove the party for the first time since the war below the 5 million mark, the P.C. has been the only opposition party that has managed a slow but steady comeback in national and local elections — until the government's warnings against the menace of "totalitarian communism" in 1968 cost the party over one-half million votes.[27] In the presidential elections of 1969, the communist candidate recouped some of the earlier losses. In the eyes of the party leadership this did not only vindicate the reassuring and good-natured campaign style of M. Duclos who played up the tribunitial themes and did not stop at chauvinistic overtones, it also justified a propaganda which derided the two leftist candidates for their utopian commitment to a socialist revolution.[28]

In each of the elections since 1958, about 70 per cent of the

[26] For details, see Table VI. Only the number of ballots cast for the P.C. is an indicator of popular sympathies; under the prevailing electoral system, the number of communist deputies in parliament depends entirely on whatever arrangements between the parties of the Left have been made for the second ballot.

[27] For a comprehensive analysis, see Frank L. Wilson, "The French Left and the Elections of 1968," *World Politics,* XXI:4 (1969), pp. 539–574.

[28] See Roy C. Macridis, "Pompidou and the Communists," *Virginia Quarterly Review,* XLV:4 (1969), p. 582.

communist vote came from working-class families, but less than one-half of the working-class population voted communist. The substantial regional variations in the political alignment of French workers can once more be traced to historical traditions. Where Catholicism has remained strong, as in the industrial centers of the East and certain districts of the North, communists and socialists combined have in the past obtained little more than one-fourth of the working-class vote.

The greatest concentration of communist strength in the working-class vote remains in the unfashionable suburbs of large cities. Within the "red belt" almost encircling Paris, 1.5 million live in districts administered by communist mayors; the communist vote amounts regularly to between 40 and 50 per cent of total votes cast. There, at least four-fifths of the vote comes from working-class families, and two-thirds of the working-class votes are cast for the P.C. The density of the working-class population favors an all-encompassing socialization by the communist subculture. The number of those who read the Sunday edition of the *Humanité* in the red belt of Paris might reach the one-half million mark.

When compared to its working-class vote, the relative strength of the communists in certain rural departments, especially in southern and central France, is on the increase. Partly these are seriously underdeveloped regions where the P.C. has long had strongholds; elsewhere it seems to have fallen heir lately to some traditionally socialist following.[29] For many years the communist weekly *La Terre* was the most widely read farm journal in the country.

During the last years of the Fourth Republic, the P.C. was, in spite of its continuing electoral appeal and its organizational strength, beset by the same kind of immobility that plagued other organizations and political life in general. By appealing simultaneously to many groups, the party became enmeshed in the

[29] For estimates of communist strength in the working class and among farmers, see Mattei Dogan in Lipset and Rokkan, *op. cit.*, pp. 131–50, and Jean Ranger, in *Fondation Nationale, op. cit.*, pp. 211–54. For communist gains and losses in the 1968 and 1969 elections, see Lancelot, *op. cit.*, *Projet* (1968 and 1969) and *RFSP* (1970), and the careful study by Goguel, *Modernisation. . ., op. cit.* which maintains that there is no definite relationship between economic development and communist voting strength.

contradictions of an unevenly developing society and fell captive to the numerous, and partly conservative, forces whose support it sought. Its leadership was more entrenched and bureaucratic than that of almost any other Communist party, with the sole exception of the state party in East Germany. For many years neither the French nor the German party entered honestly upon the process of de-Stalinization. A sclerosis of doctrine and of party life was communicated to the entire organization by an overage leadership. When Maurice Thorez died in 1964, he had been the party's Secretary General for 34 years.[30]

In the ensuing years, international as well as domestic developments loosened some of the former rigidity. Polycentrism in Eastern Europe and the Sino-Soviet split offered opportunities for a somewhat freer discussion within the party and the organizations controlled by it. Negotiations, first with the Socialist party and then with the larger Federation of the Left (see below), increased the representation of the opposition and thereby also of the communists in parliament. In February 1968, after a series of electoral successes, the new leadership of the P.C. was flexible enough to agree with the Federation on a lengthy common program. This much vaunted program however appeared so vacuous and left so many things unsaid that nobody even referred to it when, a few weeks later, a chance of toppling the Gaullist regime seemed to arise — another indication of the gap between the traditional parties and the rebels of May. But what the communists discovered at the height of the crisis was that their recent allies in the Federation envisaged a government without communist participation. In the elections that followed, the P.C. paid the price for the barricades it did not build and for the picketing it had not encouraged. Worse, its slow integration into French politics seemed to have been interrupted once more.

Shortly afterwards, the party's presidium and the communist-controlled trade unions reacted to the invasion of Czechoslovakia with a sharply worded and widely publicized reproof of the Soviet action. This was the first time since its founding that the P.C. had

[30] For a good comparative article showing the greater vitality of the Italian Communist party in almost every respect, see Thomas H. Greene, "The Communist Parties of Italy and France. A Study in Comparative Communism," *World Politics,* XXI: 1 (1969), *pp.* 1–28.

turned against Moscow; even the Hitler-Stalin pact had been swallowed. In 1968, many months of intra-party squabbling followed; in the end, the party bureaucracy succeeded in bringing the party apparatus into line and in enforcing the limits which it set for permissible criticism. The previous censure of the Soviet Union was softened, and many of its arguments in favor of the intervention were accepted. The P.C. may no longer swear unconditional fealty to the Moscow party, but it remains a member of the family, a son that has reached manhood and has some ideas of his own, yet does not consider breaking old-established ties.[31]

Its course cost the party most of the intellectual following it long enjoyed but which had gradually drifted away even before the party's attitude during the May Events had infuriated many intellectuals. One of the outstanding representatives of the intelligentsia in the party leadership, Roger Garaudy, a party-faithful of almost forty years and long a specialist in building bridges to progressive Catholics, indicted the party for its past and recent errors until he was finally expelled.[32] But at the head of the party, Thorez' ailing successor, the aged Waldeck Rochet, was in fact replaced by a much younger party official, Georges Marchais, a metal worker who had rapidly risen in the party hierarchy without even being identified with a definite political viewpoint. He became known to outsiders during the May Events when he denounced the "adventurism" of the students and their allies in particularly vehement terms.

Within the forces of opposition, because of the decline of the noncommunist Left (see below), the relative weight of the P.C. and of its vassal organizations was bound to increase. The party's tactics during the 1969 presidential elections showed that it preferred at that time the discomfort of continuing Gaullist rule to a weak left-of-center government which would have tried to isolate the communist opposition. This, of course, happened in the Fourth Republic. But since the party also does not wish to be identified with the Pompidou regime and the social injustices with which the

[31] Excellent on this point as well as on the following is the special issue on "Les Communistes au Carrefour" of the journal *Esprit,* XXXVIII:5 (1970), pp. 865–914.

[32] His *Toute la vérité* (Paris: Grasset, 1970) summarizes his arguments. His more theoretical *Le Grand Tournant du Socialisme* (Paris: Gallimard, 1969) opens with the words: "It is no longer possible to be silent."

regime is likely to be charged, the P.C. must seek to become the core of a broader opposition without scaring its weak opposition partners.

Opinion polls seem to indicate that a fairly large part of the electorate views such a possibility with equanimity. Between April 1968 and December 1969 sympathies for the P.C. did not substantially decrease nor hostility violently increase.[33] Close to 70 per cent of the respondents approved (with only 21 per cent opposed) of the idea that communist Ministers were to participate in a future government of the Left, only the positions of the Prime Minister and of the President should be withheld from them. From answers to various questions it became clear that while the public viewed with grave misgivings communist control of the state, it did not believe that a sharing of power with the communists was disastrous. In 1969 45 per cent (as against 35 per cent in 1968) did not feel that at the time of the poll the communists were having an undue influence among the opposition forces. On all these questions the 21 to 34 age group was more favorable to the communists than all others.

Conversely it is no longer true, as it once was, that communist voters persist in attitudes that set them apart from the main body of political opinion. When voters are asked which policies France should follow in regard to the two super-powers, the United States and the Soviet Union, the opinions of communist voters do not vary drastically from those of the national averages.[34] They are hardly more desirous than other Frenchmen of seeing their country enter into a military alliance with the Soviet Union, nor are they more hostile toward the United States. In regard to other questions, such as the European Common Market and the Near East, variations are even slighter.

One might conclude that, after temporary disturbances, the

[33] Explicit sympathies for the party fell from 20 to 16 per cent; hostility rose from 34 to 36 per cent, but almost half of the respondents remained "neutral or indifferent" towards the P.C. See SOFRES, *Polls of 5 and 10 December 1969,* for these and all following data. For earlier findings, see also IFOP, *Les Français devant le Communisme* (mimeographed, Paris, February, 1966).

[34] See also for the following, SOFRES, *Polls of 16–22 January, 1970,* pp. 16 ff.

P.C. has once more achieved its goal of leaving the political ghetto to which it has been long confined and of being considered part and parcel of French politics. Which role it will actually be able to play may depend, at least in part, on its own internal development. What is decisive, however, for the future of the P.C. is the future of the party system.

The Noncommunist Left. In terms of electoral strength, of membership, and of traditions, even a greatly weakened Socialist party remains the most important of the organizations designated for want of a common structure as "noncommunist Left." [35] In comparison with the solid Social-Democratic parties in other European countries, the French Socialist party has lacked muscle almost since its beginnings in 1905. (The initials S.F.I.O., by which it was known for more than sixty years, express an idealistic commitment to the cause of international solidarity; they stand for *Section Française de l'Internationale Ouvrière.*)

The slow and uneven industrialization, paired with a reluctance to organize, has not only clogged the development of labor unions. By the same token the S.F.I.O. has been deprived of that base of working-class strength which has come to other Social-Democratic parties from their affiliation with a valid trade-union movement. Moreover, deeply engrained syndicalist traditions, which have survived in all "Latin" countries, have prevented the existing trade unions from collaborating too closely with any political party. When the communists came on the scene, an end was put to such prejudices; they also diverted, for a time, a substantial part of the socialists' membership and electoral following.

Since very few socialist leaders had a working-class or trade-union background, the workers' distrust of the bourgeois and intellectuals representing them in parliament weakened the party. It is true that the S.F.I.O. has had throughout its history more than its share of renegades who bolted the party in which they had started

[35] For an overall journalistic account see Jean A. Faucher, *La Gauche Française sous de Gaulle* (Paris: Didier, 1969); more historically oriented with interesting biographical sketches covering the leadership of an entire century, Daniel Mayer, *Pour une historie de la Gauche* (Paris: Plon, 1969).

their political careers, and who continued to hold elective office under another label.

Differently from British Labour, the S.F.I.O. also failed to absorb the middle-class radicals, the equivalent of the liberals in England. Here a French version of doctrinaire Marxism prevented the fusion with the neighbor to the right. For many years the wide gap between a constantly reaffirmed Marxist ideology and a political practice which was frequently at odds with professed ideals created additional difficulties for the S.F.I.O. The problem as to whether and under what conditions a socialist party could participate in a bourgeois government was endlessly debated within the party, especially during the interwar years when Léon Blum was the party's respected leader. Outstanding intellectual and distinguished lawyer that he was, he had drunk deep from the wells of Marxism and of French democratic tradition.[36] His attempts to merge both amounted frequently to exercises in sophistry lost on the working-class audiences he addressed. The discussions would have been less poignant if the party had ever been strong enough to assume control of the government. Since its weakness reduced it to becoming at best one of several partners in a coalition government, doctrinaire principles were marshaled to replace the wanting power.

When in 1956 Guy Mollet took over the leadership of the party, a post he was to occupy for twenty-three years, he did so to prevent the "decline of Marxist doctrine" in the S.F.I.O. A former professor of English, he was in many ways the prototype of the "political class" (as described above, Chap. V). Punctilious in matters of political doctrine, open to pragmatic bargaining in power and in opposition, endowed with talents and given to tactics quite similar to those of an American political boss, he never lost control of the party machine. But under his leadership, the party's membership and electoral following dwindled steadily. From a share of 23 per cent of the votes in the first post-war elections, the socialist vote plummeted to 10 per cent in 1967 and 8 per cent in the elections

---

[36] Joel Colton, *Léon Blum, Humanist in Politics* (New York: Knopf, 1966), gives a good account of the development of the S.F.I.O. during the long leadership of Blum. For the post–World War II period, see also Henry W. Ehrmann, "The Decline of the Socialist Party, in Earle, *op. cit.*, pp. 181–99.

of 1968.[37] Before the S.F.I.O. made way for a new socialist party in 1969, it was estimated that about one-sixth of the working class still voted the socialist ticket and that about one-fifth of its dues-paying members were workers. Most of the working-class following of the S.F.I.O. was concentrated in a few regions of traditional strength, but the party had some strongholds elsewhere. Almost from its beginnings it has had a large following among the wine-growers of the South, fervent devotees of republican ideals, of anti-clericalism, and of producers' cooperatives. The proportion of civil servants, especially of teachers, and of other people living on fixed income has at all times been far higher in the ranks and among the voters of the S.F.I.O. than the population at large. This made for a deliberate but not particularly dynamic following, especially since the young were no longer attracted by the party. With a total membership variously estimated at between thirty and sixty thousand, financial resources were constantly strained.

In one respect only, albeit an important one, the socialists continue to outshine their communist competitors: their positions in local government remain strong, due to experienced personnel and honored traditions. In 1965, seven years after the socialists had been driven into opposition, forty-one mayors of cities over thirty thousand in population in almost all parts of the country and forty thousand members of town and city councils were still socialists.[38] These positions of strength provided substantial patronage and held the party together when a dwindling membership, leadership clashes, and a changing constellation in the French Left started to tear at the foundations of the old S.F.I.O.

The approval of the referendum of 1962 by the electorate made it obvious that the Fifth Republic was not merely an interlude that, after ending the war in Algeria, would make room for the more traditional forms of a representative regime. If nothing else, the election of the President by popular suffrage would necessitate a regrouping within the multi-party system. A first attempt to fuse all

[37] This is the approximate share of socialist votes cast for the lists of the broader alliance, the Federation of the Left, entered on Table VI. In the 1968 parliament there were 42 socialist deputies as against 146 in 1945.

[38] For these and other data on the socialists, see Harvey G. Simmons, "The French Socialist Opposition in 1969" *Government and Opposition,* IV:3 (1969), pp. 294 ff.; and Goguel and Grosser, *op. cit.,* p. 132 ff.

opposition forces, with the exception of the communists, into a strongly structured federation failed because the old parties and their leadership reacted against the threat to their survival.[39] With the approach of the presidential elections of 1965, François Mitterand succeeded where Defferre had failed because, rather than insisting on the ultimate fusion of the parties, he contented himself with forming a looser electoral alliance. He also appeared as a less dangerous competitor since he had no traditional party apparatus at his disposal.

When he announced his candidacy he had the support of an agglomeration of political clubs, the *Convention des Institutions Républicaines* (C.I.R.). For a few years the belief was held in many quarters that the political clubs might play the roles of softening up and possibly exploding and replacing former party structures. They were the political expression of the same impetus which had led to the formation of the *"forces vives"* in the group universe (see Chap. VII). Many of the clubs, indeed, wished to be considered as a form of general interest groups.

By their very name, the clubs drew on traditions of the French Revolution. At that time, when political parties had not yet come into being, the clubs had sought simultaneously to undertake the "patriotic" education of the citizenry and to direct their political activities. Since their renaissance in the 1950s, the clubs have wavered between the same two poles.[40]

Most clubs never had a total membership of more than a few hundred and actually were adverse to mass recruiting. Usually, they prided themselves on their efforts to develop a coherent program, and in so doing they did not shun ideological commitment. To them this was not to be understood as a revival in new garb of the traditional doctrinairism of French politics, but as a recognition, in as pragmatic a fashion as possible, that all political

---

[39] The new leader-designate was Gaston Deferre, the socialist Mayor of Marseilles. Jean-Jacques Servan-Schreiber (see below) was among the principal sponsors of the enterprise.

[40] On the phenomenon and the development of the clubs see Jean-André Faucher, *Les Clubs Politiques en France* (Paris: 1965), and, vastly more reliable, Georges Lavau, "Les Clubs Politiques," *RFSP,* XV:1 (1965), pp. 103–13; and *ibid.,* XV:3 (1965), pp. 555–69. As it appears now, both writers were too sanguine in their expectations of the clubs' possible future role.

solutions are based on attitudes and choices that ought to be defined rather than concealed.

Yet, for all their efforts and partial success, the clubs were unable to channel their energies into the creation of those institutions which are needed for the running of a renovated political system. Whenever the clubs were compelled to join efforts with the traditional parties, as they did in 1965, they were concerned, and not without reason, that the immobility of the existing structure would compromise their own commitment to renovation.

Between 1965 and 1968 the Federation of the Left,[41] composed of the S.F.I.O., the Radical party (see below), and the C.I.R. added through an electoral alliance with the communists, a near-victory in the parliamentary elections of 1967 to the respectable record of Mitterand in his challenge of General de Gaulle. For the Socialist and Radical parties, well aware of their diminished attractiveness, the time seemed to have come to enlarge their basis and to transform the Federation into a more unified organization to which members could adhere directly. Such a regrouping of the entire noncommunist Left into what was to be a new Socialist party would have been tantamount to a transformation of the French party system and might have aroused interest among young voters whose number increased but who felt estranged from party life. Of necessity, it would also have had an impact on the Communist party since at the very least, it would have created a more valid partner for the attempts to form a coherent opposition to the Gaullist regime.

Nothing has come of these plans. The inability to take advantage of the May Events and the invasion of Czechoslovakia — which was followed by deep rifts among the partners as to the risks of a continuing rapprochement with the communists — rapidly undid the progress that had been made in previous years. At General de Gaulle's resignation from the Presidency the disarray became complete, disagreements over the best tactics broke into the open, so that the Left went into the first ballot of the elections with not less than five candidates. None of them was less followed by the clientele on which he counted than the socialist Defferre. About one-third of the socialists must have voted for the communist Duclos; one-third of the Federation's voters of 1968 voted immediately for

[41] Its official title was: Federation of the Democratic and Socialist Left.

Poher without waiting for the second ballot. Defferre's earlier image as a political innovator was destroyed during a mediocre campaign.

Neither the radicals nor the Convention felt that the new Socialist party in the process of formation was either sufficiently novel or promising to join with it. Moreover, in the meantime, the political clubs had lost all significance so that the Convention was reduced to a loose union of individual politicians. M. Mitterand himself, whose popularity has not ceased declining, has been listed since 1968 on the parliamentary roster as "nonaffiliated."

At its first convention, the new Socialist party — left to itself — changed its name, adopted a new platform, and replaced M. Mollet with Alain Savary, who was a long-time socialist but never a party bureaucrat and who had been in disagreement with the S.F.I.O. for several years. In parliament the new party left the Federation and established once more its own socialist group. The membership of the new party (an official figure of 75,000 appears highly inflated) is essentially the same as that of its predecessor. Whether in the end tradition or renovation of doctrine and action will win out, whether the new party will become a pole of attraction for various opposition elements, is at least doubtful. Much will depend on the socialists' relations with other forces on the Left, above all with the communists. Local elections will show whether the new party will be able to hold on to the city halls which had been the strength of the old for so long.[42]

The *Parti Socialiste Unifié* (P.S.U.) continued another old French (and European) tradition, that of a small party situated between the socialists and communists, critical of both and, at least verbally, more militant than either. For a short time, Pierre Mendès-France, himself impatient with the established parties, had belonged to it and represented it in parliament. During the Events of May it was the only political party which backed the students' revolt wholeheartedly and also the only party to which some of the student leaders had belonged beforehand. In the elections that followed it was also the only opposition party to increase its vote (by about 400,000) ; some of the dissatisfied younger socialists and communists seemed to have flocked to it, although its

---

[42] There is one city in the Southwest where the office of the mayor has been controlled for seventy-five consecutive years by (a total of three!) socialists.

gains were inferior to the losses of the other parties on the Left and its share in the total vote was below 4 per cent. In the presidential elections of the following year, the two left wing candidates (P.S.U. and Trotskyites) obtained a total of slightly over one million votes, possibly one of the flash movements which in the past have usually emerged on the Extreme Right.

The extraparliamentary influence of the P.S.U. is somewhat larger, since some of its members have leadership positions in unions belonging to the C.F.D.T., in the *Jeunes Agriculteurs,* and in the U.N.E.F. (the national students' organization). The party's leader, Michel Rocard, member of the top administrative *corps,* the Inspectorate of Finance, entered parliament in 1969 through a brilliantly fought by-election. The party recruits its fluctuating membership, amounting to about 15,000, mostly from students and intellectuals. Ideologically, it harbors every form of Marxism and neo-Marxism; its annual conventions are given over to a joust between conflicting dogmas.

Parties of the Center. It is quite characteristic that, in the parliament of 1967 and, for a time, in that of 1968, the radicals belonged to a Federation of the Left, but that they have since then, and without new elections, rejoined the center of the political spectrum. This most typical of all French political parties was rightly considered the very incarnation of the Third Republic; it showed astonishing staying power under the Fourth Republic, and has so far survived into the Fifth Republic.

Even during its height of power the Radical party had no formal organization except on paper; its annual conventions were gatherings of politicians holding elective office on the national or local level, whose reelection was based on personal reputation and on the services they had rendered to their constituencies. The complete freedom from party directives and party programs which radical representatives enjoyed made their parliamentary groups into a collection of individuals whose orientation toward day-to-day political decisions could differ widely. In general, a radical Senator was far more conservative than his colleague in the lower house. This added to the confusion of coalition alignments — and made the party's phraseology all but meaningless.

Radical liberalism, which at times affects outright libertarianism, likes to trace its ancestry back to the Jacobins and to the republicans of 1848. Its political strength, however, dates from the era when it fought clericalism in all its forms. At times the fusion between ranking personalities in the Masonic Lodges and the Radical party was complete. Once the separation of church and state was assured, the radicals became, even before the First World War, the staunch supporters of the economic and social *status quo* attractive to the middle classes which were then rising to political prominence. A doctrinaire egalitarianism flattered small interests which explains the electoral strength of the radicals in towns and countryside — mainly in areas of mediocre economic development in the South and the Southeast. But wherever circumstances demanded it, a principled Jacobinism was perfectly capable of adjusting itself to policies perpetuating differences of wealth and existing class structures. A leftist "sensibility," adverse to the concentration of power in the hands of the executive, was the main criterion by which ambitious and able leaders (or leaders-to-be) were recruited for a career in the radical camp. The writings of Alain (see above) provided a convenient rationalization for an attitude seemingly coherent on a philosophical level but utterly contradictory in its political consequences.[43]

When the Fourth Republic came into being, the fate of the radicals seemed sealed. A party that had identified itself completely with the discredited institutions and political mores of the Third Republic and that was still adverse to modern forms of party organization seemed unsuitable for the needs and the temper of the moment. Yet between 1948 and 1958 the radicals furnished not only numerous cabinet members but also more Premiers than any other party; for a long time the speakers of both houses of parliament were radicals.

This astonishing comeback was a consequence of the permanent features of the political system and especially of the endur-

[43] See Alain, *op. cit.,* and the excellent criticism in Kirchheimer, "The Transformation," pp. 178 f. For the history and structure of the Radical party in general see Daniel Bardonnet, *Évolution de la structure du Parti Radical* (Paris: Mont Chrestien, 1960) and an informative summary in Pierre Avril, *Le Gouvernement de la France* (Paris: Éditions Universitaires, 1969), pp. 55–58. (Now also in an English translation as *Politics of France,* Baltimore: Penguin, 1970.)

ance of an unstable party system. The solid footholds which radicals had established in local and departmental politics and historical loyalties, especially in the South, could be turned into profitable assets when the style of the Fourth Republic, both within and outside parliament, came to resemble more and more that of the Third.

Most important, however, was the fact that radicals, by composition and temperament, could play to perfection the role of the Center, of the "swamp" whose importance in the French multi-party system has been described. After 1946, the Radical party's electoral strength never exceeded 11 per cent, but it was capable of participating in all government coalitions and soon became indispensable to most. Because it offered opportunity for office and power, it was again attractive to young and able men, although there was no rejuvenation of ideas or methods.

In the Fifth Republic, the radicals were confined to the camp of the opposition and lost further strength in every national election while still holding on to important positions on the level of local government and politics. For a time the newly formed Federation of the Left was for the radicals a welcome means of concealing their weakness behind a larger coalition.

When the Federation broke apart, the radical group in the National Assembly was reduced to 13 deputies. (A corresponding group in the Upper House still has 41 Senators as members.) As before, the individuals who appear at the party's annual conventions are active in national and local politics but neither share political convictions nor agree even on tactics. At a moment when the Radical party appeared once more to face extinction, Jean-Jacques Servan-Schreiber was installed as its Secretary General. Wealthy son of a family with diversified holdings in the publishing field, himself a gifted journalist, he pledged to endow the old party with a new style and a new program. His book containing the program and entitled *Heaven and Earth* seeks to rival its author's earlier best seller, *The American Challenge*,[44] by its controversial proposals and imaginative language. The boldness of the program for reform is far greater than what the French Left published during the preceding years: confiscatory

[44] (New York: Atheneum 1968.)

inheritance taxes; cessation of economic subsidies, and other drastic measures for the redistribution of national wealth, all subordinated to the needs of rapid economic growth and further industrialization. Little of this appears congenial to the temper or the interest of the party notables. Servan-Schreiber's efforts could be likened to those of Pierre Mendès-France who during the last years of the Fourth Republic had waged a similar and entirely unsuccessful effort at making over the Radical party in his own image of a modernizing reformer. In the summer of 1970, M. Servan-Schreiber used a by-election for a vacant parliamentary seat in Nancy to challenge the Gaullist candidate in a staunchly Gaullist region which felt neglected by the policies of the national government. Without any previous connection in the constituency he won a surprise victory (45 per cent of the votes in the first, 55 in the second ballot with, it is true, a record-high number of abstentions) at the expense of all of his competitors with the significant exception of the communists who bettered their previous record.

Whatever the possible political significance of popular sympathies for a somewhat Kennedy-like, untraditional candidate and for a campaign which made modernization a nonpartisan objective, the radicals will profit little by Servan-Schreiber's victory. Sensing that an identification with any party was costing him votes, the candidate let it be known that he would resign shortly his leadership position in the Radical party thereby returning to that pattern of independence which had been customary for successful politicians in the Third and Fourth Republics.[45]

The group "Progress and Modern Democracy," (P.M.D.), is another loose union of thirty-three deputies in the Assembly who lack even the ties that are still binding the radicals to each other, namely those of a common political past. Conservatives and

[45] Some well-informed observers have attributed to the Nancy election a far greater importance than is suggested here. See, for instance, Pierre Viansson-Ponté, "L'Enjeu de Nancy," *Le Monde,* June, 25, 1970. The outcome of another by-election by which he sought to challenge the Prime Minister in Bordeaux was disastrous for M. Servan-Schreiber. It made it appear more than dubious that the reform of the French party system can be brought about by the methods inaugurated by a wealthy political amateur.

liberals, some of them with a long parliamentary experience, have joined those who once represented the *Movement Républicain Populaire* (M.R.P.).

In 1946, the M.R.P. had emerged for a time as the strongest political party in terms of electoral appeal and the only truly new creation of the postwar political scene. The explicit purpose of the M.R.P. had been to overcome the schism between the republic and faithful Catholics by offering a program of bold economic and social reform. Since it wanted to compete with the socialists and communists with whom it shared governmental office in the immediate post-Liberation period, it laid the foundation for a mass party, and at one time had a membership of over 200,000. For a time it was also able to impose on its representatives in parliament a far stricter discipline than had been customary beyond the benches of the Extreme Left.

The party furnished the governments of the Fourth Republic with five Prime Ministers and an impressive number of gifted and youthful Ministers. Since its support was sought by most cabinets, whatever their political orientation, the M.R.P. acquired the typical qualities of a French center movement: soon enough it was wading, like the radicals, into the "swamp." When the postwar eagerness for sweeping reforms had receded, the M.R.P. was in part unwilling and in part unable to turn into the broadly based conservative mass party which the Christian-Democratic parties in Germany and Italy have become.

The decline in membership and votes had set in before General de Gaulle's return to power. It intensified in the Fifth Republic when the M.R.P.'s following was won over by the leaders and the institutions of the new republic. Former M.R.P. senators, Lecanuet and Poher, presented themselves as unsuccessful candidates in both presidential elections. But this only accelerated the disintegration of the party, which officially dissolved to permit its elected representatives to merge with the P.M.D. This group claims from its members neither adherence to a program nor any voting discipline.[46] Before General de Gaulle's resignation, its tactics amounted to those of a loyal opposition, trying to influence governmental policies from without, occasionally

[46] For details on the democratic center, see Jean-Luc Parodi, "Les Paradoxes du Centre Démocrate," *RFSP,* XVI:4 (1966), pp. 957 ff.

pressing for social reforms and regularly for a greater commitment to European unity. The battle for the referendum and the Presidency in 1969 found the group divided between the advocates of the "Oui" and the "Non" and the partisans of Poher and of Pompidou.

When the smoke of electoral battle had cleared and M. Chaban-Delmas formed his first Cabinet under the Pompidou administration, three prominent members of the P.M.D. entered it and occupied the important Ministries of Justice, Agriculture, and Labor (Messrs. Pleven, Duhamel, and Fontanet).[47] Some of their colleagues on the benches of the P.M.D. continued to vote with the opposition, but with the disappearance of General de Gaulle against whom some of them held personal grudges, they too might some day be willing to join a government coalition. The P.M.D. has therefore become the classical "nonparty" of French conservatism with considerable strength left in the Upper House and in the municipal councils of towns and of some important cities. However with a change in attitude towards the government they have become less and less distinguishable from the Independent Republicans.

The *Républicains Indépendents* (R.I.) originated as a separate group in 1962 when the conservatives in parliament divided over the question of constitutional reform. The R.I. who sided with General de Gaulle on that occasion have regularly voted with the Gaullist party since then and have furnished a number of Ministers to all the governments in power since 1962. The new party was saved from showing the sparseness of its electoral following when President and Prime Minister insisted that even in the first ballot of 1967 elections and for most constituencies in the 1968 elections only a single candidate was to run for the majority in each constituency. Yet in both elections the number of deputies elected on the common list but affiliated with the R.I. has increased (see Table VI).

The leader of the party, M. Valéry Giscard d'Estaing, was Finance Minister under two of General de Gaulle's Prime Ministers. Temporarily eliminated from the government he is once more occupying this important post in the Chaban-Delmas government. Born in 1926, scion of an old family whose members

---

[47] The Foreign Minister, Maurice Schumann, was one of the outstanding postwar leaders of the M.R.P. before joining the Gaullist party.

have for a long time combined careers in banking with service to the state, Giscard d'Estaing became one of the most brilliant graduates the E.N.A. has produced since its founding. He is a member of the most distinguished corps of civil servants, the Inspectorate of Finance, as were before him his father, his grandfather, and one of his uncles.

For a time M. Giscard d'Estaing was considered as the favorite "outsider" for General de Gaulle's succession.[48] This probably explains why he and others among the R.I. deputies came out in opposition to the referendum of 1969 which opened chances for such a succession. But Pompidou's candidacy and his initial emphasis on broadening the basis of his support beyond the Gaullist party, left the R.I. no choice but to abandon at least for this election the idea of a candidate of their own. Once more well-represented in the government and rewarded by fairly important committee assignments in parliament, the R.I. has not gone far in developing a party organization in the country beyond its positions in local governments which however are substantial: close to 90 per cent of its deputies in parliament are also mayors. If this too corresponds once more to the customary pattern of conservative politics, the economic and social policies advocated by the R.I. are undoubtedly more progressive, more concerned with industrial and technological development than those of classical French conservatism which were mostly though never exclusively oriented towards laissez-faire.

Union des Démocrates pour la République (U.D.R.). The U.N.R., as the Gaullist party was then known,[49] thrown hastily

[48] On the various groups of indépendents and on Giscard d'Estaing's efforts, see Marielle Bal, "Les Indépendents," *RFSP*, XV:3 (1965), pp. 537–55, and Marie-Christine Kessler, "M. Valéry Giscard d'Estaing et les républicains indépendants: réalités et perspectives," *ibid.*, XVI:5 (1966), pp. 940–57.

[49] The Gaullist party has changed names even more often than initials. What had been at its founding the *Union pour la Nouvelle République* (U.N.R.) became in 1967 the *Union Démocratique pour la Ve République* (UDV^e) and the party outside of parliament has kept that designation. But in 1968, the Gaullists campaigned under the name *Union des Démocrates pour la République* and are now largely known by the initials U.D.R. In order to simplify matters, the discussion of the Gaullist party following in the text will use exclusively these initials even though, where developments before 1968 are mentioned, they amount to a neologism.

together after General de Gaulle's return to power in 1958, is the one true novelty in French party politics. Novel it is first and foremost by the extent and durability of its success. It has already been the leader and the core of a stable governing coalition for a far longer period than has any other political movement in the history of French republics. When, only weeks after its birth, it won over 20 per cent of the vote and, more surprisingly, almost 40 per cent of the seats in the first parliament of the new republic, it benefited largely from the floating vote which in the past had swelled, but never for long, other surge movements. The plethora of seats in the National Assembly, with which the party found itself blessed after the run-off elections, resulted from a bandwagon effect which the electoral system chosen by General de Gaulle was expected to prevent.

From then on, and in each parliamentary election, the U.D.R. increased its share of the total vote (see Table VI), until in 1968 the Gaullists and their allies commanded in the first ballot an electoral following of over 10 million Frenchmen, 46 per cent of the votes cast and 36 per cent of the registered votes — a record never obtained under a republican regime in France. The social stratification and regional distribution of the Gaullist vote as it evolved over the first decade of the regime is at least equally remarkable. (For details on the 1968 election, see Table VII.) Initially confined to the traditionally conservative regions of the country, especially in the Northeast and Northwest, the party has swept south of the Loire and conquered many historically progressive bastions. While in the beginning the U.D.R. did better in urban centers and in constituencies most touched by the modernization of the economy, it has since increased its following also in backward rural regions. Because of the phenomenon of shifting abstentionism, it is difficult to tabulate how many voters the U.D.R. has won away from parties of the Left — most estimates conclude that this gain must amount to at least 1.5 million or 15 per cent of the present Gaullist vote. Many Gaullist voters still come from the urban and rural middle classes. But at least under the impact of the 1968 events, the working-class vote for Gaullist candidates was for the first time equal and possibly larger than that for the communists. It must however be kept in mind that in all social categories and from 1958 on, women have voted more heavily Gaullist than men, which blurs the picture somewhat.[50] (For details see Table VII.)

In spite of the broad range of its following the party has continued to be regarded, by many of its friends and foes alike, as a party of the Right: in 1966, 53 per cent of the respondents to a public opinion poll classified it as belonging to the "Right" or "Extreme Right" (with only 17 per cent undecided how to answer). In the spring of 1969 the attitude of the U.N.R. voters towards some social problems such as strikes and trade unions was more conservative that that of all other respondents.[51] It is true, that in the preceding elections voters of the Extreme Right had joined the Gaullist ranks which they had left under the impact of the government's Algerian policy. In subsequent months, one of the Cabinet ministers spoke with concern about a right wing radicalism operating partly from within the confines of the Gaullist party.

All this does not make the U.D.R. into a conservative party "like the others." Its political origin as an instrument in the service of a leader who had little use for any party, including his own; its progressive development as a structure to ensure General de Gaulle's succession; and the new trends to which it has been submitted since the father figure has left the scene are all of importance in explaining the political orientation of the U.D.R. and the role that it will be called upon to play in the France of the seventies.

"The innermost thought of General de Gaulle is not all there is to Gaullism," it has been said. ". . . But, on the other hand, the motives [of the millions of U.D.R. voters] have sometimes only a rather loose relationship with the essence of Gaullism." [52]

What then is the essence of Gaullism? Another astute observer has remarked that de Gaulle has regarded at all times the French state with the eye of a "great Jacobin cardinal" [53] — his views

[50] For details see the election studies by Lancelot quoted previously (Ch. IV n. 34) and François Goguel, "Bipolarisation ou rénovation du Centrisme?" *RFSP*, XVII:5 (1967), pp. 927 ff. and "Les Élections législatives des 23 et 30 juin 1968," *ibid.*, XVII:5 (1968), pp. 852 ff.

[51] See Deutsch, Lindon et Weill, *op. cit.*, p. 113 and *Sondages* XXXI:1:2 (1969), p. 81.

[52] René Rémond, *La Droite* . . . etc., *op. cit.*, p. 279. See *ibid.*, pp. 280 ff. also for the following.

[53] Lacouture, *op. cit.*, p. 170.

TABLE VII.   *Sociological Composition of the Gaullist Electorate in 1968*

	(1) % in the adult population	*(2)* % in the votes for UDR/RI	% of difference between (1) and (2)
Men	48	46	—2
Women	52	54	+2
Ages:			
Voters between 21 and 34 / Voters between 35 and 49	56	55	—1
Voters between 50 and 64 / Voters 65 and older	44	45	+1
Occupations:			
Farmers	17	18	+1
Professionals and Management	5	6	+1
Industrialists and Businessmen	10	14	+4
White Collar, Lower Civil Servants, etc.	15	18	+3
Workers	31	25	—6
Retired and Without Profession	22	19	—3
Places of Residence:			
Rural Communities	37	40	+3
Towns of less than 20,000	13	16	+3
Towns of 20,000 to 100,000	13	11	—2
Towns of more than 100,000	19	19	0
Region of Paris	18	14	—4

Adapted from Jean Charlot, *Le Phénomène Gaulliste* (Paris. Fayard, 1970), p. 69.

represented indeed a mixture of Richelieu and Robespierre. Such cult of the state had nothing in common with the obsolete dreams of monarchists and counterrevolutionary doctrinaires, such as Maurras and the *Action Française*. He was out of sympathy with their longings for corporatist organizations in a decentralized state. To him not only parties but also all other organized inter-mediaries standing between the citizen and the state were what the "categories" were to Richelieu, the "particular societies" to Jean-Jacques Rousseau, and the parties to Napoleon: disturbers of the national interest and particularly disastrous in a nation full of volatile centrifugal trends.

Like Rousseau, de Gaulle was convinced that there is a dor-mant general will which only needs awakening, that the people want what is right even if they are not always able to see what they want without proper guidance. Like Napoleon, he liked to admonish his compatriots, of whatever political camp, to be "good Frenchmen with him." The resolve to take major ques-tions of national concern out of the political realm, to "depoli-ticize" them as de Gaulle's first Premier Michel Debré has put it, denoted of course a definitely political purpose. It was a policy which before de Gaulle not only the first Bonaparte but also Napoleon III had vowed to pursue.[54]

General de Gaulle's aversion to all political parties was con-firmed by the debacle of the *Rassemblement du Peuple Français* (R.P.F.) which he himself had founded in 1947 to attack the institutions of the Fourth Republic. As a mass movement, the R.P.F. had not been free of rightist radicalism distasteful to its leader. Its parliamentary representatives had not withstood the temptations of cabinet seats; finally the party had succumbed to the centrifugal forces of day-to-day politics.

When in 1958, upon de Gaulle's return to power, it became necessary to seek a parliamentary representation for Gaullist ideas, the U.D.R. prospered from the first by its complete identi-fication with the General's views. Among such views were the insights the young officer had won as a student of military stra-tegy: what counted was to reach limited objectives with the help of available resources. "There exists," he wrote later, "no absolute truth, either in politics or in strategy. There are only the circum-stances."[55] To master "the circumstances" dictated in part by

[54] See Marcel Merle, who speaks about "organized depolitization" in his article "Inventaire des apolitismes," Association Française de Science Politique, *La Dépolitisation, mythe ou réalité?* (Paris: Colin, 1961), pp. 48 ff.

[55] *War Memoirs, III,* p. 136.

the domestic and international environment, in part by the new constitution which had not wanted to depart entirely from the parliamentary form of government, it was first of all necessary to enforce strict discipline on the party representatives in parliament.

Because of deep divergences over the solution of the Algerian conflict, this led to the expulsion from the party of some of de Gaulle's earliest and most prominent supporters. But unlike what happened to political apostates in the past, anathema from the U.D.R. leadership ended the careers of the dissidents. Whenever they sought elective office, they were always soundly defeated. This was enough to discourage any further thought of defection among Gaullist deputies and senators.

Of ideas or ideologies, there was little discussion among party leaders or militants, at least not in the open. Undoubtedly General de Gaulle's concept of *grandeur* was a loadstar for the movement; it permitted the party to decide which road to take when political alternatives appeared and to "manipulate ideology for the maximum general appeal." [56] De Gaulle's concept of *grandeur* has been judged an antiquated and hence quixotic disturbance for present-day international relations. But its function was also, if not primarily, domestic: designed to heighten pride and belief in a great destiny, it is an antidote to disunity and a diversion from discord. After the Third Republic had ignominiously collapsed in 1940, and the Fourth had become the "sick man of Europe" in the fifties, France had to be healed of a dangerously low self-esteem. The great leader, de Gaulle, had to become the healer, enabling France to live up to her "exalted destiny." His speeches as a wartime exile or as the President of the Republic were to many outsiders — and to critical Frenchmen as well — at times exasperating because they heap exaggerated praise on the nation and its leader for past achievements. But, the speaker frequently treated Frenchmen as if they had already done things which remain to be done. His exhortations were designed to coax his listeners into efforts and changes of which he believed them to be capable, with proper guidance.[57]

[56] Kirchheimer, "The Transformation of the Western European Party Systems" in La Palombara and Weiner, *op. cit.*, p. 187.

[57] On this point see the excellent essay by Stanley Hoffmann, "De Gaulle's Memoirs. The Hero as History." *World Politics*, XIII:1 (1960), p. 151.

Until his reelection in 1965 General de Gaulle was successful in discouraging all attempts to develop the U.D.R. into the structured and disciplined Conservative party which France has never known. The upper echelons of the party hierarchy constituted almost without exception a "peer group." All of its members had belonged directly, or indirectly through a single intermediary, to General de Gaulle's entourage during the days of the Free French movement in London and Algiers, during the immediate post-Liberation period, or during the R.P.F. episode.[58] Since those troubled times had attracted men of widely different background to General de Gaulle, the ties that bound them to each other consisted mostly of their personal loyalty to the leader.

De Gaulle's second Prime Minister, Georges Pompidou, had never run for political office and was not himself a member of the U.D.R. But as chief of the government majority he drew the lessons of the presidential election of 1965 and of a near-defeat for Gaullism in the parliamentary elections of 1967: after the disappearance of the charismatic leader and whenever it might occur, only a better organized party would be able to manage an orderly succession and to ensure the survival of Gaullism *sans* de Gaulle.

New by-laws, adopted by the party convention in 1967, gave muscle to the party organization at all levels; they also secured the unity of party and government by stipulating that the Prime Minister, a member of his cabinet designated by him and all former Prime Ministers belonging to the U.D.R. were ex-officio members of the party's executive. Similar liaisons were effected between the Gaullist group in the two houses of parliament and the party directorate.[59] The party's apparatus became ever better equipped to furnish such services as information, propaganda

[58] For details on this and on the structure and history of the U.D.R. in general see the excellent study by Jean Charlot, *L'U.N.R., étude du pouvoir au sein d'un parti politique* (Paris: Colin, 1967). On more recent developments see also the same author's, *Le Phénomène Gaulliste* (Paris: Fayard, 1970). For interesting biographical details (written in a lighter vein but entirely reliable) on the Gaullist leadership, see the book by Pierre Viansson-Ponté, *The King and His Court* (Boston: Houghton Mifflin Co., 1965).

[59] For the text of the by-laws, see Goguel and Grosser, *op. cit.*, pp. 162–7. General de Gaulle, who has never appeared at a party convention, referred only indirectly to those important rules at one of his Press Conferences.

material and detailed advice to candidates and elected representatives at various levels of government.

Since that time, the U.D.R. has taken on more and more the
characteristics of what has been called a modern "catch-all"
party. For parties of this kind, the widest possible audience and
immediate electoral successes remain the principal goal.

> If the party cannot hope to catch all categories of voters, it may
> have a reasonable expectation of catching more votes in all these
> categories whose interests do not adamantly conflict . . . Even
> more important is the heavy concentration on issues which are
> scarcely liable to meet resistance in the community. National
> societal goals transcending group interests offer the best sales
> prospect for a party intent on establishing or enlarging an appeal
> previously limited to specific sections of the population.[60]

Table VIII shows how successful the U.D.R. has been with such
tactics. At the beginning of the Fifth Republic there was a wide
gap between the number of voters identifying with the Gaullist
party and those, far more numerous, who were swayed by the
plebiscitarian appeal of the national hero. With each succeeding
election, the differences narrowed until in 1968–69 the scissors
had closed. One is tempted to conclude that once this happened
the leader became expendable; the succession "without chaos"
was prepared. It also explains why the triumph of the 1968 elections (a triumph of Pompidou as some have said) was unsatisfactory to de Gaulle himself who therefore went on to seek, but not
to win, another direct confirmation from the electorate (see
above Chap. IV).

Since the replacement of de Gaulle by Pompidou, the U.D.R.
has been facing some of the difficulties all parties of this kind
must know, but aggravated by its own historical origins. De
Gaulle himself who had provided a bond of common loyalty for
a rather disparate following had not been lifted to his eminent
position by the party such as an Adenauer in the German Christian-Democratic Union or a Disraeli in the British Conservative

---

[60] Kirchheimer, *op. cit.*, p. 186. Specifically on the U.D.R. as a party
of this kind, the excellently informed studies by John S. Ambler, "The
Democratic Union for the Republic: To Survive de Gaulle," *Rice University Studies* LIX:3 (1968), pp. 1–51; and Charlot, *Le Phénomène
. . . etc., op. cit.*, pp. 63 ff.

Table VIII. *Presidential and Parliamentary Gaullism*[a] (*in percentages of votes cast*)

	Referendum Sept.1958	*Referendum Oct.1962*	*First ballot pres. elections Dec.1965*	*Referendum Apr.1969*	*First ballot pres. elections June 1969*
Presidential Gaullism	79.2	61.7	43.7	46.7	43.9
	First ballot: elections Nov.1958	*Elections Oct.1962*	*Elections Mar.1967*	*Elections June 1968*	
Parliamentary Gaullism	20.4	31.9	37.8[b]	46.0[b]	

[a] Suggested by Alain Lancelot, "Les Élections des 5 et 12 mars 1967," *Projet* 15 (1967), p. 551.
[b] These figures are slightly misleading since they include the votes for the U.D.R.'s coalition partners.

party, both parties of comparable orientation and structure. Moreover neither he nor some of his closest collaborators who continue to occupy leadership positions in the U.D.R. and the government were much given to recognize a party as the proper vehicle for the required political bargaining and logrolling.

Of leadership divisions there are many and some over seemingly fundamental issues.[61] This however is not unusual in catch-all parties. The important question is whether they break apart over existing differences or whether they hold together in spite of these differences in order not to lose their position as the dominant or government party. The latter has been the attitude of the Italian Christian-Democrats and *mutatis mutandis* of the major U.S. parties. In the past, French conservatives never really had such a choice because they never came close to dominance and therefore saw little reason to sacrifice the beliefs (or the career) of the individual politician on the altar of party discipline.

The first and unavoidable quarrels among the Gaullist epigones (or "orphans" as they are called in Paris) have not led to major dislocations of party cohesion. Some groups and personalities, especially those identified with the Gaullist Left and who claim to have the monopoly on faithfulness to General de Gaulle's ideas on social reform, have been dealt with summarily. Some were expelled; others chose to submit. This was done all the easier as even in its changed form, the U.D.R., unlike catch-all parties in other countries, does not have a mass membership. Hence, leadership divisions have not necessarily had repercussions or meaning for the *militants* and even less for a hardly existing rank and file.[62]

However what could provide a more lasting cement is lacking: there is no threat from a credible and coherent opposition which would force the present majority to shore its strength and forget

[61] Roy Macridis, *op. cit.,* pp. 589 ff. lists them with great, and quite amusing, completeness.

[62] Official membership figures are not available. General estimates are about 1 member per 1,000 voters, which would mean a membership of between 80,000 and 100,000. Charlot, *Le Phénomène Gaulliste,* estimates that in 1970 the membership could reach about 160,000, an as yet unconfirmed assumption. An inquiry conducted in 1968 reported that in the city of Grenoble, a center of fairly intense political activity, the U.D.R. had "virtually no members." Berger, *op. cit.,* p. 450.

its division. The U.D.R.'s very plethora of votes in parliament loosens the need for discipline. How to turn the present breathing spell (to last until the next parliamentary elections in 1973, unless there is premature dissolution) to permanent advantage, has given rise to yet another division of opinion. Here the most prominent Gaullists appear to be on different sides of a controversy which mirrors fundamental trends in French representative traditions. Characteristically enough French observers with their never failing sense for historical memories see here the reappearance of the Jacobin and the Girondist mentality.[63]

The Jacobins, among them Michel Debré, de Gaulle's first Prime Minister and the father of the Gaullist constitution, and now also President Pompidou want to see the U.D.R. as the well-structured and muscled core of the majority and as the palladium of a powerful state. A strong hand over its representatives might be necessary to enable it to fulfill its mission. In a speech on which he has elaborated since, President Pompidou emphasized the need for a "structured opposition possessing its cadres and its doctrine" so that "useful confrontation" could take place in the country as well as in parliament. But he added significantly that neither opposition nor majority should be shapeless formations which one joins or leaves at any moment and at will.[64]

The Girondists — and Pompidou's first Prime Minister Chaban-Delmas is considered their spokesman — want to open the gates of the majority even wider until possibly nobody but the communists are left outside a coalition comprising parties and personalities. Like the majorities grouped around the radicals of the Third Republic, the government coalition would recommend itself to political activists and to the voters by a record of practical performance. The U.D.R. would still be the core of the majority. But a more traditional cadre party exclusively composed of notables would be adequate for such a role.

It may be assumed that temperamentally both camps are represented among the leaders and the *militants* of the present U.D.R. What deprives, at least for the time being, the Girondist perspective of its persuasiveness is the U.D.R.'s continuing lack

[63] See Pierre Vianisson-Ponté, "Les Gaullismes," *Le Monde,* April 11, 1970.

[64] See *Le Monde,* June 30, 1970.

of strong roots in local politics and administration. The radicals, the Center, and the socialists as well, were partly judged on their performance and continuous experience in municipalities; on the basis of such judgments they were able to somewhat survive disaster on the national scene. It has been calculated[65] that in six selected departments where after the 1968 elections the U.D.R. deputies occupied 71 per cent of the seats in parliament, Gaullists furnished only 10 per cent of the mayors, while the socialists with only 9 per cent of the seats representing these same departments were mayors in 17 per cent of the municipalities. The Gaullists control only 25 of the 159 cities over 30,000 population and only two of the twenty largest. (It is true that Chaban-Delmas himself is mayor of one of them, Bordeaux, where in the sixteenth century Michel Montaigne had been among his distinguished predecessors.)

Whether this situation will substantially change during the next years might be of importance for the future of the party, its structure and its expectations. For the time being such weakness is above all organizational. Differently from the traditional parties, the U.D.R. is not organized on the basis of the *commune* and the canton but on the basis of legislative constituencies, in part because the party simply lacks the manpower to mount extensive local organizations. "Such," M. Kesselman concludes, "is the price a catch-all party may have to pay for directing its energies and resources to other (i.e., national) concerns." Here the Gaullists are paying the price for not having built a party with a large membership. Whether this decision is going to be reversed remains to be seen. In other countries too the trend seems to be away from large membership organizations.

But as long as the Gaullist party lacks a solid foothold in the *communes* a serious setback in national elections would be most critical for it. Hence the Gaullist deputies are fearful that governmental policies might hurt constituency interests and hence their chances for reelection. Such fears are heightened because the role of parliament in the decision-making process remains limited (see below Chap. X). Policies which in the future will divide the French community will also divide the party, and the tensions

[65] See, also for the following, Kesselman, "Over-Institutionalisation . . ." *op. cit.,* pp. 36 f.

which are bound to develop between the government and its majority might prove more dangerous to the unity of the U.D.R. than dissertations on the correct interpretation of Gaullist thought. Here it might become of importance whether the President of the Republic, no longer the charismatic founder of the party, will be able to play not only the role of a national arbiter but that of an effective majority leader as well.

CONCLUSION: MUTATIONS IN THE PARTY SYSTEM?

The party system has been indicted, with many good reasons, for the malfunctioning of the parliamentary system in the Third and Fourth Republics. Yet, in spite of their discredit, parties responsible for the previous stalemate have survived in more or less their old form, if sometimes under new labels; whatever little there is of party life and party organization has kept many of the old characteristics. As before some of the more outstanding figures in parliament speak and act in their own name rather in that of any party. During both presidential election campaigns most of the candidates have found it opportune to distance themselves from all parties even if they have relied on a party apparatus for the organization of their campaign. The one new party, the U.D.R., is still undecided as to which structure will be most appropriate for its future role.

The old parties are not only reproached for their past failure, but also for their lack of present significance. The doctrines around which they were formed are exhausted. What voters and, above all, political activists are seeking are not so much new doctrines as the assurance of fair representation for their interests and values, a meaningful choice of alternatives, and at the same time satisfactory possibilities for political participation. Nothing of this is provided by the existing parties except by the communists and, to an extent, by the U.D.R. None of the others seems worthy of the affective support which actual or potential activists want to lend to the party of their choice. "Those interested in political reform are not willing to join traditional parties, and those who are in traditional parties are usually not interested in reforming them." [66]

Fortunately for the future of French democracy such a dis-

[66] Berger, etc., *op. cit.,* p. 451.

satisfaction has not led to a wholesale condemnation of a system of competing parties as such. While opinion polls continue to reveal a certain ambivalence towards the role of parties in the political process, in the fall of 1969 69 per cent of respondents believed that it would be "very grave" or "grave" if the freedom of parties were interfered with. (It is true that liberty for trade unions and parliament ranked higher in the scale of public concern.) [67]

As we have seen, hopes for mutations in the party system have not been lacking. The so-called *forces vives*, reorganized and rejuvenated interest groups and the political clubs were at one time considered as possible heirs to the parties. Yet, the new structures proved too fragile when they came into contact with such realities as elections or the administrative process. While they might have taken on some of the recruiting functions of traditional parties, they were altogether unable to represent or to effectively aggregate and transmit the concerns of the electorate to the political process.

Other hopes for a restructuring and simplification of the party system arose from expectations that the new institutional framework, created by the Fifth Republic, was bound to transform the parties. It is quite true that parties are shaped, and perhaps predominantly so, by the structure of the political system within which they operate.[68] The new mode of presidential elections by popular suffrage and the new rules of parliamentary procedures (see below Chap. X) furthered a regrouping and an apparent simplification of the party system. Under such conditions, even the electoral system reintroduced in 1958, which in the past often resulted in protracted atomization of both majority and opposition in parliament, for a time furthered the formation of what

[67] See SOFRES, *Polls of Oct. 29 to Nov. 3, 1969*, pp. 78–83. These opinions are held fairly uniformly by all socio-economic groups and by those in different political camps, except that those on the Extreme Right are less and those of the Extreme Left are more concerned for such freedoms than the average. Another polling organization found that in 1967–68 only 15 to 19 per cent wished to see the parties play a "less important role," see *Sondages*, XXXI: 1–2 (1969), p. 32.

[68] This is the main thesis of the masterly analysis of the British party system by R. T. McKenzie, *British Political Parties* (2nd ed.; New York: Praeger, 1964).

has been called political dualism, i.e., a clearer confrontation of majority and opposition.

But such simplification as seemed to have been obtained did not survive the shock of the May Events and of the subsequent elections. The confusion which befell the opposition at the time of the presidential election and the temptations to which the present majority is subjected are only variations on recurrent difficulties.

The most serious among them is for the time being the lack of a valid opposition and therefore of a credible alternative to those who have been the "ins" since 1958. Even in June 1968, at a moment when the Gaullists were able to maximize their appeal to a frightened silent majority,[69] more than 50 per cent of the voters (or 11.2 million) cast in the first ballot a vote against the present majority. The electoral system translated this into a Gaullist landslide, leaving to the opposition less than one-fourth of the seats in parliament. Political developments after General de Gaulle's resignation moved representatives who had been elected on an opposition ticket over to the majority without a new consultation of the electorate — the exact phenomenon which in the eyes of the voters had marked the preceding republics as hopelessly unrepresentative.

Even at a time when hopes for a dualism — or "bipolarization" — run high, chances for a two-party system appeared mediocre.[70] As in Italy, the existence of a strong Communist party does not just add another piece to the political chessboard but transforms the conditions and the rules of the game. If the forces left of center seek a firmer alliance with the communists, they will antagonize their own more conservative following which then will see no alternative but to join forces with the present majority.

[69] General de Gaulle had his own, untranslatable description of that phenomenon when he spoke of *"le calme raisonné de la profondeur fran-çaise."*

[70] The best summary of the various points made in an earlier debate is to be found in a symposium, "La France, va-t-elle au bipartisme?" *France-Forum,* No. 80 (1967), pp. 1–20. See also an article with the same title by Alain Duhamel in *Le Monde,* June 14, 1967. More skeptical and obviously more realistic about the chances for a classical or modified two-party system was the excellently informed article by Fran-çois Goguel, "Bipolarisation ou rénovation du Centrisme?" *RFSP,* XVII:5 (1967), pp. 927 ff.

If the noncommunist Left wants to avoid such a narrowing of its base and turns resolutely away from the communists, the latter will prove attractive for all who distrust the Center because of its defense of vested rights. Such considerations and the doubts they raise have destroyed time and again the cohesion of the Left and have discouraged the formation of truly new, less anachronistic parties. It is true that clashes of personalities and the weight of historical memories have aggravated the difficulties. There is of course one way out of these difficulties: to reduce the Communist party to an insignificant sect by providing through other parties the needed vehicle for the "plebeian" interests[71] in society. That such a course is no longer regarded as a realistic alternative in either France or Italy points to fundamental differences between these countries and all other European democracies which do not have to reckon with any significant communist movement.

This difference explains why in terms of organizational strength and representativeness the often quoted statement by André Malraux remains correct: "There is nothing between us (the Gaullists) and the communists." It has already been shown that this situation has an impact on the future of the U.D.R. as well. In its present form that party has been able to manage successfully the Algerian and the succession crisis. But the continuing success of representative government calls for the emergence of parties (or of a stable coalition of parties) which would be able to alternate in power. Lacking such a system, the channels for communication and integration might again be found blocked and protest might find its only expression in violence.

[71] Plebeian in the sense given to this term by Lavau, see above, n. 25.

CHAPTER IX

Policy Processes — I

THE PRESIDENT OF THE REPUBLIC:
MULTIPLICITY OF FUNCTIONS AND OMNIPOTENCE

When General de Gaulle returned to power in 1958, it was generally expected that the Presidency of the Republic would be invested with a novel significance in the policy processes of the new republic. De Gaulle's Bayeux speech in 1961,[1] his subsequent writings, and the Gaullist propaganda in the following years constantly emphasized the need for a widely visible Chief of State. He was to be placed "above the parties" and empowered to represent effectively the unity rather than the diversity of the national community. In conforming to this concept and departing from earlier republican traditions, the text of the new constitution puts the office of the President first among the organs of government, immediately after the tribute to the principle of popular sovereignty, as if to symbolize what so far has, in fact, been the essence of the Fifth Republic: the alliance between the *homme providentiel* and the people.[2]

There is, however, a fundamental difference between the role which the constitution and those who had drafted it assigned to the Presidency and the actual significance which the office

[1] This speech of de Gaulle is indispensable for an understanding of his own constitutional thinking and that of his principal advisors. An English translation can be found in William G. Andrews (ed.), *European Political Institutions* (Princeton: Van Nostrand, 1966), pp. 40–43.

[2] See Philip M. Williams and Martin Harrison, *De Gaulle's Republic* (London: Longmans, Green, 1960), p. 214.

has taken on in the process of decision-making. Its development presents a fascinating example of how within a short time a conjunction of circumstances and of personality can thoroughly transform constitutional institutions and their underlying ideas. (Ironically enough, but not at all accidentally, the constitution of the Third Republic underwent very early a similar and thorough transformation. But then politics traveled in the opposite direction, namely towards parliamentary omnipotence.)

The constitution had left the determination of policies to the Prime Minister and his government (arts. 20–23), and the role of the President was to be that of the guardian of the constitution, "who by his arbitration" was to "ensure the regular functioning of the public authorities" (art. 5). In a brilliant exegesis of the constitutional text he had authored in large part, Michel Debré explained that it was the proper function of the arbiter to do little else than to appeal to another power, be it parliament, the Constitutional Council, or the people. The President's right to dissolve parliament (art. 11) would permit nothing more than "a short dialogue" between the Chief of State and the nation. An electoral college, composed of local notables, should designate the President, for "the President who is elected by universal suffrage is a political leader bound by the daily work of government and command." [3] In Debré's design this was not to be the domain of the French President, who should assume the executive powers of a constitutional dictator only in times of grave trouble (art. 16).

That things have turned out so differently is partly due to the fact that the heavily ideological concept of an arbiter serving the cause of national integration "beyond politics" is even more unrealistic today than in the nineteenth century when it was developed as an underpinning for the constitutional monarchies of France and England. Neither the tensions generated by the Algerian war nor, in spite of some appearances, the personality

[3] A translation of M. Debré's address is to be found in Andrews, *op. cit.*, pp. 43–55. For historical antecedents to Debré's constitutional thinking, see Nicholas Wahl, "The French Constitution of 1958: The Initial Draft and Its Origins," *American Political Science Review*, LIII:2 (1959), pp. 358–82. It is worth noting that the second incumbent of the Presidency, Georges Pompidou, participated in the drafting of the constitutional text as head of General de Gaulle's staff.

of General de Gaulle permitted him to remain solely that republican monarch whom Debré described as the "keystone of a parliamentary regime."

Even before and again upon assuming presidential office, General de Gaulle introduced a new term to describe the task that awaited him. By claiming that he was not only Chief of State but also "France's *guide*," he undertook to play the role which Jean-Jacques Rousseau, in his *Social Contract,* assigned to him who will formulate for the people what the general will truly is. Such a function foreshadowed a permanent rather than the "brief" dialogue between the Chief of State and the people which Debré had foreseen for certain specified situations. In this dialogue, moreover, the *guide* would be able to make fullest use of modern communications media.

Less than a year later the speaker of the National Assembly, who in 1969 was to become Prime Minister, explained to the U.D.R. Congress that certain policy domains, such as Algeria, foreign and military matters, were reserved to presidential decision-making and hence no longer subject to parliamentary scrutiny[4] since only the government, not the President, was responsible to parliament. The vertical separation of power thus established had no foundation whatsoever in the constitution, but it was generally accepted because a majority in the country and in parliament wished that at least one crucial question, that of the Algerian conflict, be solved by presidential fiat. The Hanoverian monarchy intended by Debré was rapidly evolving into the kind of consular dictatorship to which the Romans turned whenever the country was judged to be in danger.

From then on, a chain of events led to the gradual absorption of most decision-making by the Chief of State. The President himself became aware of the fact that the inefficiency of problem solution in the sectors to which he paid no attention (he liked to refer to them summarily as "the price of milk") endangered decision-making in the "reserved" domains. Because he was operating in a highly centralized system, the Chief of State was compelled, not only by choice but also by necessity, to hold a close rein on all matters. Soon the day came when a new Prime

[4] See *A. P. 1959,* pp. 134–35.

Minister, Georges Pompidou, declared that the concept of the two domains was no longer realistic.

When the referendum of 1962 laid the foundations for a popularly elected President, such a modification of the text and the spirit of the four-year-old constitution not only acknowledged the changes which "the circumstances" (a favored term in de Gaulle's vocabulary) had brought about. It also endowed the Presidency with the legitimacy of a direct popular vote which, it was hoped, would accrue to the office when it was occupied by a less charismatic personality than General de Gaulle.

Almost two years before the voters were asked to renew their confidence in General de Gaulle by electing him for a second term, the incumbent explained in starkly realistic terms the nature of his office and its significance for the policy process.[5] To be sure, he still was prepared to play the role of the supreme arbiter whenever this was necessary. But otherwise almost every word of his interpretation of the constitution invites comparison with the totally different summary given less than six years earlier by the principal author of the text, Michel Debré. Compared with General de Gaulle's emphatically pragmatic explanation of what is, Debré's exposé of the constitutional construct had strongly ideological overtones. Power, General de Gaulle said in 1964, "emanates directly from the people, which implies that the Head of State, elected by the nation, is the source and holder of this power." He insisted, ". . . that the individual authority of the State is entrusted completely to the President by the people who elected him, that there is no other authority — either ministerial, civilian, military, or judicial — which is not entrusted or maintained by him." As to the government, he described it as merely "sitting around him for the determination and application of policy and directing the administration."

During the same press conference General de Gaulle rejected, as Michel Debré had done before him but for different reasons, an American-type presidential system as unsuitable for France. In fact, the differences in the policy process in the two countries are enormous. There exists in present-day France no effective provision for a system of checks and balances. By holding the

[5] In his press conference of January 3, 1964, see Andrews, *op. cit.*, pp. 56–60.

threat of dissolution over parliament (art. 12) and by having at his disposal a number of other disciplinary devices which he can employ in conjunction with the government, the President is able to interfere directly with parliamentary organization and activities. He can invoke the jurisdiction of the Constitutional Council (arts. 56–63) when in his opinion parliament has transgressed its constitutional limitations. The control which the Council exercises over the constitutionality of legislation can in no way be compared to that of the American Supreme Court: it can never be invoked by a private citizen, nor can a minority in parliament appeal to it for a decision. The members of the Council are distinguished men but are selected primarily for political reasons.[6]

In situations where the Constitutional Council cannot be or has not been appealed to, General de Gaulle claimed that as guardian of the constitution he could sanction political practice by authoritative interpretation. Such a claim had its disquieting aspects all the more as the first incumbent of the Presidency had declared repeatedly that legalistic scruples (*"juridisme"*) should never stand in the way when the public good and common sense demanded a constitutional interpretation in which lawyers did not see fit to concur.[7]

The enormous concentration of actual and potential power in the office of the Presidency has so far taken place without invoking for more than a relatively short interlude the emergency powers attributed to the Chief of State by article 16. At the time the constitution was drafted, this provision was most arduously discussed. Its every word was fought over in a wrangle between the government and the Consultative Constitutional Committee which wished to safeguard as many guarantees as possible against the article's misuse.

In case of grave threat "to the institutions of the republic" (and in a number of other situations broadly and vaguely described), article 16 gives the President wider powers than even

---

[6] See Maurice Duverger, *Institutions Politiques et droit constitutionnel* (Paris: Presses Universitaires, 1966), p. 653. The most incisive and richly documented analysis of constitutional law and constitutional practice during the Fifth Republic is to be found in Jean Gicquel, *op. cit.*

[7] See Tournoux, *La Tragédie etc., op. cit.,* p. 437, and *Le Mai . . . op. cit.,* p. 474.

the Weimar constitution of Germany provided in its article 48 which served as a convenient cloak for legalizing the Nazi revolution. According to the constitution the French President may be indicted for high treason by a majority vote in the two houses of parliament and then tried by a High Court of Justice (art. 68). Since as soon as a state of emergency is declared parliament meets automatically and cannot be dissolved, a President who abuses his rights under article 16 could be brought to trial. But historical experience indicates that in a situation of dramatic tension he who holds power and controls the means of communication will be in the likeliest position to forestall an indictment by open ballot in parliament.

No other judicial controls limit the exercise of emergency powers as is the case in the United States.[8] While the French President must consult with other organs of government before and during an emergency, he is under no constitutional obligation to heed the advice that might be tendered him.

Yet General de Gaulle used his powers under article 16 only once, in 1961, at a moment when the rebellion of the generals in Algiers clearly justified such use.[9] The mutiny collapsed after a few days, not because a constitutional provision provided residual powers but because General de Gaulle's authority was unimpaired and hence left the rebels isolated and impotent.

When during the Presidency of General de Gaulle fears were expressed that such a plenitude of powers might become a danger to the democratic process especially under a successor without the temperamental inhibitions of the first incumbent, the defenders of the regime replied that the system was the very incarnation of democracy. Their arguments drew on the traditions of that plebiscitarian democracy which in France has frequently claimed preeminence over the model of a representative system (see Chap. I). According to their views, the dualism of a parliament and executive checking on each other was crowned by what Frenchmen in the tradition of Rousseau like to call the

---

[8] See, e.g., the well-known decision rendered during President Truman's administration: *Youngstown Sheet & Tube Co. et al. v. Sawyer*, 343 U.S. 579.

[9] Excellent on that important episode is Martin Harrison, "The French Experiment of Exceptional Powers: 1961," *Journal of Politics*, XXV:2 (1963), pp. 139–58.

monism of popular sovereignity. Its supreme manifestation is the popular election of the Chief of State. His authority is at all times subject to the commands of universal suffrage. Although the President is neither responsible to parliament nor subject to checks or controls by any other constitutional organ, he is nevertheless responsible to the sovereign people and to it alone. Presidential elections and referenda become expressions of the general will and legitimize the concentration of power in one hand. It was in accordance with such a concept of his rule that General de Gaulle relinquished power after failing to win majority approval for his referendum in 1969.[10]

As General de Gaulle's Prime Minister for more than six years, Georges Pompidou had ample opportunity to observe at close range the workings of the constitutional system as it had emerged between 1958 and 1969 and on whose virtues he himself had commented frequently within the confines of parliament and outside. Almost immediately upon assuming office he made it clear that he would maintain and further develop some important features of the system, while he let it be understood that the most personal of General de Gaulle's contributions might not fit his own, of necessity greatly changed, style of authority.[11]

[10] For the most comprehensive statement of the Rousseauan justification of General de Gaulle's exercise of power, see René Capitant, "L'Aménagement du pouvoir exécutif et la question du chef de l'État," in *Encyclopédie Française X* (Paris: Sté. Nouvelle, 1964), pp. 142–62. Understandably enough the same author considered de Gaulle's resignation in 1969 a necessity; see above Chap. IV, fn. 42. In a different vein, Georges Pompidou characterized in his first Press Conference the way in which his predecessor had relinquished power: "a personal decision, an entirely free decision."

[11] He expounded his views most clearly in his Press Conferences of July 10, 1969, and July 2, 1970, published by the Ambassade de France, Service de Presse et d'Information; also in a speech at Strasbourg quoted above Chap. VIII, fn. 64. His earlier opinions on the constitution are recorded in Pierre Rouanet, *Pompidou* (Paris: Grasset, 1969), pp. 165 ff, and *passim*. This remains so far the only, at least partially, satisfactory biography of Pompidou. Excellent is the evaluation of Pompidou's character and personality in Pierre Viansson-Ponté, *Après de Gaulle, qui?* (Paris: Éd. du Seuil, 1968). Merry Bromberger, *Le Destin Secret de Georges Pompidou* (Paris: Fayard, 1965) is not without interest but painfully superficial. Characteristically enough, M. Pompidou cannot be classified either with the political class or with the bureaucracy, the two usual reservoirs for recruitment into political leadership (see above Chap. VI). It was the accident of his encounter with General de Gaulle

He accepts the existing set-up as a "half-way point between a strictly presidential and a strictly parliamentary system." [12] To him this implies a balance at times "difficult, but allowing for firmness and durability as well as flexibility." Also in his eyes such a regime endows the President with the double function exercised by the head of state in a classical presidential system: "He is both," Pompidou has described his role, "arbiter and holder of the highest responsibility in the nation," that is, "supreme head of the Exectuive . . . providing the fundamental drives, defining the essential directions and ensuring and controlling the proper functioning of the government." There is no "reserved domain" since the President can and must concern himself with the direction of all affairs of state. There is also no "dyarchy" by the President and the Prime Minister. For the "primacy of the Chief of State . . . stems from his national mandate," that is, from the verdict of the popular suffrage. Pompidou is undoubtedly well aware that in the two high functions he has held in the state, he derived authority from different sources: he owed his Premiership to de Gaulle, and to him alone, but the Presidency to the electorate organized in his favor by the Gaullist party.

For the Prime Minister the system leaves, again in the words of Pompidou, a "very weighty role . . . in the conduct of affairs, in the direction of administration and in the relations with Parliament." When designating his first Prime Minister, the new President was careful to use approximately the same formula which de Gaulle had chosen to make it quite clear that while according to the constitution no government could survive a vote of censure in parliament, it could also neither assume nor con-

---

in 1944 that steered him into politics. It is futile to speculate whether otherwise this *agrégé* of classics and literature would have pursued a scholarly and professorial or a literary career, or whether he would have risen to the very top of a business calling, which he pursued for a few years in the Rothschild Bank. For a quarter of a century his life revolved around the destiny of General de Gaulle even though his independence, his style of life, and his intelligence never made him into the satellite other followers of de Gaulle's have become.

[12] It is often pointed out that a similar amalgamation had been tried by the constitution of the German Republic which succumbed to the Nazi assault.

tinue in office without the approval of the President.[13] Should
in his opinion the circumstances demand it, Pompidou is likely
to compel his Prime Minister's resignation, just as he himself was
in fact dismissed after his brilliant victory in the elections of
1968. (De Gaulle's first Prime Minister, Michel Debré, had met
a similar fate after the end of the Algerian war.)

By choosing as his first Prime Minister M. Chaban-Delmas, a
long-time deputy and for ten years the speaker of the National
Assembly, Pompidou wanted to give proof of his frequently
expressed determination to ensure a closer collaboration between
the President and parliament than had been obtained under de
Gaulle. But he also acknowledged that the smooth functioning of
the system necessitated a close unity of views between the President and the Prime Minister. What would happen in case the
President and the Prime Minister were at odds and a majority in
parliament expressed its confidence in the latter? In such a situation, Pompidou has declared, he would dissolve parliament and
call for new elections, which is indeed the constitutional procedure according to article 12.[14]

Hence the new President envisages the possibility that after a
dissolution of parliament the "short dialogue" between the Chief
of State and the voters might take place, about which Debré had
spoken in 1958. In a parliamentary system the right to dissolve
the Lower House is indeed generally regarded as a weapon, or
at least a threat, by which the executive may attempt to counter
the power of parliament to overthrow the government. While
this right had fallen into desuetude in the Third and Fourth
Republics (see below Chap. X), it was used twice, in 1962 and
in 1968, under de Gaulle's administration.

But in his exegesis of the living constitution, Pompidou has
never mentioned the referendum, praised by his predecessor, as
the vehicle of direct communication between the President and
the people, and used as a channel that permits the President to
circumvent all intermediaries, including the members of parliament. Conceivably, such reluctance will not outlast memories

[13] See with interesting details on this point, Goguel and Grosser, *op. cit.*,
pp. 262 ff.
[14] With the proviso however that there may not be a second dissolution
within a year — a possibly important guarantee against wearing the
electorate out.

that it was de Gaulle's defeat in a referendum which brought his successor to power. It is, however, more likely that Pompidou considers the outspokenly plebiscitarian aspects of General de Gaulle's rule inappropriate. The style of a man who advertises himself as "a Frenchman like any other" is of necessity different from that of the "most illustrious of Frenchmen," though one should not forget the historical lesson that nothing can change the style of an officeholder as much as holding office. More weighty is the fact that when charisma recedes, questions of legality become more important to establish a regime's legitimacy. Although not a lawyer himself, Pompidou has been a member of both the Constitutional Council and of the highest administrative tribunal in France, the respected Council of State. It is widely assumed that he had misgivings when in both 1962 and 1969 General de Gaulle used the referendum to circumvent the amendment procedures of the constitution. If continued such practice would make the constitutional structure extremely flexible in the hands of a wilful president using his powers of persuasion over the heads of the elected representatives. It is quite natural that a President who wishes to play, unlike General de Gaulle, the role of a strong and vigilant majority leader (see above Chap. VIII) would not wish to antagonize parliament by a repeated, direct appeal to the people. In this respect Pompidou does indeed return to some of the principles and assumptions of the constitution as laid down in 1958.

The distribution of tasks between the President of the Republic and the Prime Minister will change according to the needs of the moment. But it will always be the President who determines what this distribution will be; it is he who delegates authority even if he might share the exercise of power. The situation is particularly clear-cut in foreign affairs which Georges Pompidou wishes to conduct as directly as did his predecessor, although he is probably personally far less interested in them than de Gaulle was. To demonstrate this almost immediately after having assumed his new function, it was he, and neither his Prime Minister nor his Foreign Minister, who negotiated the future conditions of European unity with the chief executives of the other Common Market countries.

Since the early days of the de Gaulle administration, the office of the Chief of State has been organized so as to institutionalize the processes by which policy is not only initiated and elaborated but frequently also executed. In terms of function the staff at the Élysée Palace, composed of a General Secretariat and the presidential cabinet, has become similar to the Executive Office of the American President, yet much smaller in size — a total of about thirty persons. The staff is composed almost entirely of high civil servants. All the administrative elite *corps* are now represented.

Staff members are not formally assigned to supervise each of the ministries, but there exists a roughly functional division. Even in de Gaulle's time this frequently led to parallel elaboration of policies by members of the Elysée staff and by the Ministries. While this created delays and confusion, as it does in Washington, it enabled the President to let possibly conflicting policy proposals confront each other until he chose between alternate solutions. Since it was known that de Gaulle did not always side with his own staff, the competition between ideas, techniques, and priorities was frequently lively up to the moment of final presidential decision.

Under Pompidou the mechanics of the decision-making process have not changed; it remains characterized by the constitutionally grounded coexistence of a presidential and a governmental staff. What seems to have changed are the conditions determining its output. By temperament or design de Gaulle's successor leaves to his staff at the Elysée a far greater autonomy than it had under the close scrutiny of a forever dynamic and suspicious Chief of State. The autonomy it has acquired is used by the Élysée staff, without fear of presidential interference, to strike down governmental initiatives with which it disagrees. Conflicts between competing government bureaus and the ensuing stalemate are not new in French administration; but the pattern customary between and within ministries is now repeated at the very top of the decision-making apparatus. On the whole the staff of the President of the Republic is known for being more cautious and less given to reform than those of the Prime Minister and of some other cabinet Ministers.

THE GOVERNMENT: RULE-MAKING
AND RULE APPLICATION

Since all powers proceed from the President of the Republic, the government headed by the Prime Minister has become essentially an organ of execution, notwithstanding a totally different description of its role in the constitution (art. 20). Its paramount function is to provide whatever is needed for the application of the policies conceived by the Chief of State. This means above all legislative enactments, whether they emanate from parliament or directly from the executive, and procurement of budgetary means either by parliamentary vote or by substitutes. In many respects the position which the government thus occupies resembles far more that of the cabinet in a presidential regime such as the United States, than that of a government in a parliamentary system such as Great Britain and the earlier French Republics.

In France as in most modern democracies the task of initiating legislation had long passed, from parliament to the executive. This function is now shared between the President and the government; but it is up to the President to determine in which affairs he wishes the government to exercise its share of rule initiation. Most notable however are the changes, even though they sometimes concern form more than substance, which the new regime has brought to the enactment of all legislative rulings. A number of constitutional provisions and of practices have seriously amputated the prerogatives of parliament (for details see Chap. X). By the same token and as would have been expected, broader legislative powers have accrued to the Executive. In many fields the government is able to implement presidential policies by legally enforceable enactments without recourse to parliament.[15]

The fact that no domain of governmental activity escapes presidential initiative and control does not mean that the members of the government are deprived of all autonomy and spontaneity. There is a great deal of interaction between the President and the government, the presidential and ministerial staffs, and between the various cabinet members. The weekly meetings

[15] For a succinct treatment of the complicated terminology of rule-making in present-day France, see Ridley and Blondel, *op. cit.*, pp. 22 ff.

of the Council of Ministers under the chairmanship of the President have not only kept the decorum of earlier days, but are still a forum for deliberation and confrontation of viewpoints.[16] This was true under General de Gaulle's Presidency; it has become even more so under Pompidou and not only because of differences in the personalities of the two Presidents. With an increase in the number of experienced politicians among cabinet members, it was to be expected that their meetings would have more significance in the weighing and endorsing of decisions than, for instance, corresponding meetings in the White House. It is quite normal that these meetings are prepared for by the more frequent gatherings of interministerial committees and by audiences which the President grants to the Prime Minister or to individual Ministers.

Inasmuch as the Prime Minister is clearly more than a *primus inter pares* among his ministerial colleagues, the Fifth Republic continues and reinforces a development which has been underway at least since the end of the Second World War. The same is true of the expanding role which the General Secretariat of the Government plays in preparing, coordinating and accrediting policies. Its personnel has been astonishingly stable from one republic to another — in twenty-five years, it has been headed by only three men; it forms the nucleus of the much larger Office of the Prime Minister. However, in contrast to former times, it has now an influential counterpart in the General Secretariat of the President.

During General de Gaulle's presidency it fell to the Prime Minister, more than to any other member of the government, to provide the parliamentary majority which the system, because of its characteristics as a parliamentary regime, needs for its correct functioning. He customarily defended the governmental, i.e., the presidential, program before the National Assembly. The first incumbent of the post under Pompidou, Jacques Chaban-Delmas, has been given an even more conspicuous place and more exposure to the public outside of parliament, than his pre-

---

[16] An excellent description of the sense and nonsense of Council meetings by a participant observer is given by Buron, *op. cit.*, pp. 218 ff. Interesting on the job of being a Minister under General de Gaulle is Bernard Chenot, *Être Ministre* (Paris: Plon, 1967).

decessors. He holds his own press conferences, appears rather frequently on radio and television and engages in a good deal of speech-making throughout the country. This not only suits his personality and his experiences gathered during a political career.[17] As long as the Prime Minister does not overstep the bounds set for him by the President, such activities also correspond to the character and image M. Pompidou wants to lend to the regime.

There seems to exist in the first government of the Pompidou administration more of a hierarchy between various Ministers than in previous cabinets. It is grounded either in the personalities of the ministers or in their function or in both. Michel Debré, a senator in the Fourth Republic, the first Prime Minister of the Fifth, a past Minister of Finance and of Foreign Affairs, and at almost all times de Gaulle's confidant, is Minister of State for National Defense with broader prerogatives than the previous Minister of the Armed Forces. As Minister of Economic Affairs and Finance, a post he has held in several governments of de Gaulle's administration, M. Valéry Giscard d'Estaing presides over a ministry and over an administrative corps which decide the fate of most policies usually long before the matter reaches the final stage of decision-making.[18]

The cabinet which M. Chaban-Delmas formed after his nomination by Pompidou was composed of 39 members and is slightly larger than customary. Most of the Ministers are in charge of an administrative department. The Secretaries of State (a total of

[17] An excellent and not really dated sketch of Chaban-Delmas is to be found in Pierre Viansson-Ponte, *Les Gaullistes, rituel et annuaire* (Paris: Éditions du Seuil, 1963), pp. 87–92. More complete biographies are Jean-Claude Guillebaud and Pierre Vuilletet, *Chaban-Delmas ou l'art d'être heureux en politique* (Paris: Grasset, 1969) and Gaston Marchon, *Chaban-Delmas* (Paris: Albin Michel, 1969). Differently from Pompidou, his first Prime Minister may be considered the very prototype of a successful member of the present-day political class: continuing success as mayor of a prospering municipality, rapidly moving back and forward through all political parties just right and left of Center, and including the Gaullist R.P.F. He belonged to several governments of the Fourth Republic, before becoming in the Fifth the constantly reelected Gaullist Speaker in the National Assembly. As a young man he had been talented enough to win, while an active member of the Resistance, entrance into the highly competitive Inspectorate of Finance.

[18] See Buron, *op. cit.*, pp. 214–17 for the relationship between the Ministry of Finance and the other administrations.

twenty) are all attached to the office of a senior Minister and correspond therefore to an Undersecretary in the United States, but they too are members of the regular cabinet and participate in its sessions.

In their composition all the cabinets of the Fifth Republic have represented a political make-up reminiscent of the coalition building in the preceding regime and even of the "balanced ticket" in an American election. Not only are there three parties of the coalition represented (the U.D.R. with 29, the R.I. with 7, and the P.D.M. with 3 members), but also the various political tendencies within these parties have all received recognition in the distribution of more or less exalted posts in the cabinet.[19]

In the first cabinet of the Fifth Republic about 40 per cent of the Ministers had never stood for a parliamentary election, most of them being career civil servants. In the last cabinet of General de Gaulle's, headed by M. Couve de Murville as Prime Minister, that number was down to a little over 3 per cent and all members of the Chaban-Delmas Cabinet without exception had at one time been elected to a seat in one of the houses of parliament, usually in the National Assembly rather than the Senate. This development suggests that even General de Gaulle had abandoned earlier intentions to have technicians rather than politicians serve as cabinet members. Increasingly, members of the government have been encouraged to have a firm rooting in a constituency, and therefore, of necessity, to join a party. There are many indications that the voters expect, as they have in the past, special benefits from the fact that "their" deputy belongs to the government. And in fact the Ministers of the Fifth Republic including the Prime Minister see to it that their constituencies are given special consideration. Moreover, a number of Ministers have also newly won or kept local government positions, as mayors or as members of Municipal and Departmental Councils.

In part, this development reflects somewhat disappointing experiences with the technician-civil servants in the cabinet. It

---

[19] For an explanation of the party initials, see the previous chapter. For short biographical sketches of the members of the government, see Ambassade de France, Service de Presse et d'Information, *The Chaban-Delmas Cabinet* (New York, 1969).

first became apparent to the ranking bureaucrats in their own Ministries, that a Minister with no support outside the civil service did not have enough political weight in the councils of government, especially in negotiations with the Ministry of Finance and the staff of the Élysée. Then some of the Ministers themselves understood what advantages for their own effectiveness and authority they could derive from a political mandate.

All this has cast doubts on the wisdom of another widely heralded innovation of the constitution of 1958. Its article stipulated that a position in the government is incompatible with parliamentary office. Within one month of taking office, members of government must give up their seats for good until the end of the legislative period. In order to avoid frequent by-elections, the ballots for election to the National Assembly list in addition to the candidate a replacement who takes over the seat in parliament if it falls vacant because of such compulsory resignation.

This provision satisfied a dogmatic insistence on a clear distinction between the executive and the legislature. In the previous regimes in which the lines between government and opposition were never clearly drawn, members of a government were known to plot for the downfall of the cabinet to which they themselves belonged. Certain as they were of always returning to their seats in parliament, they did not risk much. Indeed, by such maneuvers they could hope to reach a better place in the ministerial hierarchy of a future government.

In the midst of antiparliamentarian sentiment such as prevailed in 1958, the incompatibility provision was heralded as a step towards the purification of political morals. From other sides the provision could be denounced as an anomaly in a parliamentary regime. For differently from the presidential or congressional system, it is normal in and mandatory in most parliamentary regimes that the members of government hold seats in the elected assemblies.

The described developments proved unfounded both fears and hopes that the new arrangement might alter drastically the recruitment of parliamentary and ministerial personnel and thereby the conditions of the political process. Not all of the defenders of the incompatibility clause have ceased praising its virtues.[20] But upon assuming office President Pompidou himself has let it be known publicly that he saw no reason to maintain a constitutional provision which was out of tune with experiences. Yet he wants obviously to see such a change brought about through the regular channels of a constitutional amendment.

What might be described as a victory of politics over technocratic illusions does not mean that the present (and future) cabinets of the Fifth Republic will be manned entirely by members of the traditional political class. Rather, the personnel of the government represents a new breed and, with some exceptions, a somewhat youthful one. The average age of the members of the Chaban-Delmas cabinet at the time of their appointment was 53 years. Of the 39 members, 10 had been cabinet Ministers under the Fourth Republic, and most of these could be classified as belonging to the "political class." Sixteen belonged to one or the other of the elite administration corps,[21] about half of the latter being graduates of the E.N.A. But during their careers, before as well as after 1958, these high administrators have wandered in and out of political appointments and sometimes elective office. The variety of their assignments indicates that they are temperamentally unwilling to be content with a life of bureaucratic routine. Of course, as members of the Council of State, the diplomatic, prefectoral, and other corps, they also enjoy the undiminished prestige of choice positions. If this amalgam of politics and of administration appears to be a significant development, the Fifth Republic has merely accelerated it, for it was well underway before.

Governmental "stability" is one of the most striking differences between the present and the preceding regimes. In the eleven years and five months of its life, the Fourth Republic experienced a total of twenty cabinets and disquietingly lengthy periods of *crises* during which an interim government held office between the fall of one Prime Minister and the designation of his successor. Under de Gaulle, there have been but three Prime Ministers and each of the cabinets over which they presided identified

---

[20] See the fairly interesting discussion of the pro and con by Leon Noël "Ministres et députés," and Marcel Prélot, "Rapport sur la proposition de loi etc." in *RFSP*, XVIII:2 (1968), pp. 213–37.
[21] In some cases the two groups overlap.

closely with the policy of a single Chief of State. The point has been made that to highlight these facts exaggerates the difference between the two systems. Before 1958, it is true, the combination of the French party system and the habits of the political class made the overthrow of Ministries unavoidable; nonetheless, the same personnel appeared in many cabinets, and the permanence of policies was quite impressive. On the other hand, in the Fifth Republic, there has been a frequent and quite extensive reshuffling of ministerial posts under the same Prime Minister. The important Ministry of Agriculture and Ministry of Education have not only changed hands but also policies many times. Even in the Ministry of Finance, the replacement of one Minister by another resulted in an overturn of orientation and, to a certain extent, of personnel.

Moreover, the very structure of the government and of the ministries has frequently been altered.[22] This in turn has resulted in uncertainties and a loss of effectiveness, so that at least in certain fields the permanent civil service or a ministry's clientele have complained that they were as little governed as before. The difficulties arising from the juxtaposition of the staff at the Élysée, of that of the Prime Minister, and of the different Ministries have already been described.

Another traditional institution of governmental practice of considerable importance for the policy process has also continued into the Fifth Republic. Each French Minister has long surrounded himself with a group of personal collaborators, his *cabinet* (the ministerial *cabinet* is, of course, to be distinguished from the cabinet which is the government as a whole). The members of his *cabinet* have always served as the Minister's eyes and ears in the agency which he directs, whereas in other countries the top civil servants in each Ministry are entrusted with such a task. In the past, the frequent changes of government justified an institution which gave to the Minister some leverage with a bureaucracy always suspected of seeking to sabotage policy directives which it knew to be ephemeral.

But although under the present regime the life span of minis-

---

[22] For the make-up of the first two cabinets headed by Pompidou, see Ridley and Blondel, *op. cit.,* pp. 11 ff, 314 ff. Since then the structure has again been changed substantially.

terial office has been lengthened, the ministerial *cabinets* have proven as indispensable as before — some Ministers have even enlarged their *cabinets* beyond the legal limit of ten members. The particularities of French bureaucratic organization and the obstacles it puts in the way of innovation explain much of this phenomenon. Insufficient communication between different strata within the same agency leaves the holder of power so isolated that he is unable to overcome inflexible habits and to make a break in routine even when changes in the environment make such a breakthrough necessary. Here the members of the ministerial *cabinet* are called upon to overcome an isolation that would otherwise condemn a Minister to impotence. For analogous reasons, the practice of attaching a *cabinet* to the office of those holding positions of command has become fairly generalized in large-scale organizations in both the public and the private sector.

At the ministerial level, the *cabinets* form a link between politics and administration and between administration and the outer environment; the latter comprising other administrations and organized or potential interests, especially those in the Minister's own constituency.[23] Before the war, and for a short time at the beginnings of both the Fourth and Fifth Republics, Ministers frequently appointed their own political friends, journalists, and other "experts in communication," to *cabinet* positions. But gradually, for the sake of greater effectiveness, an increasing number of high civil servants have entered the *cabinets* and today dominate them, to the extent that about 90 per cent of the members of the various *cabinets* are civil servants. Their intimate knowledge of the workings of the bureaucratic machinery has proven indispensable. If they were mere line officials they might be unable or unwilling to overcome inertia; hence they are usually on detached service from other administrations, one-third of them are members of the *grands corps*. Forty per cent of all *cabinet* members have graduated from the E.N.A. The solidarity between alumni of that training experience appears to be particularly strong at this level. In a period of sustained modernization the skills and working

---

[23] The literature on the *cabinets* is rich and interesting. Much of it is quoted in H. W. Ehrmann, "French Bureaucracy," pp. 545 ff., and "Bureaucracy and Interest Groups," pp. 279–80. For more recent data, see also Debbasch, *op. cit.,* pp. 59 ff.

methods of the elite corps are in great demand. What distinguishes them from other civil servants, and this is especially true of those who have made careers in several different *cabinets,* is a special political sensitivity. The fact that the same quality characterizes the numerous Ministers who combine administrative experience with political office facilitates collaboration. In addition, a common social origin and educational background enhance lateral connections between the members of various ministerial *cabinets.*

All this explains why of late the *cabinets* have become a training ground and a source of recruitment for high political office, including junior Ministers in the government.

THE CIVIL SERVICE: MOTOR OR INSTRUMENTALITY?

Because of its frank emphasis on the prestige and the procedures of the administrative state, and because of its dislike for "party politics," it was expected that the Gaullist regime would greatly increase the weight of the bureaucracy in the policy process. What has come about is, in fact, a seemingly contradictory but internally quite consistent development. On the one hand, the executive has subjected the bureaucracy to more stringent political controls, but, on the other, the domain open to decision-making by the technicians in the civil service has been enlarged considerably.[24]

As Table IX shows, the number of civil servants rose rather steeply during the first years of the Fifth Republic; since 1965 the rise has slowed somewhat because of budgetary limitations.

Inasmuch as the rule-making power of the government has been extended, numerous rulings, whether of primary or secondary importance, have been formulated and codified by the civil service. At the start of the Fifth Republic, the staff of most ministries produced out of their desk drawers legislative texts which had lain

---

[24] This proposition was first put forward by Georges Vedel in his contribution to a roundtable concerned with "Technocracy and the Role of Experts in Government," organized by the Fifth World Congress of the *International Political Science Association* and held in Paris in 1961. Since then his thesis has been widely accepted as essentially correct. See also Victor Silvera, "Réflexions sur la stabilité gouvernementale et l'action administrative depuis 1958," *La Revue Administrative,* XVII (1964), pp. 545–55.

TABLE IX.   *Growth of the Public Service*

Full time civilian public employees[a]	*1956*	*% Total labor force*	*1965*	*% Total labor force*
National Government:				
Civil Servants	953,000	4.89	1,171,000	6.01
Workers with civil service status	156,000	0.80	139,000	0.71
Local Government:				
All levels	437,000	2.24	552,000	2.83
Total	1,546,000	7.93	1,862,000	9.55

[a] These figures do not include those employed by nationalized enterprises, such as coal mines, railroads, and by the social security system (total of about 1,000,000).

Source: Roland Drago, *Cours de Science Administrative. Faculté de Droit de Paris* (Paris: Les Cours de Droit, 1966–1967), pp. 181–182.

there for months if not for years. For contrary to widespread belief, the bureaucracy had not been able to rule the Fourth Republic at will while ministries toppled; at the approach of every governmental crisis all projects of more than routine nature were shelved. During the first months after the promulgation of the new constitution and in conformity with its temporary dispositions (arts. 91, 92), a substantial number of long-delayed reform bills was enacted into law by the Council of Ministers.

Since then, top-ranking bureaucrats have prepared important policy decisions in every detail without consulting parliament or other elective bodies. Some of the measures for which the technicians in the government bureaus assumed *de facto* responsibility and about which there was little or no discussion in parliament, were the currency reform of 1958 and the host of economic measures accompanying it; the stabilization plan of 1961 with its far-reaching consequences; the thorough reforms of the court and of the social security systems. The complete revamping of the administrative structure of the Paris region, affecting more than nine million people and far more important than the changes introduced by Baron Haussman during the days of Napoleon III, was briefly debated in parliament, but in all essentials shaped by gov-

ernmental bureaus.[25] Many important *ad hoc* committees advising
the government on long-range policy planning have been manned
exclusively by civil servants. It is true that by submitting the modernization plan to parliament at various stages of its elaboration,
the government of the Fifth Republic took a step which the preceding regime had not dared to take for fear of seeing its objectives
assaulted by special interests. But what has been said earlier (see
above Chap. II) must not be forgotten: the entire planning enterprise is now obviously on the decline.

In most administrative quarters, the lessening of controls and of
interference by members of parliament was generally welcomed as
a boon to administrative efficiency. Nationalized enterprise and
the entire public sector of the economy have been freed almost
completely from parliamentary supervision. The taste of the
regime for secrecy and its preference for carefully channeled information correspond well to the working methods of the French
bureaucracy. And even though a change of Ministers has been a
fairly frequent occurrence, the civil service has on the whole welcomed the greatly increased governmental stability. Even those
civil servants who were inimical to Gaullism on political grounds
have in general greeted with satisfaction the restoration of governmental authority.

But such a restoration has by the same token strengthened executive controls in many respects. For all his exaltation of technical
expertise and his depreciation of politics, one of the most articulate spokesmen of the regime, Michel Debré, has long insisted that
it was not the bureaucracy's role to rule but to serve a strongly
governed state. During de Gaulle's Presidency the manner in
which the Office of the President of the Republic issued policy
directives and followed up on their transformation into administrative rulings corresponded to such a model. With increasing
frequency the Élysée, by presidential directive, unceremoniously
overruled some long-established technicians and their coteries in a
number of Ministries. The possibly different situation under

[25] The contrasting routes to metropolitan reform followed by Greater
London and Greater Paris offered a striking example of the enormous
differences between the policy process in present-day Britain and France.
For London, see Frank Smallwood, *Greater London: The Politics of
Metropolitan Reform* (Indianapolis: Bobbs-Merrill, 1965).

Pompidou where such directives are apparently less single-minded has been mentioned earlier.

In the relationships between the Ministers, the members of their *cabinets,* and the administrative personnel, the lines separating the initiation and the execution of policies are of necessity never neatly drawn. For reasons that have been explained previously, there exists on these levels considerable homogeneity of functions and of mentality. Frequently a Minister and his staff become mere executive agents of presidential policies. But where leeway is left, the Ministers as well as the civil servants (whether they be line officials or belong to a *cabinet*) become directly involved in establishing political priorities and thereby in decision-making. Edgar Faure, an eminent politician of the Fourth Republic and twice Minister during General de Gaulle's administration, has spoken about a powerful "technostructure" comprising certain (but not all) Ministers, some staff members of the Presidential Office and of selected ministerial *cabinets,* and some of the most influential bureau chiefs in the line administration.

Whether such an amalgamation of the political and the technical has resulted in greater bureaucratic efficiency cannot be determined in any generalized fashion.[26] Seemingly technical conflicts may lead to deadlocks in decision-making. The immobilism thus caused is no longer blasted apart, as it might have been in the past, by the dynamics of a frankly political decision coming from outside the bureaucracy.[27]

So far the Fifth Republic has been unable to undertake the often announced thorough reform of the country's administrative structures. Hence the perennial trend towards an almost spontaneous centralization has continued (for details see Chap. VI). Nonetheless, the increasing involvement of the bureaucracy in tasks concerned with the development of economic and human resources has motivated the one major administrative reform which the new regime has initiated, in addition to the reorganization of the Paris region: the regionalization of the country.

[26] For strenuously critical views see the books by Debbasch and by Mignol, *op. cit.,* and the latest study by Crozier, *La Société etc., op. cit.*

[27] This point was forcefully made by one of the outstanding technocrats in the high civil service, Bloch-Lainé. For his statement and a similar one by Viansson-Ponté, see Pierre Avril, *Le Régime Politique de la Ve République* (Paris: Librairie Générale de Droit, 1964), p. 196.

Regionalization — How and When? When in 1962 the Modernization Plans began to attack seriously the imbalance in economic development between various regions, it soon became apparent that the organization of the country into 95 departments, most of them carved out in the eighteenth century, was cramping the needed effort. Conceived as a more rational division of the territory and as a counterweight against excessive centralization, regionalism in France has a long and honorable tradition.[28] The Fifth Republic seems to have given no consideration to plans of merging departments and thereby undermining the departmental power structure, headed by the prefects, but who themselves depend entirely on the central administration in Paris, the Ministry of Interior. Quite to the contrary, whenever President de Gaulle traveled through the French countryside, he paid tribute to the particularities of each individual department and to its traditional elites, the prefect and notables surrounding him.

A true decentralization would call for at least two major interconnected reforms in territorial organization: on the one hand the areas should be large enough so at to be able to develop and live, at least in part, on their own human and financial resources; on the other, the authorities in charge of the newly created regions should become more truly autonomous, less dependent on binding directives from the capital. Either as a precondition for or as a consequence of these reforms, it would also be necessary to proceed, as France's neighboring countries have done, with a merger of many of the historical pygmy communes and their local government units which prove grossly inappropriate to their tasks in a modernizing economy.

Proposals of this kind or of similar nature have not been lacking.[29] Certain forces within the Gaullist regime, governmental as

---

[28] See Stanley Hoffmann, "The Areal Division of Powers in the Writings of French Political Thinkers," in Arthur Maas (ed.), *Area and Power, A Theory of Local Government* (Glencoe, Ill.: Free Press, 1959), pp. 113–49, and the fairly complete review of past thinking and efforts, by Lawrence Gladieux, "Regionalism in France," *Public and International Affairs,* V:1 (1967), pp. 135–57.

[29] See e.g., Club Jean Moulin, *Les Citoyens au pouvoir. 12 Regions, 2,000 communes* and *Quelle Réforme? Quelles Régions?* (Paris: Éditions du Seuil, 1968 and 1969); Club Nouvelle Frontière, *Le Dossier du 27 Avril* (Paris: Grasset, 1969) and, with many critical comments on governmental policy, Debbasch, *op. cit.,* pp. 167–211, a chapter entitled: "La V⁰ République et les collectivités locales."

well as administrative, have resisted them since in their more radical forms the suggestions run indeed counter to habits of centralization. The Jacobin temperament of a man like Michel Debré saw in truly strong regions, especially if they were endowed with an elected executive and a representative assembly, the danger of enfeebling the national government.[30]

After many hesitations a series of decrees issued in 1964 attempted to strike a compromise which, even if fully implemented, would amount at most to a deconcentration, not to a true decentralization of administrative function. The country is now divided into twenty-one regions,[31] each comprising several departments (see Map, p. 122), but, according to critics, still too numerous and too uneven in resources for the vigorous development of all. In each region one of the prefects is designated prefect of the region. His very extensive responsibilities (which he carries on in addition to his normal duties as prefect of a department) consist in implementing the government's policy for regional development and the objectives set for the region by the Planning Office. It is he who supervises and coordinates the numerous field services of the national administrations, operating either on the regional or the departmental level.[32]

In order to enable the prefect of the region to discharge his manifold functions, a number of new institutions have been created, fashioned partly after the working methods of the Planning Office in Paris. The prefect of the region is materially assisted by a *mission,* a brain trust composed of high (although generally young) civil servants detached from various central administrations. In addition, he has to consult regularly the Regional Development Board, the CODER. Depending upon the importance of the region, the CODER is made up of between twenty and fifty members, half of them designated by interest groups, chambers of

[30] See his *La Mort de l'État Républicain* (Paris: Gallimard, 1947) a fascinating treatise which strikes the outsider as not free from paranoid fears.

[31] Of late the island of Corsica has been treated, at the urging of its population, as a separate unit without acquiring the full status of a 22nd region. Corsicans still refer to France as "the continent."

[32] For a complete account of the new institutions, see Jean Hourticq, "La vie administrative dans les circonscriptions d'action régionale," *International Review of Administrative Sciences,* XXXI:1 (1965), pp. 8–12, with a summary in English, pp. ii–iii. For the earlier attempts at regional development, see Ridley and Blondel, *op. cit.,* pp. 225–32.

commerce, and the like, one-fourth appointed by the Prime Minister, and the other fourth composed of traditional leaders such as mayors and members of the departmental councils. One of the foremost tasks incumbent upon the regional prefect, his staff and his advisory body, is to decide on the proper distribution of the public investments available for regional development.

On paper this scheme looks like an ingenious if deliberately ambiguous blending of old and new. It seeks to further the collaboration between the hierarchy of line officials and the younger technocrats whose training and interest are more functionally oriented, and between local government authorities and organized interests. It could be hoped that the regional missions would at the very least help spread administrative talent: it is estimated that of the 1,500 top civil servants graduated from the E.N.A. since the war, all but 200 have been stationed permanently in the capital.

From the very beginning it has been difficult to decide whether and to what extent the intended reforms amount to more than organizational façades and generous declarations of intent. Spontaneous and organized resistance to the arrangement has made itself felt almost immediately and over time it has multiplied rather than abated.[33] Much of the resistance has come from the prefects of the single departments and of the subprefects in the *arrondissements,* the departmental subdivisions. To them the institution of a regional prefect, even though they share his training and career, is a violation of the principle of equality of all prefects before their common "sovereign," the Minister of the Interior. In the past, this equality had been safeguarded by the virtual isolation of each prefect in his department, an isolation which the regional institutions wish to overcome. The prefect of the region is suspected of seeking preferential treatment for his own department, since he controls the channeling of all economic information concerning the entire region to the Ministries in Paris. Certain prefects seem to fear that a long-established equilibrium, already endangered by urban growth and industrial deconcentration, will be further and definitely upset.

[33] For an account see Pierre Grémion, "Résistance au changement de l'administration territoriale: le cas des institutions régionales," *Sociologie du Travail,* VIII:3 (1966), pp. 276–95. At an earlier stage of his careful inquiry, the same author had been far more optimistic, see his *La Mise en place des institutions régionales* (Paris: Centre de Recherche de Sociologie des Organisations, 1965).

Prefectural antagonism have condemned many of the regional brain trusts to ineffectiveness. In their opposition, the prefects and their staffs can frequently count on local notables as their allies. The generally underrated solidarity between the prefects and the local government authorities (described above Chap. IV) has found new terrain in a common front against the staff of the regional prefect.

Even after they were fully manned (a total of 920 members) the effectiveness of the CODER has varied greatly from one region to the next. The local notables, who have found themselves in a minority on the Boards, suspect them for ursurping the powers traditionally held by local government and such suspicions are systematically fanned by the communists. At the same time many of the more active and reform-mongering members of the CODER are frustrated because they have only advisory powers while municipal and departmental councils, for all their limited resources, are able to make decisions. How little the CODER as a going institution has attracted public attention or succeeded in explaining their activities became evident in a public opinion poll in which 15 per cent of the respondents replied that they felt rather badly informed and 74 per cent that they were very badly informed about the CODER — no other public institution fared that poorly.[34]

Nonetheless the reform of 1967 can not be considered an overall failure. Especially where there has been a conjunction of forceful personalities on the staff of the regional prefect and a satisfactory amount of regional investments, the new instituions have functioned fairly well and have transmitted to some participants in the new structure at least an incipient sense of belonging to a wider area than that of the departments. The regional set-up is far too weak, and possibly not even eager, to provide any sense of participation to a wider group. But municipalities and citizens, accustomed to wait an inordinate time for the most trivial decision, while the files were traveling up to Paris and back again, have seen here some hope of a somewhat more rapid satisfaction of their needs.

When in March 1968 General de Gaulle relaunched the re-

---

[34] See SOFRES, *Poll of October-November 1969,* p. 27. For a sharp criticism of the CODER, see also Mignot, *op. cit.,* p. 45.

gional reform in a widely noted speech he probably wanted to capitalize on such beginnings of a "regionalist solidarity." When he proclaimed that the "century-old effort at centralization" had seen its day and ought to be replaced by giving to the national effort a new balance through the regions, he probably also wanted to voice (as he was increasingly given to do, though mostly in private conversations) his frustrations about the ineffectiveness of the policy process.

After governmental inefficiency had been amply demonstrated during the May Events, de Gaulle instructed various ministries to prepare a new regional reform which after thorough, if confusing, discussion in parliament, was submitted to the electorate in April 1969.[35] If enacted, the bill would have gone further in the direction of true decentralization although again it stopped far short of the thoroughgoing reforms advocated by many. The new legislation would still not have created larger regions; the stronger Regional Assemblies which were to be constituted in each of the twenty-one regions would still not have been elected nor would there have been an elected executive at the top; the regions would have continued to live on grants-in-aid by the government rather than on taxes levied by them. Altogether the text, a compromise between many bureaus and personalities with conflicting views, was the prototype of that tentative and in the end rather timid experimenting in which the French administration has been engaging frequently over the last years.

Such however were hardly the reasons why the referendum failed to rally popular approval (For the reasons of its defeat, see above Chap. IV). It is likely that of the two questions asked in the referendum, regional organization was viewed with more sympathy than the proposed reconversion of the Senate. But it is noteworthy that during the referendum campaign, only 33 per

[35] The debate was one of the most interesting ever held in the National Assembly of the Fifth Republic, see Journal Officiel, *Assemblée Nationale, Débats,* Dec. 11–14, 1968, pp. 5323–5420; 5461–5491; 5507–23. During the campaign, an official commentary was sent to each voter under the heading: "Declaration of General de Gaulle, President of the Republic, concerning the Reasons for the Projected Law Relating to the Creation (sic!) of Regions and the Renovation of the Senate." The regions had of course been created years earlier, but this was a way of dramatizing the new proposals.

cent of the respondents considered the regional reform of true importance for the future.[36]

It is as yet impossible to foretell whether the regional reform will resume or whether the institutions created in 1964 will merely be permitted to survive. There is widespread agreement among the country's elite, and this includes at least part of the administration, that without a dismantling of the hypercentralized structure of the bureaucracy, reform efforts in many domains will remain sluggish. But opinions are divided as to whether the defeat of the referendum has meant no more than a temporary setback for regionalization as a way towards true decentralization, or whether here, like elsewhere, there is grave risk that a traditional mentality is winning out.[37]

Admittedly the Sixth Modernization Plan pays scant attention to the problems of regional as against national development, but this may be taken as a consequence of the general decline of attention to planning. In his first Press Conference, President Pompidou has declared in deliberately vague terms that he favored "a regional reform" which however could only be undertaken "through parliamentary channels." But a year after these observations, the Chief Editor of the *Monde* concluded that nothing had been done in this domain "because the political will at the helm is lacking." [38]

A Place for the Military? During the first years of the new regime, it appeared likely that the military bureaucracy, the career officers' corps, would claim a leading role in the political process.

---

[36] *Sondages,* **XXXI**:3 (1969), p. 10. 36 per cent of the respondents did not answer, probably mostly out of indifference. By contrast at the time of the preceding referendum, 53 per cent had considered the question of the popular election of the President as being of great importance.

[37] For interesting arguments on both sides, see optimistic views by Louis Joxe (former Minister of de Gaulle's and now head of an interest group for regional reform), "La Région, une affaire qui est mûre," *Preuves,* 2ième trimestre (1970), pp. 88–94; and (pessimistic) Pierre Grémion and Jean-Pierre Worms (systematic students of the problem), "L'État et les collectivités locales," *Esprit,* **XXXVII**:1 (1970), pp. 20–34. More balanced and tying the problems of regionalization to those of local government reform, E. Pisani, J. Hourticq, P. Grémion, "Réforme régionale et démocratie locale," *Projet,* No. 44 (April, 1970), pp. 393–429.

[38] Jacques Fauvet, "Un État," *Le Monde,* June 30, 1970.

A number of generals stationed in Algeria had played an important part in the events which brought General de Gaulle back to power. At least some expected that their vision of a "forever French" Algeria and their views on the proper running of the French state would be given commensurate recognition.

The relationship between the French Republic and its standing army has been frequently beset by tensions. Both sides, the military as well as the political class, have felt mutually estranged. After the Dreyfus Affair had discredited the officers corps, the army retreated to the position of a "great mute," until its defeat in the Second World War brought it back to prominence in the armistice regime of Marshal Pétain. It is worth noting that political muteness, which should be the normal stance of the armed forces in a democracy, was frequently regarded in France as a remarkable phenomenon even by those who acknowledged it with relief.

The military and political events of the Second World War, followed by years of rearguard fighting in colonial wars, threw the officers corps into deep crisis. It took long to heal the split between those who had sided with the Vichy regime and those who had fought for the Free French. When General de Gaulle attempted after the war to bring about the amalgamation of both sides with those who had participated as military men in the resistance movement, he failed. Instead, his own act of insubordination in June of 1940 became a lodestar for officers who wished to justify disobedience to authority by claiming a higher legitimacy for their actions. Many officers who found it difficult to adjust to the political and moral climate of postwar France found solace in the campaigns of Indochina and Algeria. Feeling more and more misunderstood by the political elites and by large sectors of the population, the "military society" grew apart from society at large. It formed a subsystem, with its own norms of behavior, values, and symbols.[39] However much the officers were opposed to

[39] See R. Girardet (ed.), *La Crise Militaire Française, 1945–1962* (Paris: Colin, 1964). For the mentality and politics of the officers corps during the period of the Vichy regime, see the study by Robert O. Paxton, *Parades and Politics at Vichy: The French Officers Corps under Marshal Pétain* (Princeton: Princeton University Press, 1966). For a complete and competent account of the political engagement of the army during the Fourth and the first years of the Fifth Republic, see John S. Ambler, *The French Army in Politics 1945–1962* (Columbus: Ohio State University Press, 1966).

communism, their isolation resembled in many respects that of the working class in sympathy with the P.C.

It is however incorrect to assume that a homogeneous mentality distinguished the officers corps. The officers' ideas were frequently found to vary according to different experiences in the wars and in prisoner-of-war camps, or according to the services to which they belonged. Nevertheless, a lack of understanding for political realities, both national and international, characterized many of their divergent viewpoints. Their isolation from society was maintained and aggravated by a process of self-selection. Today almost 40 per cent of those attending officers' candidate schools are the sons of officers. But promotions from the ranks of noncommissioned officers are also a frequent occurrence. On a more limited scale, the career of an army officer has become, like that of other civil servants, a means of social promotion. For this reason, today's officers corps is more representative of the country's social structure than the officers of the past who came largely from aristocratic or upper bourgeoisie backgrounds. It is ironical that the feudally oriented army of earlier days had on the whole remained loyal to republican institutions, while a more democratic officers corps took it upon itself to challenge the democratic basis of both the Fourth and the Fifth Republics.[40]

A high army officer greeted General de Gaulle's return to power in terms which were indicative of the political role certain general officers felt entitled to play in this and any crisis situation: "At grave hours when the sovereign voice of the people can no longer express itself, the ARMY suddenly becomes aware of what it is: the people under the Flag. Then the Army takes responsibility for the People." [41] (Capitals in the original.)

After it turned out that such was not the place General de Gaulle was willing to reserve to the army, the latter challenged the government once more, most dramatically in the Algerian uprising of 1961, only to find out at once that its isolation was complete.

The generals' ambition and the junior officers' dream of a new Algerian community uniting Frenchmen and Arabs had estranged

---

[40] See Hoffmann, in *In Search of France,* p. 52.
[41] Admiral Ortola, "Le Général de Gaulle: soldat-écrivain-homme d'État," *Revue de la Défense Nationale,* IX:4 (1959), pp. 565–587.

the army activists from practically everybody: not only from the government authorities in Paris and Algiers but also from the white settlers, not only from liberal but also from right wing politicians, and last but not least, from the conscript soldiers. The rebellion did not extend beyond a few elite units (if the Foreign Legion can be regarded as such). Their defeat not only sealed the fate of the putsch but put once more an end to the political role of the officers corps.

Undoubtedly the professional soldiers were more embittered against General de Gaulle than they had been against the political leadership of the Fourth Republic, since in their eyes de Gaulle had betrayed hopes which the previous regime had never truly raised. When rebellious officers and members of the military organizations carrying out terrorist acts were brought to trial, the defendants spoke the language of fundamental revolt against the existing state. The feelings they voiced were quite similar to those of the rightist extremists in pre-Hitler Germany. But while the German fanatics were hero-worshiped and, if convicted, regarded as martyrs by broad strata of public opinion, the French officers felt at best surrounded by indifference. The repeated plebiscitarian approval of de Gaulle's policies was tantamount to popular disapproval of an autonomous army position.

With the actual end of fighting in Algeria, special legislation drastically reduced the number of professional officers and men in the army, robbing them of a sense of career security. At present the total number of professional soldiers amounts to about 300,000 men. New recruitment of capable officer material has become difficult; voluntary resignations from the officers corps are said to be numerous, although exact data are not made available. But contrary to certain expectations (and again contrary to what happened in Germany after the First World War), the reintegration of officers into civilian life and occupations has generally been easy. This seems to indicate that the cleavage between the military and civil society has not been deep enough to prevent individuals from passing from one into the other.

Morale among those who have stayed on is not high. New weaponry, especially atomic, holds fascination for only a relatively small number of officers. For others, the failure of the high command to provide updated equipment and to overhaul the organization of the armed forces has meant simply more broken promises. The disengagement of the army from NATO forces seems to have been accepted with mixed feelings, since the officers corps was not of one mind regarding Atlantic defense policies.

During 1970 it appeared as if the latent crisis in the army might become more acute. True enough the opposition which is being voiced, more and more loudly, is speaking the language of an interest group concerned with the security and welfare of its members. However the malaise was widespread enough for the Minister to open an inquiry into the causes of serious disaffection of many officers.[42] On the other hand, such dejection as exists has facilitated the return to political muteness. Even the most highly placed officers remain voluntarily distant from the process of policy formation.

To be sure, it was the new Chief of Staff, General Fourquet who, a few months before General de Gaulle's resignation from office, announced in a lecture before the War College a drastic reversal of the overall military strategy of France.[43] But according to all indications this was a change fully approved of if not initiated by the President of the Republic.

[42] See an article by Jacques Isnard, "M. Debré veut mieux connaître les raisons du mécontentement de certains cadres d'actives," *Le Monde,* July 17, 1970.

[43] Reprinted as "Emploi des différents systèmes de force dans le cadre de la stratégie de dissuasion," *Revue de la Défense Nationale,* XXV:5 (1969), pp. 757–67. This journal published by the Army is making a rather successful effort at building bridges between the officers corps and other elite communities.

CHAPTER X

Policy Processes — II

PARLIAMENT: THE NATIONAL ASSEMBLY —
FROM OMNIPOTENCE TO IMPOTENCE

The constitution-makers of 1958 had the announced ambition of endowing France with a "true" parliamentary regime, with "a Parliament," in the words of General de Gaulle, "intended to represent the political will of the nation, to enact laws and to control the executive, *without venturing to overstep its role.*" [1] Ever since the establishment of the Third Republic, constitutional and political discussions had centered on the question of the proper role of parliament in the policy process. The prevailing distrust of executive authority had tipped the balance in favor of tight and continuous supervision of the government by both houses of parliament. Techniques to make such supervision effective were developed early and steadily refined over time.[2] Their major purpose was to make the government dependent for its survival on a, however heterogeneous, majority of deputies. In both the Third and the Fourth Republic the power of the government to counteract a vote of censure, i.e., a threat to its own existence, by dissolving parliament and calling for new elections was constitutionally granted. But one early misuse of this right by a military President

[1] Speech of General de Gaulle of Sept. 4, 1958 (italics supplied), Andrews (ed.), *op. cit.,* p. 42.
[2] Williams, *Crisis,* pp. 208 ff., gives the most complete account of parliamentary activities in the Fourth Republic. For the same period, see also MacRae, *op. cit.,* pp. 181 ff. and *passim.*

(General MacMahon in 1877) had been enough to deprive this governmental privilege of its republican respectability and legitimacy. Hence it fell into disuse.

In the French republics the concept of parliamentary "sovereignty" included more than the right to cause the downfall of the government. It also left parliament at all times in complete control of its own proceedings and gave it the choice of topics to be debated. Its committees were entitled to alter the text of bills proposed by the government, even before they were considered by the Assembly. Like congressional committees, and unlike the corresponding bodies in the House of Commons, the standing committees of both houses were highly specialized, which facilitated the access of interest groups to the center of decision-making. The constant watch which parliamentary committees kept over each of the ministries was all the more effective because the chairman of an important committee was often regarded as the most likely successor to the incumbent Minister. Such an assumption would hold even where committee chairman and Minister belonged to the same party.

Besides its other effects, the political harassment of the government led to the physical and mental exhaustion of its members — this has been described by many politicians of the period in their memoirs, and it perturbed Colonel Charles de Gaulle in his encounters with the leaders of the Third Republic.[3] Yet formal supremacy was not sufficient to give to the parliaments of the Third and Fourth Republics that power which institutions derive from an effective handling of their functions. Having sought to fuse parliamentary and executive functions, a parliament desirous of keeping the executive weak weakened itself in the process. Since there was no longer any clear focus for decision-making, the resulting loss of momentum communicated itself to all parts of the policy machinery, to parliament as well as to government.

The way in which parliament discharged its role as lawmaker illustrates the impotence of seeming omnipotence. In French constitutional doctrine, every single law is the expression of the general will — by which the people through their representatives manifest their sovereignty. At least on the level of

[3] De Gaulle, *War Memoirs, I*, p. 26 ff.

theoretical considerations, every statute takes on the same symbolic significance which the constitution has in the United States.
Since only parliament can enact a law, only another act of parliament can rescind it.[4] But political realities have deprived the
legislator of so exalted a place.

When after the First World War and especially during the
depression of the Thirties a more active role was thrust upon the
state, a parliament which lacked stable majorities proved unable
to provide the needed legislation. In order to avoid chaos, it
periodically abandoned its legislative authority to the government. During the interwar years, eleven governments obtained
special powers from parliament to override existing laws and to
enact new legislation by so-called decree-laws. "While decree-
laws enabled the executive to act where the legislature would
not, they encouraged evasion of responsibility by the deputies
and of parliamentary control by the administration . . . the
authority given was very widely drawn and still more widely
interpreted." [5] Because of an unsteady party system, the composition and political orientation of a government never conformed
for long with the wishes which the electorate might have expressed in tht previous elections. To give but one example:
although no new elections had taken place, in 1938 decree-laws
annulled important parts of the social legislation which the
Popular Front government had enacted two years earlier, and
deputies who had turned over an essential part of their functions
to an unrepresentative cabinet lost the respect of their constituents.

The constitution of the Fourth Republic sought to forestall
such practices and their political consequences by addressing a
stern prohibition to the National Assembly against delegating its
legislative authority. But since the reasons for political disorder
had not been removed and no disciplined majority emerged in
parliament, constitutional provisions were flouted. Using only
slightly different techniques than before the war, parliament

---

[4] For a classical (and remarkable) statement of the exalted role of the
law in French constitutional thinking, see R. Carré de Malberg, *La Loi,
expression de la volonté générale. Étude sur le concept de la loi dans la
Constitution de 1875* (Paris: Recueil Sirey, 1931).

[5] Williams, *Crisis,* p. 270. See *ibid.,* pp. 271 ff. for interesting details on
the practice followed in the Fourth Republic.

found ways to surrender its sovereign powers as the law-making authority to the executive. Yet as if to compensate for such weakness, it continuously shortened the life span of succeeding governments.

In line with previously developed Gaullist principles, the constitution of 1958 strove to put an end to the subordination of the government to parliament. The framers of the new text were in exactly the opposite position from that in which the founding fathers of the new Bonn constitution had found themselves about a decade earlier. After the experiences of the Nazi regime and of the Weimar Republic, the Federal Republic of Germany wished to give its parliament, the *Bundestag,* a central role in the political system,[6] while the Fifth Republic was to divest the National Assembly of such a role. Debré's acknowledged model was the political system of Great Britain where the place of parliament in policy-making is as well defined (though by custom rather than by law) as it is strictly limited. Whether Debré fully understood that such limitations are primarily an outcome of the party discipline which permits the Cabinet to control the majority in the House of Commons, is a moot question.[7] He simply started with the assumption that the French voter could never be expected to send coherent majorities to the National Assembly.

Therefore the constitution and the so-called organic laws, enacted in conjunction with the constitution, fitted strict rules of behavior, something like a steel corset, on each individual deputy and on parliament as a body. This, it was hoped, would ensure what Debré and General de Gaulle have repeatedly described as the needed equilibrium between parliament and the executive.

Now the cabinet, not parliament, is effectively in control of proceedings in both houses and can require priority for bills

[6] See Gerhard Loewenberg, *Parliament in the German Political System* (Ithaca: Cornell University Press, 1966), p. 432.

[7] The foremost British expert on French politics concludes that the makers of the 1958 constitution set out to import "mainly from Britain, institutions they understood very imperfectly in detail and not at all in spirit." Philip Williams, *The French Parliament. Politics in the Fifth Republic* (New York: Praeger, 1968), p. 114. See *ibid. passim,* for many examples showing how singularly uninformed M. Debré was about the most elementary facts of the British parliamentary system.

which it wishes to push. While previously both the National Assembly and the upper house, the Senate, sat almost permanently, they are now confined to sessions of closely regulated length (amounting to a maximum of six months), so that "the government has time to reflect and to act." [8] It is true that the constitution foresees the possibility of parliament's meeting in special session on a specific agenda at the request of either the Prime Minister or of the majority of the deputies (art. 29). But when in 1960 the required number of deputies expressed the wish to meet in a special session to deliberate on farmers' grievances, President de Gaulle advised the speaker of the Assembly that he would refuse to accede to this demand since in his opinion the deputies' request had been made under pressure from agricultural interest groups. As guardian of the spirit of the constitution he considered it his role to ward off such pressures when they were brought to bear on the representatives of the nation.[9] Hereby a precedent was set, requiring, in spite of the wording of the constitution, the assent of the President of the Republic to any demand for parliament to meet in special session.

It is still the parliament's function to enact laws. But the domain of the "law" is strictly defined (art. 34): major areas of modern life such as the regulation of civil liberties, the budget, important treaties, and at least the principles governing state intervention in economic and social life belong to this domain. But everything not specifically listed is subject to rule-making by the government. Such a distribution of tasks between the cabinet and the assemblies is designed to avoid what Debré has described with telling realism as the "double deviation of our political organization: a parliament overwhelmed by bills and rushing in disorder towards a multiplication of detailed speeches, [and] a government treating without parliamentary interference the gravest national problems."

While there were nineteen standing committees in the National Assembly of the Fourth Republic, their number is now

[8] Speech by M. Debré before the Council of State, reprinted in Andrews (ed.), *op. cit.,* p. 46. Other quotations from Debré's statement are taken from the same speech.

[9] For the text of the letter by the President, see *A.P., 1960,* p. 640. Because of what he considered a flagrant violation of the constitution by the General, Vincent Auriol resigned his seat on the Constitutional Council which he held *ex officio* as a former President of the Republic.

reduced to six in each house. With a membership ranging from 60 to 120 representatives, the committees are made intentionally large so as to prevent interaction between highly specialized deputies or senators who could become effective counterparts to the Ministers. By the same token, the possible influence of pressure groups is diluted.

Both at the stage of deliberation by the competent committees and in plenary sessions, deputies and government are entitled to move amendments to a bill under consideration. But unlike what has happened in the past, the government has the power to force the final vote on a bill with only those amendments which it has been willing to accept. When the budget is being discussed, amendments which would reduce receipts or increase expenditures are out of order. Should parliament fail to accept the budget submitted by the government within the constitutionally allotted time of seventy days, the cabinet can enact the budget by ordinance — a procedure which so far has not been applied since parliament has hastened its deliberations to meet the prescribed deadline. According to a Gaullist former Senator who became a member of the Chaban-Delmas government, the organization of the budget debates "since 1959 seems to be dominated by a single objective: speed. This horror of losing time consumes the managers of the National Assembly, the *rapporteurs-généraux* and the government." [10]

Among the parliaments of Europe, the French Assembly has long been known more for its archaic than for its dignified aspects (although the latter are not entirely lacking). Hence a number of rules, which the new regime introduced and which were above all designed to rationalize and modernize the work of the elected representatives, were generally greeted with satisfaction. But, intentionally or not, these improvements were not associated with modern facilities which would make the work of parliament more efficient. Most deputies have neither working space nor staff. Their means of information are seriously limited: what they do not unearth by themselves has to be passed on to them by the government.

It is not surprising that the new constitution spelled out in detail the conditions under which the National Assembly could

[10] Léon Hamon, here quoted from Williams, *The French Parliament.* etc., *op. cit.*, p. 77.

overthrow a government. Since on the one hand the principle of parliamentary responsibility of the cabinet was to be maintained, and since on the other there was unanimous agreement that the previous frequency of cabinet crises was harmful to the policy process, possibilities for a vote of censure were left open but strictly regulated. Previously the constitution of the Fourth Republic stipulated that a government need resign only when a majority of the National Assembly had voted its downfall. That provision proved unrealistic; governments resigned voluntarily as soon as they had no positive majority behind them. Now the rule was given muscle and stated in more elaborate terms (arts. 49, 50). Yet more important: it was made clear that in the event of a motion of censure the President of the Republic would make use of his solemnly stated right to dissolve the National Assembly and to call for new elections (art. 12).

It is true that many of the reform proposals suggested before 1958 also envisaged the "automatic dissolution" of the parliament which had caused a cabinet crisis. What came as a surprise was that now the vote of censure, as it turned out, was the only means by which parliament could effectively criticize the conduct of government. As in the past, parliament can normally obtain information from the government by means of debate, confrontation of the Prime Minister or of members of his cabinet, written and oral questions, or formal investigations. However, backed by rulings of the Constitutional Council, the government made it clear that under the new regime the deputies would never have the right to express their appraisal of the information thus obtained by a vote or a resolution.[11] Such votes, the government explained, would bring back the practices of harassment which had proved so detrimental in the past because they had led to the gradual weakening of most cabinets. If the National Assembly wished to voice its displeasure with the government, it should gather sufficient votes for a motion of censure. As long as this major weapon was not wielded, no poisoned arrows should be shot in the direction of the benches occupied by cabinet members.

[11] For an English translation of some interesting phases of the discussion pertaining to the new standing orders of the National Assembly, see Andrews (ed.), *op. cit.*, pp. 377–85. The minutes of the entire debate fill 200 pages of the *Journal Officiel*.

Such rules were quite obviously designed as a substitute for disciplined majority voting. Considered in their entirety, they did not necessarily make the role of parliament in the policy process a more limited one than that of the British "mother of parliaments" or of the *Bundestag* in West Germany. But during the early years of the Fifth Republic, the players on both sides, i.e., the members of the government as well as of parliament, adopted attitudes which narrowed the scope of parliamentary activities far more than might have been intended or necessary. The new constitutional provisions and standing orders were interpreted by the President, the Prime Minister, and the Constitutional Council with such harshness that the "no trespassing" signs which were erected always warned parliament, never the executive, to stay within its bounds. It might no longer be true, as it was in the early days of the new regime, that the Constitutional Council seldom rules against the government. Yet, it has at all times guarded firmly the boundary between legislative and executive spheres against any encroachment from the parliamentary side.[12] The government would argue that so painful a process of "reeducation" was necessary in order to forestall a return to the folkways of the political class. But on their side the deputies felt so uneasy in acting out roles that were new to them that they left unused many of the opportunities open to them for the exercise of their functions (see below).

The new imbalance between the executive and parliament resulted in part from the preeminence of the President of the Republic in the policy process. The way in which General de Gaulle appointed the very first government of the new republic indicated that the flow of power and of policy initiative was to be channeled in unaccustomed ways (see Chap. IX). It is true that Debré attempted to set a precedent by appearing before parliament, shortly after his appointment with a declaration of policy which the Assembly could have rejected in the manner which the constitution prescribes for the vote of censure. But his successors failed to follow the precedent and refused to present their program and the members of their government to parliament. Nothing has changed in this respect under the Pompidou administration. After his appointment as Prime Minister, Chaban-

---

[12] For details, see Williams, *The French Parliament* . . . , *op. cit.*, pp. 58 ff.

Delmas waited several weeks before appearing before the National Assembly with his cabinet and program. This has brought the procedures ever closer to those prevalent in a presidential system.

As long as the Algerian crisis was not resolved, parliament was anxious to have the President rather than the government carry the burden of responsibility for political decisions. Such a shift absolved parliament from responsibility as well, since only the government, not the President, is accountable to the National Assembly. But it also shook the very foundations of the parliamentary regime which the constitution was dedicated to strengthening.

The legislative output of parliament under the new regime has not been negligible. In mere quantitative terms the number of laws voted annually by parliament has been reduced rather drastically. But if one weighs their content, the parliaments of the Fifth Republic have enacted statutes of great importance for all aspects of national life. It is true that the initiative for legislation has rarely come from a plenary debate in parliament or from a bill proposed by a deputy. More important were direct contacts between a Minister and an executive of an interest group, talks between a Prefect and a local notable. But this had been the case long before 1958.[13]

The constitution had foreseen that in extraordinary situations normal legislative channels could be bypassed either by a direct appeal to the people, the referendum (art. 11), or by the exercise of presidential emergency powers (art. 16). But unless these provisions are abused, they can shortcircuit parliament only in brief, dramatic situations and hence do not basically affect the balance between executive and parliament. What did prove detrimental to the latter's role in the policy process was the way in which the government handled the means at its disposal to exact voting discipline from the deputies or to obtain from parliament a temporary but sweeping transfer of legislative privilege to the executive.

Whenever the government wished to avoid a vote on a troublesome amendment, it made frequent use of the so-called blocked or package vote (art. 44) which compels parliament to vote on

[13] See Wahl, in *Lawmakers etc., op. cit.,* p. 53.

a bill only in that form which the government considers acceptable. An even more drastic means of obtaining acceptance of
legislation for which there is clearly no majority in parliament is
the possibility of making such approval a question of confidence
(art. 49). Debré at one time stated that this procedure should be
used rarely, but once more events exploded good intentions.
Frequently the deputies were faced with a choice of either giving
in to the government's wishes or censuring it. They also knew
that a vote of censure would most likely lead to the dissolution
of the Assembly, and that, at least during de Gaulle's Presidency,
the subsequent elections would have all the characteristics of a
plebiscite. Those who had voted the motion of censure would
have to bear the onus of having opposed not only a government
whose popularity might well have been waning, but the President
of the Republic himself whose support waxed particularly strong
whenever he could appeal to the electorate against the fomenters
of disunity, the "old parties."

Important bills, such as that establishing France's nuclear
striking force, have become laws in this manner. The preceding
debate had made it clear that in the National Assembly of 1960
abstentions and negative votes would be numerous enough to
defeat the government's intention of launching France on its
career as a nuclear power. But since the motion of censure clos-
ing the debates was not carried by the required vote of half of the
Assembly's total number of deputies, the Speaker could announce
that "in consequence the bill for the program relating to certain
military equipment [sic!] is considered adopted . . ."

If one expected that the package vote would be used less frequently once the government acquired, as it did for the first time
in the election of 1962, a reliable majority, such hopes were frustrated. In fact, although its difficulties in parliament had diminished, the government used the package vote more freely and
more harshly — frequently "for purely tactical purposes on con-
tentious subjects." [14]

[14] Williams, *The French Parliament etc., op. cit.*, p. 67. This of course
failed to enhance the self-confidence of the National Assembly and drove
even the majority to dejection. It was during that period that the
Assembly's speaker (M. Chaban-Delmas) spoke about the government
(then under the Premiership of M. Pompidou) as behaving like an
"autocrat."

During the first three legislatures (1959–1968), parliament was induced more than once a year to authorize the government to pass, by executive ordinances, measures which were and are ordinarily in the domain of the law and should therefore have been voted upon by parliament (art. 38). This provision was fashioned after the practices which during the Third and Fourth Republics had enabled the legislative machinery to function by decree-laws in the absence of a coherent majority in parliament. To continue such practices under the changed conditions of the new regime was first considered advisable in connection with Algerian affairs. Later the authorization given to the executive concerned mostly more technical but equally important matters, such as the legislation necessitated by the association of France with the economies of the other Common Market countries.

In other modern democracies, parliament can regulate a number of questions by broad enabling legislation and leave it to the government to fill in the necessary details. But in France, for a parliament struggling to regain its prestige and not to lose the foothold in the decision-making process which the constitution has provided, a further limitation of the parliamentary legislative function is of necessity more harmful than in a system where over the years the various organs of government have achieved mutual accommodation.

At times the French government combined a demand for new and rather sweeping enabling powers with a challenge to parliament to either accede to this demand or to vote a motion of censure. By combining the powers which it held under two articles of the constitution (articles 38 and 49), the government was not violating the wording of the constitution, but in the opinion of many, it was acting against its spirit. Unwilling to make parliament a channel of information and a sounding board, the government required from parliament and from public opinion no other response than an expression of confidence. Since experience under previous regimes has shown that confidence in the government was difficult to obtain, and more difficult to maintain, parliament was still considered an incommodious rival rather than a partner in the exercise of power. The government asserted that it was merely continuing a tradition developed by the decree-laws of the Third and Fourth Republics. But those traditions were the outgrowth of an instability which the new constitution had set out to correct by other means than by limiting the bounds of free debate and communication between the government and the governed.

A particular instance of the government's high-handedness in its dealings with parliament occurred after the elections of 1967 and turned out to have, by delayed effect, grave consequences. Georges Pompidou, then Prime Minister, had included among the laws to be enacted by ordinance a controversial reform of the social security system. Neither parliament nor public opinion were given an opportunity to discuss the reform. Organized labor capitalized on the widespread hostility toward the measures by a widely observed general strike, clearly directed against the government and hence political in character. In more than one way that twenty-four-hour work stoppage appeared later as a rehearsal for the sweeping strike movements of the following year. By then the workers and their trade unions felt that they were taking revenge for the unpopular measures that had been passed without sufficient consultation of parliament or of public opinion.

Another important milestone on the way to a decline of parliamentary powers was the referendum in the fall of 1962 which divested parliament of its constitutional role in the amending process. To avoid expected parliamentary opposition to his proposed introduction of popular suffrage for the Presidency, General de Gaulle submitted the constitutional amendment directly and without prior parliamentary debate or vote to a referendum. Article 11 which he invoked to justify this procedure was clearly not designed to amend the constitution. After a majority of the electorate had approved the text of the amendment, the Constitutional Council rejected an appeal by the Speaker of the Senate to declare the procedure unconstitutional. The Council declared that it lacked jurisdiction in cases where the *vox populi* had spoken.[15]

However, when de Gaulle tried to use the same procedure to reorganize the regions and the Senate and to circumvent parliament once more, his attempt misfired (see above Chap. IV). It may therefore be assumed that at least for the foreseeable future,

[15] For the text of the terse decision by the Constitutional Council, see *AP, 1962,* pp. 687 ff.

the two houses of parliament have regained through this reaction of the electorate their constitutional place in the amending process.

The style and working methods of a parliament hemmed in on many sides by constitutional rules and by the authoritarian manners of the executive could be expected to vary greatly from those developed during times of parliamentary strength. In the past, as in other Western democracies, the political class was successful in giving to both houses of parliament a club-like atmosphere which neither acrimonious debate nor, on occasion, a duel between temperamental members could spoil. The longevity of the membership in elective office established solidarity between deputies and senators of all parties, with the sole exception of the communists; political opponents would frequently address each other by the familiar *"tu,"* not always used between husband and wife when both belong to the upper bourgeoisie. New members of parliament were rapidly socialized into the established framework, its *esprit de corps,* and its style, which all contributed to making parliament into a subsystem of the political process.

In the Fifth Republic, the changes in personnel and radically changed expectations and attitudes have altered the atmosphere and have made internal socialization far less intense than previously.[16] The boredom and indifference of many deputies can be measured by an absenteeism which is as rampant as ever, although the government has tried to counter it by granting rather degrading pay premiums for those who do attend. Such absenteeism is not restricted, as it is in the United States Congress, to plenary sessions but extends also to most committee meetings, which deputies and senators regard as futile. Even the parliamentary group of the U.D.R. finds it easier to produce unanimity than to compel attendance. Elaborate restrictions on the vote by proxy have been evaded with dexterity, so that it is practiced as frequently (and in many cases as scandalously) as before. The work load of the deputies belonging to the majority is very unevenly distributed. Whatever committee work there is, is man-

[16] For an interesting description of present-day parliamentary behavior, see the series of articles by André Laurens, "Le Métier de Député," *Le Monde,* Oct. 4, 5, 6, 8–9, 10, 1967.

aged firmly by the majority so that many opposition leaders consider their own participation a waste of time. One committee which has preserved a certain luster and importance is that of Finance and Economics, long presided over by Giscard d'Estaing. That he has alternated between the committee chairmanship and the Ministry conforms to the pattern customary in the Third and Fourth Republics.

Altogether the deputies make meager use of those techniques and instrumentalities which are still at their disposal to control the government and to serve as a sounding board for public sentiment. For different reasons, both majority and opposition seem to compete in bringing about the self-effacement of the institution to which they belong.

One of the means by which members of parliament are able to extract information from the government and to search out dark corners of executive behavior is questions addressed to the Ministers. Written questions and answers thereto are published, as before, in the *Journal Officiel,* the French equivalent of the *Congressional Record.* They continue to fulfill the function of a gigantic service of free and official legal consultation. Often five thousand items are disposed of in a single year.

In order to give prominence to more politically pointed, oral questions, the new constitution stipulated that they and the replies by the government be made a weekly priority item (art. 48). The avowed intention in introducing this novelty was once more the desire to emulate British practice. But it was also hoped that the question period would take the place of the "interpellation" by means of which, under previous regimes, the deputies had harassed the government. The vote taken at the end of frequently lengthy debates on such interpellations had been a convenient way of gauging the cabinet's vanishing support. Hence the new standing order of the National Assembly saw to it that the exchanges between deputies and government arising from a question period could never lead to a vote or a resolution.

In the eyes of representatives accustomed to embarrassing a government rather than to scrutinizing its actions such an arrangement deprived the question period of its major interest. Measured by their potential usefulness in as tightlipped a regime as the Fifth Republic, oral questions have been an unmitigated failure: there is none of the lively give-and-take of the British model; sessions devoted to questions are even more poorly attended than others; the deputies are inclined to clothe their questions in lengthy speeches, just as the members of the government read lengthy answering statements prepared for them by their staffs; and often Ministers will send an assistant to represent them, just as President de Gaulle was known to have prevented senior cabinet members from appearing before certain parliamentary committees. If so far neither opposition nor majority has made appropriate use of the question period, the reasons for such failure are to be found in the lack of any tradition for a constructive dialogue between executive and parliament. Both sides have difficulty in believing that a confrontation, instead of precipitating the downfall of a government, could serve the ends of compromise and correction. Some procedural reforms introduced in 1969 are designed to give eventually more life to the institution of oral questions.

The possibility of controlling the executive machinery by *ad hoc* committees of investigation or of preparing legislation by other special committees has fared, if possible, even worse. Although committees of this kind have often been organized in the past, they have rarely been used effectively and have never been able to overcome administrative reluctance to disclose the truth.[17] At present their proceedings are strictly regulated. Committees can at all times exclude press and public from their hearings and do not need to publish their findings. Moreover, the majority is able to determine the membership at will, which makes the committees meaningless to the opposition. All this has meant that only a few trivial matters have been made the subject of investigations; when the opposition suggested that seemingly scandalous situations be investigated, the government was able to prevent the organization of a committee of inquiry.[18]

Also, parliamentary debates have lost much of their interest. Since victory or defeat for the government is seldom at stake,

[17] For the situation prevailing under the Third Republic, see Henry W. Ehrmann, "The Duty of Disclosure in Parliamentary Investigation: A Comparative Study," *The University of Chicago Law Review*, XI:1 and 2 (1943/44), pp. 1–25, 117–53.

[18] For examples, see Williams, *The French Parliament etc., op. cit.*, p. 51.

attendance is spotty. It is true that even before 1958 timidity and conformism had characterized many debates in the "House without Windows," the parliamentary building. If this trend has been amplified, it is not solely due to the government's ability to control the agenda. Only occasionally does a discussion on foreign policy still arouse some interest and provide arguments for debate in the information media.[19]

Under the conditions created by the Fifth Republic, the relationship between the government and its own majority in parliament is of special importance. For, as in Great Britain, the opposition cannot really alter policy as long as the majority party does not lose cohesion. But in England much political bargaining between the cabinet and its own backbenchers precedes formal policy announcements and the submission of governmentally sponsored legislation. Even during General de Gaulle's Presidency, the parliamentary caucus of the U.D.R. and to a lesser extent that of its coalition partner, the Independent Republicans, were fairly regularly consulted by the government. At least certain "study groups" of the U.D.R. served as links between the government and organized interests. Occasionally the study groups appeared to have swayed a governmental decision; they claimed to have played a role in shaping some of the agricultural and educational reforms.[20] When the deputies of the majority pleaded with the government and the bureaucracy to show consideration for the interests of their constituents, their arguments have assumed increased weight, once it had been decided that the U.D.R. should seek a firmer footing in the constituencies (see above Chap. VIII).[21]

Under a new administration and with an enlarged majority, relations between the executive and parliament (or at least the parliamentary majority) have substantially improved. Shortly

[19] For an extensive albeit not very meaningful statistical summary of parliamentary debates during the first eight years of the regime, see François Platone, "Le contenu des débats parlementaires sous la Cinquième République, Étude quantitative, 1959–1967," *RFSP,* XX:1 (1970), pp. 93–104.

[20] Interesting details and a careful evaluation are given in Charlot, *op. cit.,* pp. 153 ff., and Williams, *French Parliament etc., op. cit.,* pp. 102 ff.

[21] See *Le Monde,* June 27 and July 12, 1969. For a good case history of the U.D.R.'s influence on the final shaping of the educational bill of 1968 see Charlot, *Le Phénomène etc., op. cit.,* pp. 149 ff.

after his election to the Presidency, Georges Pompidou pledged increased collaboration between the two branches. He specifically encouraged parliament to make the widest possible use of its legislative functions and of its "right to control governmental policies." While he served as de Gaulle's Prime Minister, Pompidou was less favorably inclined towards parliamentary prerogatives. Yet the Events of 1968 and 1969 may be a sufficient explanation for his change of mind.

The relations between the deputies and the government have been institutionalized by a liaison committee meeting regularly with the Prime Minister and composed of representatives of the three coalition parties. These meetings have not been free of tensions — an unavoidable and salutary consequence of the slow awakening of the National Assembly from years of enforced torpor.

Quite generally deputies of all political persuasions have pursued the traditional defense of constituency interests as energetically as ever. The decline in importance of other parliamentary activities, the new-old electoral system, and the centralization of executive decision-making in a period of rapid economic development has encouraged the most energetic representatives, young or old, to be first of all agents of their constituents in the capital. Even more than previously it is true that the deputy is "a lawyer with a monthly salary, an interpreter, an indefatigable broker . . . and also an extremely busy and often the most efficient social worker in his department." [22] While they may no longer be sought out by those interest groups which have decided to seek direct access to the civil service, many deputies find it worthwhile to negotiate in the name and for the sake of local government authorities. In a system where a local savings bank might need an authorization from Paris to finance the paving of a village street, the services of the deputy are highly appreciated. A number of representatives have made themselves the champions of regional development, acting either through the newly established CODER and through the prefects of the region or through more conventional channels. The by-election in

---

[22] Buron, *op. cit.,* pp. 81 ff. The enthusiastic and yet realistic account by the author who has been a long-time deputy and minister under both the Fourth and Fifth Republics, remains extremely valuable.

Nancy which sent M. Sevan-Schreiber to the Assembly was the result of the frustrations of a Gaullist deputy who by resigning his seat had wished to dramatize the government's neglect of his constituency. In this instance, however, the voters felt that their interests might be better defended by a vigorous member of the opposition.

PARLIAMENT: WHICH UPPER HOUSE?

There were several reasons why the new regime wanted to create a "powerful second chamber." [23] Because they assumed that coherent majorities would never emerge in the "purely political body," as they called the National Assembly, General de Gaulle and Debré attributed to the upper chamber an important role in supporting the government. A house whose members were to be elected, as in the past, mostly by the municipal and department councilors would not only mirror "one of the fundamental aspects of French sociology" — namely the continuing existence of an inordinate number of small communes. It was also expected to bring into parliamentary activities an element of "administrative order." Whenever the National Assembly might yield to perennial temptations to overstep its boundaries, the government hoped to turn to the Senate for support.

Once more the hope of diminishing the realm of the political proved unrealistic. A thinly disguised lack of confidence in the representative expression of universal suffrage had to be paid for dearly. Almost from the beginning of the Fifth Republic the Senate has failed to play its assigned role. And the more it disappointed unwarranted expectations, the more drastically it was excluded from any meaningful participation in the policy process.

The composition of the Senate and the methods of its election have remained essentially unchanged from what they were at the beginning of the Third Republic, when a republican leader called the upper house, not without scorn, the "Great Council of the *Communes.*" He might as well have spoken of the *petites communes,* for at all times the small communities have been heavily represented in the electoral college which designates the

[23] Debré in his speech before the Council of State, in Andrews (ed.), *op. cit.,* p. 50. The quotations following in the text are either from Debré's address or from General de Gaulle's speech at Bayeux, *ibid.,* p. 38.

Senators for a nine-year term of office. (Like the Electoral College choosing the American President, this body never meets, its members voting, as it were, "at home.") All countries without a federalist structure are forever in a quandary as to which units of government or which elements of political life their upper chambers should represent. In a highly centralized system such as that of France, the difficulties are multiplied and lead to a continuous ambivalence towards the legitimacy of an indirectly elected assembly. This explains why every new constitution has determined anew the powers and functions of the upper house.

At present the delegates of municipal councils are still the predominant element among the electors: more than 100,000 of them cast their ballots together with about 3,000 members of the departmental councils, the next higher local government unit. (In this sea of votes, those contributed by the deputies of the National Assembly are without significance.) Because of the lilliputian size of so many local government units, 53 per cent of the delegates of the municipal councils represent units with less than 1,500 inhabitants, or 33 per cent of the total French population.[24] In the Senate itself, the sparsely populated regions are overrepresented: more than half of the 255 senators represent 40 per cent of the population.[25]

Because of the weight of the country's rural sector, the Senate has long been dubbed by its critics the "Chamber of Agriculture." Quite unavoidably, a body whose political roots are particularly strong in the economically least developed parts of the country tends towards parochial conservatism which is frequently out of touch with the problems of a rapidly modernizing country. Yet, in the past, the Senate has not invariably been found on the Right of the political spectrum. Its hostility to social and economic change has been balanced by a forthright defense of traditional republican liberties, and by a stand against the Catholic church and against demagogic appeals to latent antiparliamentary feelings.

---

[24] See Duverger, *Institutions,* p. 584.

[25] In the Upper House of a federal system such discrepancies are more functional than in a unitary system such as France, since even small or thinly populated states, "sovereign" as they are, might have a claim to "equal treatment."

In the Fifth Republic, neither the local elections which determine the membership of the electoral college nor the senatorial elections themselves have so far been touched by the Gaullist groundswell characteristic of all elections to the National Assembly. To speak here of a "revenge of the notables" is no exaggeration. The insufficient local implantation of the U.D.R. is more a consequence than a cause of this phenomenon. While during the first years of the new regime, classical "republican instincts" against a providential leader and a strong executive were a reason for the hostility of many notables, especially south of the Loire River, even more fundamental sociological reasons bolster their resistance. The overwhelming majority of the electoral college — the mayors and municipal councilors of small towns in predominantly rural areas — feel that their status and influence are undermined by the personalization of political power, by the modern mass media and its use by the government, indeed by the well-presented weeklies which more and more supplant the local press proper. These local notables transmit their own and their voters' outlook to senatorial candidates of similar leanings. In turn, numerous senators covet a seat in the upper house mainly because of the advantages they derive from it for the exercise of their functions as mayors or other local government officials.

All this explains why at first electoral support for the new regime was stronger in the cities and urban areas than in the countryside and why the overrepresentation of rural areas in the Senate was bound to weaken its Gaullist contingent. Although party labels in the upper house are often meaningless, it is nonetheless striking that the U.D.R. and the Independent Republicans which since 1962 have held a majority of seats in the National Assembly have never been able to claim more than thirty Senators as definitely committed to their cause.

The Senate, usually defending traditional positions, has disagreed with the government on many major policy decisions. In certain cases their opposition can be traced directly to the Senators' role of defenders of the least developed rural regions. A majority of Senators preferred price supports for agricultural products to structural reforms of rural holdings; they viewed the reorganization of the departments, the creation of the CODER, with great misgivings. The conflict over the revision of the constitution in 1962 led to a pitched battle between the upper house and the President of the Republic. The speaker of the Senate, Alain Poher's predecessor, used his constitutional position to denounce in the Senate and before the Constitutional Council the violation of the constitution by President and government.

Ever since then General de Gaulle and his Prime Minister saw to it that the government was represented at Senate sessions not by the Minister with jurisdiction over the questions under discussion, but by a junior member of the cabinet, usually an Undersecretary. This provided a constant irritant to the Senators who reacted by rejecting or by amending copiously the bills approved by the National Assembly. However, this did not prove a lasting handicap to the government as it would have in the Third Republic when the Senate was able to hold up any text in which it did not concur. The constitution of 1958 provides that if there is disagreement between the two houses concerning pending legislation, the government can appoint a joint committee (art. 45). If the views of the two houses are not reconciled, it is up to the government to decide which will prevail. A weapon originally designed to discipline an unruly lower house could now be turned against the Senate.

On bills of juridical or technical rather than political nature, the senators' opinion was usually taken into consideration. But some legislation of great importance, such as the atomic striking force, the organization of military tribunals in cases involving high treason, statutes regulating municipal elections and strikes in public services was enacted in spite of senatorial dissent. The debates in the upper house frequently showed the senators' earnest concern for the defense of civil liberties. But the amendments they proposed regularly failed when the government opposed them. Like the British House of Lords, "the senatorial opposition could always win the battle, never the war." [26]

In view of such developments, it was not surprising that proposals for a thorough reform of the upper house were heard frequently. The Senate did not really provide the balance which advocates of a bicameral system consider desirable; yet it was so unrepresentative of a modernizing country that to entrust it with

[26] Williams, *The French Parliament etc., op. cit.,* p. 110.

additional powers was likely to lead to deadlock rather than to progress and growth.

From many sides it was argued that the most appropriate solution would be a chamber in which the major economic, social, and cultural interests of the nation would be represented. In his speech at Bayeux, General de Gaulle himself had spoken about including into the upper house of parliament the representatives of such interests "so that within the state itself, the voices of the great activities of the country can make themselves heard." When in 1958 the time for constitution-making had come, General de Gaulle was prevailed upon to abandon such a scheme, to give to the upper house its traditional form and leave interest representation to another body already in existence.

An Economic and Social Council has functioned, under slightly different names and under a variety of statutes, almost continuously since 1924 in spite of the constitutional vicissitudes of the period. Appointed either by major interest groups or by the government, the members of the Council deliberate on all bills which have an impact on economic and social matters and on the Modernization Plan. The Council also studies weighty problems before they have reached the stage of proposed legislation. After extensive debates in plenary sessions and committees, the Council formulates its advice, publishing if need be majority and minority reports. There is general agreement that since its beginnings, but especially since it was reconstituted in 1946, the Council's work has been generally of high quality; its debates have often been more interesting than those in parliament. But it is also general knowledge that neither government nor parliament pay any attention to the Council's labors and advice. Its contribution to the policy process is negligible if not nil.[27] One of the more positive aspects of the Council's work has been the socialization of its members into practices of consultation and cooperation. But those group representatives who might have

[27] On the functioning of the Economic and Social Council, see J. E. S. Hayward, *Private Interests and Public Policy: The Experience of the French Economic and Social Council* (New York: Barnes and Noble, 1966), pp. 36–50. Opinion polls reveal that the public is very badly informed about the functions and the work of the Economic and Social Council — almost as badly as about the CODER (see above Chap. IX at n. 34).

acquired a somewhat changed outlook through their participation in the Council's activities were likely to find themselves at odds with the leadership of the organizations they represented.

The question whether and how to give to the Economic and Social Council more weight in the decision-making process was often discussed earnestly with not always well-informed reference to the experiences made with similar bodies in other European countries (Holland, the Weimar Republic, etc). In European constitutional tradition, suggestions that the representatives of organized interests be invested with decision-making powers belong to the arsenal of authoritarian concepts. Corporatist chambers are usually devised as a defiance of the parliament based on universal suffrage. But in France more than elsewhere, anticapitalist syndicalism has frequently been very close to corporatist concepts, and the latter were shared by socially progressive industrialists, usually themselves influenced by the ideas of an earlier social catholicism. This explains why since 1958 conservatives as well as authentic liberals have backed the idea of transforming the Upper House into a forum for interest representation.[28] The arguments advanced by the protagonists of such a body usually ignored the many and weighty reasons that have long been voiced against this solution. More than anything else, the proposals, and the urgency with which they were made, expressed a widespread uncertainty about the place of parliament in the policy process and about the idea of representation in a modern democracy. Quite typically, all sides professed the hope that an upper chamber of this kind would diminish the dominant role of the bureaucracy — a forlorn hope if past experience is a guide.[29]

When after the Events of 1968 General de Gaulle decided that the time had come for another "revolution from above," his design included a thorough renovation of the upper house.

[28] See e.g. the importance which Pierre Mendès-France attributes to the institution in *A Modern French Republic* (New York: Hill and Wang, 1963), pp. 78–81.

[29] When similar proposals were ventilated in Germany after the First World War, Max Weber expressed the contrary opinion: the position of the bureaucracy would be strengthened whenever it had to settle unavoidable conflicts between parliament and a chamber representing economic and social interests. See *Gesammelte Politische Schriften* (Tübingen: Mohr, 1958), p. 384.

The new proposal reverted to the suggestions made more than twenty years earlier in the Bayeux speech, modified by the lessons which the recalcitrant notables of the Senate had taught the Gaullist regime. Just under one-half of the new Senators (146) were to be interest representatives, chosen by their groups, rather than elected. A majority of the members of the new house (173) would represent, as before, local constituencies, except that in the electoral college selecting them, more weight would be given to the regions rather than to the old-established local government units. All legislation, including constitutional amendments, would have to be submitted to this hybrid body. It could deliberate, formulate suggestions and amendments, but would have been deprived of any power of decision. It did not need to be overruled; it could not rule. In this respect at least, it was closer to the Economic and Social Council than to the old Senate. By its composition and functions it was similar to the Regional Assemblies, proposed in other parts of the referendum (see above Chap. IX). Those assemblies would therefore have been something like twenty-one mini-Senates.[30]

The project for a new upper house was well suited to conjure the opposition, rational as well as instinctive, of traditionalists and progressives, of conservatives and liberals. It was seen as another attack against parliamentary sovereignty, weakening the defenders of republican liberties at the expense of the executive.[31] The local notables saw their status diminished, the center and left wing parties considered the bill as an assault against their positions in the municipalities. Even though the respondents admitted that they hardly understood the technicalities and the full implications of the new legislation, public opinion polls re-

[30] For a favorable commentary of the proposal, see Club Nouvelle Frontière, *Le Dossier etc., op. cit.,* pp. 114 ff. Highly critical Hayward, "Presidential suicide etc.," *op. cit.,* pp. 291 ff., mentioning that the Council of State to which all legislation has to be submitted for technical advice, concluded that the text of the referendum on the Senate was the worst drafted bill it had ever considered.

[31] In his Press Conference of September 9, 1968, President de Gaulle explained that it was no longer necessary to have an Upper House endowed with legislative powers to "counter-balance" the National Assembly, in as much as "since 1958 the Chief of State himself has had the responsibility and the means of preventing excesses and of maintaining the balance."

vealed from the very beginning of the campaign, that this part of the referendum never gathered majority support and eventually took the regional reform down to defeat as well: the defense of the old Senate had assumed a symbolic value which the actual role of the institution in the policy process hardly deserved.

With the survival of the *status quo,* the only reform of the upper house that might now be envisaged is a limited redistribution of Senate seats which could be enacted by ordinary legislation and which would give to the urban population a somewhat more adequate representation. More important for the effectiveness of the upper house would be a renewed willingness on the part of the government to consider more patiently the amendments proposed by the Senate and to use less frequently the government's constitutional powers to override the upper house with the assistance of a majority in the National Assembly. Of this, the first government of the Pompidou administration has given assurances. At the same time, the Prime Minister has promised the Economic and Social Council that its labors would be lent the utmost attention and publicity.

THE FUTURE OF PARLIAMENTARY GOVERNMENT

From the outset, its functions and its freedom have been so circumscribed that the parliament of the Fifth Republic could hardly be regarded as "sovereign." In a number of essential respects, the new regime has departed from a classical parliamentary system. Under de Gaulle parliament suffered a further decline of role and prestige when, instead of arbitrating between decisions that had been reached by the elected representatives and other organs of government, the President became the principal fountainhead of decision-making, and when, instead of being elected by an electoral college of notables, he competed with parliament for the direct suffrage.

In other European democracies there has also been a gradual decline of the role of parliament in the policy process. But for French deputies, at least for those who did not owe their seat to an identification with General de Gaulle, such a drastic and sudden break with previous traditions was difficult to endure. To them, the functions remaining within the purview of parliament appeared frequently as vacuous.[32] To them, the legitimization of policies and of laws initiated by the government was tantamount to useless "rubberstamping." This is in fact what a disciplined majority in a parliamentary regime is expected to do; but in France it has never been fully accepted as a fundamental rule of the political game.

To escape frustration, deputies and senators have turned their full attention to the defense of constituency interests. By so doing they hoped to regain prestige and possibly authority for the institution to which they belong; this in turn preserved a democratic atmosphere. But such activities also were keeping alive the habits of atomistic representation, and on their reverse side are those "games, poisons, and delights" for which General de Gaulle had always chided the political class.

At one time a Gaullist Minister resigning his post in the Pompidou cabinet expressed the fear that the two major branches of government might continue to run on different tracks: a popularly elected President who uses all the techniques of a plebiscitarian democracy, and a parliament which, for lack of strong parties, perseveres in the practices of an exclusively atomistic representation.[33] Such a situation explains why during the Events of 1968, when the authority of the President was near collapse, neither parliament nor parties were looked upon as meaningful channels through which a solution of the massive conflicts could be attempted.

Too little time has elapsed since General de Gaulle's retirement to evaluate the future role of parliamentary institutions in the successor regime. The de-emphasis of plebiscitarian features, the announced resolve to put the collaboration between the executive and the elected representatives on a new basis, the greater attention given to the building of better structured parties, whether of the majority or the opposition, all this would create new conditions for the participation of parliament in the policy process. In carrying out their intentions the new administration can, if it chooses to, find support in the fact that large

---

[32] For an interesting discussion of this question, see Association Française de Science Politique, *Le Parlementarisme, peut-il être limité sans être annihilé* (mimeographed: Paris, 1965).

[33] Edgar Pisani, "Sur une Démission," *Le Monde,* May 13, 1967.

segments of public opinion are now expressing rather strong sympathies for parliament as such and for a broadening of its functions. Under the impact of the crisis which had brought about the downfall of the Fourth Republic, sympathies for the institutions and the men held responsible for the regime's failure were at first rather slight. Between 1959 and 1966 the number of those who regretted that parliament was then playing so small a role had slowly risen from 31 to 43 per cent; but in 1964, 38 per cent declared that the question was without interest to them and 13 per cent refused to answer.[34]

Late in 1969 — at a time when some adjustments in favor of parliament had already been made — 48 per cent of the respondents wished to see parliament play a greater role than heretofore, with only 18 per cent indifferent to the question.[35] Criticism of the parliaments of the Fourth Republic has abated although preference is given to the style of parliamentary activities in the Fifth. As far as those activities are concerned, strong preferences are voiced which are not always well informed about the limits and the possibilities of a parliamentary body in modern times. Legislative and budgetary powers are still valued very highly. The respondents are ambivalent concerning the role of parliament in forming and then supporting a majority government. But there is little hesitation in attributing to parliament the primary task of protecting the citizens and safeguarding their freedoms. Hence, any suppression of parliament or even a limitation of its privileges [36] is viewed as extremely grave. About two-thirds of the respondents believe that deputies have plenty to do and 51 per cent that they are conscientious in the performance of their duties (32 per cent disagree on this point). When asked who "ideally" should be in charge of the overall orientation of policy, 33 per cent wish the parliament to assume this function, 36 per cent would leave it to the government, and only 24 per cent to the President of the Republic. In case of conflict between parliament and government, a majority holds to the traditional solution: 60 per cent find it "normal" that parliament overturns

[34] See Brulé and Piret, *Les Transformations sociales,* pp. 17, 18, and *Sondages,* XXVIII:1 (1966), p. 38, and XVII:1 (1965) pp. 69–72.

[35] SOFRES, *Poll of Oct.-Nov. 1969,* pp. 66. All subsequent data in the text are from the same poll, *passim.*

[36] On this point the question asked in the poll is somewhat vague.

the government (with 22 per cent opposed), but only 46 per cent (with 33 per cent of different opinion) approve in such a situation the dissolution of parliament by the government.

In regard to all of these questions, differences of opinion between different groups of respondents are fairly uniform: women are generally less inclined than men to favor strong parliamentary institutions; the young more so than the older generations; industrialists, professional people, managers, and executives have a higher than average inclination to give parliament a greater role. From the perspective of political stratification, sympathies for parliament are strong on the Extreme Left and go in descending order from Left to Right. U.D.R. voters reveal their usual right of center attitudes: they are less friendly toward parliament and more inclined than the average respondent to look to the executive as the most important branch of government. But they are not violently antiparliamentarian.

Such results seem to indicate that, at least in a period of relative political quiet, popular sympathies have not massively turned away from republican traditions after a decade of Gaullist rule. It is quite possible that more than its share of sympathies has accrued to parliament, just because the latter has been given a diminished status in the policy process and is therefore considered as less of a threat to the individual than the executive.

Whether and in which direction such attitudes could change, will undoubtedly depend on satisfaction or discontent with the overall performance of the system.

CHAPTER XI

Political Modernization and Legitimacy

THE DYNAMICS OF MODERNIZATION IN FRANCE

When political modernization is understood as the adaptation of the political process to changing functions, then even the most advanced countries are still modernizing.[1] In France as elsewhere, modernization takes place in an infinite continuum, and even though certain transitions deserve the scrutiny to which this and other studies have submitted them, they are never quite as dramatic as they might appear at certain moments to actors and onlookers alike. Why the French have a great ability for dramatizing the controversies generated by the modernization process has been explained in previous chapters. But similar and often identical controversies have occurred in numerous societies, reflecting everywhere reactions not only to political but also to intellectual, psychological, economic, and social problems.[2]

The particularities of the French political culture, while in no way preventing adaptation and change, have lent themselves to an alternation between periods of immobilism, when the process of modernization was blocked or unduly slowed, and "crisis-liquidation regimes."[3] Periods of purposeful activity have been

[1] Cf. C. E. Black, *op. cit.,* pp. 7, 9. This essay by a historian has been very helpful in the discussion which follows.

[2] See also *ibid.,* p. 78.

[3] This term was coined by Almond and Powell, *op. cit.,* p. 310; see *ibid.,* p. 319 for a discussion of the Weimar Republic which is also helpful for an understanding of French politics.

followed by those of frustrating confusion and immobility. Decades during which nothing really new was tried were interrupted by brief and bold experimentation.

Frequently, the change from one stage to the other was abrupt instead of continuous and incremental. As a consequence, no French regime has had the capacity for thorough self-reform since the decline of the *Ancien Régime,* i.e., for almost two centuries. This in turn has magnified almost every political crisis, many of which centered around problems arising from modernization, into a constitutional crisis. It has also meant that each of the sixteen constitutional texts which France has known since 1791 has had to seek a new legitimacy for the institutions it established and the values it sought to represent. In one way or another each French constitution became a victim of French politics, yet this bestowed legitimacy on neither. Such discontinuity, to be sure, has proved traumatic and time and again a threat to democratic government. But discontinuity has also seemed unavoidable if one wanted to overcome a stability that was tantamount to stalemate. When pressures from the international environment left only the choice between permanent decline or adaptation to changing circumstances, stability was eventually sacrificed.

The Third Republic (1870–1940) offers a foremost example of the fact that longevity and staying power are not tantamount to that stability which permits the needed adaptation of institutions to newly accruing functions. At times it survived mainly because of the ineptness of its opponents. It operated differently in times of normalcy and in times of crisis, but it has been characterized with equal justification as a "system of democratic politics and nondemocratic government," or as offering "the paradox of a weak government with a strong state." [4] Its rapid collapse in the Second World War was due largely to a lack of modernization in the broad sense in which the term is employed here.

Those who believed that the significant demographic, economic, and social changes which the country underwent after the end of the war would result in a more or less automatic adaptation of political institutions and processes to the needs of the

[4] See Eckstein, *op. cit.,* p. 229, and André Siegfried, *De la IIIième à la IVième République* (Paris, Grasset, 1956), p. 251.

society saw their hopes frustrated, especially when it turned out that the party system remained obsolete (see Chap. VIII). When first the Indochina and then the Algerian war dramatized the problem of decolonization — another phase in the modernization process — the low threshold for crisis solution by the regime became apparent.

What remains to be examined is whether the Fifth Republic, especially now that it has entered a new phase, will be able to accomplish the changes required by a continuous process of modernization, and whether its rules and procedures will be accepted as legitimate. While General de Gaulle was at the helm, this query was particularly pertinent. Lessons of history suggest that regimes which begin, as did the Gaullist Republic, in a near-revolutionary situation, and which center for a considerable time around a charismatic personality, are usually of the most transient type.[5] Yet, after de Gaulle's retirement, the often dreaded succession crisis did not occur. The "chaos" predicted by the General himself, was nowhere to be found. Competitors in an orderly electoral contest congratulated each other in good American fashion. Majority and opposition leaders agreed that the "war of the republics was over" (Chaban-Delmas), and that the "period of the permanent coup d'etat had been terminated" (Mitterand). But a collective sigh of relief is not all that is needed to enable a political community to solve its problems in a rapidly changing environment.

LEGITIMACY FOR THE NEW INSTITUTIONS?

According to General de Gaulle's expressed beliefs, the twin problems of legitimacy and authority are deceptively simple, even if modern political science might characterize his beliefs as delusions. To him authority is characteristic only of the state and never of anything outside of it. All it takes to make this monopoly effective and thereby legitimate is that the state be strong. In periods when parties and other intermediary bodies are influential enough to besiege the state and weaken its output, legitimacy ceases to exist.

Upon returning to power in 1958, General de Gaulle himself

[5] See Eckstein, *op. cit.*, p. 274.

considered it the foremost task of the new regime once more to liquidate a crisis in which legitimacy was floundering. When, especially during the first years of the Fifth Republic, he consistently tied legitimacy to his own person, he did so because he knew that neither the new men, his collaborators, nor the new institutions commanded authority. Only the authority he had earned by past deeds and merits enabled the state to overcome the strains and centrifugal tendencies which, in General de Gaulle's opinion, were artificially created by forces active from outside the government.[6]

In subsequent years, when circumstances made it no longer necessary nor even possible to identify the new regime with an acute crisis situation, the President of the Republic based the claim for legitimacy on other grounds. Instead of personally acquired historical title, he stressed that the quality of the constitution, the dignity, stability, and efficiency of the regime will ensure wide acceptance and survival after his own demise. When he praised the institutions as being adapted to present-day conditions, he emphasized their modernity. When he predicted that eventually the constitution "with its effective separation of powers" and "with all that it entails will have become as second nature to us," he offered indeed a pragmatic and not necessarily undemocratic definition of legitimacy.[7]

What had not changed was General de Gaulle's conviction that "politics" could be divorced from the "state" and consequently that the policy-making process in the Fifth Republic had nothing to do with the solving of political conflicts. In that sense, he still considered himself, as have providential leaders before him, as a satisfactory substitute for both politics and participation.[8] The Events of 1968 proved him wrong on both points with the result that his prestige declined. This however, as it

[6] To date, the most important evaluation of de Gaulle's lasting contribution is to be found in Stanley and Inge Hoffman, "The Will to Grandeur: de Gaulle as a Political Artist," *Daedalus,* IIIC:3 (1968), pp. 829–87.

[7] See various press conferences of General de Gaulle and especially that of November 27, 1967.

[8] See Hoffmann, in *In Search of France,* p. 113, and also the same author's "Heroic Leadership: The Case of Modern France," in Edinger (ed.), *Political Leadership in Industrialized Societies* (New York. Wiley, 1967), pp. 108–154.

turned out, did not shake the legitimacy of the institutions which de Gaulle had sought to accredit.

The transition from one Presidency to another was an example of that metamorphosis which the French philosopher Charles Péguy had described at the beginning of the century: "Everything begins as *mystique,* and everything ends as politics." By considering the presidential elections as a normal act of political participation even though General de Gaulle was no longer a candidate,[9] and even more so by attitudes observed since then, Frenchmen showed that in their eyes the successor regime had indeed acquired a widely accepted title to rule — a commonsense definition of legitimacy. Opinions voiced in various polls not only expressed confidence that the essential institutions of the Fifth Republic would survive de Gaulle; ambivalence and inconsistencies in the voters' attitudes correspond largely to those of the institutions themselves.[10] The popularity of the election of the Chief Executive by direct suffrage is unshaken. To have made the popular election of the Executive democratically respectable, after it had been tainted for more than a century by the suspicion of serving the ends of dictatorship, remains one of the historical achievements of the regime. In the country which continues to have the weakest of all party systems among the democracies of Western Europe, the direct election of the Head of State compensates for some of the shortcomings of parliament as a representative body.

Nonetheless, an understanding of the political implications of this mode of designating the Chief Executive is growing only slowly. As in the United States and in Latin American republics, a popularly elected President must play a paramount political role; if, as in France, the regime is half-presidential, half-parliamentarian he cannot help being at the same time, either directly

[9] It has been explained earlier (see Chap. IV) that the high rate of abstention, due largely to communist directives to its followers, was tantamount to a political decision, not to a withdrawal from the system.

[10] Already in 1964, systematic interviews among various elite groups revealed that a majority of respondents accepted the constitutional system of the Fifth Republic even while taking exception to some of the interpretations General de Gaulle had given to it. See Karl W. Deutsch, et. al., *France, Germany and the Western Alliance* (New York: Scribner's, 1967), pp. 44 ff.

or indirectly, the leader of the majority. Georges Pompidou has accepted these consequences of the institutional set-up. A majority of the electorate is still uncomfortable with them: in May, 1969, 49 per cent believed that the President should *not* be the leader of a political majority, 35 per cent thought he should, with 16 per cent not voicing any opinion. 57 per cent attributed to him the single role of arbiter and guardian of the constitution, with 32 per cent preferring that he take important decisions concerning long-range policies.[11]

Previously discussed data have indicated how uncertain and in part misinformed a large part of the electorate appears to be about the respective weight of the President, the government, and parliament in the decision-making process. When the respondents are asked to divide the various domains of governance between the three organs, very few believe that the President should have an important say in economic and social questions; in the opinion of a majority, these matters are better left to government and parliament which corresponds somewhat to constitutional arrangements. In regard to foreign affairs, preferences and reality are not in accordance. 51 per cent wish to see parliament, 25 per cent the President to be in charge — about six months after General de Gaulle's retirement this might be an expression of aversion against the style in which the country's foreign policy had been conducted rather than against its content.

At about the same time, a large number of Frenchmen let it be known that for them the merits of the "savior" were rapidly dropping into oblivion. Forty-nine per cent expressed no or "very few" regrets about General de Gaulle's disappearance from the public stage; not more than 19 per cent (far fewer than the Gaullist electorate) were truly unhappy about it. In the case of a hypothetical grave crisis, only 38 per cent wanted to see him return

[11] *Sondages,* **XXXI**:3 (1969), pp. 46. It is true that this poll was taken during the electoral campaign which by the tension it produced might have falsified opinions somewhat. At any rate, opinions had already changed rather significantly when compared with the spring of 1967 when 62 per cent could not conceive of the President as majority leader, with only 21 per cent of the opposite opinion. For the data following in the text, see SOFRES, *Polls Oct.-Nov. 1969,* esp. p. 101.

to power, 62 per cent were definitely opposed to such a reenactment of 1958.[12]

These reactions should not be interpreted as just another example of French capriciousness. They indicate, rather, that a substantial majority of the electorate felt safer with a routine than with a heroic leadership and that they had ceased enjoying the sequence of dramatic surprises.

A democracy characteristically is legitimized more by its form than by its substantive results or by the self-restraint of its temporary ruler. General de Gaulle's vast authority had not been exercised constitutionally if one understands this term to mean (at the very least) that authority is exercised "within a framework of widely accepted and well-understood limits and rules, including, for example, the rule that authority inheres always in a collective structure." [13] At important junctures, not even the French cabinet minister, to say nothing of the electorate, understood either the rules which the Chief of State was about to establish or the limits which he set for himself.

As long as General de Gaulle's performance had been stunning, politics in France had become more than ever a spectator sport, and to be spectators "together" might even have been pleasing to egalitarian instincts. With the decline in performance, satisfaction with the established pattern of nonparticipatory authority declined too. But also in the future, the government's performance will determine what it can legitimately expect from its citizens. For, just as it makes a significant difference in a political system what expectations the members have as to what the government ought to do *for* them, so it makes a crucial difference what they believe the government ought to or can do *to* them.[14]

A MODERN DEMOCRACY? — CHANCES AND SHOALS

Resource allocation is one of the most important issues in the management of industrial society. A redirection away from costly policies serving the nation's prestige and rank in international

[12] See *Le Monde,* November 27, 1969. It is noteworthy that on these questions working-class respondents were slightly more sympathetic to de Gaulle than the average.

[13] See Eckstein, *op. cit.,* pp. 198 and 235.

[14] See Verba in Pye and Verba, *op. cit.,* p. 541.

affairs was underway during the last months of General de Gaulle's administration. Further changes can be expected to be slow because of the pledged fidelity to policies of *grandeur* whose implications for domestic politics have been discussed earlier; but changes there will be. The Minister of Defense has announced that by the end of the seventies France's thermonuclear arsenal will be perfected; yet it is also expected that by 1975 military expenditures which ten years ago represented 5.6 per cent of the GNP will amount to only about 3 per cent. The rather vast foreign aid program, which has benefitted above all the French-speaking countries of Africa, is not to be abandoned but scaled down.

Economic and financial policies will be scrutinized as to whether they serve the foremost developmental goal: the speed-up of industrialization. In language sometimes reminiscent of that of Soviet leaders during the time of the first five-year plans, President Pompidou and some members of his first government insist that during the next decade industrial output must be doubled. For the time being this remains vague as national planning is relaxed rather than geared to a more intensive program of investments and production quotas. The announced policies have already provoked the renewed onslaught of special interests, claiming continuing subsidies and privileges, the granting of which can only disturb whatever program for the reallocation of resources might exist.

In the judgment of many (some of them on Prime Minister Chaban-Delmas' staff) the problems of investment, modernization, and participation are more intimately interrelated in present-day France than in other countries of similar development. Participation is a key term which the new administration has inherited from the old. After the Events of May, General de Gaulle wished to move participation into the center of governmental preoccupation, for he belatedly recognized that politics cannot be eluded and that the only true alternative is one between politics with and politics without participation. Where participation is described, as it continues to be in official propaganda, as the midway point between "totalitarianism and savage capitalism," the concept suffers easily from overuse for political ends. Yet the desire for effective participation was in fact not absent from the strikes and from the street movements in May, 1968. It expresses a strongly felt but badly articulated need for communication and cooperation for which there has been little room in a hierarchically ordered political culture, as rich in privileges as it is in egalitarian pretensions.

To lift participation from the verbal level to that of reality and activities, the government has pleaded with groups and firms for "concertation," a new-old formula for intensive and long-term bargaining and it has sought to encourage such understandings by some appropriate legislation.[15] Success and failures in this pursuit have been described earlier (see above Chap. VII). But the point has been made that to make participation solely dependent on the frequently flagging good will of the social partners will remain insufficient unless investment policies are systematically turned to fields which will call forth and enrich participatory practices.[16] In the United States such demands have evoked discussions about the need for greater emphasis on social investments designed not just to spread affluence but to enhance the quality of life. In the American context, investments of this kind are called for in order to relieve the strains which a fitfully expanding but still modernizing economy produces. In France, it is argued, sustained growth and modernization will be blocked if the pattern of decision-making, ill-adapted to present demands, is not replaced by a resolute turn to collective action, encouraged by an appropriate investment policy.

France is not the only country where the pressures and the anxieties created by postindustrial society result in an understandable craving for security and protection even though such concerns might be in contradiction with long-term goals. Moreover it is not a novel phenomenon, and again not one confined to France, that value systems frequently lag behind economic

---

[15] Interesting statements by representatives of important groups before a Committee of the National Assembly have been published in Commission des Affaires culturelles, familiales et sociales, *Qu'est-ce que c'est que la participation?* (Paris: Plon, 1969). For a bitter (communist) critique, see Jacques Kahn, *La Participation. Ce que de Gaulle cache,* (Paris: Éditions Sociales, 1969).

[16] On this see especially the recent writings by Crozier, quoted above Chap. 6, n. 32. In a similar vein, but far more optimistic about the find outcome one of the members of the Prime Minister's staff Jacques Delors, "La Nouvelle Société," *Preuves* (2nd Trim. 1970) pp. 95–107.

and social developments, just as national wealth and economic growth impinge on democratic structures only through the often delayed impact which they have on the general pattern of social forms.[17] Both value systems and social forms are of paramount importance for political modernization. When one seeks to generalize about French attitudes toward change, one can hardly avoid the pitfalls of such generalization. Tocqueville recognized in the Frenchmen of his time the traits which Caesar had drawn some 2,000 years earlier when he described the Gauls as *rerum novarum cupidi,* eager for all things new. Many of the great French novels of the nineteenth century are concerned with social change and illustrate masterfully the conflicts between traditional and modern values. Today, the same careful observer — who has explained why the bureaucratic and bourgeois system of France has favored the blossoming of a highly individual culture clinging to its preindustrial ways — considers it untrue that Frenchmen dislike change. "What they fear is not change itself, but the risks they may encounter if the stalemate that protects them (and restricts them at the same time) were to disappear." [18] Another French sociologist (who was soon thereafter to face confrontation with his students at Nanterre) concluded on the basis of several case studies that "Frenchmen are very much interested in themselves and very little in their society." [19]

Since in the last analysis problems of long-term structural changes must always be resolved in terms of the inherited political culture of each society, such attitudes have their importance. But attitudes and institutions interact. In discussions on the general problems of political development, it has been suggested not only that social and economic mobilization — that is, increasing participation — is an important variable in the process of development, but also that the growth of political institutions, able to accommodate, channel, and contain increased participation, determine success or failure of modernization.[20] In many transitional or modernizing polities (the so-called underdevel-

[17] See Black, *op. cit.,* p. 89, and Eckstein, *op. cit.,* p. 188.

[18] Cf. Crozier, *The Bureaucratic Phenomenon,* p. 226.

[19] Alain Touraine, "La Société française: croissance et crise," in Société Française de Sociologie, *Tendances, op. cit.,* p. 474.

[20] See especially Samuel Huntington, *Political Order in Changing Societies* (New Haven: Yale University Press, 1968).

oped countries) political order may erode because the growth of political institutions does not keep pace with mobilization. A contrasting picture can be observed in some highly developed systems. Here the political landscape may be so clogged with some previously successful institutions which refuse to give way that political participation is stifled by institutional abundance rather than scarcity. Modern French society has many of these features.[21] If in developing countries mobilization may be too rapid for institutions to assimilate it and hence society may "overwhelm the state," in a country like France certain highly developed public institutions may, as it were, overwhelm society by preventing meaningful participation.

In France, the rigidly hierarchical (if internally disunited) bureaucracy has been successful in keeping the state together amidst the vagaries of party and parliamentary politics. But as has been remarked, "for any organization the time may come when its triumph over function after function will become a pyrrhic victory." [22] It has been explained earlier why at various stages of development the French high civil service had to become the main promoter of change. But the fate of some of the more recent major reforms also shows that this very origin invariably hampers their rootedness and thereby endangers their eventual success. The history of the educational and regional reforms, both before and since 1968, are cases in point. The solution of other problems, such as urbanization and the reform of the communes, has run on shoals even earlier and for similar reasons: everywhere the line of command runs down from the Ministries to subprefects and mayors, to the labor inspectors and to the school inspectors; everywhere seemingly strong, long-established institutions assume direction and discourage initia-

---

[21] This is the main thesis of Kesselman's highly suggestive article "Over-institutionalization etc. . . ." *op. cit.,* esp. pp. 24 ff. Bernard E. Brown, "The French Experience of Modernization," *World Politics,* XXI: (1969), pp. 366–91, concludes an excellent essay on historical developments in a rather different vein. But both authors agree that because of its special features, not because the country is underdeveloped, a comparison between modernization in France and in some of the underdeveloped nations suggests some parallel difficulties.

[22] Dankwart A. Rustow, "The Organization Triumphs over its Function: Huntington on Modernization," *Journal of International Affairs,* XXIII:1 (1969), p. 131.

tive. But where in the past some kind of order ensued, at present the result is frequently chaos. Therefore a true decentralization not a mere deconcentration of administrative functions appears imperative to insure modernization. For power is not merely overcentralized; it is also frozen at various levels into patterns inimical to change. Hence, decentralization to be effective would have to amount to a redistribution of power within the various decision-making elites, the administrative corps, as well as the political class. It also would have to bring new groups into the decision-making process without frustrating them, as were the *forces vives* on which so many hopes were pinned in the early sixties. These forces failed not so much because they were unable to mobilize new energies, but because they could not mesh their energies with old and lordly institutions.

When Prime Minister Chaban-Delmas addressed the National Assembly for the first time, he indicted French "blocked society," its "backward social structure," and the "inefficient" as well as "overbearing" machinery of the state in rather similar terms.[23] The "new society" he went on to describe had many of the ear-marks of a "concrete utopia" which intellectuals, within and outside the high bureaucracy, had been developing for some time.[24] The politically relevant question which has been asked from many sides and which remains open is whether the government, even assuming that it has the will to do so, can gather enough strength to carry through the announced reforms.

The heterogeneity of the dominant party, the U.D.R., has been described. The governing coalition, being broader, comprises men of yet more widely differing viewpoints on social, economic, and administrative reforms. There is no indication that President Pompidou now has more faith in the virtue of reforming traditional structures than he had when he was Prime Minister. The desire of M. Chaban-Delmas to build the largest

[23] For a discussion of other parts of the speech, see above Chap. II, at n. 10. The term *"société bloquée,"* now very widely used, is admittedly an adaptation of the "stalemate society" which an American scholar, Stanley Hoffmann, coined to characterize the Third Republic in its years of decline. See his contribution to *In Search of France . . . , op. cit.,* pp. 3 ff.

[24] For a thoughtful example, see François Bloch-Lainé, a widely respected high civil servant, "Bâtir des utopies concrètes," *Projet* No. 45 (May 1970), pp. 507–20.

possible coalition for progress indicates that he realizes how unwilling the conservatives in his own party might be to follow him on the path he has traced. But the continuing shapelessness of the Center and the disorganization of the noncommunist Left could still turn any alternative to the present coalition into a hazardous venture. If the "swamp" at the Center has not really been drained,[25] the old situation could be resurrected: a number of deputies whose votes are needed for the support of a coalition government could be sent to parliament by their constituents to pursue one set of policies, and then feel inclined to vote for and to follow other if not opposite policies. As in the past, this could once more destroy the representativeness of parliament and the aggregative function of parties as well. In order to prevent such a recurrence of the former pattern, Pompidou insists on preserving a coherent and disciplined, if conservative, party and invites the emergence of a better structured opposition. The future of the French party system, including the special problems created by the existence of a large Communist party, remains therefore one of the factors that will decide the future of the required reforms.

In his address to the National Assembly in 1969, the Prime Minister discussed additional difficulties that reforms traditionally encounter in France: ". . . we never manage to push through reforms except by pretending to make revolutions. French society has not yet been able to advance in any way except by a major crisis." Frenchmen are indeed fascinated by a crisis, and at the next moment they are panicstricken by one.[26] The Events of 1968 gave renewed evidence of this phenomenon. During the days of the revolt, a large majority of citizens, in most districts of Paris, applauded the students and their goals, even where they were revolutionary; high church officials — both Catholics and Protestants — expressed sympathies for the rebels. Many blamed the university authorities and the police for being responsible for the violent clashes.[27] But only weeks later the ballots in the elections expressed little else but fear of disorder.

[25] This was the skeptical conclusion reached by Goguel in 1967 in "Bipolarisation," *op. cit.*

[26] So Crozier, "Pourquoi la France . . ." *op. cit.,* p. 138.

[27] According to polls taken during the events, see *Sondages,* **XXX**:2 (1968), pp. 73 ff.

If France is bound to advance primarily by crises then "crisis management" becomes imperative. How to use a crisis for feeding into the legislative and administrative machinery tangible reforms and yet avoid serious civil disturbances likely to provoke reactions hostile to any progress, calls for a strategy to be developed by trial and error. Recent experiences have shown that the present presidential regime has greater capabilities for overcoming an acute crisis than previous regimes. On the other hand the centralization and concentration of power easily results in the generalization of even a local conflict and magnifies thereby the effect of an outbreak of violence anywhere. That potentials for violence remain close to the surface at the very time when the government has some tangible success in its call for collaboration and concerted action, has also been noted previously (see Chap. VII). Citizens for whom the exalted promises of a "new society" remain empty slogans feel inclined to take their demands to the streets and highways.

So that it might be well-equipped to meet future disorders, the government has obtained from parliament new "law and order" legislation; under a harmless name it could infringe seriously upon civil liberties and the freedom of association. The so-called *"anti-casseurs"* law insists that those who in the course of any public commotion destroy property be made to pay for it and possibly be punished by fines or imprisonment. In fact, existing provisions in the Civil and Penal Code provide for such sanctions. What the new legislation adds are possibilities for prosecuting the leadership of any organization engaged in illicit manifestations or even in authorized demonstrations that lead to spontaneous violence. Heavy fines against the organizations themselves could destroy them financially. The government reasons that it needs stronger weapons in order to forestall the backlash that must be expected if radicals are permitted to roam at will. But in the hands of an illiberal government, provisions of the new legislation could quite easily be used to discourage if not suppress dissent.

It may be taken as another illustration of contradictory governmental policies that almost simultaneously with the *anti-casseurs* law, the Minister of Justice submitted a bill which could become a milestone in liberalizing criminal procedures. A series of judicial scandals drew public attention to the fact that under existing regulations — which date from the Napoleonic period — the privileges of defendants in criminal trials, and especially the rights of those suspected of criminal activities, are badly safeguarded. Insufficient provisions for bail has resulted in the fact that at least one-third of the total prison population are people awaiting trial and who in some cases are behind bars for as much as eight months or more before the examining magistrate concludes his investigation. The new law reinforces the protection of the accused at many stages of criminal procedure and in several ways seeks to change judicial habits.[28]

It will indeed be a foremost task for the government to establish confidence in the functioning of the judicial system. The existence of such trust has been considered rightly an indicator of a regime's legitimacy, for it is a yardstick for the esteem in which the citizenry holds system performance. On these grounds the French judiciary fares extremely poorly. In 1969, 52 per cent of respondents in a public opinion poll thought that the judicial system functioned badly (with a mere 30 per cent satisfied).[29] Such figures, evoking the bitter drawings of a Daumier, undoubtedly mirror another lag in the modernization of institutions. They also indicate the alienation of a large body of citizens in regard to an important aspect of government output.

The bemused truism with which Robert Dahl concludes a celebrated symposium on political opposition has often been quoted: ". . . one perennial problem of opposition is that there is either too much or too little." [30] In another age, and in a passage quoted before, Alexis de Tocqueville has indicated how perfectly this applied to his country. Whether the present study is written (and will be read) at a time of the "too much" or of the "too little" is difficult to tell.

While the constitutional crisis, opened in the thirties, seems to

[28] Since this has been tried before without much success, doubts about the possible effects of the legislation have already been expressed. See Jean-Marc Théolleyre, "Au delà des réformes, les hommes," *La Nef*, No. 39 (1970), pp. 75–84.

[29] *Sondages* XXI: 1–2 (1969), p. 35. These opinions have varied but little over the lifespan of the Fifth Republic. By contrast the police is held in far higher esteem.

[30] "Epilogues" in Robert A. Dahl, (ed.), *Political Opposition in Western Democracies* (New Haven: Yale University Press, 1966), p. 397.

have been overcome, there are other systemic problems besetting and dividing the community in its search for modernity. That search cannot be eluded. For in more ways than one, the challenge of modernization and the attack on the structures of the stalemate are coming either from the outside or from developments which Frenchmen are no longer able or willing to prevent. The incorporation of the economy into the Common Market has done more than to sustain prosperity and to provide a more orderly set of relations with the country's neighbors. It has also afforded an opportunity to relieve the tensions generated by the modernization process within France. Many who originally feared competition in a larger market have defended themselves with remarkable success. The new conditions have forced many a French entrepreneur to abandon established routines; in both industry and agriculture obsolescent units are hard pressed. When such changes affect the tactics, outlook, and personnel of trade associations and other interest groups, the inputs into the political system are altered significantly. Similarly, the onrush of the younger generation has shaken the foundations of an educational system which had remained the bottleneck in the modernization not only of social but also of political structures.

The outcome is uncertain on many grounds. As long as French politics remain democratic, they will move rather more vigorously than the politics of other communities between the poles of cohesion and of diversity. This makes for their fascination. It also makes any prediction concerning the course of political change a hazardous undertaking.

Suggestions for Further Reading

The footnotes of this book provide a rather complete and updated bibliography of books and articles in English and French. Hopefully, it will prove useful to both the undergraduate and the graduate student engaged in specialized research. The reader in search of factual information, either current or historical, will find indispensable the Paris daily *Le Monde* (of which a weekly "Selection" is available outside of France both in French and in English) and *L'Année Politique,* published every spring (Presses Universitaires de France). The journal of the French Political Science Association, *Revue Française de Science Politique,* contains a regular section *"Les Forces Politiques en France"* that is of great value.

The following bibliography lists, quite selectively, some books, all in English, which the reader may find useful when he wishes to familiarize himself with a variety of viewpoints on various periods and aspects of French politics.

Ambler, J. S., *The French Army in Politics, 1945–1962* (Columbus: Ohio State University Press, 1966)

Ardagh, J., *The New French Revolution* (New York: Harper & Row, 1968)

Aron, Raymond, *France: Steadfast and Changing, The Fourth to the Fifth Republic* (Cambridge: Harvard University Press, 1960)

Aron, Robert, and Georgette Elgey, *The Vichy Regime, 1940–1944* (New York: Macmillan, 1958)

Brinton, Crane, *The Americans and the French* (Cambridge: Harvard University Press, 1968)

Brogan, Denis W., *France under the Republic* (New York: Harper & Row, 1940)

Campbell, Peter, *French Electoral Systems and Elections Since 1789* (New York: Praeger, 1958, 2nd edition, 1965)

Crawley, A., *De Gaulle* (London: Wm. Collins, 1969)

Curtius, Ernst R., *The Civilization of France: An Introduction* (New. York: Vintage Books, paperback ed., 1962)

Gilpin, Robert, *France in The Age of the Scientific State* (Princeton: Princeton University Press, 1968)

Grosser, Alfred, *French Foreign Policy under de Gaulle* (Boston: Little, Brown and Company, 1967)

Harrison, Martin, (ed.), *French Politics* (Lexington: Heath & Company, 1969)

Hoffmann, Stanley, et al., *In Search of France* (Cambridge: Harvard University Press, paperback ed., 1965)

Kesselman, Mark, *The Ambiguous Consensus: A Study of Local Government in France* (New York: Knopf, 1967)

Lichtheim, George, *Marxism in Modern France* (New York: Columbia University Press, paperback ed., 1968)

Lorwin, Val, *The French Labor Movement* (Cambridge: Harvard University Press, 1954)

MacRae, Duncan, *Parliament, Parties and Society in France, 1946–1958* (New York: St. Martin's Press, 1967)

Rémond, René, *The Right Wing in France from 1815 to de Gaulle* (Philadelphia: University of Pennsylvania Press, 1969)

Ridley, F., and J. Blondel, *Public Administration in France* (New York: Barnes and Noble, 1964, 2nd edition, 1969)

Siegfried, André, *France: A Study in Nationality* (New Haven: Yale University Press, 1930)

Thomson, David, *Democracy in France Since 1870* (New York: Oxford University Press, paperback ed., 1964)

Waterman, Harvey, *Political Change in Contemporary France. The Politics of an Industrial Democracy* (Columbus: Charles Merril, 1969)

Werth, Alexander, *De Gaulle: A Political Biography* (Baltimore: Penguin Books, 1965)

Williams, Philip M., *Crisis and Compromise: Politics in the Fourth Republic* (New York: Anchor Books, paperback ed., 1964)

Williams, Philip M., *De Gaulle's Republic* (London: Longmans, 1961)

Williams, Philip M., *The French Parliament: Politics in the Fifth Republic* (New York: Praeger, 1968)

Wright, Gordon, *France in Modern Times, 1760 to the Present* (Chicago: Rand McNally and Company, 1962)

Chronology of Events

1789	*July 14*, Fall of the Bastille
	August, Declaration of the Rights of Man
	November, Nationalization of Church property
1791	*September*, First constitution voted
1792	*September*, Abolition of Monarchy, First Republic
1793	*June*, Second constitution voted
1794	Fall of Robespierre
1795	Rule of Directory begins
1799	Coup d'état of 18 brumaire, Napoleon First Consul
1804	Proclamation of Empire
	Promulgation of the Civil Code
1808	Establishment of the University
1814	Abdication of Napoleon
	Constitutional Charter of the restored Bourbon Monarchy
1815	Napoleon's Hundred Days
1830	*July*, Revolution in Paris; fall of the Bourbon dynasty
	Constitutional Charter of the July Monarchy (Louis-Philippe)
1848	*February*, Revolution in Paris
	Proclamation of universal suffrage
	June, Bloody suppression of workers' insurrection in Paris
	Constitution of the Second Republic
	Louis Napoleon Bonaparte elected President
1851	Coup d'état by Louis Napoleon
1852	Proclamation of the Second Empire
1867	Napoleon III announces constitutional changes to inaugurate the "Liberal Empire"

1870   Franco-Prussian War; Surrender of Napoleon III at Sedan; Government of National Defense

1871   *March to May,* Paris Commune

1875   Constitutional Laws of the Third Republic

1879–82   Educational reforms terminating clerical control and banning religious instruction from the public schools

1889   Movement in favor of General Boulanger collapses with Boulanger's flight

1890   Charles de Gaulle born in Lille

1892   High-tariff policy inaugurated by J. Méline, Minister of Agriculture

1894   Captain Dreyfus convicted for treason

1899   Dreyfus pardoned

1905   Law for separation of Church and State

1914   *July,* Assassination of the socialist leader Jaurès on the eve of the French mobilization for the First World War
September, Battle of the Marne

1917   Clemenceau government with extensive wartime powers

1919   *June,* Treaty of Versailles

1923   *January,* Occupation of the Ruhr

1934   Stavisky scandal; Attempted coup d'état by the right wing Leagues

1936   Electoral victory of the Popular Front; Léon Blum Prime Minister

1937   Fall of the Popular Front government

1938   Munich agreement on the dismemberment of Czechoslovakia

1939   England and France declare war on Germany

1940   *June 18,* General de Gaulle calls from London for continued resistance
June 22, Pétain Government signs the armistice with Germany
July, Vote in Vichy of constitutional laws establishing the French State

1942   *November,* Allied landings in North Africa; Germans move into unoccupied France

1944   *June,* Allied landings in Normandy
August, General de Gaulle enters Paris

1945   The Constituent Assembly confirms General de Gaulle as head of the Provisional Government

1946   *January,* Commissariat of the Modernization Plan established; General de Gaulle resigns his office

June, Speech at Bayeux, outlining General de Gaulle's constitutional ideas

October, Constitution of the Fourth Republic approved by referendum

1947   *May,* Dismissal of the communist Ministers from the government

October, A newly formed Gaullist party (R.P.F.) gains 40 per cent of the votes in municipal elections

1949   NATO Treaty ratified by France

1951   Law (Barangé) granting state subsidies to parochial schools

Ratification of the treaty creating the European Coal and Steel Community

1954   *May,* Defeat of the French Army in Indochina at Dien Bien Phu

June, Mendès-France government invested

July, Geneva Accords on Armistice in Vietnam

November, Nationalist insurrection in Algeria begins

1955   *February,* Mendès-France government falls on North African policy

June, General de Gaulle announces his total retirement from public life

1956   Independence for Morocco and Tunisia; French troops participate in the attack on the Suez Canal.

1957   Ratification of the Rome Treaties establishing the European Common Market

1958   *May 13,* Insurrection of French settlers in Algiers; formation of a Committee of Public Safety demanding the return to power of General de Gaulle

June 1, General de Gaulle government invested

September, Constitution of the Fifth Republic approved by referendum

December, General de Gaulle elected President of the Republic

1959   *September,* General de Gaulle proposes self-determination for Algeria

1960   *January,* Collapse of French settlers' revolt in Algeria; gradual independence for French Black Africa accomplished

1961   *April,* Collapse of Army revolt in Algeria

1962   *March,* Cease-fire agreement for Algeria signed at Evian

July, Independence for Algeria approved by referendum

October, Amendment to the constitution, introducing the popular election of the President, accepted by referendum

1965 General de Gaulle reelected President of the Republic

1966 France leaves the North Atlantic Treaty Organization and demands the withdrawal of all foreign troops stationed on her territory

1968 *May*, The "Events": student riots and mass strikes

   June, Massive Gaullist victory in parliamentary elections

1969 *April*, Constitutional Referendum defeated; General de Gaulle resigns as President

   June, Georges Pompidou elected President of the Republic.

1970 *November*, Death of General de Gaulle

The French Constitution of 1958

(This abridgment includes only those parts which are referred to in the text of this book. A complete version of the constitution may be obtained from the Press and Information Division of the French Embassy, New York.)

The French people hereby solemnly proclaims their attachment to the Rights of Man and the principles of national sovereignty as defined by the Declaration of 1789, reaffirmed and completed by the Preamble to the Constitution of 1946.

· · · · · ·

TITLE I — ON SOVEREIGNTY

Article 2. France is a Republic, indivisible, secular, democratic and social. It shall ensure the equality of all citizens before the law, without distinction of origin, race or religion. It shall respect all beliefs.

The national emblem is the tricolor flag, blue, white and red.

The national anthem is the "Marseillaise."

The motto of the Republic is "Liberty, Equality, Fraternity."

Its principle is government of the people, by the people and for the people.

Article 3. National sovereignty belongs to the people, which shall exercise it through their representatives and by way of referendum.

No section of the people, nor any individual, may attribute to themselves or himself the exercise thereof.

Suffrage may be direct or indirect under the conditions stipulated by the Constitution. It shall always be universal, equal and secret.

All French citizens of both sexes who are of age and who enjoy civil and political rights may vote under the conditions to be determined by law.

Article 4. Political parties and groups shall play a part in the exercise of the right to vote. They shall be formed freely and shall carry on their activities freely. They must respect the principles of national sovereignty and of democracy.

Title II — The President of the Republic

Article 5. The President of the Republic shall see that the Constitution is respected. He shall ensure, by his arbitration, the regular functioning of the governmental authorities, as well as the continuity of the State.

He shall be the guarantor of national independence, of the integrity of the territory, and of respect for Community agreements and treaties.

Article 6.* The President of the Republic shall be elected for seven years by direct universal suffrage.

The procedures implementing the present article shall be determined by an organic law.

Article 7.* The President of the Republic shall be elected by an absolute majority of the votes cast. If no such majority obtains on the first ballot, a second ballot shall take place on the second Sunday following the first ballot. Then only the two candidates who have received the greatest number of votes on the first ballot, after taking into account, if need be, better placed candidates who have withdrawn, may present themselves.

The Government shall be responsible for organizing the election.

The election of the new President of the Republic shall take place at least twenty days and not more than thirty-five days before the expiration of the powers of the current President.

In the case of vacancy of the Presidential office for any reason whatsoever, or if the President is declared incapable of exercising his functions by the Constitutional Council, the question being referred to the latter by the Government and the decision being taken by an absolute majority of the members of the Council, the functions of the President, with the exception of those listed in Articles 11 and 12,

* [Adopted by referendum of October 28, 1962.]

shall be temporarily exercised by the President of the Senate, or, if the latter is in turn incapable, by the Government.

In case of vacancy or when the Constitutional Council declares the President permanently incapable of exercising his functions, the ballot for the election of the new President shall take place, except in case of *force majeure* officially noted by the Constitutional Council, at least twenty days and not more than thirty-five days after the beginning of the vacancy or the declaration of the permanent character of the incapability.

In case of vacancy of the Presidency of the Republic or during the time between the declaration of the incapability of the President of the Republic and the election of his successor, Articles 49, 50 and 89 may not be invoked.

Article 8. The President of the Republic shall appoint the Prime Minister. He shall terminate the functions of the Prime Minister when the latter presents the resignation of the Government.

On the proposal of the Prime Minister, he shall appoint and dismiss the other members of the Government.

Article 9. The President of the Republic shall preside over the Council of Ministers.

Article 10. The President of the Republic shall promulgate the laws within fifteen days following their final adoption and transmission to the Government.

Before the end of this period he may ask Parliament for a reconsideration of the law or of certain of its articles. This reconsideration cannot be refused.

Article 11. The President of the Republic, on the proposal of the Government during Parliamentary sessions, or on joint motion of the two Assemblies, published in the *Journal Officiel,* may submit to a referendum any bill dealing with the organization of the public authorities, entailing approval of a Community agreement, or authorizing the ratification of a treaty that, without being contrary to the Constitution, might affect the functioning of the institutions.

When the referendum decides in favor of the bill, the President of the Republic shall promulgate it within the time limit stipulated in the preceding article.

Article 12. The President of the Republic may, after consultation with the Prime Minister and the Presidents of the Assemblies, declare the dissolution of the National Assembly.

General elections shall take place twenty days at the least and forty days at the most after the dissolution.

The National Assembly shall convene by right on the second

Thursday following its election. If this meeting takes place between the periods provided for ordinary sessions, a session shall, by right, be held for a fifteen-day period.

There may be no further dissolution within a year following these elections.

. . . . . .

Article 16. When the institutions of the Republic, the independence of the Nation, the integrity of its territory or the fulfillment of its international commitments are threatened in a grave and immediate manner and when the regular functioning of the constitutional public authorities is interrupted, the President of the Republic shall take the measures required by these circumstances, after official consultation with the Prime Minister, the Presidents of the Assemblies and the Constitutional Council.

He shall inform the nation of these measures by a message.

These measures must be inspired by the desire to ensure to the constitutional public authorities, in the shortest possible time, the means of fulfilling their assigned functions. The Constitutional Council shall be consulted about such measures.

Parliament shall meet by right.

The National Assembly may not be dissolved during the exercise of emergency powers.

. . . . . .

Article 19. The acts of the President of the Republic, other than those provided for under Articles 8 (first paragraph), 11, 12, 16, 18, 54, 56, and 61, shall be countersigned by the Premier and, should circumstances so require, by the appropriate ministers.

TITLE III — THE GOVERNMENT*

Article 20. The Government shall determine and direct the policy of the nation.

It shall have at its disposal the administration and the armed forces.

It shall be responsible to Parliament under the conditions and according to the procedures stipulated in Articles 49 and 50.

Article 21. The Prime Minister shall direct the operation of the

*[The Constitution uses the term "government" in the narrow sense of the responsible ministry, the cabinet.]

Government. He shall be responsible for national defense. He shall ensure the execution of the laws. Subject to the provisions of Article 13, he shall have regulatory powers and shall make appointments to civil and military posts.

. . . . . .

Article 23. Membership in the Government shall be incompatible with the exercise of any Parliamentary mandate, with the holding of any office at the national level in business, professional or labor organizations, and with any public employment or professional activity.

An organic law shall determine the conditions under which the holders of such mandates, functions or employments shall be replaced.

TITLE IV — THE PARLIAMENT

Article 24. The Parliament shall comprise the National Assembly and the Senate.

The deputies to the National Assembly shall be elected by direct suffrage.

The Senate shall be elected by indirect suffrage. It shall ensure the representation of the territorial units of the Republic. Frenchmen living outside France shall be represented in the Senate.

. . . . . .

Article 28. Parliament shall convene by right in two ordinary sessions each year. The first session shall begin on October 2nd and last eighty days.

The second session shall begin on April 2nd and may not last longer than ninety days.

Article 29. Parliament shall convene in extraordinary session at the request of the Prime Minister, or of the majority of the members of the National Assembly, to consider a specific agenda.

When an extraordinary session is held at the request of the members of the National Assembly, the closure decree shall take effect as soon as the Parliament has exhausted the agenda for which it was called, and at the latest twelve days from the date of its meeting.

Only the Prime Minister may ask for a new session before the end of the month following the closure decree.

. . . . . .

Title V — Relations between Parliament and the Government

Article 34. All laws shall be voted by Parliament.

Laws shall establish the regulations concerning:

— civil rights and the fundamental guarantees granted to the citizens for the exercise of civil liberties; the obligations imposed by national defense upon the persons and property of citizens;

— nationality, status and legal capacity of persons, marriage contracts, inheritance and gifts;

— definitions of crimes and misdemeanors as well as the penalties applicable to them; criminal procedure; amnesty; the creation of new types of jurisdictions and the statute of the judiciary;

— the basis, the rate and the methods of collecting taxes of all types; the currency system.

Laws shall likewise determine the rules concerning:

— the electoral system for the Parliamentary and local assemblies;

— the creation of categories of public corporations;

— the fundamental guarantees granted to civil and military personnel employed by the State;

— the nationalization of enterprises and the transfer of property from the public to the private sector.

Laws shall determine the fundamental principles of:

— the general organization of national defense;

— the free administration of local communities, the extent of their jurisdiction and their resources;

— education;

— property rights, civil and commercial obligations;

— labor law, trade-union law and social security.

Finance laws shall determine the resources and obligations of the State under the conditions and with the reservations to be provided for by an organic law.

Laws pertaining to national planning shall determine the objectives of the economic and social action of the State.

The provisions of the present article may be developed in detail and completed by an organic law.

Article 35. Parliament shall authorize the declaration of war.

Article 36. Martial law shall be decreed in a meeting of the Council of Ministers.

Its prolongation beyond twelve days may be authorized only by Parliament.

Article 37. Matters other than those that fall within the domain of law shall be subject to rule-making.*

. . . . . .

Article 38. The Government may, for the implementation of its program, ask Parliament to authorize it, for a limited period, to take by ordinance measures that are normally within the domain of law.

The ordinances shall be enacted in meetings of the Council of Ministers after consultation with the Council of State. They shall come into force upon their publication, but shall become null and void if the bill for their ratification is not submitted to Parliament before the date set by the enabling act.

At the expiration of the time limit referred to in the first paragraph of the present article, the ordinances may be modified only by law in those matters which are within the legislative domain.

. . . . . .

Article 40. Bills and amendments introduced by members of Parliament shall not be considered when their adoption would have as a consequence either a diminution of public revenues, or the creation or increase of public expenditures.

Article 41. If it appears in the course of the legislative procedure that a private member bill or an amendment is not within the domain of law or is contrary to a delegation of authority granted by virtue of Article 38, the Government may request that it be ruled out of order.

In case of disagreement between the Government and the President of the assembly concerned, the Constitutional Council, upon the request of either party, shall rule within a time limit of eight days.

. . . . . .

Article 44. Members of Parliament and of the Government shall have the right of amendment.

After the opening of the debate, the Government may oppose the examination of any amendment which has not previously been submitted to a committee.

If the Government so requests, the assembly concerned shall decide, by a single vote, on all or part of the bill under discussion, retaining only the amendments proposed or accepted by the Government.

* [i.e., by the cabinet]

Article 45. Every bill is discussed successively in the two assemblies with a view to agreement on identical versions.

When, as a result of disagreement between the two assemblies, a bill has not been passed after two readings in each assembly, or, if the Government has declared the bill urgent, after a single reading by each assembly, the Prime Minister is entitled to have the bill sent to a joint Committee composed of equal numbers from the two assemblies, with the task of finding agreed versions of the provisions in dispute.

The version prepared by the joint committee may be submitted by the Government to the two assemblies for their approval. No amendment may be accepted without the agreement of the Government.

If the joint committee does not produce an agreed version, or if the version agreed is not approved as provided for in the preceding paragraph, the Government may ask the National Assembly, after one more reading by the National Assembly and by the Senate, to decide the matter. In this case, the National Assembly may adopt either the version prepared by the joint committee or the last version passed by itself, modified, if necessary, by one or any of the amendments passed by the Senate.

. . . . . .

Article 47. Parliament shall pass finance bills under conditions to be stipulated by an organic law.

Should the National Assembly fail to reach a decision on first reading within a time limit of forty days after a bill has been introduced, the Government shall refer it to the Senate, which must rule within a time limit of fifteen days. The procedure set forth in Article 45 shall then be followed.

Should Parliament fail to reach a decision within a time limit of seventy days, the provisions of the bill may be put into effect by ordinance.

Should the finance bill establishing the revenues and expenditures of a fiscal year not be filed in time for it to be promulgated before the beginning of that fiscal year, the Government shall immediately request from Parliament the authorization to levy the taxes and shall make available by decree the funds needed to meet the Government commitments already voted.

The time limits provided for in the present article shall be suspended when Parliament is not in session.

The Court of Accounts shall assist Parliament and the Government in supervising the implementation of the finance laws.

Article 48. The discussion of the bills submitted or agreed upon by the Government shall have priority on the agenda of the assemblies in the order determined by the Government.

One meeting each week shall be reserved, by priority, for questions asked by members of Parliament and for answers by the Government.

Article 49. The Prime Minister, after deliberation in the Council of Ministers, may pledge the responsibility of the Government before the National Assembly with regard to the program of the Government, or if it be so decided with regard to a declaration of general policy.

The National Assembly may call into question the responsibility of the Government by the vote of a motion of censure. Such a motion shall be in order only if it is signed by at least one tenth of the members of the National Assembly. The vote may only take place forty-eight hours after the motion has been introduced. Only votes favorable to the motion shall be counted. It shall be considered adopted only if supported by a majority of the members of the Assembly. Should the motion of censure be rejected, its signatories may not introduce another motion in the course of the same session, except in the case provided for in the next paragraph.

The Prime Minister may, after deliberation in the Council of Ministers, pledge the Government's responsibility before the National Assembly on the vote of all or part of a bill or motion. In that case, the text shall be considered as adopted, unless a motion of censure, filed in the succeeding twenty-four hours, is voted under the conditions laid down in the previous paragraph.

The Prime Minister shall be entitled to ask the Senate for the approval of a general policy declaration.

Article 50. When the National Assembly adopts a motion of censure, or rejects the program or a declaration of general policy of the Government, the Prime Minister must submit the resignation of the Government to the President of the Republic.

· · · · · ·

TITLE VII — THE CONSTITUTIONAL COUNCIL

Article 56. The Constitutional Council shall consist of nine members, whose term of office shall last nine years and shall not be renewable. One third of the membership of the Constitutional Council shall be renewed every three years. Three of its members shall be appointed by the President of the Republic, three by the President of the National Assembly, three by the President of the Senate.

In addition to the nine members provided for above, former Presidents of the Republic shall be members ex officio for life of the Constitutional Council.

The President shall be appointed by the President of the Republic. He shall have the deciding vote in case of a tie.

. . . . . .

Article 61. Organic laws, before their promulgation, and the rules of procedure of the Parliamentary assemblies, before they come into application, must be submitted to the Constitutional Council, which shall decide whether they conform to the Constitution.

To the same end, laws may be submitted to the Constitutional Council, before their promulgation, by the President of the Republic, the Prime Minister or the President of either assembly.

In the cases provided for by the two preceding paragraphs, the Constitutional Council must make its ruling within a time limit of one month. Nevertheless, at the request of the Government, in case of emergency, this period shall be reduced to eight days.

In these same cases, referral to the Constitutional Council shall suspend the time limit for promulgation.

Article 62. A provision declared unconstitutional may not be promulgated or implemented.

The decisions of the Constitutional Council are not subject to appeal. They are binding on public authorities and on all administrative and judicial authorities.

. . . . . .

Title VIII — On Judicial Authority

Article 64. The President of the Republic shall be the guarantor of the independence of the judicial authority.

He shall be assisted by the High Council of the Judiciary.

. . . . . .

Article 66. No one may be arbitrarily detained.

The judicial authority, guardian of individual liberty, shall ensure the respect of this principle under the conditions stipulated by law.

. . . . . .

TITLE X — THE ECONOMIC AND SOCIAL COUNCIL

Article 69. The Economic and Social Council, at the request of the Government, shall give its opinion on such Government bills, ordinances and decrees, as well as on the private members' bills as are submitted to it.

. . . . . .

Article 70. The Economic and Social Council may likewise be consulted by the Government on any problem of an economic or social character of interest to the Republic or to the Community. Any plan, or any program-bill of an economic or social character shall be submitted to it for its advice.

. . . . . .

TITLE XIV — AMENDMENT

Article 89. The initiative for amending the Constitution shall belong both to the President of the Republic on the proposal of the Prime Minister and to the members of Parliament.

The proposed amendment must be passed by the two assemblies in identical terms. The amendment shall become effective after approval by a referendum.

However, the proposed amendment shall not be submitted to a referendum when the President of the Republic decides to submit it to Parliament convened in Congress;* in this case, the proposed amendment shall be approved only if it is accepted by a three-fifths majority of the votes cast. The Bureau of the Congress shall be that of the National Assembly.

No amendment procedure may be initiated or pursued when the integrity of the territory is in jeopardy.

The Republican form of government shall not be subject to amendment.

* [i.e., a joint meeting of both Assemblies]

Index